Miguel Sales Dias   Sylvie Gibe
Marcelo M. Wanderley   Rafael _____ (____)

Gesture-Based Human-Computer Interaction and Simulation

7th International Gesture Workshop, GW 2007
Lisbon, Portugal, May 23-25, 2007
Revised Selected Papers

Springer

Series Editors

Randy Goebel, University of Alberta, Edmonton, Canada
Jörg Siekmann, University of Saarland, Saarbrücken, Germany
Wolfgang Wahlster, DFKI and University of Saarland, Saarbrücken, Germany

Volume Editors

Miguel Sales Dias
Microsoft and ISCTE, Microsoft Language Development Center
C1/C2, Av. Doutor Aníbal Cavaco Silva, Tagus Park, 2744-010 Porto Salvo, Portugal
E-mail: miguel.dias@microsoft.com

Sylvie Gibet
Université de Bretagne-Sud, Laboratoire Valoria
Centre de Recherche Yves Coppens, Campus de Tohannic, 56000 Vannes, France
E-mail: sylvie.gibet@univ-ubs.fr

Marcelo M. Wanderley
McGill University, Schulich School of Music
555, Sherbrooke Street West, H3A 1E3 Montreal, QC, Canada
E-mail: marcelo.wanderley@mcgill.ca

Rafael Bastos
ADETTI/ISCTE
Av. das Forças Armadas, 1600-082 Lisboa, Portugal
E-mail: rafael.bastos@adetti.iscte.pt

Library of Congress Control Number: Applied for

CR Subject Classification (1998): I.2, I.3.7, I.5, I.4, H.5.2, H.5.5

LNCS Sublibrary: SL 7 – Artificial Intelligence

ISSN   0302-9743
ISBN-10   3-540-92864-2 Springer Berlin Heidelberg New York
ISBN-13   978-3-540-92864-5 Springer Berlin Heidelberg New York

springer.com

© Springer-Verlag Berlin Heidelberg 2008

Typesetting: Camera-ready by author, data conversion by Scientific Publishing Services, Chennai, India
Printed on acid-free paper   SPIN: 12593873   06/3180   5 4 3 2 1 0

Preface

The International Gesture Workshop is an interdisciplinary event where researchers working on human gesture-based communication present advanced research currently in progress and exchange ideas on gesture across multidisciplinary scientific disciplines. This workshop encompasses all fundamental aspects of gestural studies in the field of human–computer interaction and simulation, including all multifaceted issues of modelling, analysis and synthesis of human gesture, encompassing hand and body gestures and facial expressions. A focus of these events is a shared interest in using gesture in the context of sign language analysis, understanding and synthesis. Another stream of interest is the user-centric approach of considering gesture in multimodal human–computer interaction, in the framework of the integration of such interaction into the natural environment of users. In addition to welcoming submission of work by established researchers, it is the tradition of the GW series of workshops to encourage submission of student work at various stages of completion, enabling a broader dissemination of finished or on-going novel work and the exchange of experiences in a multidisciplinary environment.

Gesture Workshop 2007 (GW 2007) was the 7th European Gesture Workshop in the GW series initiated in 1996. Since that date, the Gesture Workshops have been held roughly every second year, with fully reviewed proceedings typically published by Springer. GW 2007 was organized by ADETTI at ISCTE-Lisbon University Institute, during May 23–25, 2007. In GW 2007, from the 53 contributions that were received, 15 high-quality full papers were accepted, along with 16 short papers and 10 posters and demos, showing on-going promising gesture research. Two brilliant keynote speakers honored the event with their presentations. Andrew Wilson, member of the Adaptive Systems and Interaction group at Microsoft Research, Redmond, USA, explored gesture recognition from video and other sensors in machine learning and human–computer interaction frameworks, specially oriented to table-top, surface and ubiquitous computing. Joaquim Jorge, Full Professor of Computer Science at Instituto Superior Técnico (IST/UTL), and head of Intelligent Multimodal Interfaces Group at INESC, Lisbon, Portugal, described how gesture can be used for sketch-based and multimodal human–computer interfaces.

This book is a revised selection of papers presented at Gesture Workshop 2007, containing 20 full papers and 10 short papers, offering the most recent advances in gesture research and its application to human–computer interaction and simulation. The book covers all core topics of gesture studies, organized in eight sections of the following thematic areas:

- Analysis and Synthesis of Gesture
- Theoretical Aspects of Gestural Communication and Interaction
- Vision-Based Gesture Recognition
- Sign Language Processing
- Gesturing with Tangible Interfaces and in Virtual and Augmented Reality

- Gesture for Music and Performing Arts
- Gesture for Therapy and Rehabilitation
- Gesture in Mobile Computing and Usability Studies

The GW2007 workshop was organized by ADETTI and supported by a number of institutions, namely, ISCTE, the Lisbon University Institute, FCT, the Foundation for Science and Technology of the Ministry of Science and Higher Education, the Portuguese Group of Computer Graphics – Eurographics Portuguese Chapter, and the City Hall of Lisbon. The submission procedures were managed by Openconf, by the Zakon Group.

The editors would like to express their thanks and appreciation to the Local Organizing Committee, particularly Ana Rita Leitão from ADETTI, who was the mastermind behind all the logistical aspects of the organization of GW2007, including the website design (www.adett.iscte.pt/events/GW2007/), the submission procedure and most of the workshop local organization activities, with the close aid of Rafael Bastos also from ADETTI, Ricardo Jota, from IST/Technical University of Lisbon, the Poster and Demo Chair, and Jean-François Kamp, from VALORIA, University of Bretagne Sud, who helped in the organization of GW 2007 with his prior GW 2005 experience. Our thanks to Nelson Carvalho from ADETTI, for the creation of the logo of this volume.

Finally, the editors would like to thank to the contributing authors of this book, for their high-level scientific work, as well as the panel of international reviewers. Their valuable feedback and recommendations helped the authors in creating this volume as a state-of-the-art reference for researchers and academics interested in all aspects of gesture studies.

October 2008

Miguel Sales Dias
Sylvie Gibet
Marcelo W. Wanderley
Rafael Bastos

Reviewers

Marjie Baalman	Concordia University, The Netherlands
Mark Marshall	McGill University, Canada
Matthieu Aubry	CERV, ENIB, France
Miguel Sales Dias	Microsoft & ISCTE, University Institute of Lisbon, Portugal
Nicolas Courty	University Bretagne-Sud, France
Nicolas Rasamimanana	IRCAM, France
Nuno Correia	FCT/New University of Lisbon, Portugal
Patrice Dalle	IRIT, University Paul Sabatier, France
Peter Wittenburg	Max Planck Institute for Psycholinguistics, The Netherlands
Philippe Gorce	LESP, University of Toulon-Var, France
Pierre-François Marteau	Valoria, University Bretagne-Sud, France
Rafael Bastos	ADETTI/ISCTE, Portugal
Richard Kennaway	University of Norwich, UK
Ronan Boulic	EPFL, Switzerland
Seong-Whan Lee	Korea University, Korea
Sylvie Gibet	Valoria, University Bretagne-Sud, France
Teresa Chambel	FC/New University of Lisbon, Portugal
Thomas Moeslund	Aalborg University, Denmark
Timo Sowa	Bielefeld University, Germany
Vincent Verfaille	McGill University, Canada
Winand Dittrich	University of Hertfordshire, UK
Sha Xin Wei	Concordia University, Canada
Ying Wu	Northwestern University, Evanston, USA
Zsofia Ruttkay	University of Twente, The Netherlands

Table of Contents

Sign Language Processing

Gesturing with Tangible Interfaces and in Virtual and Augmented Reality

Gesture Recognition Based on Elastic Deformation Energies

Radu-Daniel Vatavu[1,2], Laurent Grisoni[1], and Stefan-Gheorghe Pentiuc[2]

[1] Laboratoire d'Informatique Fondamentale de Lille, Villeneuve d'Ascq 59650, France
[2] University Stefan cel Mare, Suceava 720229, Romania
vatavu@eed.usv.ro, laurent.grisoni@lifl.fr, pentiuc@eed.usv.ro

Abstract. We present a method for recognizing gesture motions based on elastic deformable shapes and curvature templates. Gestures are modeled using a spline curve representation that is enhanced with elastic properties: the entire spline or any of its parts may stretch or bend. The energy required to transform a gesture into a given template gives an estimation of the similarity between the two. We demonstrate the results of our gesture classifier with a video-based acquisition approach.

Keywords: gesture recognition, elastic matching, deformation energies, video, gesture acquisition.

1   Introduction

Gestures have been given considerable attention lately as an effective mean for human computer interaction. The motivation lies in naturalness and efficiency: people use gestures in the real-world in order to interact with real objects and to convey information. A gesture-based interface would thus provide the net advantage of familiarity and intuitiveness with respect to other input devices. That is of course if one considers the ideal gesture framework that does not importunate, distract or add cognitive load [1,2].

A successful implementation of a gesture-based interface requires the selection of an appropriate technology for the acquisition process, a gesture representation technique that will suit the implemention of a robust classifier and finally, providing appropriate and efficient feedback to the user. Many of the above issues have been widely discussed in the literature. Good overviews on the state-of-the-art in gesture-based interaction including gesture taxonomies for HCI, existing technologies, recognition and interpretation techniques are given in [3,4]. An important problem that may be particularly identified relates to gesture motion trajectories. Trajectory recognition is difficult due to the variability that comes with gesture execution: different users will input different patterns for the same gesture type and even more, the same user will perform the same gesture differently at different moments in time by unwillingly including a certain degree of variability. Robust approaches are hence needed in order to support variations which translate into local deformations of the trajectory parts such as stretching or extra bending, articulations or any other small differences.

M. Sales Dias et al. (Eds.): GW 2007, LNAI 5085, pp. 1–12, 2009.

We propose in this paper a motion trajectory recognition method based on previous results on deformable shapes [5,6,7,8]. Robust energy measures for local deformations are discussed together with a procedure that allows automatic computation of templates from a given set of training samples. In order to demonstrate our gesture classifier we equally built a video-based acquisition system for detecting hands and retrieving their motion trajectories in a tabletop-like scenario. The paper is organized as follows: section 2 gives an overview of related work on gesture-based interfaces with a focus on video acquisition; section 3 provides details on the acquisition of hands and motion trajectories as well as on the gesture representation method using spline curves; the elasticity concepts of the deformation approach are presented in section 4 together with the classification method and recognition results; we believe that the elastic view on gestures may lead to interesting new future work as stated under the conclusions section.

2   Related Research

Gesture recognition research has been extensively conducted lately and the idea of interacting by gestures received support among public as it was induced by various media. A great variety of devices for acquiring gestures have been developed such as trackers, pointing and whole hand or body movements sensing and acquisition apparatus [9]. Among all, video-based acquisition presents the main advantage of not being intrusive and not requiring users to wear additional equipments or devices. The final feeling is thus of comfortability and naturalness. Video-based acquisition comes however with several drawbacks such as: high processing power required by the real-time interaction demand especially when more video cameras are involved; dependency on the working scenario and environment conditions such as lighting, user skin color, changing background; hands occlusion. Surveys on visual gesture recognition may be found in [9,10].

When it comes to detecting and recognizing gestures performed by hand, common approaches are to follow colored gloves [11], detect skin color [12,13] and track local features [14,15] and active shape models [16]. KLT features, named after Kanade, Lucas, Tomasi are *good features* to track [14]; sets or *flocks* of KLT features have been used by Kolsch and Turk [15] for achieving robust hand tracking and their technique is available in the HandVu system. Recognition was performed using Markov models [17], finite state machines [18], temporal motion templates [19], geometric features [20], probability signatures [21] and various shape similarity measures [22].

In what concerns the recognition of motion trajectories, many researchers have considered shape analysis approaches that make use of local parameters such as the curvature: CSS (Curvature Scale Space) representations [22], detection of high curvature points [23], similarity measures based on curvature differences [24] or various curvature-based representations [25]. Trajectory recognition remains a difficult problem as already mentioned in the introduction due to the variability that comes with each gesture execution.

3 Gesture Acquisition and Representation

We consider a gesture as a point moving in time $gesture(t) : [t_0, t_1] \rightarrow \Re^2$ in the continuous domain as well as a series of points sampled at a given resolution r in the discrete case: $gesture = \{p_i/p_i \in \Re^2, i = \overline{1,r}\}$. We are only interested in the motion trajectory that is associated with gestures performed by hand and discard all information related to postures.

3.1 Video Acquisition of Hand Gestures

Hand gestures are acquired using a top-view mounted video camera that monitors the surface of a table as illustrated in Figure 1. Hands segmentation is achieved using a simple low-cost skin filtering in the HSV color space on the Hue and Saturation components:

$$pixel\ p\ is\ skin \Leftrightarrow Hue\,(p) \in [H_{low}, H_{high}] \wedge Saturation\,(p) \in [S_{low}, S_{high}] \quad (1)$$

where p is the current pixel submitted to classification and $H_{low}, H_{high}, S_{low}, S_{high}$ are the low and high thresholds for the Hue and Saturation components. The homogeneous blue colored background of the table was chosen as it provides contrast with the users' skin color which allows for a robust hand and forefinger detection in real-time at 25 fps. The values for the Hue and Saturation thresholds were chosen experimentally as $H_{low} = 180, H_{high} = 240, S_{low} = 20, S_{high} = 150$ where Hue varies from 0 to 359 and Saturation from 0 to 255. We preffered to use this simple low-cost solution for detecting hands in a controlled environment for real-time processing purposes although there are other skin modeling approaches that deal very well with various scenario conditions [12,13] but which go beyond the scope of this paper. We are only interested at this stage in retrieving an accurate motion trajectory of gestures performed by hand.

The gesture trajectory corresponds to the forefinger of the user's hand while it is pointed. Our one-video camera acquisition approach will generate 2D curves yet all the following discussion is also relevant and may be equally extended to 3D curves as stated under the conclusions section.

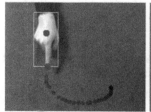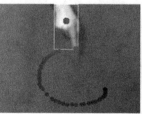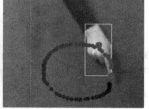

Fig. 1. Gesture acquisition above the table surface using a top-view video camera

3.2   Spline-Based Motion Representation

The acquired raw trajectory of the hand motion is simplified with a fast version of the Douglas-Peucker polyline reduction algorithm [26] into a series of 2D points $\{p_i, i = \overline{1,n}\}$ and modeled using a Catmull-Rom spline representation [27]. We perform data simplification followed by spline modeling in order to reduce and attenuate small variations that may occur in gesture execution and that may affect the performance of classifiers at later stages.

The Catmull-Rom splines are a family of cubic interpolating splines defined such that the tangent at each control point p_i is calculated using previous and next neighboring points:

$$t_i = r_i \cdot [p_{i-1}p_i] + (1 - r_i) \cdot [p_i p_{i+1}] \qquad (2)$$

where $[p_{i-1}p_i]$ denotes the vector from point p_{i-1} to p_i. The spline is completely defined by the control points p_i and their associated tangents t_i, $i = \overline{1,n}$. The ith segment of the spline is defined between the control points p_i and p_{i+1} as $p(u) = \sum_{k=0}^{3} c_k \cdot u^k$ where u is a local parameter that varies in the $[0, 1]$ interval. The coefficients $c_k, k = \overline{0,3}$ are computed for each segment using end-continuity conditions:

$$p(0) = c_0, \, p(1) = c_0 + c_1 + c_2 + c_3, \, p'(0) = c_1, \, p'(1) = c_1 + 2c_2 + 3c_3 \qquad (3)$$

Catmull-Rom splines have C^1 continuity and local control [27]. The parameters r_i are known as tensions and affect how sharply the curve bends at the interpolated control point p_i (common value is 0.5). We have chosen r_i to be $r_i = |p_i p_{i+1}| / (|p_{i-1}p_i| + |p_i p_{i+1}|)$ where $|\cdot|$ denotes the Euclidean distance, which allows for each segment $[p_i p_{i+1}]$ to be weighted inversely proportional to its length and thus giving much smoother curve shapes. Examples of a few gesture trajectories and their corresponding spline representations are given in Figure 2.

Fig. 2. Raw gesture trajectory (in red) and spline representation (in green, control points displayed) for three gesture types: rectangle, star and triangle

3.3   Curvature Functions

The fundamental theorem of differential geometry of curves [28] states that the curvature signature function $\kappa(s)$ of a planar curve $C(s)$ parameterized by arc-length s fully prescribes it up to a rigid motion transformation. The curvature

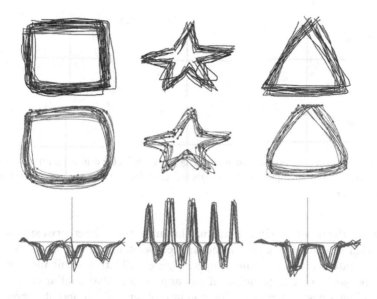

Fig. 3. Different gesture representations: raw acquired trajectories (top), spline representations (middle) and curvature functions from spline representations (bottom). Multiple executions from the same user are displayed superimposed.

functions describe the shape of gestures completely and may be used for shape matching. Moreover, plotting the curvature functions for multiple instances of the same gesture visually confirms high inter-class and small intra-class variances. Figure 3 illustrates plotting the curvature functions of several gesture trajectories. The figure also gives an idea of the variability that exists within gestures while they are executed: all gestures were performed by the same user at different moments in time. The intra-class variance is given by variations in length and bending while executing gestures.

4 An Elastic Deformation Approach for Gesture Recognition

4.1 Deformation Energies

Deformation-based approaches for the purpose of curve matching consider the transformation of one curve into another by minimizing a performance functional of energies in accordance with elastic theory [5,6,7,8]. Ideal alignments between curves will allow for similar parts to be compared together, leaving out errors that may be caused by articulations, deformation of parts or other variations in the curves' shapes.

A gesture curve is being viewed as a chain of connected elastic springs with infinitesimal lengths. Each spring may be subjected to stretching and bending. The amount of stretching is measured by the difference in length while bending

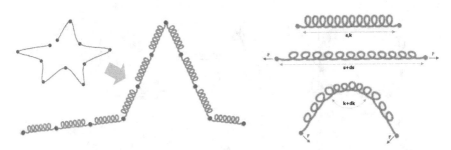

Fig. 4. Elastic gesture representation: the gesture trajectory is a chain of connected elastic springs (left); springs may be subjected to deformations such as stretching and bending (right)

accounts for the difference in curvature. The larger these differences are the larger the associated energy measure is be and consequently, the cost of deforming one spring into another becomes bigger. Figure 4 illustrates this idea for a star shaped-like gesture. The principle of the approach is that similar curves would need small energies for transforming one into other while different curves would require bigger deformation costs.

The stretching energy required to deform one spring of length ds into one of length $\overline{ds}$ may be given in analogy with Hookes' law from the elastic theory [29]:

$$E_{stretching} = \frac{1}{2}\alpha \left(ds - \overline{ds}\right)^2 \tag{4}$$

where α is the stiffness coefficient of the springs. Similarly, instead of considering springs of length we consider springs of angle between tangents at the spring extremities. The energy needed to bend a spring of angle $d\phi$ into another of angle $\overline{d\phi}$ may be expressed in terms of curvatures as:

$$E_{bending} = \frac{1}{2}\alpha \left(d\phi - \overline{d\phi}\right)^2 = \frac{1}{2}\alpha \left(dk \cdot ds - \overline{dk} \cdot \overline{ds}\right)^2 \tag{5}$$

where curvature is defined as $dk = \frac{d\phi}{ds}$. We may further express the total energy cost needed to transform one spring into another as:

$$E_{deformation} = E_{stretching} + R \cdot E_{bending} \tag{6}$$

where R is a coefficient that controls the distribution of the two energy terms.

4.2   Aligning Curves

Let $C(s)$ and $\overline{C}(\overline{s})$ be two curves indexed by arc-lengths s and $\overline{s}$ where $s \in [0, L], \overline{s} \in [0, \overline{L}]$ and $L, \overline{L}$ are the lengths of the curves. Let a mapping $g : [0, L] \to [0, \overline{L}], g(s) = \overline{s}$ represent an alignment of the two curves. The principle of elastic alignment may be described by finding the best alignment g that minimizes the total stretching and bending energy [6]:

$$\mu[g] = \int_C (C(s) - \overline{C}(\overline{s}))^2 + R \cdot (k(s) - \overline{k}(\overline{s}))^2 ds \qquad (7)$$

where $k(s), \overline{k}(\overline{s})$ are the curvatures along the $C, \overline{C}$ curves and R is the parameter that controls the contribution of each energy term. The optimal match is given as $\mu[C, \overline{C}] = \mu^* = \min_g \{\mu[g]\}$. A premise of the approach is that the goodness of the optimal match is the sum of the goodness of infinitesimal matches. The above functional is asymmetrical but it may be transformed into a symmetrical one by expressing both s and $\overline{s}$ as functions of a new parameter as in [5]. Furthermore, [5] shows that the optimal alignment of the two curves respects the properties of a metric function.

In the discrete case, the two curves $C, \overline{C}$ are sampled into n and m points respectively, $C = \{s_i / i = \overline{1, n}\}$, $\overline{C} = \{\overline{s}_j / j = \overline{1, m}\}$ and the alignment becomes a sequence of ordered pairs $\alpha_k = (s_{i_k}, \overline{s}_{j_k})$ with $(s_1, \overline{s}_1)$ and $(s_n, \overline{s}_m)$ being the first and last pairs of the sequence, $i_k \in \{1, n\}$ and $j_k \in \{1, m\}$. The optimal alignment is found via dynamic programming by considering an energy cost propagation scheme. Let $cost_{i,j}$ be the total cost of transforming the first i springs of curve C into the first j springs of curve $\overline{C}$. Also let $e_{i \to j}$ be the energy term required to transform the ith spring of curve C into the jth spring of curve $\overline{C}$:

$$e_{i \to j} = e_{stretching, i \to j} + R \cdot e_{bending, i \to j} = (ds_i - \overline{ds}_j)^2 + R \cdot (dk_i - \overline{dk}_j)^2 \quad (8)$$

We also define the energy of removing the ith spring by transforming it into a void/nil spring of 0 length and 0 curvature: $e_{i \to nil} = ds_i^2 + R \cdot dk_i^2$. The final energy cost propagation scheme is given by:

$$
\begin{cases}
cost_{1,1} = e_{1 \to 1} \\
cost_{1,j} = cost_{1,j-1} + e_{j \to nil} \\
cost_{i,1} = cost_{i-1,1} + e_{i \to nil} \\
cost_{i,j} = \min \begin{cases} cost_{i-1,j-1} + e_{i \to j} \\ cost_{i-1,j} + e_{i \to nil} \\ cost_{i,j-1} + e_{j \to nil} \end{cases}
\end{cases}
\qquad (9)
$$

We use the elastic deformation approach based on the notion of the alignment curve in the discrete case and apply it directly to the curvature functions. An illustration of the alignment result between the curvature functions of two star gestures is given in Figure 5.

4.3   Gesture Matching

Gesture recognition is performed by matching new gestures against pre-defined templates in the form of average curvature functions. Let $C_i(s_i)$, $i = \overline{1, N}$ be N curves representing multiple executions for the same gesture type. The curves

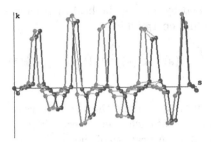

Fig. 5. Elastic alignment of the curvature functions for two star gestures

are parameterized by arc-lengths $s_i \in [0, L_i]$ with L_i being the length of the ith curve. The average curve $\tilde{C}$ is computed by averaging the lengths and curvatures of the corresponding subsegments (springs) as they are paired during the alignment procedure of each curve to a reference. We are selecting as reference the curve C_{i*} that produces the minimum total alignment cost:

$$\min_{i^*=1,N} \left\{ \sum_{i=1, i \neq i^*}^{N} \mu[C_i, C_{i^*}] \right\} \tag{10}$$

The average curve $\tilde{C}$ will have the same sampling resolution as the reference curve $\tilde{n} = n_{i^*}$ while the arc-length and curvature values are averaged during the alignment process:

$$\tilde{s}_j = \frac{\sum\limits_{t=1, t \neq i^*}^{N} \sum\limits_{\alpha_r^{i^*} = \left(s_j^{i^*}, s_{j_r}^t \right)} s_{j_r}^t}{\sum\limits_{t=1, t \neq i^*}^{N} 1}, \quad \tilde{k}_j = \frac{\sum\limits_{t=1, t \neq i^*}^{N} \sum\limits_{\alpha_r^{i^*} = \left(s_j^{i^*}, s_{j_r}^t \right)} k_{j_r}^t}{\sum\limits_{t=1, t \neq i^*}^{N} 1} \tag{11}$$

where $j = 1, \tilde{n}$ and $\alpha_r^{i^*} = \left(s_j^{i^*}, s_{j_r}^t \right)$ denotes the part of the alignment between C_{i*} as reference curve and C_t that considers only those points $s_{j_r}^t$ from C_t that are aligned to the point $s_j^{i^*}$ from C_{i*}. Figure 6 shows the average curvature function as computed from multiple examples of the rectangle gesture.

The averaging process outputs the curve $\tilde{C}$ sampled in $\{\tilde{s}_j, j = \overline{1, \tilde{n}}\}$ with curvatures $\{\tilde{k}_j, j = \overline{1, \tilde{n}}\}$, $\tilde{s}_1 = 0$ and $\tilde{s}_{\tilde{n}} = 1$. Classification of a new gesture C

Fig. 6. Average curvature function computed from multiple rectangle gestures

sampled in $\left\{s_i, i = \overline{1,n}\right\}$ with curvature values at sampled points $\left\{k_i, i = \overline{1,n}\right\}$ into a particular class of already pre-defined types is done by computing an alignment and a cost of match with respect to the average curvature function of each class in a nearest-neighbor approach. Let $\tilde{C}_1, \tilde{C}_2, \ldots \tilde{C}_k$ be the set of gesture templates (or curvature functions averages) representing k gesture types. The new gesture C is classified as being of type $j \in \{1, k\}$ where j is the index of the class that minimizes the alignment cost:

$$j = \min_{i=1,k}\left\{\mu\left[C, \tilde{C}_i\right]\right\} \tag{12}$$

4.4 Performance Results

Classifier performance. We acquired a data set of $2,000$ gesture samples from 10 subjects. Each subject performed each of the 10 gesture types from Figure 7 several times. Figure 8 lists several matching results given twice: as numerical values and using visual cues. The gray-levels range from white to black where black stands for maximum difference while white shows a perfect match.

We had a total of 200 samples for each gesture type. Out of these samples, we chose T that made up the training set. We performed the training stage 100 times by randomly choosing the T samples. The rest of 200 - T samples were added to the testing set. From each testing set and for each of the 10 gesture types, one sample was randomly selected and classified against the trained classifiers. We performed these steps 100 times and updated each time the classification error rate (10 x 100 = 1,000 tests were computed for a specified T value). We varied T from 2 to 10 samples which led to an error rate of 6% (or 94% accuracy) when using only 2 training samples and 2.5% (97.5% accuracy) for 10 training samples (or 1 sample from each user).

Discussion. The main cause for classification errors was related to wrongly classifying down-left gestures as right-arrows, down-right gestures as left-arrows and vice versa. This was due to the fact that our classifiers are rotation invariant hence the only difference between these gesture types stands in their turn angle (which is 90 degrees for down-left and down-right gestures and smaller for right- and left- arrows). By selecting only 2 stroke samples from the entire dataset acquired from 10 users (or 0.2 samples per user), the achieved accuracy performance was of 94%. The accuracy percent went up to 97.5% with 10

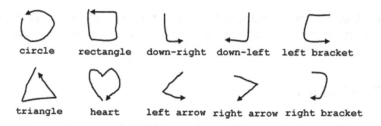

Fig. 7. Set of 10 gesture types

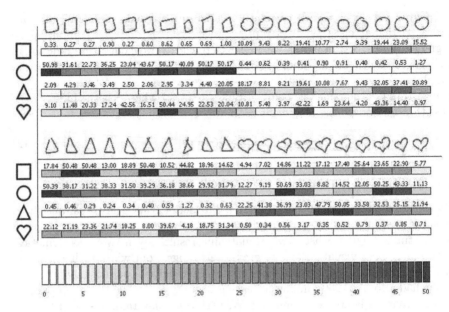

Fig. 8. Matching results for several gesture types

stroke samples (or 1 sample from each user) which makes our method suitable for multi-user gesture recognition.

System performance. Video-based acquisition was performed on a dual core P4 2.66GHz machine at a video rate of 25fps with a 320x240 image resolution. The CPU load varied around 25-30% mainly due to video processing (15-20%). The maximum time interval allowed for executing a gesture was of 5 seconds which limited the spline representation to maximum 125 control points at 25fps. The resolution step chosen for the spline segments (i.e. the number of elastic springs per segment) was 5 giving in the end a maximum dimensionality for the algorithm data of order $n \approx 600$ with an average of $n \approx 250$. The complexity of our classification algorithm for a gesture set composed of $|G|$ templates is $O(|G| \times n \times m)$ where n and m represent the resolutions of the two sampled gestures. Although the complexity is quadratic, the domain range is limited, n and m being of order 250 in the average case.

Video. A demonstrative video of the system running including acquisition and classification for the purpose of creating virtual objects may be downloaded from http://www.eed.usv.ro/~vatavu.

5   Conclusions

We presented in this paper a method for recognizing gestures based on a spline representation for motion trajectories. The classification algorithm is invariant to translation, scale and rotation due to the use of curvature functional representation however it depends on the starting point and direction of execution (due to the fact that the curvature function changes sign when direction changes). Also, we were interested in our approach solely on the recognition of gesture shapes and discard other execution parameters such as speed. However, it may prove interesting to investigate how execution speed may help classification.

Although we only demonstrate 2D gesture recognition, we believe that the method can be extended to the 3D case by taking into account another parameter, i.e. the torsion. Similar to the fact that a planar curve is completely described (up to translation) by its curvature function, a space curve is equally defined by the pair curvature and torsion. We believe that extending our method to the 3D case is interesting as future work while the analysis of the relationship between the two components curvature and torsion may reveal useful facts with regards to gesture execution.

Acknowledgments. The work presented in this paper was partially supported by IRCICA funding, the AUF Bourse de Formation a la Recherche Ref. No. 1021FR58ML/2006 and the Research of Excellence funding grant Ref. No. CEEX 131/2006.

References

1. Cerney, M.M., Vance, J.M.: Gesture recognition in virtual environments: A review and framework for future development. Iowa State, TR ISUHCI-2005-01 (2005)
2. Nielsen, M., Moeslund, T., Storring, M., Granum, E.: A procedure for developing intuitive and ergonomic gesture interfaces for HCI. In: Proc. 5th Int. Workshop on Gesture and Sign Language based HCI, Genova, Italy (2003)
3. Jaimes, A., Sebe, N.: Multimodal human computer interaction: a survey. In: Proc. of IEEE Int. Workshop on HCI, Beijing, China, pp. 1–15 (2005)
4. Watson, R.: A survey of gesture recognition techniques. TR TCD-CS-93-11, Trinity College Dublin (1993)
5. Sebastian, T.B., Klein, P.N., Kimia, B.B.: On Aligning Curves. IEEE Trans. Pattern Anal. Mach. Intell. 25(1), 116–125 (2003)
6. Cohen, I., Ayache, N., Sulger, P.: Tracking Points on Deformable Objects Using Curvature Information. In: Sandini, G. (ed.) ECCV 1992. LNCS, vol. 588, pp. 458–466. Springer, Heidelberg (1992)
7. Basri, R., Costa, L., Geiger, D., Jacobs, D.: Determining the similarity of deformable shapes. Vision Research 38, 2365–2385 (1998)
8. Azencott, R., Coldefy, F., Younes, L.: A distance for elastic matching in object recognition. In: Proc. 13th Int. Conf. on Pattern Recognition, pp. 687–691 (1996)
9. LaViola, J.: A survey of hand posture and gesture recognition techniques and technology. TR CS-99-11, Brown University (1999)
10. Pavlovic, V., Sharma, R., Huang, T.: Visual interpretation of hand gestures for human-computer interaction A review. IEEE Trans. on PAMI 19(7) (1997)
11. Dorner, B: Chasing the colour glove: Visual hand tracking. Master's thesis, Simon Fraser University (1994)
12. Jones, M.J., Rehg, J.M.: Statistical color models with application to skin detection. Cambridge Research Laboratory, TR 98/11 (1998)

13. Lee, J.Y., Yoo, S.I.: An elliptical boundary model for skin color detection. In: Proc. Int. Conf. on Imaging Science, Systems and Technology, Las Vegas, USA (2002)
14. Shi, J., Tomasi, C.: Good features to track. In: Proc. IEEE Conference on Computer Vision and Pattern Recognition, Seattle (1994)
15. Kolsch, M., Turk, M.: Fast 2d hand tracking with flocks of features and multi-cue integration. In: Proc. IEEE Workshop on Real-Time Vision for HCI (2004)
16. Chang, J.S., Kim, E.Y., Jung, K., Kim, H.J.: Real time hand tracking based on active contour model. In: Gervasi, O., Gavrilova, M.L., Kumar, V., Laganá, A., Lee, H.P., Mun, Y., Taniar, D., Tan, C.J.K. (eds.) ICCSA 2005. LNCS, vol. 3483, pp. 999–1006. Springer, Heidelberg (2005)
17. Wilson, A., Bobick, A.: Realtime online adaptive gesture recognition. In: Proc. ICPR 2000 (2000)
18. Hong, P., Turk, M., Huang, T.S.: Constructing finite state machines for fast gesture recognition. In: Proc. 15th ICPR Barcelona, Spain, vol. 3, pp. 691–694 (2000)
19. Bobick, A.F., Davis, J.W.: The recognition of human movement using temporal templates. IEEE Trans. Pattern Anal.Mach. Intell. 23(3), 257–267 (2001)
20. Fonseca, M.J., Pimentel, C., Jorge, J.A.: CALI: An Online Scribble Recognizer for Calligraphic Interfaces. AAAI Sketch Understanding, 51–58 (2002)
21. Martin, J., Hall, D., Crowley, J.L.: Statistical gesture recognition through modelling of parameter trajectories. In: 3rd Gesture Workshop, France (1999)
22. Mokhtarian, F., Abbasi, S.: Shape Similarity Retrieval under Affine Transforms. Pattern Recognition 35(1), 31–41 (2002)
23. Deriche, R., Faugeras, O.: 2-D curve matching using high curvature points: application tostereo vision. In: Proc. 10th Int. Conf. on Pattern Recognition (1990)
24. Femiani, J.C., Razdan, A., Farin, G.: Curve Shapes: Comparison and Alignment. TPAMI (November 2004)
25. Gatzke, T., Grimm, C., Garland, M., Zelinka, S.: Curvature Maps For Local Shape Comparison. In: Proc. Int. Conf. on Shape Modeling and Applications (SMI) (2005)
26. Hershberger, J., Snoeyink, J.: Speeding Up the Douglas-Peucker Line-Simplification Algorithm. In: Proc. of 5th Symposium on Data Handling, pp. 134–143 (1992)
27. Catmull, E., Rom, R.: A class of local interpolating splines. In: Barnhill, R.E., Reisenfeld, R.F. (eds.) Computer Aided Geometric Design. Academic Press, London (1974)
28. Do Carmo, M.: Differential Geometry of Curves and Surfaces. Prentice-Hall, Englewood Cliffs (1976)
29. Kosevich, A.M., Lifshitz, E.M., Landau, L.D., Pitaevskii, L.P.: Theory of Elasticity, 3rd edn., Butterworth-Heinemann (1986)

Approximation of Curvature and Velocity for Gesture Segmentation and Synthesis

Sylvie Gibet[1] and Pierre-François Marteau[2]

[1] IRISA, Campus de Beaulieu, F-35042 Rennes Cedex
`Sylvie.Gibet@irisa.fr`
[2] VALORIA, Université de Bretagne Sud, Université européenne de Bretagne,
Campus de Tohannic, rue Yves Mainguy,
F-56017 Vannes, France
`Pierre-Francois.Marteau@univ-ubs.fr`

Abstract. This paper describes a new approach to analyze hand gestures, based on an experimental approximation of the shape and kinematics of compressed arm trajectories. The motivation of such a model is on the one hand the reduction of the gesture data, and on the other hand the possibility to segment gestures into meaningful units, yielding to an analysis tool for gesture coding and synthesis. We show that the measures of the inverse of the distance between adaptive samples and velocity estimated at these points are respectively correlated to the instantaneous curvature and tangential velocity directly computed on motion capture data. Based on these correlation results, we propose a new way to automatically segment hand gestures. We show also that this approach can be applied to a global analysis / synthesis framework, useful for automatic animation of virtual characters performing sign langue gestures.

1 Introduction

Numerous approaches have been developed for the representation of human gesture. These studies sensibly differ, whether the emphasis is placed on the search of structural features used for example for gesture transcription or coding, or signal-based features used for example to represent the movement kinematics.

The first class of studies relies most of the time on a thorough knowledge of gestures, leading to a semantic, or a symbolic description using different types of codes. For example, the Laban notation was defined for describing dance or martial art gestures 1]. In the same way, HamNoSys notation was defined to represent sign languages gestures [2]. Other studies propose a segmentation of human gestures into a sequence of discrete phases or motion units of different types, based for example on velocity or acceleration profiles [3, 4, 5].

The second class of studies is related to the analysis of human motion, which has become feasible with the recent development of new technologies for motion capture. The analysis is supported by signal processing or statistical techniques, and has yielded to data-based methods for gesture recognition, motion retrieval, or computer animation. The representation and understanding of motion followed two distinct approaches: the first one can be characterized by the identification of regularities in

M. Sales Dias et al. (Eds.): GW 2007, LNAI 5085, pp. 13–23, 2009.

motion, expressed in terms of analytical motion laws [6], and the second one is dedicated to the characterization of the variability in motion, due for instance to variations in styles [7]. Among the motion laws, we retain two specific ones which can be used for trajectory segmentation. In particular, the two-third power law, expressing a power relation between velocity and curvature [8] was proposed for segmenting three dimensional unconstrained drawing movements, on the basis of abrupt changes of the velocity gain factor. Another segmentation hypothesis was based on the observation that endpoint trajectories of human arm movements tend to be piecewise planar [9]. These segmentation hypotheses are largely discussed in the neuroscience community.

One major problem in representing gesture from recorded data is that these data are multidimensional. Motion capture data generally consist indeed of sampled trajectories for each degree-of-freedom characterizing the position and orientation of the different joints of the human skeleton. Consequently, direct access and use of motion data is rather time consuming. Moreover, motion data are produced by systems which are redundant, which means that there is an excess of degrees of freedom in the motion representation. In order to efficiently represent gesture, it is therefore useful to compress the original information. Different categories of techniques are classically used for the dimensionality reduction. One category consists in projecting motion into other bases, using for example the Principal Component Analysis [10]. This method extracts the main axes which maximize the variance of the motion. Another category of methods proposes a compression of trajectories by curves and surfaces approximations. Few works concern motion trajectories. Polygonal approximation provides characteristics points to represent the geometry of the trajectory. These points, which correspond to local curvature extrema, can be connected by line segments. This method has been used by [11] for non-uniform sub-sampling of motion time-series. Another method proposes curve approximation using active contours [12]. These methods are developed for dance gesture recognition.

Independently of the data reduction method, we propose in this paper to characterize gesture trajectories expressed in a reduced space by approximated measures of curvature and velocity. Curvature mainly represents the geometry of the trajectories, and velocity represents the kinematics. The data reduction method is presented in [13].

We are mainly interested by structured gestures conveying meaningful information, such as French sign language gestures. These gestures generally use the visuo-gesture channel. In other words, they use the 3D space to sketch specific patterns expressed by Cartesian trajectories. We assume that hand gestures are well characterized by their shape (change of curvature), as well as by their kinematics (change of velocity). In sign language, the signer can indeed draw the shape of the symbol as an icon representing some feature of the object or the activity to be symbolized (Fig. 1). Expressive gestures may also implicitly contain some velocity or acceleration profiles. In particular variations in velocity are responsible for the aggregation of samples in some areas of the trajectories.

We propose here to study both these spatial and kinematics characteristics in the reduced representation space. In order to illustrate the method, we implement it on arm end-point trajectories. Nevertheless, the method can be extended to multidimensional motion trajectories the dimension of which is higher than three. Basing our work on a compressed representation of trajectories [13], we define approximations of adaptive velocity and curvature. We show that these approximations can be strongly

Fig. 1. Three first pictures: sign language gestures using the visuo-gesture channel; right: corresponding 3D end-point trajectory of the right arm with the target location

related to curvature and tangential velocity, not only in 3D space, but in any multidimensional space. These measures provide new tools to automatically analyse gestures, and can be applied to noisy data. An interpretation is given for the segmentation of sign language gestures and its possible use for gesture synthesis.

The paper is mainly composed of four sections. Section 2 gives an overview of the analysis method. Section 3 presents an evaluation of the method applied on 3D arm end-point trajectories, in terms of correlation and compression rate. After illustrating some results about the segmentation of sign language trajectories, section 4 presents some results concerning a global analysis / synthesis framework. The paper concludes and gives some perspectives in section 5.

2   Analysis of Arm Movements

The gestures consist of raw data composed of 3D Cartesian trajectories, each trajectory representing the evolution with time of one coordinate x, y, or z expressing the position of a specific joint. For our study, we consider $X(t)$ as constituted of time-series in $3.p$ dimensions, represented by spatial vectors $X(t) = [x_1(t), y_1(t), z_1(t) x_2(t), y_2(t), z_2(t)... x_p(t), y_p(t), z_p(t)]$. In practice, we deal with the sampled trajectory at a constant frequency of 120 Hz: $X(n)$ where n is the time-stamp index.

In this analysis method, we rely on the method *DPPLA* algorithm, an implementation of a reduced search dynamic programming approach described in [15], which provides a linear piecewise curve approximation, based on an optimization process. This algorithm finds samples in the time series $X(t)$, not regularly located in time.

The method *DPPLA* consists in seeking an approximation $X_{\hat{\theta}}$ of $X(n)$, θ being the set of discrete time location $\{n_i\}$ of the segment endpoints. The selection of the optimal set of parameters $\hat{\theta} = \{\hat{n}_i\}$ is performed using a recursive dynamic programming algorithm. The result of this method is the optimal identification of discrete X_{Ti} keypoints – we call them spatial targets – delimitating the segments, for a given compression rate ρ.

The time complexity of the optimal dynamic programming algorithm is $O(k.n^2)$ [14] where n is the number of samples, and k the number of segments. DPPLA, relying on the reduced search dynamic programming algorithm, has a $O(n^2/k)$ time complexity. Note that recently a multi-resolution algorithm based on DPPLA in $O(n)$ time

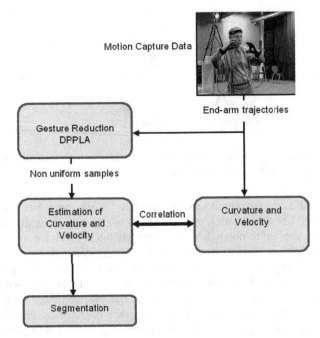

Fig. 2. An approximation of the end-point trajectory using the non uniform sampling algorithm

complexity has been proposed relaxing a bit more the optimality [16, 17]. For detailed description of the method, see [13].

The general approach is illustrated in figure 2. We propose to extract an estimation of the curvature and the velocity from the non uniform samples obtained thanks to the *DPPLA* algorithm. This estimation is evaluated through a correlation measure between the estimated measures and the analytical calculus of both the curvature and the velocity.

In this paper our work is based on 3D end point trajectories $X(t) = [x(t), y(t), z(t)]$, the coordinates being calculated in the shoulder frame. For any smooth trajectory parameterized with t, we express the instantaneous velocity $v(t)$ and the absolute value of the instantaneous curvature $\kappa(t)$:

$$v(t) = \left\| \dot{X}(t) \right\| = \sqrt{\dot{x}^2 + \dot{y}^2 + \dot{z}^2} \qquad (1)$$

$$\kappa = \frac{\left\| \dot{X}(t) \times \ddot{X}(t) \right\|}{\left\| \dot{X}(t) \right\|^3} \quad and \quad R(t) = \frac{1}{|\kappa|} \qquad (2)$$

where R is the radius of curvature. The curvature measures how fast a curve is changing direction at a given point.

These variables have been extensively studied for a variety of goal-directed experimental tasks. In particular, a number of regularities have been empirically observed for end-point trajectories of the human upper-limb, during 2D drawing movements.

However, for 3D movements with great spatial and temporal variations, it can be difficult to directly extract significant features from these signals. Moreover, computing the radius of curvature raises a problem, when the velocity is too high, or when there are inflexion points in the trajectories. In particular for noisy data the radius of curvature may be difficult to compute. Finally, for higher dimensions, the curvature is not defined, prohibiting its use in the angular space in particular.

We propose to approximate these velocity and curvature by empirical measures calculated from the adaptive samples identified through the *DPPLA* algorithm.

We define the target-based velocity by the expression:

$$V_{T_{gi}}(n_i) = \frac{\|X(n_{i+1}) - X(n_{i-1})\|}{n_{i+1} - n_{i-1}} \qquad (3)$$

where n_{i+1} and n_{i-1} are temporal indices of the associated targets Tg_{i+1} and Tg_{i-1}.

As the targets are not regularly located, the addition effect of this measure, homogeneous to a velocity, is to filter the raw data. The filtering depends on the compression rate.

We define as well the inverse distance between adjacent targets as:

$$\kappa_{T_{gi}}(n_i) = \frac{1}{\|X(n_i) - X(n_{i-1})\|} \qquad (4)$$

With this formulation, we assume that this last quantity might be linked to a measure of aggregation points on the trajectory: when the movement velocity decreases, the distance between original samples decreases and the curvature appears to be important. Therefore, $\kappa_{T_{gi}}(n_i)$ expresses a spatial quantity which might be correlated to curvature at time-index n_i.

In the next section, we will study the correlation between the target-based approximations and the instantaneous values. We will also study the influence of the compression parameter k of the compression algorithm.

3   Analysis of 3D Endpoint Arm Data

One deaf signer performed the gestures. He signed sequences of French sign language gestures representing several versions of bulletin weather performed with different styles, relative to the subject's dynamics and emotional state. The sequences were composed of 12 phrases; the whole duration was about 30 s. The subject was asked to perform the gestures with variations of the geometry (large vs. small amplitude), kinematics (high vs. low speed) and dynamics (smooth vs. jerky).

Raw data are first filtered by a low pass Butterworth filter with a cutoff frequency of 10.0 Hz. We consider sequences of about 10000 frames.

The analysis of correlation is achieved, on the one hand between the log of target-based velocity and the log of its instantaneous value, and on the other hand between the inverse of the distance between targets and the instantaneous curvature. The results concerning the velocity are shown in figure 3 (a).

They illustrate an excellent correlation between the two variables, thus allowing us to use target-based velocity as a good approximation of instantaneous velocity. We may also compute the acceleration of arm end-point trajectories on the basis of this target-based velocity. The correlation between the log of the inverse target distances and the log of its instantaneous curvature is also very good, as illustrated in figure 3 (b). The points with abrupt changes are located at the same place, but the target-based signal

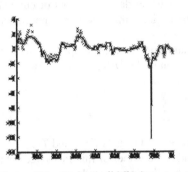

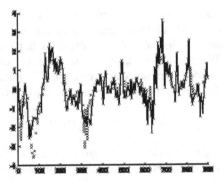

a) Tangential velocity (solid line) vs. target-based density (dotted line)

b) Curvature (solid line) vs. target density (dotted line)

Fig. 3. Correlation for 3D end-point trajectories of arm movements; a) Correlation between instantaneous tangential velocity (solid line) and target-based velocity (dotted line); b) Correlation between instantaneous curvature (solid line) and inverse target density (dotted line); for each signal x, we computed: $(\log(x) - \text{mean}(\log(x)))/\text{std}(\log(x))$.

seems less noisy than the original one. This makes possible to approximate curvature as the inverse of target density.

The influence of the compression factor characterizing the adaptive sampling algorithm is analyzed at the light of the correlation coefficient. The results can be seen in figure 4. It shows that for the target-based velocity, the correlation coefficient remains very close to 1, independently of the compression rate (from 50% to 95%). For the target-based acceleration, the correlation coefficient is very good (0.9), for a compression rate varying until 70%. Beyond this limit, the correlation coefficient abruptly falls. The correlation coefficient is lower for the inverse distance, but still high (.85), even for a high compression rate (until 80%). These results support the assumption that target-based variables can be used without a significant loss of data for the analysis of 3D end-point trajectories.

4   Gesture Segmentation and Data-Driven Synthesis

Studies on gesture [3,4] showed that human gestures can be segmented into distinct phases. Some researches assumed that objective measures can be used to segment hand movement. In particular, Kita et al. showed that abrupt changes of direction, accompanied by a velocity discontinuity indicate phase boundaries in hand trajectories. These observations have been exploited by [5], who proposed a new distance metric to detect phase boundaries, based on the sign of the first and second derivatives of endpoint trajectories. The analysis method described above can be used for automatically segmenting 3D arm motion. Moreover, it can be used for a compact gesture representation and for data-driven synthesis.

4.1   Segmentation

Our segmentation is based on the observation that phase boundaries may appear when the radius of curvature becomes very small, and the velocity decreases at the same time, indicating a change of direction. Our segmentation algorithm is based on the product variable $v(t).\kappa(t)$, and on its approximation, based on the approximated target-based variables : $v_{Tgi}(n_i).\kappa_{Tgi}(n_i)$.

A color-coding method allows to quantify the variations of the variable, according to an equally distribution of its values. The meaning of this coding is presented in table 1.

Table 1. Coding values for the color coding

coding	Variable values	Interpretation
black	---	lowest values
blue	--	very low values
cyan	-	low values
green	0	average values
yellow	+	high values
magenta	++	very high values
red	+++	highest values

The color-coding is reported on 3D trajectories, as can be seen in figure 4.

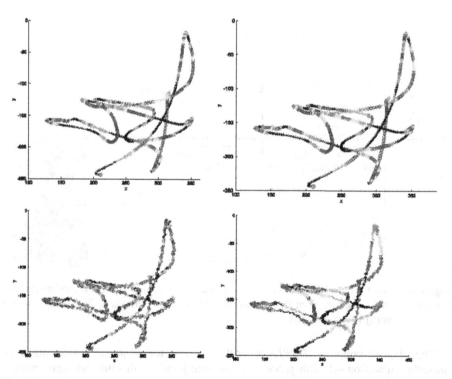

Fig. 4. Example of end-point trajectories segmentation (in the xy plane) using a color-coding of quantified variables (different color or gray levels); up-left: segmentation using the product $\kappa(t).v(t)$; up-right: segmentation using the product $\kappa_{Tgi}(t).v_{Tgi}(t)$; down-left: using the product $\kappa(t).v(t)$ for noisy data; down-right: segmentation using the product $\kappa_{Tgi}(t).v_{Tgi}(t)$ for noisy data.

When the velocity is very low, the color is green (clear gray). In the contrary, when the velocity is high and the curvature low, the color is red (dark gray). The level of quantification indicates the size of the segmental units. A great similarity can be observed between the segmentation of the curve $v(t).\kappa(t)$ and $v_{Tgi}(n_i).\kappa_{Tgi}(n_i)$ (see figure 4 up-left and up-right).

We observe also in figure 4 (down-left and down-right) that the method is well adapted to noisy data, the segmentation using the target-based measures of curvature and velocity being more filtered, while keeping the main motion phases.

4.2 Gesture Analysis / Synthesis Framework

The analysis algorithm described above can be used for representing in a compact way gesture trajectories. These trajectories can be just 3D end-point trajectories, or multidimensional trajectories. In the latter case, the trajectories may be represented by angular postures or Cartesian positions at each joint of the articulated chains.

We define an analysis / synthesis framework which separates the adaptive sampling (DPPLA) and segmentation off-line process and the in-line data-based synthesis process, as illustrated in figure 5.

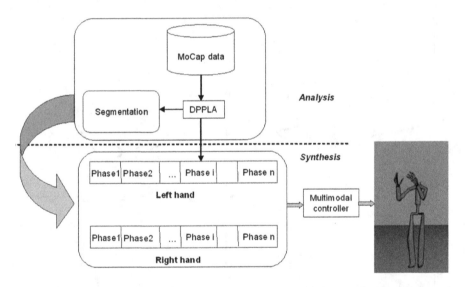

Fig. 5. Analysis / synthesis framework: up) Off-line analysis using *DPPLA* algorithm and the derived automatic segmentation; down) In-line synthesis using the phase description and the adaptive sampling within each phase.

The adaptive sampling (*DPPLA* algorithm) is used for automatic segmentation, as presented in section 4.1. This process can be used jointly with a manual segmentation process to identify phases within the gesture trajectories.

For each phase, the synthesis is achieved by an inverse kinematics process, applied for the arms on adaptive samples of end-point trajectories, and a tracking process for the rest of the body. The inverse kinematics is based on a sensory motor approach with biological relevance, as described in [18] and [19]. When applied to 3D end-point trajectories (hand motion), the discrete representation which is provided by the *DPPLA* algorithm is directly used to deal with the co-articulation between the motion segments.

The synthesis is achieved for body, hand and arm gestures. This will be soon extended to a complete multimodal system, including the synthesis of the head motion and gaze direction.

Note that the segmentation method can be extended to multidimensional trajectories, representing angular or Cartesian trajectories. It has already been experimented for 6D trajectories, representing wrist and elbow Cartesian trajectories. The results are similar to the ones obtained with 3D trajectories: we are able to identify segments along the sequence, with a varying compression factor. But the necessity to take into account more degrees of freedom still needs to be experimented and evaluated, both for segmentation and synthesis purposes.

5 Conclusion and Future Perspectives

This paper presented a method for computing an approximation of the curvature and velocity characterizing arm trajectories. This method is applied on compressed data, obtained from a non uniform sub-sampling algorithm which automatically extracts discrete target patterns from raw data, for a given compression rate. Given a desired trajectory, we already showed that the targets patterns represented in an optimal way the original trajectories.

We showed that the target-based approximations are correlated with the instantaneous tangential velocity and curvature. They can therefore be used as an alternative means of representing both the geometry and the kinematics of end-point trajectories. Moreover, this representation can be adjusted by adapting the compression rate, according to its influence on the correlation. The results obtained for 3D trajectories are very promising. This method for analyzing the shape and kinematics of gesture trajectories leads to a new analysis tool for multidimensional data.

These empirical approximations provide a significant way to segment gestures. The measure proposed in this paper, in terms of the product of the target-based velocity by the target-based curvature, gives us indeed an original means of delimitating segments which are more or less short, depending on our algorithm parameterization. In order to affirm that these segments represent meaningful components, we should compare them with those obtained through manual segmentation, for larger sequences of gestures containing multiple representations of motion segments. Nevertheless, for gestures composed of chunks whose kinematics strongly discriminate them (with different profiles of acceleration and curvature), it would by interesting to use our segmentation algorithm as an alternative method to the classical geometrical ones.

Manual and automatic segmentation are combined in a more general analysis / synthesis framework. This leads to the proposition of a data-based synthesis process, which associates tracking and inverse kinematics, according to the phases implicitly contained in gestures.

In future works, we will use this approach to identify meaningful units of semantic gestures (for instance sign language gestures). We will thus determine an optimal compression rate, by temporally aligning the proposed segmentation with a semantically interpretable segmentation. Other variables should also be tested for segmentation, and confronted to manual segmentation. Furthermore, we intend to experiment this approach for dealing with co-articulation aspects of gestures. The evaluation of the synthesis methods will be conducted both for the understanding of sign language gestures and for the realism of the produced gestures.

References

1. Maletic, V.: Body, Space, Expression: The Development of Rudolf Laban's Movement and Dance Concepts. Mouton de Gruyte, New York, NY, USA (1987)
2. Prillwitz, S., Leven, R., Zienert, H., Hanke, T., Henning, J., et al.: HamNoSys, version 2.0 - Hamburg Notation System for Sign Languages, an introductory guide. In: International studies on Sign Language and communication of the Deaf, vol. 5. Signum Press, Hamburg (1989)
3. Kendon, A.: How gestures can become like words. In: Poyatos, F. (ed.) Crosscultural perspectives in nonverbal communication, Toronto, Hogrefe, pp. 131–141 (1988)
4. McNeill, D.: Hand and Mind – What Gestures Reveal about Thought. The University of Chicago Press, Chicago (1992)
5. Kita, S., van Gijn, I., van der Hulst, H.: Movement Phase in Signs and Co-speech Gestures, and their Transcriptions by Human Coders. In: Wachsmuth, I., Fröhlich, M. (eds.) GW 1997. LNCS, vol. 1371, pp. 23–35. Springer, Heidelberg (1998)
6. Gibet, S., Kamp, J.-F., Poirier, F.: Gesture Analysis: Invariant Laws in Movement. In: Camurri, A., Volpe, G. (eds.) GW 2003. LNCS, vol. 2915, pp. 1–9. Springer, Heidelberg (2004)
7. Héloir, A., Gibet, S., Multon, F., Courty, N.: Captured Motion Data Processing for Real Time Synthesis of Sign Language. In: Gibet, S., Courty, N., Kamp, J.-F. (eds.) GW 2005. LNCS, vol. 3881, pp. 168–171. Springer, Heidelberg (2006)
8. Viviani, P., Terzuolo, C.: Trajectory determines movement dynamics. Neuroscience 7, 431–437 (1982)
9. Soechting, J.F., Terzuolo, C.A.: Organization of arm movements in three dimensional space. Wrist motion is piecewise planar. Neuroscience 23, 53–61 (1987)
10. Alexa, M., Müller, W.: Representing Animations by Principal Components. Computer Graphics Forum 19(3) (2000)
11. Chenevière, F., Boukir, S., Vachon, B.: A HMM-based dance gesture recognition system. In: Proceedings of the 9th international workshop on systems, signals and image processing, Manchester, UK, pp. 322–326 (2002)
12. Boukir, S., Chenevière, F.: Compression and recognition of dance gestures using a deformable model. Pattern Analysis and Applications 7(3), 308–316 (2004)
13. Marteau, P.F., Gibet, S.: Adaptive sampling of motion trajectories for discrete task-based analysis and synthesis of gesture. In: Gibet, S., Courty, N., Kamp, J.-F. (eds.) GW 2005. LNCS, vol. 3881, pp. 168--171. Springer, Heidelberg (2006)
14. Pikaz, A., Dinstein, I.: An algorithm for polygonal approximation based on iterative point elimination. Pattern Recognition Letters 16, 557–563 (1995)
15. Kolesnikov, A., Franti, P.: Reduced-search dynamic programming for approximation of polygonal curves. Pattern Recognition Letters 24, 2243–2254 (2003)

16. Marteau, P.F., Ménier, G.: Adaptive multiresolution and dedicated elastic matching in linear time complexity for time series data mining. In: Sixth International Conference on Intelligent Systems Design and Applications (IEEE ISDA 2006), Jinan Shandong, China, October 16-18 (2006)
17. Marteau, P.F., Ménier, G.: Speeding up Simplification of Polygonal Curves using Nested Approximations. Pattern Analysis and Applications (June 3, 2008), doi: 10.1007/s10044-008-0133-y
18. Gibet, S., Marteau, P.F.: A Self-Organized Model for the Control, Planning and Learning of Nonlinear Multi-Dimensional Systems Using a Sensory Feedback. Journal of Applied Intelligence 4, 337–349 (1994)
19. Gibet, S., Marteau, P.F., Julliard, F.: Models with Biological Relevance to Control Anthropomorphic Limbs: A Survey. In: Wachsmuth, I., Sowa, T. (eds.) GW 2001. LNCS (LNAI), vol. 2298, pp. 105–119. Springer, Heidelberg (2002)

Motion Primitives and Probabilistic Edit Distance for Action Recognition

Preben Fihl, Michael B. Holte, and Thomas B. Moeslund

Laboratory of Computer Vision and Media Technology
Aalborg University, Denmark
tbm@cvmt.dk

Abstract. The number of potential applications has made automatic recognition of human actions a very active research area. Different approaches have been followed based on trajectories through some state space. In this paper we also model an action as a trajectory through a state space, but we represent the actions as a sequence of temporal isolated instances, denoted primitives. These primitives are each defined by four features extracted from motion images. The primitives are recognized in each frame based on a trained classifier resulting in a sequence of primitives. From this sequence we recognize different temporal actions using a probabilistic Edit Distance method. The method is tested on different actions with and without noise and the results show recognition rates of 88.7% and 85.5%, respectively.

1   Introduction

Automatic recognition of human actions is a very active research area due to its numerous applications. As opposed to earlier the current trend is not as much on first reconstructing the human and the pose of his/her limbs and *then* do the recognition on the joint angle data, but rather to do the recognition directly on the image data, e.g., silhouette data [20,21,23] or spatio-temporal features [1,4,15].

Common for these approaches is that they represent an action by image data from all frames constituting the action, e.g., by a trajectory through some state-space or a spatio-temporal volume. This means that the methods in general require that the applied image information can be extracted reliably in every single frame. In some situations this will not be possible and therefore a different type of approach has been suggested. Here an action is divided into a number of smaller temporal sequences, for example movemes [6], atomic movements [7], states [5], dynamic instants [16], examplars [11], behaviour units [9], and key-frames [8]. The general idea is that approaches based on finding smaller units will be less sensitive compared to approaches based on an entire sequence of information.

For some approaches the union of the units represents the entire temporal sequence, whereas for other approaches the units represent only a subset of the original sequence. In Rao *et al.* [16] dynamic hand gestures are recognized by searching a trajectory in 3D space (x and y-position of the hand, and time) for certain dynamic instants. Gonzalez *et al.* [8] look for key-frames for recognizing actions, like walking and running.

M. Sales Dias et al. (Eds.): GW 2007, LNAI 5085, pp. 24–35, 2009.

Approaches where the entire trajectory (one action) is represented by a number of sub-sequences are Barbic *et al.* [2] for full body motion, where probabilistic PCA is used for finding transitions between different behaviors, and Bettinger *et al.* [3] where likelihoods are used to separate a trajectory into sub-trajectories. These sub-trajectories are modeled by Gaussian distributions each corresponding to a temporal primitive.

2   Paper Content and System Design

In this paper we address action recognition using temporal instances (denoted primitives) that only represent a subset of the original sequence. That is, our aim is to recognize an action by recognizing only a few primitives as opposed to recognition based on the entire sequence (possibly divided into sub-trajectories).

Our approach is based on the fact that an action will always be associated with a movement, which will manifest itself as temporal changes in the image. So by measuring the temporal changes in the image the action can be inferred. We define primitives as temporal instances with a significant change and an action is defined as a set of primitives. This approach allows for handling partly corrupted input sequences and, as we shall see, does not require the lengths, the start point, nor the end point to be known, which is the case in many other systems.

Measuring the temporal changes can be done in a number of ways. We aim at primitives that are as independent on the environment as possible. Therefore, we do not rely on figure-ground segmentation using methods like background subtraction or personalized models etc. Instead we define our primitives based on image subtraction. Image subtraction has the benefit that it measures the change in the image over time and can handle very large changes in the environment.

Concretely we represent our primitives by four features extracted from a motion-image (found by image subtraction). In each frame the primitive, if any, that best explains the observed data is identified. This leads to a discrete recognition problem since a video sequence will be converted into a string containing a sequence of symbols, each representing a primitive. After pruning the string a probabilistic Edit Distance classifier is applied to identify which action best describes the pruned string. The system is illustrated in figure 1. The actions that we focus on in this work are five one-arm gestures, but the approach can with some modifications be generalized to body actions. The actions

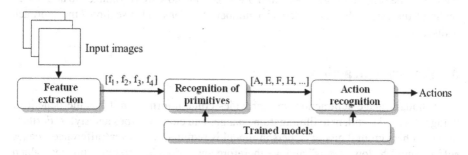

Fig. 1. System overview

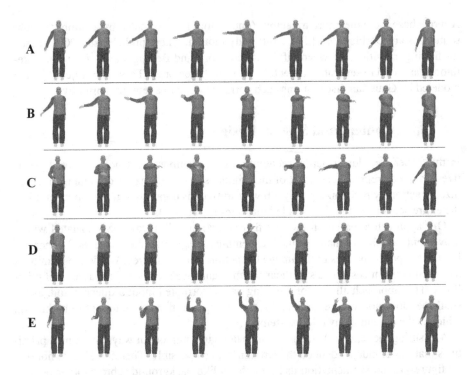

Fig. 2. Samples from the five actions. The following describes the actions as seen from the person performing the action. **A - Point right:** A stretched arm is raised to a horizontal position pointing right, and then lowered down. **B - Move left:** A stretched arm is raised to a horizontal position pointing right. The arm is then moved in front of the body ending at the right shoulder, and then lowered down. **C - Move right:** Right hand is moved up in front of the left shoulder. The arm is then stretched while moved all the way to the right, and then lowered down. **D - Move closer:** A stretched arm is raised to a horizontal position pointing forward while the palm is pointing upwards. The hand is then drawn to the chest, and lowered down. **E - Raise arm:** The arm is moved along the side of the person, stretched above the head, and then lowered again.

are inspired by [10] and can be seen in figure 2. The paper is structured as follows. In section 3 we describe how our features are extracted. In section 4 we describe how we recognize the primitives, and in section 5 we describe how we recognize the actions. In section 6 the approach is evaluated on a number of actions and in section 7 the approach is discussed.

3   Feature Extraction

Even though image subtraction only provides crude information it has the benefit of being rather independent to illumination changes and clothing types and styles. Furthermore, no background model or person model is required. However, difference images suffer from "shadow effects" and we therefore apply double difference images, which are known to be more robust [22]. The idea is to use three successive images in order to

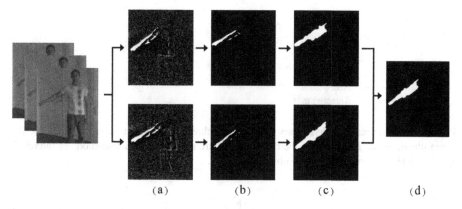

(a)   (b)   (c)   (d)

Fig. 3. An illustration of the motion extraction process. (a) Difference images are calculated from a set of three input frames yielding noisy gray scale images. (b)+(c) The hysteresis thresholds T_1 and T_2 are applied. (d) The two thresholded images from (c) are ANDed together resulting in a single connected motion-cloud.

create two difference images. These are thresholded and ANDed together. This ensures that only pixels that have changed in both difference images are included in the final output. The motion extraction process is illustrated in figure 3. Multiple steps between the three successive images used to generate the double difference image have been investigated (frames 1-2-3, frames 1-3-5, and frames 1-4-7, etc.). The approach is rather invariant to this choice, i.e., invariant to the frame-rate and the execution speed of the actions. Frames 1-3-5 are used in this work.

When doing arm gestures the double difference image will roughly speaking contain a "motion-cloud". However, noise will also be present. Either from other movements, e.g., the clothes on the upper body when lifting the arm (false positives), or the motion-cloud will be split into a number of separate blobs, e.g., due to the shirt having a uniform color (false negatives). Since the two noise sources "work against each other", it is difficult to binarize the difference image. We therefore apply a hysteresis principle consisting of two thresholds T_1 and T_2 with $T_1 > T_2$. For all difference pixels above T_1 we initiate a region growing procedure which continues to grow until the pixel values falls below T_2, see figure 4. The resulting connected motion components are further sorted with respect to their size to obtain robustness towards noise. This hysteresis threshold helps to ensure that noisy motion-clouds are not broken up into multiple fragments and at the same time eliminates small noisy motion blobs. The result is one connected motion-cloud.

We model the motion-cloud compactly by an ellipse. The length and orientation of the axes of the ellipse are calculated from the Eigen-vectors and Eigen-values of the covariance matrix defined by the motion pixels. We use four features to represent the motion cloud. They are independent of image size and the person's size and position in the image. To ensure the scale invariance two of the features are defined with respect to a reference point currently defined manually as the center of gravity of the person. The features are illustrated in figure 5 and defined as follows. Feature 1 is the eccentricity of the ellipse defined as the ratio between the axes of the ellipse (e_2/e_1). Feature 2

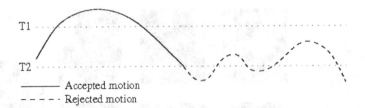

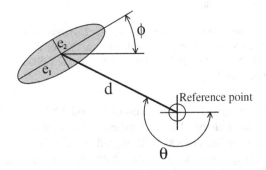

Fig. 4. An illustration of the hysteresis with an upper threshold T_1 and a lower threshold T_2. The figure illustrates the advantage of the hysteresis, where most of the "motion-blob" of interest is accepted while the smaller "noise-blobs" are rejected.

Fig. 5. An illustration of the features used for describing the motion-cloud. See text for details.

is the orientation of the ellipse defined as the angle between the x-axis of the image and the major axis of the ellipse (ϕ). Feature 3 is the size of the ellipse defined as the ratio between the length of the major axis and the distance from the reference point to the center of the ellipse (e_1/d). Feature 4 is the angle between the x-axis of the image through the reference point and the line from the center of the ellipse to the reference point (θ).

4   Recognition of Primitives

Each incoming frame is represented by the four extracted features described above. This feature vector is then classified as a particular primitive or as noise with a Mahalanobis classifier. From a set of training examples we extract representative feature vectors for each primitive. The primitives are then formed by the mean and covariance of the representative feature vectors, see below. The four features are not equally important and therefore weighted in accordance with their importance in classification. Experiments yielded features 2 and 4 as the most descriminative and feature 1 as the least descriminative. This gives the following classifier for recognizing a primitive at time t:

$$\text{Primitive}(t) = \arg\min_i \left[(\boldsymbol{W} \cdot (\boldsymbol{f}_t - \boldsymbol{p}_i))^T \Pi_i^{-1} (\boldsymbol{W} \cdot (\boldsymbol{f}_t - \boldsymbol{p}_i)) \right] \qquad (1)$$

where f_t is the feature vector estimated at time t, p_i is the mean vector of the ith primitive, Π_i is the covariance matrix of the ith primitive, and W contains the weights and are included as an element-wise multiplication.

The classification of a sequence can be viewed as a trajectory through the 4D feature space where, at each time-step, the closest primitive (in terms of Mahalanobis distance) is found. To reduce noise in this process we introduce a minimum Mahalanobis distance in order for a primitive to be considered in the first place. Furthermore, to reduce the flickering observed when the trajectory passes through a border region between two primitives we introduce a hysteresis threshold. It favors the primitive recognized in the preceding frame over all other primitives by modifying the individual distances. The classifier hereby obtains a "sticky" effect, which handles a large part of the flickering.

After processing a sequence the output will be a string with the same length as the sequence. An example is illustrated in equation 2. Each letter corresponds to a recognized primitive (see figure 7) and $\emptyset$ corresponds to time instances where no primitives are below the minimum required Mahalanobis distance. The string is pruned by first removing '$\emptyset$'s, isolated instances, and then all repeated letters, see equation 3. A weight is generated to reflect the number of repeated letters (this is used below).

$$\text{String} = \{\emptyset, \emptyset, B, B, B, B, B, E, A, A, F, F, F, F, \emptyset, D, D, G, G, G, G, \emptyset\} \quad (2)$$
$$\text{String} = \{B, A, F, D, G\} \quad (3)$$
$$\text{Weights} = \{5, 2, 4, 2, 4\} \quad (4)$$

4.1 Learning Models for the Primitives

In order to recognize the primitives we need to have a prototypical representation of each primitive, i.e., a mean and covariance in the 4D feature space. As can be seen in figure 2 the actions are all fronto-parallel. Ongoing work aims to generalize this work by allowing for multiple viewpoints. One problem with multiple viewpoints is how to train the system - it will require a very large number of test sequences. Therefore we have captured all training data using a magnetic tracking system with four sensors. The sensors are placed at the wrist, at the elbow, at the shoulder, and at the upper torso (for reference). The hardware used is the Polhemus FastTrac [18] which gives a maximum sampling rate of 25Hz when using four sensors. The data is converted into four Euler angles: three at the shoulder and one at the elbow in order to make the data invariant to body size. An action corresponds to a trajectory through a 4D space spanned by the Euler angles.

The data is input to a commercial computer graphics human model, Poser [19], which then animates all captured data. This allows us to generate training data for any view point and to generate additional training data by varying the Euler angles (based on the training data) and varying the clothing of the model. Figure 6 shows a person with magnetic trackers mounted on the arm, two different visualizations of the 3D tracker data from Poser, and an example of the test data. Based on this synthetic training data we build a classifier for each primitive.

Fig. 6. An illustration of the different types of data used in the system. From left to right: 1) 3D tracker data is acquired from magnetic trackers mounted on persons who perform the five actions. 2) The tracker data is animated in Poser from a fronto-parallel view. 3) The tracker data can be animated from any view point with different clothings and models. 4) After training the primitives on semi-sythetic data we recognize actions in real video.

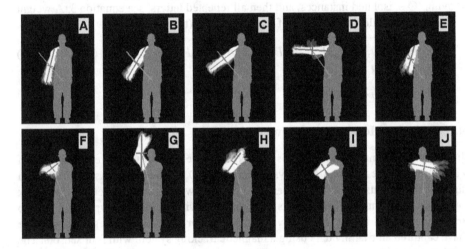

Fig. 7. The figure of each primitive contains the silhouettes of the 20 samples added together which gives the gray silhouette. The 20 motion clouds from the double difference images of the samples are added on top of the silhouette as the white cloud. The figures furthermore illustrates the mean of the four features for each primitive by depicting the axes of the fitted ellipse and the distance and direction from the reference point to the motion cloud.

4.2   Defining the Primitives

Defining the number of primitives and their characteristics ("human movement") is quite a significant optimization problem. We are aiming at automating this process [17], but in this work the definition of primitives was done manually.

The primitives are defined based on an evaluation of video sequences showing three different people performing the five actions. The criteria for defining the primitives are 1) that they represent characteristic and representative 3D configurations, 2) that their projected 2D configurations contain a certain amount of fronto-parallel motion, and 3) that the primitives are used in the description of as many actions as possible, i.e., fewer primitives are required. In this way we find 10 primitives that can represent the five actions. Each primitive is appearing in several actions resulting in five to eight primitives for each action.

To obtain the prototypical representation we randomly select 20 samples of each primitive and render the appropriate motion capture data to get a computer graphics representation of that sample. The double difference images of these samples are calculated and each of the motion-clouds are represented by the four features. The 20 samples then yields a mean vector and a 4x4 covariance matrix for each primitive. In figure 7 the 10 primitives and their representations are visualized together with the letter denoting the primitive. We can use the computer generated version of the training samples in stead of the original real video since the resulting double difference images are comparable and with this approach we achieve the possibility of generating new training data in a fast and flexible way without recording new training video.

5   Recognition of Actions

The result of recognizing the primitives is a string of letters referring to the known primitives. During a training phase a string representation of each action to be recognized is learned. The task is now to compare each of the learned actions (strings) with the detected string. Since the learned strings and the detected strings (possibly including errors!) will in general not have the same length, the standard pattern recognition methods will not suffice. We therefore apply the Edit Distance method [12], which can handle matching of strings of different lengths. Furthermore, training in the Edit Distance method is insignificant compared to for example HMM.

The edit distance is a well known method for comparing words or text strings, e.g., for spell-checking and plagiarism detection. It operates by measuring the distance between two strings in terms of the number of operations needed in order to transform one into the other. There are three possible operations: *insert* a letter from the other string, *delete* a letter, and *exchange* a letter by one from the other string. Whenever one of these operations is required in order to make the strings more similar, the score or distance is increased. The algorithm is illustrated in figure 8 where the strings *motions* and *octane* are compared.

The first step is initialization. The two strings are placed along the sides of the matrix, and increasing numbers are place along the borders beside the strings. Hereafter the matrix is filled cell by cell by traversing one column at a time. If the letters at row i and column j are the same then cell $c_{i,j}$ is assigned the same value as cell $c_{i-1,j-1}$. Otherwise cell $c_{i,j}$ is assigned the smallest value of the following three operations:

$$Insert: \quad c_{i-1,j} + cost \tag{5}$$

$$Delete: \quad c_{i,j-1} + cost \tag{6}$$

$$Exchange: c_{i-1,j-1} + cost \tag{7}$$

In the original edit distance method the *cost* equals one.

Using these rules the matrix is filled and the value found at the bottom right corner is the edit distance required in order to map one string into the other, i.e., the distance

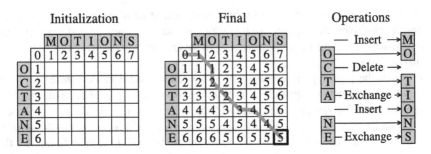

Fig. 8. Measuring the distance between two strings using edit distance

between the two strings. The actual sequence of operations can be found by back-tracing the matrix. More than one path is often possible.

The edit distance is a deterministic method but by changing the cost of each of the three operations with respect to likelihoods it becomes a probabilistic method. The edit distance method has several variations that define cost functions in different ways, e.g. the Weighted Edit Distance where a cost function is defined for each operation or the Needleman-Wunsch algorithm [14] where a cost matrix is used to define the similarity between the symbols (letters) of the applied set of symbols (alphabet). In stead of defining a fixed cost for an operation or each symbol-pair we define the cost of applying operations to a primitive based on the actual observations at any given time. The number of repetitions of a primitive to some extent represent the likelihood of that primitive being correct. This means, in terms of a cost function, that the cost of deleting or exchanging a primitive that have been observed multiple times should be increased with the number of observed repetitions. Concretely we incorporate the weights described above (see equation 4) into the edit distance method by increasing the cost of the *delete* and *exchange* operations by the weight multiplied by β (a scaling factor). The cost of *inserting* remains 1.

When the strings representing the actions are of different lengths, the method tends to favor the shorter strings. Say we have detected the string $\{B, C, D\}$ and want to classify it as being one of the two actions: $a_1 = \{J, C, G\}$ and $a_2 = \{A, B, C, D, H\}$. The edit distance from the detected string to the action-strings will be two in both cases. However, it seems more likely that the correct interpretation is that the detected string comes from a_2 in a situation where the start and end has been corrupted by noise. In fact, 2 out of 3 of the primitives have to be changed for a_1 whereas only 2 out of 5 have to be changed for a_2. We therefore normalize the edit distance by dividing the output by the length of the action-string, yielding 0.67 for a_1 and 0.2 for a_2, i.e., a_2 is recognized.

The above principle works for situations where the input sequence only contains one action (possibly corrupted by noise). In a real scenario, however, we will have sequences which are potentially much longer than an action and which might include more actions after each other. The action recognition problem is therefore formulated as for each action to find the substring in the detected string, which has the minimum edit distance. The recognized action will then be the action that has the substring with the overall minimum edit distance. Denoting the start point and length of the substring, s and l, respectively, we recognize the action present in the detected string as:

$$\text{Action} = \arg\min_{k,s,l} PED(\Lambda, k, s, l) \tag{8}$$

where k index the different actions, Λ is the detected string, and $PED(\cdot)$ is the probabilistic edit distance.

6 Results

6.1 Test Setup

Two kinds of tests are conducted: one with known start and stop time of action execution, and another with "noise" added in the beginning and end of the sequences (unknown start time). By adding noise to the sequence we introduce the realistic problem of having no clear idea about when an action commences and terminates which would be the case in a real situation. To achieve a test scenario that resembles this situation we split the five actions into halves and add one of these half actions to the beginning and one to the end of each action to be processed by the system. The added half actions are chosen randomly resulting in unknown start and end point of the real action.

We use eleven test subjects, whom each performs each gesture 10 times. This leads to 550 sequences. The weighting of the features W are set to $\{1, 4, 2, 4\}$, and $\beta = 1/8$. W and β are determined through quantitative tests. A string representation of each action is found and since the shortest string contains five primitives and the longest eight primitives, we only perform the probabilistic edit distance calculation for substrings having the lengths $\in [3, 15]$.

6.2 Tests

The overall recognition rate for the test with known start time is 88.7%. In figure 9(a) the confusion matrix for the results is shown. As can be seen in the figure, most of the errors occur by miss-classification between the two actions: *move closer* and *raise arm*. The main reasons for this confusion are the similarity of the actions, the similarity of the primitives in these actions, and different performances of the actions of different test subjects (some do not raise their arm much when preforming the *raise arm* action).

	1.	2.	3.	4.	5.
1. Point right	100				
2. Move left	6.4	90.9		2.7	
3. Move right	5.5		92.7	0.9	0.9
4. Move closer		2.7	1.8	70.9	23.6
5. Raise arm				10.9	89.1

(a) Known start and stop time.

	1.	2.	3.	4.	5.
1. Point right	99.1		0.9		
2. Move left	9.1	90.0		0.9	
3. Move right	7.3		90.0	2.7	
4. Move closer	0.9	4.5	1.8	62.7	30.0
5. Raise arm	1.8	1.8		10.9	85.5

(b) Unknown start and stop time.

Fig. 9. The confusion matrices for the recognition rates (in percent) without added noise (a) and with added noise (b). Zero values have been left out to ease the overview of the confusion.

As can be seen in figure 2 both actions are performed along the side of the person when seen from the fronto-parallel view and differs mainly in how high the arm is raised. From figure 7 it can be seen that primitives 'F', 'G', 'H', and 'I' have similar angles between the reference point and the motion cloud and 'F', 'H' and 'I' also have similar orientation of the ellipse. These two features, which are the ones with highest weights, make these four primitives harder to distinguish.

Figure 9(b) shows the confusion matrix for the test results with noise. The overall recognition rate for this test is 85.5%. The errors are the same as before but with some few additional errors caused by the unknown start and end time of the actions.

7 Conclusion

In this paper we have presented an action recognition approach based on motion primitives as opposed to trajectories. Furthermore, we extract features from temporally local motion as opposed to background subtraction or another segmentation method relying on learned models and a relatively controlled environment. We hope this makes our approach less sensitive, but have still to prove so in a more comprehensive test.

The results are promising due to two facts. First, the models are generated from synthetic data (generated based on test subjects) while the test data are real data. In fact, the test data and training data are recorded several months apart, hence this is a real test of the generalization capabilities of the action recognition process. This means that we can expect to use the same scheme when learning models for the next incarnation of the system, which is aimed at view-invariant action recognition. Secondly, the system does not break down when exposed to realistic noise. This suggests that the approach taking has potential to be expanded into a real system setup, as opposed to a lab setup which is virtually always used when testing action recognition systems.

The primitives used in this work are found manually. This turned out to be quite an effort due to the massive amount of data and possibilities. Currently we are therefore working to automate this process [17]. Another ongoing activity is to avoid manually defining the reference point, see section 3, by using the face as a reference for the features [13]. In future work we plan to include two-hand gestures, meaning that other motion features and primitives are required.

Acknowledgement

This work is partially funded by the MoPrim project (Danish National Research Councils - FTP) and partially by the HERMES project (FP6 IST-027110).

References

1. Babu, R.V., Ramakrishnan, K.R.: Compressed domain human motion recognition using motion history information. In: Proc. Int. Conf. on Acoustics, Speech and Signal Processing, Hong Kong, April 6-10 (2003)
2. Barbic, J., Pollard, N.S., Hodgins, J.K., Faloutsos, C., Pan, J.-Y., Safonova, A.: Segmenting Motion Capture Data into Distinct Behaviors. In: Graphics Interface, London, Ontario, Canada, May 17-19 (2004)

3. Bettinger, F., Cootes, T.F.: A Model of Facial Behaviour. In: IEEE International Conference on Automatic Face and Gesture Recognition, Seoul, Korea, May 17-19 (2004)
4. Bobick, A., Davis, J.: The Recognition of Human Movement Using Temporal Templates. IEEE Trans. Pattern Analysis and Machine Intelligence 23(3) (2001)
5. Bobick, A.F., Davis, J.: A Statebased Approach to the Representation and Recognition of Gestures. IEEE Trans. on Pattern Analysis and Machine Intelligence 19(12) (1997)
6. Bregler, C.: Learning and Recognizing Human Dynamics in Video Sequences. In: Conference on Computer Vision and Pattern Recognition, San Juan, Puerto Rico, pp. 568–574 (1997)
7. Campbell, L., Bobick, A.: Recognition of Human Body Motion Using Phase Space Constraints. In: International Conference on Computer Vision, Cambridge, Massachusetts (1995)
8. Gonzalez, J., Varona, J., Roca, F.X., Villanueva, J.J.: aSpaces: Action spaces for recognition and synthesis of human actions. In: Perales, F.J., Hancock, E.R. (eds.) AMDO 2002. LNCS, vol. 2492, pp. 189–200. Springer, Heidelberg (2002)
9. Jenkins, O.C., Mataric, M.J.: Deriving Action and Behavior Primitives from Human Motion Data. In: Proc. IEEE Int. Conf. on Intelligent Robots and Systems, Lausanne, Switzerland, September 30 – October 4, 2002, pp. 2551–2556 (2002)
10. Just, A., Marcel, S.: HMM and IOHMM for the Recognition of Mono- and Bi-Manual 3D Hand Gestures. In: ICPR workshop on Visual Observation of Deictic Gestures (POINTING 2004), Cambridge, UK (August 2004)
11. Kale, A., Cuntoor, N., Chellappa, R.: A Framework for Activity-Specific Human Recognition. In: Int. Conf. on Acoustics, Speech and Signal Processing, Florida (May 2002)
12. Levenshtein, V.I.: Binary Codes Capable of Correcting Deletions, Insertions and Reversals. Doklady Akademii Nauk SSSR 163(4), 845–848 (1965)
13. Moeslund, T.B., Petersen, J.S., Skalski, L.D.: Face Detection Using Multiple Cues. In: Scandinavian Conference on Image Analysis, Aalborg, Denmark, June 10-14 (2007)
14. Needleman, S.B., Wunsch, C.D.: A general method applicable to the search for similarities in the amino acid sequence of two proteins. J. Mol. Biol. 48(3), 443–453 (1970)
15. Patron-Perez, A., Reid, I.: A Probabilistic Framework for Recognizing Similar Actions using Spatio-Temporal Features. In: British Machine Vision Conference, UK (September 2007)
16. Rao, C., Yilmaz, A., Shah, M.: View-Invariant Representation and Recognition of Actions. Journal of Computer Vision 50(2), 55–63 (2002)
17. Reng, L., Moeslund, T.B., Granum, E.: Finding Motion Primitives in Human Body Gestures. In: Gibet, S., Courty, N., Kamp, J.-F. (eds.) GW 2005. LNCS (LNAI), vol. 3881, pp. 133–144. Springer, Heidelberg (2006)
18. http://polhemus.com/ (January 2006)
19. http://www.poserworld.com/ (January 2006)
20. Weinland, D., Ronfard, R., Boyer, E.: Free Viewpoint Action Recognition using Motion History Volumes. Computer Vision and Image Understanding 104(2), 249–257 (2006)
21. Yilmaz, A., Shah, M.: Actions Sketch: A Novel Action Representation. In: Proc. IEEE Conf. on Computer Vision and Pattern Recognition, San Diego, CA, June 20-25 (2005)
22. Yoshinari, K., Michihito, M.: A Human Motion Estimation Method using 3-Successive Video Frames. In: Int. Conf. on Virtual Systems and Multimedia, Gifu, Japan (1996)
23. Yu, H., Sun, G.-M., Song, W.-X., Li, X.: Human Motion Recognition Based on Neural Networks. In: Int. Conf. on Communications, Circuits and Systems, Hong Kong (May 2005)

On the Parametrization of Clapping

Herwin van Welbergen and Zsófia Ruttkay

Human Media Interaction, University of Twente Enschede, The Netherlands
{welberge,ruttkay}@ewi.utwente.nl

Abstract. For a Reactive Virtual Trainer(RVT), subtle timing and lifelikeness of motion is of primary importance. To allow for reactivity, movement adaptation, like a change of tempo, is necessary. In this paper we
investigate the relation between movement tempo, its synchronization to
verbal counting, time distribution, amplitude, and left-right symmetry of
a clapping movement. We analyze motion capture data of two subjects
performing a clapping exercise, both freely and timed by a metronome.

Our findings are compared to results from existing gesture research
and existing biomechanical models. We found that, for our subjects, verbal counting adheres to the phonological synchrony rule. A linear relationship between the movement path length and the tempo was found.
The symmetry between the left and the right hand can be described by
the biomechanical model of two coupled oscillators.

1   Introduction

Recently we have been interested in creating embodied conversational agents
(ECAs) [5] with believable expressive verbal and nonverbal behavior. One of the
applications is the RVT: an ECA in the role of a real physiotherapist, capable
of 'acting out' the exercise sequences the user is supposed to do. This virtual
trainer is reactive: she perceives the performance of the user, and adapts her reactions accordingly. The reaction often involves change of tempo of the exercises
to be performed – see [14] for more details. The RVT – similarly to real trainers
– accompanies some of the exercises with counting, to emphasize the required
tempo. In this paper we address the issue of change of tempo of rhythmic motion, particularly exercises involving the movement of the arms and hands, like
clapping. Our goal is to find the consequences of a change of the tempo on other
characteristics of the motion. We seek answers for questions like: What is the
effect of tempo change on the timing schedule of the claps? Does the amplitude
change too? Does the motion path depend on tempo? What are the individual differences? How is rhythmic counting synchronized with the motion? These
questions are essential in order to be able to generate (physiotherapy) exercises,
where subtle timing and lifelikeness of the motion is of primary importance.
We want to be sure that the user mimics the motion of the RVT to the detail, otherwise it may not achieve the envisioned positive effect, or may be even
harmful. The context of such rhythmic arm motions differs substantially from

M. Sales Dias et al. (Eds.): GW 2007, LNAI 5085, pp. 36–47, 2009.

communicative gestures accompanying casual speech. So it is interesting to compare our findings on synchronization to what is known about synchronization of speech-accompanying gestures, in general.

Our methodology is to analyze motion captured data and eventually, speech of different real people performing exercises. In this paper we give an account on our first investigation concerning clapping, a relatively simple repetitive exercise. We discuss the subtle characteristics and synchronization and timing strategies discovered in clapping. We expect that the established methodology can be used for studying other rhythmic hand motions. Moreover, we hypothesize that some of the findings on synchrony and scheduling will be valid not only for clapping, but also for other rhythmic hand motions like pulling the arms. Ultimately, we intend to use the findings based on real people's motion and motion adaptation to generate similar behavior for the RVT in a parameterized way.

In this paper we report in depth on the first stage of our ongoing work on the analysis of data gained from two subjects. Based on the findings, we plan to gather further data and perform dedicated comparative statistical analysis of the clapping of subjects of different gender and body characteristics.

1.1 Related Work

Rhythmic limb motion is studied in biomechanics [7,8,9,10,15]. While biomechanical research is typically interested in gaining deep knowledge about a single movement characteristic, we aim to obtain insight on a wider range of characteristics on an abstraction level suitable to be used as control parameters in motion generation. Biomechanical research often limits the freedom of movement to a single joint and a single characteristic of this joint is tested extensively. We do our measurements in an environment that is un-obtrusive, and allows free, natural movements. Where data from biomechanical research is already available, we relate it to our experiment.

In human motion, there are many correlations between joint actions [13]. Statistical methods [6] and machine learning [4] have been employed to find independent parameters in human motion data. These parameters can then be used to control an animation. However, the movement parameters learned in such approaches are not very intuitive to use and are highly depended on the training data. For example, [4] reports having a parameter that sets both the speed *and* the global pose.

Our approach is similar to that in [11], in which arm animations are generated using biomechanical rules of thumb, in the domain of speech-accompanying gestures. We plan to extend that work by making animations that involve the whole body, introducing movement variability (see 5.2) and parameterization.

2   The Research Issues

2.1   Synchronization of Clap and Speech

Inspired by the movement phases identified in gestures [12], we decompose a single clap into four phases (Fig. 1). The hands can be held in their starting

| Hold | Stroke | Hold | Retraction |

Fig. 1. Phases during a single clap

position in an *pre-stroke hold* phase. During the *stroke* phase, the hands move together. Note that, unlike the stroke phase in gestures, the stroke phase in repeated clapping does not express meaning. The hands can then be held together in an optional *post-stroke hold* phase. In the *retraction* phase, the hands move back to their initial positions.

Question 1. Does the phonological synchrony rule [12] for gestures also hold for the clapping exercise?

The phonological synchrony rule states that the moment of peak gesture effort (in the stroke phase) of a gesture precedes or ends at the phonological peak syllable of the speech. For our clapping exercise, this means that the clap moment, at which the hands touch, should precede or coincide with the phonological peak of a verbal count.

2.2   Time Distribution between Clapping Phases

When one claps slower, there is a longer time to be spent on a single clap. This can be used by simply linearly time-warping the normal clap. However, by observing people it became apparent that more complex strategies are used for the time distribution itself, and that the tempo change may have effect on the amount of motion performed. For instance, in a low tempo the hands may be kept still in a hold phase and the claps may be wider. The following questions address the possibilities.

Question 2. Are slow claps larger in amplitude, and fast ones smaller?

Question 3. How does the tempo change effect the distribution of the duration of the different phases of a clap?

2.3   Body Involvement

Involvement of the whole body is crucial to make an animation believable [1]. We want to know which body parts are involved in the clapping motion. These body parts could contribute to clapping itself, or are additional movements. In the latter case some, aspects of it could still be influenced by the clapping motion, comparable to how the tempo of breathing can be influenced by the tempo of a running motion [2].

Question 4. Which body parts are involved in clapping motion?

Question 5. How does body part involvement relate to tempo?

2.4   Symmetry

Rhythmic moving limbs have been modeled as self-oscillating systems [7,9,10]. They have their own preferred oscillating frequency, or eigenfrequency ω. Inter limb coordination patterns have been modeled as oscillator interaction through a coupled medium [8]. The oscillator travels a closed orbit in a coordinate system defined by its position (x) and velocity (v) [7]. x is the normalization of angle $\hat{x}$ between the hand-shoulder vector and the right-left shoulder vector (Fig. 2). v is the normalized angular velocity. The location of the oscillator in its cycle is represented as a phase angle θ (See Fig. 3). The coordination of two oscillators

Fig. 2. Angle $\hat{x}$ between the shoulder-shoulder vector and shoulder-hand vector during the clap

Fig. 3. Determining phase angle θ

is captured by the relative phase angle $\phi = \theta_{left} - \theta_{right}$. If the two oscillators are perfectly in phase, then $\phi = 0$. If they are perfectly in anti-phase, then $\phi = \pi$. Clapping is an in-phase movement. The stability of this in-phase behavior depends on the mass imbalance between limbs and the clapping frequency [7,15].

Question 6. Do the deviation of ϕ from 0 and the standard deviation of ϕ increase with an increase of the clapping tempo?

In an in-phase finger tapping task, it has been shown that right-handed individuals lead the tapping with their right finger [15]. However, such asymmetry often disappears when the task is constrained to a metronome.

Question 7. Do right handed subjects show a negative mean ϕ when clapping freely?

Question 8. Is the mean ϕ closer to 0 when clapping driven by metronome?

3   Setup of the Experiments

Two subjects (both male, right handed, and Dutch, age 25 and 24) were first asked to clap and to count from 21 to 30 in Dutch while clapping. We choose the words 21-30 rather than 1-10 because they consist of multiple syllables, allowing our subjects to choose a syllable to align their clap to. In Dutch, the words 21-30 have all have their phonological peak at the first syllable. In the remaining part of the paper we will call this the 'free clapping'. Then, the subjects were asked to clap to the beat of a metronome and to count while clapping. In the remaining part of the article, we will call this 'metronome-driven clapping'. The metronome is set at 30, 50, 70, 90, 110, 150, 180, 210 and 240 beats per minute. The subject had to clap twelve times at each tempo, after which the tempo was increased. The subjects were told that, if necessary, they could skip the first two metronome ticks to adjust to the new tempo. In our further analysis, we ignore motion data on clapping at those two ticks.

Motion capture is a technology which allows us to gain detailed information about the kinematic characteristics of the motion of a person, by tracking position of certain marked points of the body. We used a Vicon 460 [1] optical motion capture system with 6 cameras, recording at 120 fps. We placed the markers as indicated by the CMU marker placement guide. [2] However, to prevent occlusion between markers on the hands and those on the upper body, all markers on the front of the upper body were omitted. Thus, movement information on the torso is obtained only from the markers placed on the back. Also, we omitted the markers on the heel, ankle, and toes. Motion was recorded using 32 markers in total in the first test: four markers were placed on the head, seven on each arm, one on the neck, one on the right shoulder blade, one on the back, three on the hips and four on each leg. To save time and because we did not expect clapping to effect leg movement, in the second test, the markers on the legs were omitted. The sessions were recorded on video to gain information about the timing of speech.

4   Results

4.1   The Shape of the Movement Path

Figure 4 shows the movement path of the left and the right hand at 70 and 90 bpm for subject 1. The movement path for subject 2 looks very similar. Movement is not confined to a 2D plane, but the hands seem to move over a banana-shaped surface. The movement path is less curved as the tempo increases and the amplitude decreases. This is also observed in gestures [11].

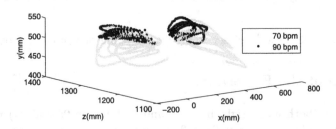

Fig. 4. Movement path of left and right hand at different speeds

---

[1] www.vicon.com/

[2] www.etc.cmu.edu/projects/mastermotion/Documents/markerPlacementGuide.doc

4.2 Synchronization of Clap and Speech

Both subjects in the pilot study counted after the clap moment during both free clapping and metronome-driven clapping. Thus for our subjects, the phonological synchrony rule was valid.

The free clap was performed at a consistent tempo very close to 60 bpm (with an average single clap duration of 1.007 s for subject 1 and 1.011 s for subject 2) by both our subjects. Because saying 21, 22, etc. takes about 1 second, it is likely that during this task, the timing of clapping became guided by that of the speech.

4.3 Time Distribution between Clapping Phases

Subject 1 kept moving his hands while clapping at all speeds. No hold phases were observed. Subject 2 used a pre-stroke hold phase at 30bpm and kept his hands moving constantly at the faster speeds.

Table 1 shows the average relative duration of the stroke phase for each of the clapping speeds and the standard deviation σ between the duration of the stroke phase of claps at the same speed. The duration of the preparation is always in between 31-39% for subject 1 and 22-34% for subject 2. No significant correlation between phase duration and tempo is found for our subjects. A correlation (significant at the 0.05 level) between σ and the metronome period was found for subject 1: σ increases with the metronome period. No such correlation was found for subject 2.

Table 1. Time distribution of the clap exercise at different speeds

Frequency (bpm)	Stroke duration		σ	
	sub. 1	sub. 2	sub. 1	sub. 2
30	34%	22%	9%	11%
50	34%	32%	3%	4%
70	36%	31%	3%	6%
90	34%	25%	2%	4%
110	37%	26%	3%	8%
150	34%	26%	3%	3%
180	31%	25%	3%	6%
210	36%	27%	1%	7%
240	36%	34%	2%	9%
Free	39%	32%	2%	5%

4.4 Amplitude

To measure amplitude, we first looked at the maximum distance between the hands. However, since the hand movement path is curved, this alone might not correctly display the amount of motion. We used the distance traveled along the movement path as another measure of amplitude in our quantitative analysis, which provided us with information on the hand's velocity profile as well.

Figure 5 shows the distance between the hands at different tempi for subject 1. Clearly, the maximum hand distance decreases, as the tempo increases. For subject 2, a similar pattern occurs. However, the hand distances during the 30 bpm clap (with the pre-stroke hold) and the 50 bpm clap were very similar. The maximum hand distance of subject 2 was smaller than that of subject 1 (see Table 2). While clapping at the same tempo for some time, the maximum hand distance seems to increase. This might indicate that the subject, once he is familiar with the clapping task, becomes able to execute it at a higher amplitude.

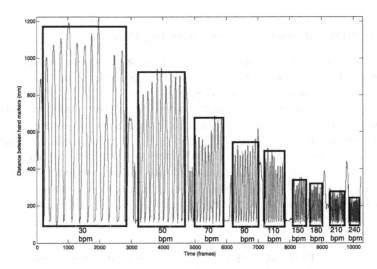

Fig. 5. Hand distance during the clapping exercise

For subject 1, free clapping has nearly the same maximum hand distance as the distance while clapping at the slowest metronome speed. This might indicate that, at least for this subject, clapping using that hand distance is 'natural' and that amplitude reduction is used as a speedup technique. For subject 2, the maximum hand distance during free clapping was much larger than that during metronome-driven clapping. However, it was still smaller than the average hand distance in subject 1's free clap.

Table 2 shows the average lengths of the path traveled through space for the hand, during the stroke (S) and retraction phase (R). The average distance traveled per minute is quite constant for the claps at the metronome. However during the free clap, the hands move at a higher speed. Possibly, this is because it is less effortful to clap freely than to exactly align the clap moment to a metronome tick. Obviously, at 30 bpm, where subject 2 makes use of the pre-stroke hold, his average clap speed is lowered. Excluding the free clap and subject 2's clap at 30 bpm, a high correlation between metronome period and movement path distance is found (Table 3, all values are significant at the 0.01 level). This

Table 2. Distance traveled along the path by the left (l) and right (r) hand during the stroke phase (S) and the retraction phase (R)

Tempo (bpm)	$R_r(mm)$ sub. 1	sub. 2	$S_r(mm)$ sub. 1	sub. 2	$R_l(mm)$ sub. 1	sub. 2	$S_l(mm)$ sub. 1	sub. 2
30	713	350	633	296	714	352	662	237
50	524	326	373	289	529	328	382	232
70	298	196	265	173	301	197	260	125
90	253	115	209	106	257	117	210	68
110	210	100	165	91	214	101	179	59
150	132	105	114	91	156	106	127	54
180	119	66	99	55	121	69	108	46
210	100	50	80	37	127	51	77	39
240	79	34	75	29	83	34	71	38
Free (60)	665	551	612	428	673	561	615	322

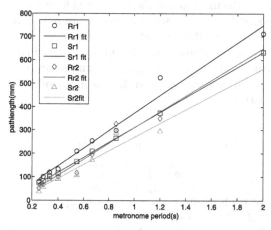

Table 3. Correlation between metronome period and movement path distance

	Pearson sub. 1	sub. 2	Spearman's ρ sub. 1	sub. 2
S_r	1.000	0.979	1.000	0.976
S_l	0.999	0.950	1.000	1.000
R_r	0.989	0.974	1.000	0.976
R_l	0.988	0.973	0.983	0.976

Fig. 6. Distance traveled along the path for the right hand of the subjects during stroke (S) and retraction (R)

indicates that there is a linear relation between metronome period and path distance:

$$pathdistance = a + b \cdot period \qquad (1)$$

a and b are very similar for the left and right hand but between the two subjects and between the retraction and stroke phase, different values for a and b are found (see Fig. 6).

4.5   Involved Body Parts

For all markers, it was annotated if they were involved in the clapping motion. For both subjects, multiple body segments besides the arms were involved in the clapping motion. Movement related to clapping was found on the head, torso and at low tempi even on the thighs and knees. At higher tempi, fewer body segments were perceivably involved.

4.6   Symmetry

The relative phase angle ϕ (see 2.4) is defined as $\text{atan2}(x_{left}, v_{left}) - \text{atan2}(x_{right}, v_{right})$, in which x_i is the normalized angle $\hat{x}$ (see Fig. 2) for limb i and v_i is the normalized angular velocity of $\hat{x}$. x_i and v_i are normalized so that their values are in between -0.5 and 0.5. Spikes in ϕ occur when the two hand touch and the collision forces the slower hand's direction into that of the faster hand, thus flipping its angular velocity. These spikes were filtered out. Table 4 shows the mean and standard deviation of the relative phase angle of the clap at different speeds, with and without the filtering.

For both subjects, the standard deviation of ϕ increases significantly (at 0.05 level) with tempo. No relation between the mean ϕ and the tempo was found. For both subjects the mean ϕ was consistently negative when no pre-stroke hold was used, indicating that the right hand was ahead of the left hand in its cycle. For both subjects, free clapping and metronome-driven clapping at the roughly the same tempo have a very similar mean ϕ. The expected larger absolute mean ϕ in free clapping was not found. Possibly this is because the verbal count introduced another timing synchronization constraint.

Table 4. Relative phase angle at different movement speeds

Frequency (bpm)	mean (°)		σ (°)		mean (°) (filtered)		σ (°) (filtered)	
	sub. 1	sub. 2	sub. 1	sub. 2	sub. 1	sub. 2	sub. 1	sub. 2
30	10.1	12.0	73.3	26.1	-6.8	11.3	2.9	6.8
50	7.3	3.4	70.3	40.9	-7.2	-0.4	2.0	3.5
70	9.8	-6.7	85.7	47.1	-12.0	-11.0	1.9	11.4
90	9.5	4.3	83.5	55.8	-11.3	-2.9	1.5	16.4
110	7.6	-19.6	81.0	66.7	-11.5	-18.0	2.7	43.0
150	9.3	-118.1	78.4	97.6	-8.8	-105.4	3.2	144.7
180	2.9	-17.5	90.0	67.9	-3.7	-10.4	5.7	44.6
210	22.7	-40.7	115.2	87.8	-21.6	-30.1	11.4	88.2
240	4.1	-14.7	70.6	101.0	-10.4	-19.0	6.1	102.6
Free(=60)	0.8	19.3	63.1	99.4	-10.4	-10.6	2.5	7.9

5   Conclusions

5.1   Summary of the Results

1. The phonological synchrony rule was obeyed for our subjects: they both counted after clapping.

2. Our experiments have shown that clapping movement is often sped up just by making the path distance shorter, keeping the average speed and the relative timing of clapping phases the same. If this speedup strategy is used, the path distance decreases linearly with the clapping speed. The average movement speed on the path is quite constant and does not change with the metronome tempo. The value of this speed is depended on the movement phase (retraction or stroke) and on the subject (or his/her clapping style), but it does not vary much between hands.

3. A pre-stroke hold can be used as a slowdown strategy.

4. Clapping is a whole body motion. Movement related to the clap is perceived on the head, torso and even down to the knees.

5. At higher clapping speeds, fewer body parts are perceivably involved.

6. The standard deviation of the relative phase angle between the left and right hand ϕ increased with the clapping frequency. No significant increase of the mean of ϕ with the clapping frequency was observed.

7. Both our right handed subjects show the expected negative mean ϕ.

8. The mean ϕ in free clapping was similar to the mean ϕ in metronome driven clapping at the same tempo.

5.2   Discussion

The present study provided in-depth insight on different aspects of clapping. Our experiment validates several models from both biomechanics and gesture research, indicating that these models might be valid in our exercising domain. We plan to gain more information on the clapping motion by further analysis of our clapping data and by capturing new subjects.

The timing of the free clap (almost exactly 60bpm) suggests that, by asking our subjects to count while clapping in the free clap, we probably introduced speech driven clapping behavior, rather than completely free clapping. In further experiments we plan to test timing and other differences between clapping with and without counting.

We have obtained motion capture of clapping humans that can be adapted given the models we have found. Ultimately, we want to generate clapping motion procedurally, given just a tempo and some personal characteristics. A virtual human Turing test (as suggested in [16]) can be used to test the importance of our findings for the believability of motion in a in a formal way.

Variability is a measure of the differences in a motion repeated multiple times by the same person [3]. To generate natural clapping motion, variability is crucial. If we repeat exactly the same clap twice, it looks artificial. We have found relationships between variability in symmetry and time distribution and tempo. However, we have not yet shown how and where variability effects the motion path. Looking at the movement data (see Fig. 5), we hypothize that variability can be modelled solely by adjusting the clap point and maximum extension of the hands.

Style is a measure conveying the difference in the motion of two subjects [3]. Our experiments clearly show motion differences between the subjects. We would like to find out which movement characteristics are caused by personality traits (for example, introvert vs. extrovert) or specific body properties (for example, right-handed vs. left-handed). Movement data of far more subjects is needed to find significant relations between movement characteristics and style.

Movement of joints other than our arms is in principle not necesary for clapping. However, the effect of the clapping movement was seen throughout the body. We would like to know if this movement is caused just by clapping, or if clapping somehow effects movement that is already there. For example: does the clapping itself influency balance and thus induce balance changing behavior, or does it merely change the tempo of balancing behavior that is already there? In [6] and [13] movement on new joints was generated from animation pieces in a mocap database, given only a motion 'sketch' on some joints. Inspired by this work, we plan to investigate if we can generate believable movement on other body parts, given just the movement on the arms.

So far we have not looked at the *transition* from one clapping tempo to another. In the recorded motion capture data the tempo changes were large and took effect immidiately. Our subjects could not adapt to this changes immidiatly and often stopped clapping to listen to the new tempo and get used to it. We expect tempo changes in the RVT to be smaller and smoother. We plan to analyze tempo transition movement by doing another metronome driven clapping experiment, in which the metrome speed increases in smaller steps.

Acknowledgments

The authors would like to thank our clapping subjects Wim Fikkert and Dimitri Heuvel. This research has been supported by the GATE project, funded by the Netherlands Organization for Scientific Research (NWO) and the Netherlands ICT Research and Innovation Authority (ICT Regie).

References

1. Badler, N.I., Costa, M., Zhao, L., Chi, D.M.: To gesture or not to gesture: What is the question? In: Proceedings of the International Conference on Computer Graphics, Washington, pp. 3–9. IEEE Computer Society, Los Alamitos (2000)
2. Bernasconi, P., Kohl, J.: Analysis of co-ordination between breathing and exercise rhythms in man. Journal of Physiology 471(1), 693–706 (1993)
3. Bodenheimer, B., Shleyfman, A.V., Hodgins, J.K.: The effects of noise on the perception of animated human running. In: Magnenat-Thalmann, N., Thalmann, D. (eds.) Computer Animation and Simulation 1999, pp. 53–63. Springer, Wien (1999) (Eurographics Animation Workshop)
4. Brand, M., Hertzmann, A.: Style machines. In: Proceedings of the annual conference on Computer graphics and interactive techniques, New York, pp. 183–192. ACM Press/Addison-Wesley Publishing Co. (2000)
5. Cassell, J.: Embodied Conversational Agents. The MIT Press, Cambridge (2000)
6. Egges, A., Molet, T., Magnenat-Thalmann, N.: Personalised real-time idle motion synthesis. In: Pacific Conference on Computer Graphics and Applications, pp. 121–130. IEEE Computer Society, Los Alamitos (2004)

7. Fitzpatrick, P.A., Schmidt, R.C., Lockman, J.L.: Dynamical patterns in the development of clapping. Child Development 67(6), 2691–2708 (1996)
8. Haken, H., Kelso, J.A.S., Bunz, H.: A theoretical model of phase transitions in human hand movements. Biological Cybernetics 51(5), 347–356 (1985)
9. Kadar, E.E., Schmidt, R.C., Turvey, M.T.: Constants underlying frequency changes in biological rhythmic movements. Biological Cybernetics 68(5), 421–430 (1993)
10. Kay, B.A., Kelso, J.A.S., Saltzman, E.L., Schöner, G.: Space-time behavior of single and bimanual rhythmical movements: Data and limit cycle model. Journal of Experimental Psychology: Human Perception & Performance 13(2), 178–192 (1987)
11. Kopp, S., Wachsmuth, I.: Model-based animation of coverbal gesture. In: Proceedings of Computer Animation, Washington, pp. 252–257. IEEE Computer Society Press, Los Alamitos (2002)
12. McNeill, D.: Hand and Mind: What Gestures Reveal about Thought. University of Chicago Press, Chicago (1995)
13. Pullen, K., Bregler, C.: Motion capture assisted animation: texturing and synthesis. In: Proceedings of the 29th annual conference on Computer graphics and interactive techniques, pp. 501–508 (2002)
14. Ruttkay, Z.M., Zwiers, J., van Welbergen, H., Reidsma, D.: Towards a reactive virtual trainer. In: Gratch, J., Young, M., Aylett, R.S., Ballin, D., Olivier, P. (eds.) IVA 2006. LNCS, vol. 4133, pp. 292–303. Springer, Heidelberg (2006)
15. Treffner, P.J., Turvey, M.T.: Symmetry, broken symmetry, and handedness in bimanual coordination dynamics. Experimental Brain Research 107(3), 463–478 (1996)
16. van Welbergen, H., Nijholt, A., Reidsma, D., Zwiers, J.: Presenting in Virtual Worlds: Towards an Architecture for a 3D Presenter explaining 2D-Presented information. IEEE Intelligent Systems 21(5), 47–99 (2006)

Improving the Believability of Virtual Characters Using Qualitative Gesture Analysis

Barbara Mazzarino[1], Manuel Peinado[2], Ronan Boulic[3], Gualtiero Volpe[1], and Marcelo M. Wanderley[4]

[1] InfoMus Lab- DIST-Università degli Studi di Genova, Italy
{Barbara.Mazzarino,Gualtiero.Volpe}@unige.it
[2] Escuela Politécnica University of Alcalá, Spain
Manupg@aut.uah.es
[3] VRLAB, Ecole Polytechnique Fédérale de Lausanne, EPFL 1015 Lausanne, Switzerland
Ronan.Boulic@epfl.ch
[4] McGill University, Montreal, Canada
marcelo.wanderley@mcgill.ca

Abstract. This paper describes preliminary results of a research performed in the framework of the Enactive project (EU IST NoE Enactive). The aim of this research is to improve believability of a virtual character using qualitative analysis of gesture. Using techniques developed for human gesture analysis, we show it is possible to extract high-level motion features from reconstructed motion and to compare them with the same features extracted from the corresponding real motions. Moreover this method allows us to evaluate whether the virtual character conveys the same high level expressive content as the real motion does, and makes it possible to compare different rendering techniques in order to assess which one better maintains such information.

Keywords: Gesture Analysis, Believability, Expressive Motion Content.

1 Introduction

Virtual Reality is improving its performance, reaching high levels of reliability, also thanks to the evolution of hardware technology, such as processor and computational power of new graphic cards. Nevertheless, these fascinating results are not followed by a comparable improvement in the believability of virtual characters, in particular for anthropomorphic avatars. Perception of artifacts from users is still present, something of unnatural is still perceived.

Believability, or more simply, plausibility of virtual characters is an important multidisciplinary aspect that becomes crucial for the improvement of Virtual Reality application.

In this direction, it is interesting the work of Neff [1] for improving the expressive body communication in VR, but it is relating only to stance.

M. Sales Dias et al. (Eds.): GW 2007, LNAI 5085, pp. 48–56, 2009.

As Jean-Louis Vercher well described [2], for improving Virtual Reality it is necessary to consider also perception of biological motion. Following this idea, we handled a research aiming at evaluating the reasons of disbelief in virtual mannequins, following an innovative approach.

In the framework of a joint collaboration within the Enactive Network, we designed and performed an experiment in which the motion of a real musician, a clarinetist, has been compared with the related avatar, reconstructed using IK techniques .

The underlying idea was to use the theories and research results on evaluation of human motion characteristics, to analyze virtual character motion. We decided to consider the virtual musician as a real human, and quantitatively evaluate the characteristics of its motion using the same techniques developed for human motion analysis.

A single clarinetist has been video recorded from the lateral side, and the related avatar has been reconstructed with the same point of view of the video camera. In this way, it has been possible to compare exactly the same motion and to individuate qualitative discrepancies focusing the attention on single gestures or postures.

The sensors on the clarinetist body were applied only on one side, the right side, occluded from the camera view.

This experimental approach demonstrated to be powerful and useful for better understanding the limits of current techniques. Moreover, preliminary results allowed us to refine the IK algorithm, used for generating the virtual character, producing a new set of movies that was evaluated in order to verify the improvement in the quality of the motion of the avatar.

2 Prioritized Inverse Kinematics

We briefly recall here the context of the musician movement recovery from a partial set of sensors (the detailed background on the IK framework can be found in [7]). In this study we recovered a clarinet player movement by exploiting only six positional sensors (markers): two for the ends of the clarinet, and the remaining four for the head, right shoulder, right hip and right knee of the player. The amount of data provided by this set of sensors is insufficient for a traditional motion recovery method. For this reason we took advantage of the possibility to associate a strict priority level to each constraint as detailed in Table1.

Table 1. Constraints and associated priority rank for the musician movement recovery

Constraint	Dimension	Total dimension	Priority rank
Keep the feet fixed on the ground (2 effectors/foot at heel and toe locations)	3/effector	12	1
Project center of mass between the feet	2	2	2
Place both hands on the clarinet	3/hand	6	3
Follow head sensor (position only)	3	3	4
Follow hip sensor (position only)	3	3	4
Attract toward preferred self-collision avoidance and singularity-free posture	Full joint space	Full joint space	5

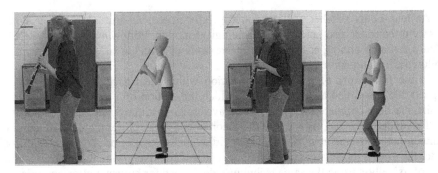

Fig. 1. Some discrepancies between the original movie and the first set of reconstructed movement detected by the qualitative analysis from DIST; (left) neck posture, (right) knee and torso posture

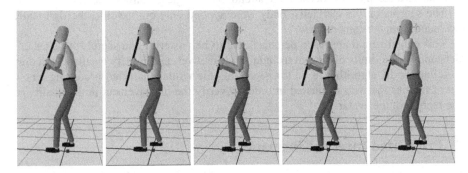

Fig. 2. A few successive postures extracted from the recovered movement with an enlarged support basis and partial guidance in the sagittal plane (only)

We have arrived at this particular ranking by trial and error. For example, it soon became apparent that the constraints used to keep the feet planted required the highest priority, otherwise the virtual player seemed to "hover". In a similar fashion, we had to assign the next-to-highest priority level to the balance constraint, to avoid visually disrupting postures in which the virtual character leaned too much while tracking the head sensor. As for the "attract reference posture" constraint, we had no option but to give it the lowest priority due to its high dimensionality (it controls all the degrees of freedom in the skeleton), which would have prevented the satisfaction of any constraints of lower priority. Overall, this organization through priority levels has strong consequences on the resulting movement as revealed by the qualitative analysis (Figure 1).

Results of the qualitative analysis suggested that the centre of mass was prevented to move freely over the supporting feet. For this reason a second set of reconstructed movements has been elaborated by guiding the centre of mass within the sagittal plane instead of being constrained to remain on its initial vertical line, between the feet. More precisely, while still being unconstrained along the vertical dimension, its projection on the floor was guided forward and backward relatively to the instrument movement. The guidance interval was limited within the support polygon to keep ensuring the balance. We also enlarged the support polygon by two but we kept the same relative priority hierarchy.

Figure 2 shows a few successive postures where we can see the forward displacement of the centre of mass projection on the floor (square on the floor).

3 Qualitative Analysis

Using the EyesWeb Expressive Gesture Processing Library (www.eyesweb.org), developed by InfoMus Lab – DIST, it has been possible to apply the same motion analysis to virtual characters and real humans.

The conducted analysis aimed at evaluating differences in motion qualities between the real subject and his avatar. The ultimate goal we pursued was to improve the believability of the virtual character's motion, in order to obtain a better approximation of the original performance.

We performed this analysis in different steps. After each one, the results were analyzed and converted into feedback for the developers of the IK algorithms. The developers took advantage of such a feedback to enhance the expressive qualities of the virtual character (and hence its believability). The data we show in this paper comes from collecting the results of each individual step.

Three sets of virtual character movies, each one corresponding to a different step of the work, were analyzed and compared with the data obtained from the videos of the original performances:

- The first set included two movies, the first one obtained from the sensor data in real-time (RT) and the other one obtained with a more computationally expensive off-line processing (OL).
- The second set consisted of five movies, each characterized by the number of IK iterations per frame of motion capture data (the more IK iterations, the more accurately the motion is recovered).
- The third set, which contained two movies, was generated after implementing the suggestions of the first qualitative analysis.

For the first set of movies a generalized analysis was performed and a wide palette of motion characteristics was extracted. Two of these characteristics, fluency and space occupation, were found to be more relevant for our believability analysis. They are described briefly in the next section.

3.1 Fluency

Two different definitions and approaches for evaluating fluency were employed in this study.

The first one is an offline evaluation based on the global segmentation of the whole motion in sequences of gesture or motion units. In this work with motion unit we mean a time interval where motion is prevalent. We call such a time intervals *motion bells* or *motion phases*. These are separated by time intervals in which motion is not relevant, i.e., pauses or stance periods, called *non-motion phases*.

Following this concept, fluency can be evaluated by analysing the sequence of motion and non-motion phases. A fluent motion can be defined as a homogeneous combination, in terms of number and shape, of motion and non-motion phases, where there is not a prevalence of non-motion phases or, on the other side, there is not an high segmentation (fragmentation of the motion). In this study we were interested in looking for the differences between real and virtual motion and not in evaluating the global fluency. So it was necessary to match the segmentation in gestures of the reconstructed movies with the segmentation of the real movie in order to identify possible mismatches.

The motion feature extracted in order to perform gesture segmentation was Quantity of Motion[1] QoM (see Camurri et al.[3]). The profile of the temporal trend of this feature consists of a series of motion bells characterizing gestures along time.

By the analysis of the sequence of the motion bells, it is possible to segment motion in areas of prevalent motion and areas of non-motion. Starting from this segmentation along time, it is possible to evaluate the global fluency of motion. Figure 3 shows an example of motion bells. It is important to underline that non-motion phases are not ignored but studied in a different way.

The second fluency evaluation technique is a runtime approach inspired by dance performance (we worked it out from experiments with dancers) and focuses on the discrepancy between movements of different body parts. In particular in standing

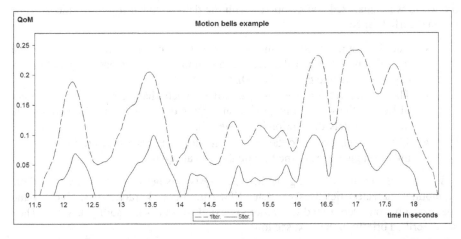

Fig. 3. Motion bells extracted from two movies of the second set. These movies differ in the number of IK iterations (1 vs 5) allowed per frame of input motion data. It is important to notice that in the case of the hatched line there is just one motion bell having a complex profile with many peaks. In the case of the continued line there are instead 4 bells for the same gesture. For this particular case, increasing the number of times the sensor data are processed implies an increase of the fragmentation of the motion.

---

[1] Quantity of Motion is a motion cue; it is a normalized measure assessable from the image sequence of a moving subject. It is proportional to energy and it is evaluated integrating along time the variations of the body silhouette (called Silhouette Motion Images). In this study the time window for integration was set to 400 ms. High frequencies were removed using an alpha filter.

tasks such as walking it is possible to define lack of fluency as a decoupling between the energy of the motion in the upper part of the body (the torso) with respect to the energy in the lower part (the legs). As an example consider a walker who moves his/her torso in order to avoid moving his/her sick leg. In such a case the motion of the torso will be bigger than necessary and, in particular, it will have a higher energy with respect to the motion of the leg.

This approach leads to a new technique for evaluation of fluency. This feature can be extracted as a first approximation by computing the ratio between the QoM evaluated on the upper part of the body and the QoM evaluated on the lower part. More generally, it is possible to compare the energy evaluated on several different body parts[2].

3.2 Space Occupation

Since the information on fluidity puts into evidence a disagreement, in the reconstructed movement, between the motions of the upper part with respect to the lower part, we decided to analyse the two body parts separately, and chose to consider the clarinet as belonging to the upper part of the body.

Following Rudolf Laban's theories [4, 5], a space occupation analysis was performed by extracting and evaluating the Contraction Index[3], *CI* (Camurri et al [3]) from the movies. Since CI depends on posture, posture problems can be detected with this feature. Results highlight that in the reconstructed character posture results to be generally more *open* with respect to the real musician.

In Laban's theory an "*open*" posture is a posture characterized by a low space occupation with respect to the surrounding space of the subject. In psychological theories [5] this feature is usually associated with a positive emotional state if the occupation is low (open postures or gestures) or with a negative one if the occupation is high (closed postures or gestures).

In the context of our work some gestures of the upper part of the body (included the clarinet) are necessary for producing music. The differences between the executions of such gestures imply a difference in the expressivity of gestures (different observers' interpretation) and normally a difference in the produced audio. In this last case, the difference corresponds to a disagreement between the gesture performed by the virtual musician and the sound produced by the real one.

4 Results and Conclusions

Table 2 shows the number of motion phases obtained with motion segmentation from the movies of the virtual and real subjects. For the first set of movies, results show a higher rate of fragmentation of motion in the virtual humanoid. This information

---

[2] For this work we chose upper and lower body parts because the subjects (real and virtual) in the movies were displayed from a lateral viewpoint.

[3] Contraction Index is a motion feature; it is a measure of the space occupation of a single posture. It is measured comparing the surrounding space area of the subject, with the area of the silhouette, i.e. the area really engaged by the subject. In this work the used approximation of the surrounding area is the bounding box of the silhouette.

Table 2. The number of motion phases obtained from segmentation analysis

	Movie	*Number of motion phases*
Real subject movie.	Real	10
First set of movies	Off Line Algorithm	17
	Real Time Algorithm	16
Second set of movies	1 Iteration	11
	2-3-5 Iterations	13
	10 Iterations, Off line	13
Last set of movies with posture correction	Off Line Algorithm	12
	Real Time Algorithm	16

seems quite relevant, since it is likely that the higher segmentation of the reconstructed motion is perceived as a lower fluidity.

Moreover, using the second definition of fluency we proposed, we could also explain the reason of such a higher segmentation rate. In fact, the curve of the ratio of QoM shows a global trend related to the particular motion performed. Such a curve can contain spikes, and each spike represents a potential non-fluent gesture. If the duration of the spike is sufficiently long to be perceived by a human observer[4] (Figure 4), the non-fluent phase is confirmed.

Table 3 reports comparables values for the QoM ratio in the real movie and in the reconstructed movies. It is possible to see the improvement of fluidity in the subsequent sets and also it is possible to identify which number of iterations, in the IK algorithm,

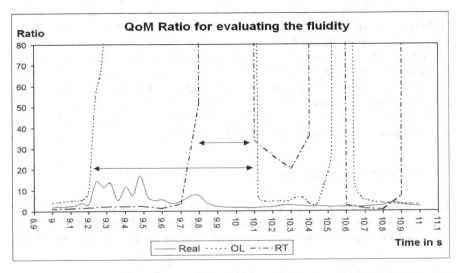

Fig. 4. A zoomed view of the fluidity curve, around second 10, for the first set of movies. The double arrows put in evidence the duration of the OL spikes and of the RT spikes.

---

[4] In this study we considered as a spike a local value in the curve, which is at least ten times higher with respect to the reference curve.

Table 3. An overview of the results obtained with real time analysis of motion fluency

	Movie	Average Value of motion fluency	Max Value of motion fluency
Real subject movie	Real	4.75	56.18
First set of movies	Off Line Algorithm	3,196.76	124,431.00
	Real Time Algorithm	1,571.12	59,626.70
Second set of movies	Worst case 2 Ite.	19.21	1,423.22
	Best case 3 Ite	18.06	776.17
	10 Iterations, Off line	20.45	1,444.72
Last set of movies with posture correction	Off Line algorithm	5.52	195.02
	Real Time Algorithm	10.78	169.64

should be the most efficient. This is due to the management of the constraints in the reconstruction algorithms: the more the algorithm performs iterations on the sensor data, the more the constraints (such as particular joint positions) are met. Moreover, the more the constraints are violated, the more motion mistakes are evident from a perceptual point of view.

In the case of the clarinetist's motion, spikes are mainly due to non-motion of the lower part of the body. This is confirmed examining the QoM curves for the two parts of the body respectively. In the real curves the QoM values for the two parts increase and decrease at the same time, with coherence along time. The reconstructed motion does not have this same coherence. This is mainly due to smooth oscillations present in the real motion, which force a motion of the legs. Moreover, when the motion is concentrated in the torso, the legs follow the motion of the torso. The reconstructed movement is different: motion is concentrated on the arms and torso, while legs have just to compensate equilibrium.

In terms of space occupation it is possible to see that the upper part of the body, for the real and the virtual subjects, performs the same sequence of gestures, but the virtual characters have a lower occupation of the surrounding space.

This means that the virtual mannequins are performing the same variations of posture in terms of contraction and expansion, but with postures that are locally more open.

The leg motion of the musician has generally a high spatial occupation (closed posture) with small local variations in order to follow the upper body motion. In the reconstructed human, on the contrary, the motion of the legs is reduced to little oscillations. For the virtual subject the posture is quite constant, perturbations are due to the equilibrium constraint.

This result is mainly observed in the first set of movies. In fact, after the identification of this motion fault, a modification to the equilibrium constraint was applied and this divergence has been reduced.

In conclusion, two main factors were identified as conveyors of unbelievability in the reconstructed motion: the occupation of the surrounding space with local unbelievable postures, and the fluidity of motion. Using techniques developed for human gesture analysis, we showed how it is possible to extract high-level motion features from the reconstructed motion and to compare them with the same features extracted from the corresponding real motions. Moreover, these features allow a qualitative comparison between different rendering techniques. This resulted in a precious complementary tool to believability studies that are currently often based on analysing solely viewer feedback through questionnaires.

5 Future Work

In the Enactive Framework the work here presented will be improved following two directions. The first direction aims at improving the analysis with other motion qualities related to believability, and aims at generalizing the method by analyzing other types of musicians (e.g., flute players). The second direction tries to extend the work in the 3D perspective. Related to these new activities some recording sessions has been organized involving a clarinetist and a violinist, with a complete motion tracking using markers on the whole body, Optotrack System, and two video cameras.

Acknowledgments

This research has been supported by the E.U. Network of Excellence on Enactive Interfaces. We would like to thank Marie-Julie Chagnon for the data from her clarinet performance.

References

1. Neff, M., Fiume, M.: Methods for Exploring Expressive Stance. In: Boulic, R., Pai, D.K. (eds.) Proc. Eurographics/ACM SIGGRAPH Symposium on Computer Animation (2004)
2. Vercher, J.-L.: Perception and synthesis of biologically plausible motion. In: Gibet, S., Courty, N., Kamp, J.-F. (eds.) GW 2005. LNCS (LNAI), vol. 3881, pp. 1–12. Springer, Heidelberg (2006)
3. Camurri, A., Mazzarino, B., Volpe, G.: Analysis of expressive gesture: The eyesWeb expressive gesture processing library. In: Camurri, A., Volpe, G. (eds.) GW 2003. LNCS, vol. 2915, pp. 460–467. Springer, Heidelberg (2004)
4. Laban, R., Lawrence, F.C.: Effort. Macdonald & Evans Ltd., London (1947)
5. Laban, R.: Modern Educational Dance. Macdonald & Evans Ltd., London (1963)
6. Wallbott, H.G.: Bodily expression of emotion. European Journal of Social Psychology. Eur. J. Soc. Psychol. 28, 879–896 (1998)
7. Boulic, R., Peinado, M., Raunhardt, D.: Challenges in Exploiting Prioritized Inverse Kinematics for Motion Capture and Postural Control. In: Gibet, S., Courty, N., Kamp, J.-F. (eds.) GW 2005. LNCS (LNAI), vol. 3881, pp. 176–187. Springer, Heidelberg (2006)

A Method for Selection of Optimal Hand Gesture Vocabularies

Helman Stern, Juan Wachs, and Yael Edan

Department of Industrial Engineering and Management,
Ben-Gurion University of the Negev, Beer Sheva, 84105, Israel
{helman,juan,yael}@bgu.ac.il

Abstract. This work presents an analytical approach to design a gesture vocabulary (GV) using multiobjectives for psycho-physiological and gesture recognition factors. Previous works dealt only with selection of hand gestures vocabularies using rule based or ad-hoc methods. The analytical formulation in our research is a demonstration of the future need defined by previous research. A meta-heuristic approach is taken by decomposing the problem into two sub-problems: (i) finding the subsets of gestures that meet a minimal accuracy requirement, and (ii) matching gestures to commands to maximize the human factors objective. The result is a set of solutions from which a Pareto optimal subset is selected. An example solution from the Pareto set is exhibited using prioritized objectives.

Keywords: hand gesture vocabulary design, multiobjective optimization, fuzzy c-means, feature selection, gesture interfaces, hand gesture recognition, human-computer interaction.

1 Introduction

Hand gestures to control systems require high learnability, usability, ergonomic design and comfort [1]. Unfortunately, most gesture interfaces are designed with the technical consideration of recognition accuracy as the central focus. The selection of hand gestures that consider recognition accuracy as well as the ease of learning, lack of stress, cognitively natural, and ease of implementation is still an open research question.

An example of intuitive hand gesture vocabulary selection can be found in [2]. The value of [2] is that it allows the user to act more naturally since no cognitive effort is required in mapping function keys to robotic hand actions. This system, like others, is based in navigation control and implements deictic gestures to make them intuitive. Many applications can be criticized for their idiosyncratic choice of hand gestures or postures to control or direct computer-mediated tasks [3]. However, the choice was probably perfectly natural for the developer of the application but may not be for others, which would show the dependence of gestures on their cultural and social environment. Within a society, gestures have standard meanings, but no body motion or gesture has the same meaning in all societies [4]. Even in the American Sign Language (ASL), few signs are so clearly transparent that a non-signer can guess their

M. Sales Dias et al. (Eds.): GW 2007, LNAI 5085, pp. 57–68, 2009.
© Springer-Verlag Berlin Heidelberg 2009

meaning without additional clues [5]. Additionally, gestures can be culturally defined to have specific meanings. Even though the naturalness of hand gestures is different from person to person, there are common gestures that are similar for a wide range of cultures. For instance, the most natural way to choose an object is to point to it. To stop a vehicle, most people open their palm towards the vehicle. To show that everything is "ok", people close their fist and extend the thumb upwards. In everyday life, it is quite unlikely that users will be interested in a device for which they have to learn some specific set of gestures and postures, unless there is an obvious increase in efficiency or ease of use. On the other hand, the economics of the marketplace may dictate such a set independent of its compatibility with existing cultural and/or social standards. For a gesture set to gain major acceptance in the market place, it is advisable to examine the tasks and semiotic functions most frequently executed, and then choose a hand gesture set that seems to appear natural, at least to a number of different people within a social group or even a culture, when executing those tasks and functions.

In [6], it was found that people consistently used the same gestures for specific commands. In particular they found that people are also very proficient at learning new arbitrary gestures. In [7] it was found that test subjects used very similar gestures for the same operations. In [6], Hauptmann, et al found a high degree of similarity in the gesture types used by different people to perform the same manipulations. Test subjects were not coached beforehand, indicating that there may be intuitive, common principles in gesture communication.

In this work the aim is to design a gesture vocabulary that is both intuitive and comfortable on the one hand, and can be recognized with high accuracy, on the other. The first step is to decide on a task dependent set of commands to be included in the vocabulary such as; "move left", "increase speed", etc. The second step is to decide how to express the command in gestural form i.e., what physical expression to use such as, waving the hand left to right or making a "V" sign with the first two fingers. The association (matching) of each command to a gestural expression is defined here as a "gesture vocabulary" (GV). These steps constitute a meta-heuristic procedure for solving the gesture vocabulary design problem. The procedure is formulated as a multiobjective optimization problem (MOP).

In the next section the problem is defined. This is followed in section 3 by a description of the solution architecture; comprised of hand gesture factor determination, gesture subset selection, command-gesture matching, and selection of pareto optimal multiobjective solutions. In section 4 an example is solved to illustrate the procedure. Section 5 provides conclusions.

2   Problem Statement

An optimal hand gesture vocabulary, GV, is defined as a set of gesture-command pairs, such that it will minimize the time τ for a given user (or users) to perform a task, (or collection of tasks). The number of commands, n, is determined by the task(s), while the set of gestures, G_n, is selected from a large set of hand postures, called the gesture "master-set". The main problem is to minimize task, performance time τ over a set of all feasible gesture vocabularies, Γ. However, since the task completion time, as a function of GV, has no known analytical form, we propose three different performance measures as proxies: intuitiveness $Z_1(GV)$, comfort $Z_2(GV)$ and recognition accuracy $Z_3(GV)$. The first two measures are user centered, while the last is machine centered. This MOP may have conflicting solutions where all the objectives can not be maximized simultaneously. As with most multiobjective problems this difficulty is overcome by allowing the decision maker to select the best GV according to his own preferences.

Problem P_1

$$Max\ Z_1(GV), Max\ Z_2(GV), Max\ Z_3(GV)$$
$$GV \in \Gamma \tag{1}$$

Each of the performance measures is described as a function of the given gesture vocabulary GV, below.

Intuitiveness is the naturalness of expressing a given command with a gesture. There are two types of *intuitiveness; direct* and *complementary*. For direct intuitiveness, let p be an assignment function where p(i)=j indicates that the command i is assigned to gesture j. The value $a_{i,p(i)}$, represents the strength of the association between command i and its matched gesture p(i). Complementary intuitiveness, $a_{i,p(i),j,p(j)}$ is the level of association expressed by the matching of complementary gestures pairs (p(i), p(j)) to complementary command pairs (i,j). The total intuitiveness is shown in (2).

$$Z_1(GV) = \sum_{i=1}^{n} a_{i,p(i)} + \sum_{i=1}^{n}\sum_{j=1}^{n} a_{i,p(i),j,p(j)} \tag{2}$$

Stress/Comfort is related to the strength needed to perform a gesture. Obviously, there are gestures that are easier to perform than others. Total stress is a scalar value equal to the sum of the individual stress values to hold the postures, and to perform transitions between them, weighted by duration and frequency of use. The value of s_{kl} represents the physical difficulty of a transition between gestures k and l. The duration to reconfigure the hand between gestures k and l is represented by d_{kl}. The symbol f_{ij} stands for the frequency of transition between commands i and j. The value K is a constant and is used to convert stress into its inverse measure comfort.

$$Z_2(GV) = K - \sum_{i=1}^{n}\sum_{j=1}^{n} f_{ij}\, d_{p(i)p(j)} s_{p(i),p(j)} \tag{3}$$

Accuracy is a measure of how well a set of gestures can be recognized. To obtain an estimate of gesture accuracy, a set of sample gestures for each gesture in G_n is required to train a gesture recognition system. The number of gestures classified correctly and misclassified is denoted as T_g and T_e, respectively. The gesture recognition accuracy is denoted by (4).

$$Z_3(GV) = \left[(T_g - T_e)/T_g\right] 100 \tag{4}$$

3 Architecture of the Solution Methodology

Maximizing each of the performance measures over the set of all feasible GVs defines P_1. Solving P_1 is difficult, especially because gesture recognition accuracy (objective Z_3)

is not an analytical function and enumeration is untenable, for even reasonable size vocabularies As such, the problem is restructured into a two stage decomposition approach, with a dual priority objective, where recognition accuracy is considered of prime importance, and the human performance objectives are secondary. By considering A_{min}, the minimum acceptable accuracy, as a constraint (6) and combining the intuitive and comfort objectives into one objective, $\overline{Z}$, using weights w_1, w_2 we obtain problem P_2.

Problem P_2

$$Max\overline{Z}(GV) = w_1 Z_1(GV) + w_2 Z_2(GV) \tag{5}$$

$$GV \in \varGamma$$

$$s.t. \quad Z_3(GV) \geq A_{min} \tag{6}$$

The architecture of the solution methodology is comprised of four modules (Fig. 1). In Module 1, human psycho-physiological input factors are determined. In Module 2, gesture subsets satisfying (6) are determined; Module 3 constitutes a command - gesture matching procedure. Finally, the set of Pareto optimal solutions is found in Module 4.

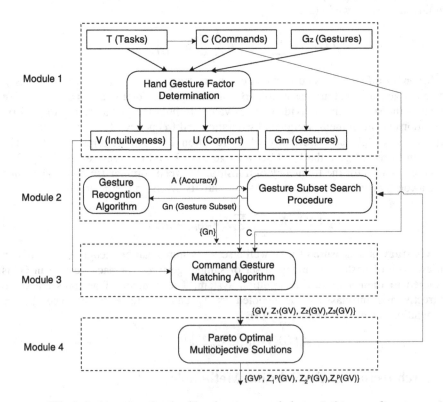

Fig. 1. Architecture of optimal hand gesture vocabulary solution procedure

3.1 Module 1: Hand Gesture Factor Determination

The task set T, a large gesture master set G_z and the set of commands C are the input parameters to the Module 1. The objective of Module 1, to find the comfort matrix based on command transitions and fatigue measures, and to reduce the large set of gestures, to the master set G_m. The intuitiveness V, comfort U, and gesture G_m, matrices values were determined through experimental studies the details which can be found in [10][11][12].

Task and Command Sets (T, C): For each task t_i , a set C of c_i commands are defined, as the union of all the task commands.

Command Transition Matrix (F): For a command set C of size n, a matrix F_{nxn} is constructed where; f_{ij} represents the frequency that a command c_j is evoked given that the last command was c_i. The frequency of command usage is determined by experiments using real or virtual models to carry out the tasks.

Large Gestures Master Set (G_z): Since the set of all possible gestures is infinite, we established a set of plausible gesture configurations based on a synthetic gesture generator using finger positions (extended, spread), palm orientations (up, down sideways), and wrist rotations (left, middle, right) as the primitives. Encodings for the sample gestures are shown in Fig. 2.

00000000000   10000000000   20000000000   02010000000   10011000100   10111111111

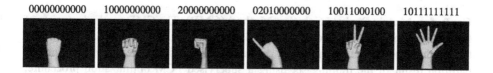

Fig. 2. Synthetic hand gestures

The direct intuitive matrix (I): The intuitiveness matrix, $I_{m \times n}$ is composed of indices a_{ik} which represent the naturalness of using gesture i for command k.

The complementary intuitive matrix (I'): The naturalness of matching up a pair of complementary commands (i, j) with a pair of complementary gestures (k,l), is represented by a complementary intuitive index of the form a_{ijkl} . The matrix of complementary intuitive indices $I'_{n,m \times n,m}$ can be quite large, but can be compacted considerably as most of the entries will be zero. Denote V=[I, I'] as the set of matrices including both the direct and complementary matrices.

The gesture master set (G_m): Each element of the intuitive matrix I indicates the number of times that a gesture i was used to represent command j. The row sums indicate how popular a gesture is. The normalized popularity of gesture i, p_i, can be used to reduce the master set of postures. Those gestures below a popularity threshold t are removed to obtain the reduced master set G_m (see (7)).

$$G_m = \{ g_i \mid p_i \geq t \} \quad , \quad p_i = \sum_{k=1}^{n} a_{ik} \bigg/ \sum_{k=1, j=1}^{n} a_{jk} \tag{7}$$

Fatigue and Comfort Matrices (S,U): The fatigue (or comfort) indices are arranged in a matrix $S_{m \times m}$, whose common element s_{ij} represents the physical difficulty of performing a transition from gesture i to gesture j. Let the coefficients u_{ijkl} be the entries of a square matrix, $U_{nm \times nm}$. An entry $u_{ijkl} = K - f_{ij} \times s_{kl}$ represents the frequency of transition between commands i to j times the stress of a command transition k to l given that i and j are paired with gestures k and l, respectively. This product reflects the concept that the total stress measure of GV depends on the frequency of use of a gesture or a gesture pair transition. The total comfort is the difference between the constant and the total stress detailed above. Note, that the diagonal entries s_{ii} represent the total stress of using a gesture repeatedly to carry out the same command.

3.2 Module 2: Gesture Subset Selection

For Module 2, the necessary inputs are the reduced master set of gestures G_m, and a recognition algorithm to determine A. This module employs an iterative search procedure to find a set of gesture subsets $\{G_n\}$, satisfying a given accuracy level as in (6). The subset search procedure is based on the properties of the confusion matrix of the multi gesture recognition algorithm, and is described below.

Confusion Matrix Derived Solution Method (CMD). The CMD method consists of three phases: (i) train the recognition algorithm for the gestures in G_m, and let $\mathcal{C}_m$ be the resulting confusion matrix[*]. The confusion matrix is obtained directly from the partition result of the training set using a supervised FCM optimization procedure, [13], (ii) find a submatrix $\mathcal{C}_n$ from $\mathcal{C}_m$ with the highest recognition accuracy whose corresponding G_n meets the minimum accuracy constraint, and (iii) Repeat (ii) until a given number of solutions are found.

Let G_k be a set of gesture indices ($k \leq n$).

Let $\mathcal{C}_{m-k}$ be a reduced confusion matrix after deleting the set of rows and columns defined by G_k.

Let N be the number of solutions requested.

A set of N feasible solutions G_n can be obtained, using the CMD algorithm described below.

The CMD algorithm obtains N solutions (or all the solutions with associated accuracy above a given minimum allowed A_{min} if less than N). Each iteration of the CMD algorithm generates a new solution by excluding each time a different gesture, from the subset of gestures of the current solution, and adding a new gesture from the master set.

Let j be the current solution number. The first time that this algorithm is called, $G_n = \phi$ and j=0.

---

[*] Without loss of generality we assume $\mathcal{C}_m$ is square.

The CD Routine (G$_k$, j, A$_{min}$)
1. Let the number of gestures k=|G$_k$|. Let n=|C| be the number of commands
2. Repeat (n-k) times: (a) Find the least confused gesture i' (break ties arbitrary) in the confusion matrix $\mathcal{C}_{m-k}$ using $\arg\max_{i=1,\ldots,m-k}\{C_{ii}\}=C_{i'i'}$. (b). $G_{k+1}=G_k\cup i$. (c) Remove the corresponding column and row i from C$_m$.
3. Find $\mathcal{C}_n^j$ according to the indices in G$_n$ and calculate A(G$_n$)
4. If A(G$_n$) ≥ A$_{min}$ then G$_n^j$ = G$_n$ is a feasible solution, and added to the set {G$_n$}, otherwise it is not.
5. Stop

The CMD Algorithm(N, A$_{min}$)
1. Initialization: $G_k=\phi$, j=0,
2. G$_n^j$=CD (G$_k$, j, A$_{min}$)
3. Calculate A using $\mathcal{C}_n$, If G$_n^j$=ϕ then exit
4. Remove the most confused gesture i from G$_n^j$, and remove the corresponding column and row i from $\mathcal{C}_m$.
5. G$_n^{j+1}$=CD(G$_n^j$, j, A$_{min}$)
6. If G$_n^{j+1}$ belongs to the feasible solution subset. (a) Take out the highest confused gesture k, from G$_n^j$. (b) Restore the corresponding column and row k from $\mathcal{C}_m$. (c) Go to 4.
10. If A ≥ A$_{min}$ then add G$_n^{j+1}$ to the feasible solution subset. Restore $\mathcal{C}_m$ to the original
12. If j<N and A ≥ A$_{min}$, return to 4.

3.3 Module 3: Command-Gesture Matching

The inputs to the third module are the matrices; intuitiveness V, comfort U, command C, and the subset of gestures {G$_n$}. The goal of this module is to match the set of gestures G$_n$ to the set of commands, C, such that the human measures are maximized. The resulting gesture-command assignment constitutes a gesture vocabulary, GV.

Given a single set of gestures G$_n$ found from module 2, the gesture-command matching can be represented as a quadratic integer assignment problem (QAP) [8] shown below as Problem P$_3$.

Problem P$_3$

$$max\ \overline{Z}(G_n^*)=w_2\sum_{i=1}^{n}\sum_{j=1}^{n}\sum_{k=1}^{n}\sum_{l=1}^{n}u_{ijkl}x_{ik}x_{jl}+w_1\left[\sum_{i}^{n}\sum_{j}^{n}v_{ij}x_{ij}+\sum_{i=1}^{n}\sum_{j=1}^{n}\sum_{k=1}^{n}\sum_{l=1}^{n}v_{ijkl}x_{ik}x_{jl}\right] \quad (8)$$

$$\sum_{j=1}^{n}x_{ij}=1,\quad i=1,..,n, \quad (9)$$

$$\sum_{i=1}^{n} x_{ij} = 1, \qquad j = 1,...,n, \tag{10}$$

$$x_{ij} \in \{0,1\}; \qquad i = 1,...,n, \qquad j = 1,...,n, \tag{11}$$

Here, the x_{ij} binary assignment variable equals to 1 if command i is assigned to gesture j, and zero otherwise. Constraint (9) insures that each command is paired with exactly one gesture. Constraint (10) insures that each gesture is paired with exactly one command. A simulated annealing approach from [9] is adopted to solve P_3. For each subset G_n found on Module 2, Problem P_3 is solved by varying the weights such that $w_1 + w_2 = 10$. This results in a set of GV solutions corresponding to each G_n in $\{G_n\}$.

3.4 Module 4: Pareto Optimal Multiobjective Solution

Let each of the N solutions (gesture subsets G_n) from Module 2, have M associated solutions. This results in a total of $N \times M$ candidate GV's, each may be represented as a point in 3D space, (Z_1, Z_2, Z_3). The total set of multiobjective candidate solutions is then $\{Z_1(GV), Z_2(GV), Z_3(GV): GV = \{1,..., N \times M\}$. From this set is possible to find a set of Pareto solutions. A Pareto solution is one that is not dominated by any other solution. That is, a Pareto solution is one in which one cannot increase one performance measure without decreasing at least one of the others. The Pareto solutions offer a reduced set of candidate solutions from which a decision maker can select the GV that meets his/her internal preferences.

4   Experiments and Results

To determine the feasibility of the approach, a robotic arm control task using hand gestures is used. The task includes fifteen commands to control the direction of movement of the robot, and additional functions to interact with the objects in the environment. The gestures will be extracted from a master set of 23 postures, and matched to the 15 commands (see Fig. 3). The master set was obtained from an empirical study in which gestures were selected by subjects in response to command stimuli. Gesture comfort indices and frequency of use were also obtained by an empirical experiment. Details of the empirical experiments may be found in [11] [12].

4.1   Obtaining the set of GV's

The algorithm CMD generated the five solutions shown in Table 1, where the minimal acceptable accuracy was set to 98.33 percent.

The set of candidate solutions associated with each subset G_n, was obtained by solving P_3 with unit changes of w_1, w_2 such that $w_1 + w_2 = 10$. The solutions generated reflect the gradual transfer of importance between intuitiveness and comfort. For each pair of weights (w_1, w_2) and a gesture subset G_n, a solution is obtained in terms of a gesture-command matching (GV) and the associated values of Z_2 and Z_3. Since there were 5 different subsets of gestures, and 11 weight combinations, a total of 55 solutions were obtained. The plots in Fig. 4 show the intuitiveness versus comfort

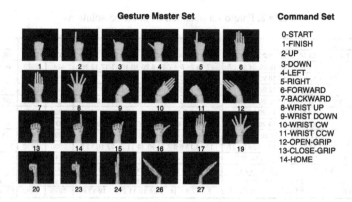

Fig. 3. Gesture master set and command set for the robotic arm task

Table 1. Subset of gestures obtained using the CMD method

id	Gn	Acc(%)
1	4 6 7 8 10 11 13 14 16 17 19 20 24 26 27	98.5
2	4 5 6 7 8 10 11 14 16 17 19 20 24 26 27	98.5
3	5 6 7 8 10 11 13 14 16 17 19 20 24 26 27	98.33
4	4 5 6 7 8 10 11 13 14 16 19 20 24 26 27	98.33
5	4 5 6 7 8 10 11 13 14 16 17 19 24 26 27	98.33

trade offs for each G_n and its associated accuracy $A(G_n)$. All the associated GV solutions for a given G_n are displayed as a connected curve. This family of curves is shown in a space orthogonal to the recognition accuracy coordinate. From this set of solutions, it is possible to find the Pareto set of GVs.

4.2 The Pareto Set

Table 2 shows the thirteen Pareto points, found from the families of curves generated using the different weights. The second column shows the G_n solution ID number from which the curve was generated. The fourth column shows the GV solution, where the order of gestures corresponds to the command to which it was matched. The next three columns show intuitiveness, comfort and accuracy values, and the last two columns are the intuitiveness and comfort weights used.

Fig. 5 shows the multiobjective value points with the pareto points indicated by circles. Each point represents a solution in terms of intuitiveness, comfort and accuracy values.

The decision maker may wish to prioritize the objectives such that accuracy Z_3, intuitiveness Z_1, and comfort Z_2 are considered as the 1st, 2nd and 3rd priorities, respectively. Using this criteria, the following solution is obtained: GV* = {14,7,17,6,4,16,24,20,10,11,26,27,19,13,8} (row 7 in Table 2). The associated objective values for this solution are $(Z_1. Z_2, Z_3)$ = (6671, 5458, 98.5%). An image of the solution GV* is presented in Fig. 6.

Table 2. Pareto set obtained from the 55 solutions

No	sol	Gn	GV	Z(i,1)	Z(i,2)	Z(i,3)	w1	w2
1	1	4 6 7 8 10 11 13 14 16 17 19 20 24 26 27	27 14 8 6 4 7 20 24 13 10 19 11 17 26 16	67	5930	98.5	0	10
2	1	4 6 7 8 10 11 13 14 16 17 19 20 24 26 27	27 14 24 6 4 7 20 8 26 10 19 11 17 13 16	424	5929	98.5	1	9
3	1	4 6 7 8 10 11 13 14 16 17 19 20 24 26 27	10 14 24 6 4 7 20 8 26 27 19 11 17 13 16	651	5927	98.5	2	8
4	1	4 6 7 8 10 11 13 14 16 17 19 20 24 26 27	10 14 17 6 4 7 24 20 26 27 8 11 19 13 16	3602	5862	98.5	6	4
5	1	4 6 7 8 10 11 13 14 16 17 19 20 24 26 27	10 14 17 6 4 16 24 20 26 27 7 11 19 13 8	6331	5645	98.5	7	3
6	1	4 6 7 8 10 11 13 14 16 17 19 20 24 26 27	10 8 17 6 4 16 24 20 26 27 7 11 19 13 14	6335	5633	98.5	8	2
7	1	4 6 7 8 10 11 13 14 16 17 19 20 24 26 27	14 7 17 6 4 16 24 20 10 11 26 27 19 13 8	6671	5458	98.5	9	1
8	2	4 5 6 7 8 10 11 14 16 17 19 20 24 26 27	10 14 8 6 4 7 24 20 26 27 19 11 17 5 16	1092	5883	98.5	3	7
9	3	5 6 7 8 10 11 13 14 16 17 19 20 24 26 27	10 14 17 6 8 7 24 20 16 11 26 27 19 13 5	3890	5710	98.333	7	3
10	4	4 5 6 7 8 10 11 13 14 16 19 20 24 26 27	10 14 8 6 4 7 24 20 26 27 19 11 5 13 16	1117	5866	98.333	3	7
11	4	4 5 6 7 8 10 11 13 14 16 19 20 24 26 27	10 14 7 6 4 16 24 20 26 27 8 11 19 13 5	5086	5687	98.333	7	3
12	5	4 5 6 7 8 10 11 13 14 16 17 19 24 26 27	10 14 17 6 4 16 24 7 26 27 8 11 19 13 5	5541	5647	98.333	5	5
13	5	4 5 6 7 8 10 11 13 14 16 17 19 24 26 27	5 7 17 6 4 16 14 24 10 11 26 27 19 13 8	6979	5287	98.333	10	0

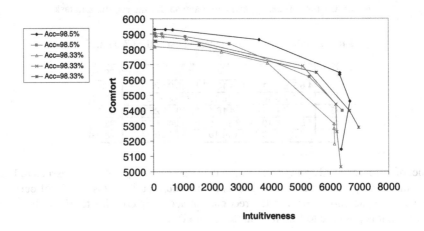

Fig. 4. Intuitiveness vs. comfort families of 5 curves

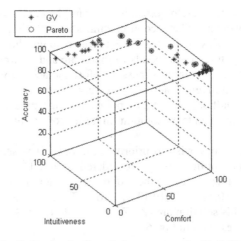

Fig. 5. 3D plot for the solutions generated with 5 GVs

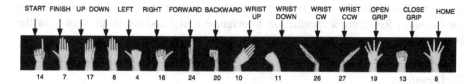

Fig. 6. A GV selected by the decision maker from the pareto solutions

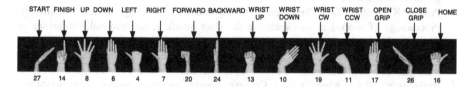

Fig. 7. A GV showing low intuitiveness from the pareto solutions

It can be seen that the resulting solution contains many complementary gesture-command pairings. For example, the left and right commands are represented by a wrist flip. Also, the commands closing and opening the gripper are represented by closing and opening of the fist. Fig. 7 shows another GV selected from the Pareto set (sol 1 of Table 2) with the same accuracy, but low intuitiveness. The resultant solution matches highly comfortable gestures with the commands used most frequently. For example, the right command has a high frequency of use and is matched with gesture 7 which is more comfortable than gesture 16.

5 Conclusions

A two stage decomposition approach is proferred for finding the solution to an optimal hand gesture vocabulary problem. The first stage finds a feasible subset of gestures from the master set, given some recognition accuracy threshold, A_{min}. The second stage finds a set of gesture vocabularies, each obtained by finding the best match between commands and gestures so that a weighted sum of the total intuitiveness and comfort are maximized. A confusion matrix derived (CMD) solution method is used to solve the first stage problem by searching for the best gesture candidates from a master set of gestures G_m. The CMD method is an approximation method for determining subsets of gestures and their associated accuracies. It requires using a supervised fuzzy c-means optimization procedure only once, and uses values from the confusion matrix to approximate the recognition accuracy of the subsets.

The CMD was used to obtain five initial gesture subsets G_n with A_{min}=98.33%, for a robotic arm task. For each G_n,va set of 55 associated GVs were obtained which constituted a set of candidate solutions. From this, set thirteen Pareto points were obtained and offered to the decision maker to select the GV according to his/her own preferences. Future work will include dynamic gestures embedded in our methodology. Also, usability tests are planned to obtain user evaluated insights for the selected Pareto solutions.

Acknowledgments. This research was partially supported by the Paul Ivanier Center for Robotics Research & Production Management at Ben-Gurion University of the Negev.

References

1. Baudel, T., Beaudouin-Lafon, M.: Charade: remote control of objects using freehand gestures. Communications of the ACM 36(7), 28–35 (1993)
2. Pook, P.K., Ballard, D.H.: Teleassistance: A gestural sign language for teleoperation. In: Proceedings of Workshop on Gesture at the User Interface, International Conference on Computer-Human Interaction CHI 1995, Denver, CO, USA (1995)
3. Baudel, T., Beaudouin-Lafon, M., Braffort, A., Teil, D.: An interaction model designed for hand gesture input, Technical Report No. 772, LRI, Université de Paris-Sud, France (1992)
4. Birdwhistell, R.L.: Kinesics and Context; essays on body motion communication. University of Pennsylvania Press, Philadelphia (1970)
5. Klima, E.S., Bellugi, U.: Language in another mode. Language and brain: developmental aspects, Neurosciences research program bulletin 12(4), 539–550 (1974)
6. Hauptmann, A.G., McAvinney, P.: Gestures with speech for graphic manipulation. International Journal of Man-Machine Studies 38(2), 231–249 (1993)
7. Wolf, C.G., Morrel-Samuels, P.: The use of hand-drawn gestures for text editing. International Journal of Man-Machine Studies 27, 91–102 (1987)
8. Koopmans, T.C., Beckmann, M.J.: Assignment problems and the location of economic activities. Econometrica 25, 53–76 (1957)
9. Connolly, D.T.: An improved annealing scheme for the QAP. European Journal of Operational Research 46, 93–100 (1990)
10. Stern, H., Wachs, J., Edan, Y.: Human factors for design of hand gesture Human - Machine Interaction. In: Proceedings of 2006 IEEE International Conference on Systems, Man, and Cybernetics, pp. 4052–4056 (2006)
11. Wachs, J.: Optimal Hand Gesture Vocabulary Design Methodology for Virtual Robotic Control. PhD Dissertation, Ben Gurion University of the Negev, Israel (2007)
12. Stern, H., Wachs, J., Edan, Y.: Designing Hand Gesture Vocabularies for Natural Interaction by Combining Psycho-Physiological and Recognition Factors. Special Issue on Gesture in Multimodal Systems, International Journal of Semantic Computing 2(1), 1–24 (2008)
13. Wachs, J., Stern, H., Edan, Y.: Cluster Labeling and Parameter Estimation for the Automated Setup of a Hand-Gesture Recognition System. IEEE Transactions on Systems, Man and Cybernetics. Part A 35(6), 932–944 (2005)

Person-Independent 3D Sign Language Recognition

Jeroen F. Lichtenauer[1], Gineke A. ten Holt[1,2], Marcel J.T. Reinders[1], and Emile A. Hendriks[1]

[1] Information and Communication Theory Group, Delft University of Technology, Mekelweg 4, 2628 CD, Delft, The Netherlands
[2] Human Information Communication Design, Delft University of Technology, Landbergstraat 15, 2628 CE, Delft, The Netherlands
{j.f.lichtenauer,g.a.tenholt,m.j.t.reinders,e.a.hendriks}@tudelft.nl

Abstract. In this paper, we present a person independent 3D system for judging the correctness of a sign. The system is camera-based, using computer vision techniques to track the hand and extract features. 3D co-ordinates of the hands and other features are calculated from stereo images. The features are then modeled statistically and automatic feature selection is used to build the classifiers. Each classifier is meant to judge the correctness of one sign. We tested our approach using a 120-sign vocabulary and 75 different signers. Overall, a true positive rate of 96.5% at a false positive rate of 3.5% is achieved. The system's performance in a real-world setting largely agreed with human expert judgement.

1 Introduction

Sign languages are natural languages that emerge in Deaf communities and possess their own grammars and vocabularies. For (pre-lingually) deaf children, sign language is the only language that can be acquired naturally, and as such is important for their development [1]. However, most deaf children are born into hearing families [1]. This means that their parents often have to learn sign language themselves first, and that the amount and quality of natural language available to a deaf child is poor compared to hearing children.

We aim to build an interactive learning environment (ELo) [2] for young deaf children to practise their sign language vocabulary. With such a system available at home or in the classroom, children would have an extra source of sign language input and extra opportunity to practise signing and receive feedback on their signs. ELo consists of several modules. In one module, the child is asked to make a certain sign, and the system gives feedback on the correctness of the sign. To realize this module, it was necessary to build a sign language recognizer that can judge the correctness of a sign. This recognizer is the subject of this paper.

Because of its purpose, there are several requirements for the recognizer. It must work real-time and person-independently. It must be mobile and work in different surroundings (at school, at home). It must be vision-based, because we do not want to encumber the children with sensors or markers. And it must

M. Sales Dias et al. (Eds.): GW 2007, LNAI 5085, pp. 69–80, 2009.
© Springer-Verlag Berlin Heidelberg 2009

deal with variation and sloppiness. Since ELo's goal is vocabulary training, the recognizer only needs to handle isolated signs.

Previous work in the field of automatic sign language recognition included approaches using Hidden Markov Models (HMMs) [3,4,5], and various machine learning techniques [6,7,8]. The recognition rates of these early systems were typically around 80-90%, and they were trained and tested on single signers (except for [6], who used six signers). More recent projects, using (H)MMs representing whole words [9,12] or parts of words [10,11], achieved better results: 85-98%. However, none of them provide person-independent test results. [13] achieved a recognition rate of 92% with whole word HMMs, but this dropped to 84% when six signers were used. Similarly, [14] achieved 98% accuracy with one signer, but only 55% with multiple signers. Clearly, the variation in sign execution between persons remains a problem for sign recognition. Current attempts to remedy this problem include adapting basic sign models to specific signers [14,15], and gathering an appropriate sign language corpus [16]. All projects described used medium-sized vocabularies (size 10-262), except [13] who worked with 5,113 signs. Some projects were vision-based, others ([4,6,7,11,13]) worked with gloves and/or trackers.

For ELo, we need person-independent sign recognition — different children must be able to work with it. It must be noted, however, that our aim is slightly different from that of the aforementioned projects: instead of distinguishing between a set of signs, we want to judge the correctness of a sign. This means that we want to distinguish each sign from "anything else". We therefore create a one-class classifier for each sign in our vocabulary. Its purpose is to take an input sign and judge whether this was the expected sign or not. This makes our task both easier and harder than simple distinguishing. Easier, because we know which sign we expect, but harder, because we must be able to exclude anything else, even movements we have never seen before.

In the next section, we give an overview of our system. The subsequent sections discuss the system's components in detail. Recognition results are given in section 6, and section 7 presents the discussion.

2   System Setup

Figure 1(a) gives an overview of the physical setup of the system. The child is seated in front of a touchscreen, through which it interfaces with the system. Above the screen, stereo cameras are placed to record the child's signs. To control the environment, the system is set inside a cube-shaped tent. This ensures that lighting, background and distance to the cameras are controlled, which makes it possible to use the system in different locations. Indirect lighting is provided by shining 4 11W-lights (with a total light emittance equivalent to a 240W light bulb) onto the white wall behind the touchscreen. The computer running the system is outside the tent. There is room for an adult supervisor on the side.

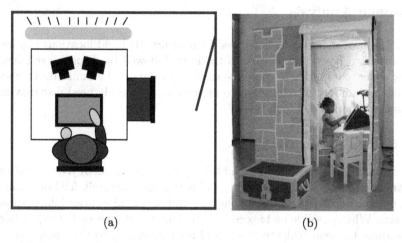

(a)   (b)

Fig. 1. (a) Overview of the system. The child is seated at a table behind a touchscreen. His/her signs are recorded by stereo cameras. Indirect lighting is provided by shining light onto the white wall. There is room for an adult supervisor. A tent (made to look like a play castle on the outside) encloses the system, ensuring no interference from other light sources/persons. (b) The setup in reality.

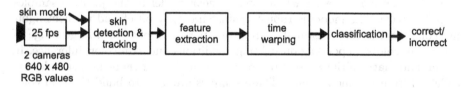

Fig. 2. Flow diagram of the sign recognition system. Input from the 2 cameras is combined to 3D features in the feature extraction step.

Since skin colour is used to track the hands, the child must wear long-sleeved clothes. Figure 1(b) shows the setup in reality.

In figure 2 the components of the recognition system are shown schematically. Signs are recorded with two calibrated digital cameras, Allied Vision Technologies 'Guppies', at 25 fps, resolution 640 x 480. Currently, the start and end of a sign must be indicated by putting the hands in a fixed position on the table top. The hands and head are found and tracked using a skin colour model and various tracking techniques, which are discussed in the next section. From the tracked hands, several properties are measured, such as position, size and angle of the hand blobs in both cameras. From these properties, a set of features can be calculated, among which are the 3D co-ordinates of the hands. Different examples of a sign must then be synchronized. These steps are described in section 4. After that, a classifier can be trained using feature selection, as described in section 5.

3   Image Analysis

The image processing operations used to measure 3D hand locations can be divided into two layers: single-camera tracking, followed by disparity refinement. In this order, computing a complete disparity map can be omitted. This saves a significant amount of redundant computation, as we only need disparity measurements of hands and face.

3.1   Single-Camera Tracking

The hands and face are found around their previous location by a combination of blob tracking and template searching. This is done separately for both cameras (2D), but the depth from the previous time frame is used as prior information on hand size. When possible and necessary, tracking is automatically (re-)initialized by assigning the skin blobs to hands and head according to their position.

Blob Tracking. Finds the blob whose center of gravity is closest to the previous hand location. Blobs are connected components of a skin color segmentation. As long as no occlusion occurs and segmentation is reliable, blob tracking is both fast and robust.

To get a reliable skin segmentation, we use our adaptive model described in [17]. The method fits a 3-part piecewise linear model to the positive samples in RGB space. The model is robust against intensity offset and ambient lighting color, and a model estimated from one person applies to a large range of other skin colors, depending on lighting conditions and skin color difference. In a semi-automatic initialization procedure, skin and other (non-skin) samples are collected from a camera image. These samples are used to build the skin color model and to find thresholds on the distributions. For that, the opposite corners of a few rectangles have to be indicated manually: one containing the inner face (positive samples) and two containing all skin regions of face and hands respectively. The negative samples are all the pixels outside the indicated rectangles.

The initialized model provides a skin likelihood for any RGB color tuple. However, simply thresholding this likelihood results in a lot of false positive skin detections. So instead, two different segmentation thresholds are applied: A high (H) and a low (L) threshold. The H segmentation contains few false positives, but many misses. L covers almost all skin area, but also contains many false positives in the background and the clothes. False positives are reduced to a minimum by using the positive detections of L only around areas with positive detections of H. This is usually done using hysteresis thresholding. To limit computation time spend on dilations, we reduced this to only one big dilation after the first threshold. Sporadic false positives in H are removed by a density filtering F_d that sets a lower threshold on the number of positive pixels in a local neighborhood around each positive pixel, using the integral image. The final skin segmentation is obtained by:

$$S_s = \mathrm{C}\left\{\mathrm{D}(\mathrm{F}_d(H)) \bigcap L\right\} \tag{1}$$

Where $\cap$ denotes a logical AND, D a dilation and C a morphological closing to connect falsely detached segments.

For computational efficiency, the H and L thresholds are applied off-line to all possible RGB tuples $C = [C_R, C_G, C_B]^T \in \{0, .., 255\}^3$ and stored in lookup tables $T_H(C_R, C_G, C_B)$ and $T_L(C_R, C_G, C_B)$, respectively. This also makes it possible to combine the likelihood model (a simplified generalization of reality) with a histogram of the positive and negative initialization samples. Negative values in T_L that coincide with a high number of positive samples are added to T_L to reduce false negatives. Positive values in T_H that coincide with a high number of negative samples are removed from T_H to reduce false positives. To reduce data size for effective caching, RGB space is quantized into 64x64x64 color bins and the boolean table values are packed into 32 bit words, resulting in 64kB of data all together. To further reduce false negatives, T_H is applied to a larger image size (320x240) and the result saved to a 160x120 segmentation in which one pixel is positive if at least one of four corresponding pixels in the larger image is positive.

Template Tracking. Finds the local maximum correlation with a template copied from the hand location in the previous frame. In the template search, the template value differences are weighted by a Gaussian function after limiting them to a maximum of 20, to reduce the effect of outlier and background pixels inside the template and search area. The template search is automatically adapted to the situation. The search grid scale is linearly dependent on the distance to the camera of each hand in the previous frame, and the grid size (number of points) is reduced significantly if no motion is detected at the previous hand location. Furthermore, only grid points within the skin segmentation are considered. When motion is detected at the previous hand location, this is further reduced to grid points at areas with both skin and motion. Motion areas are segmented by a threshold on the local sum of absolute frame differences, using the integral image method. Figure 3 (b) shows a motion segmentation example. The noise threshold for motion segmentation is determined in the same

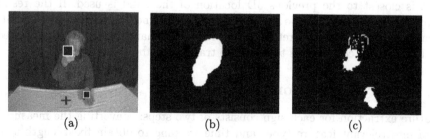

           (a)   (b)   (c)

Fig. 3. Image processing example. (a) shows the left camera image with the back-projected 3D hand positions as squares, the size of which represents the estimated depth. (b) motion segmentation. (c) the skin segmentation where a buffered face image is used to remove skin pixels of the face.

initialization procedure as in paragraph 3.1. Because it is very cumbersome and unpractical to get an image containing no moving persons at all (especially with a wide angle camera) the 50% most still regions were used for setting the threshold. This assumes that at least 50% of the image contains no motion (only noise). This is usually the case for a normal situation where only one person sits in front of the camera. It is very difficult to track a hand in front of the face. Especially when the hand changes shape. Therefore, the search area is further reduced by face segmentation. In each video frame where no hand is near the head area, the area of the head is copied from the gray image. The pixels in each new frame that are similar enough to the buffered face image are removed from the skin segmentation, resulting in a face-less skin segmentation image, used to reduce tracking search space. Figure 3 (c) shows a face-less skin segmentation example.

Combined Blob/Template Tracking. The results of blob and template tracking are combined depending on the situation. When a hand blob is free from the other hand and outside of the head/hair area, the blob center is considered most reliable. It is averaged with the template search result to get a more precise estimation, but only if the two are close enough. Otherwise, only the blob center is used. When a hand blob is merged with the other hand blob, or close to the head/hair, only the template search result is used. When two hand blobs are merged, and their difference in depth is large, only the hand closest to the camera is tracked, while the other is assumed to be still.

3.2　Disparity Refinement

For the result of single-camera tracking in one camera, the stereo disparity is measured by a coarse-to-fine block search of the located hand patch along the epi-polar curve (distorted line) in the other camera image, with a range slightly wider than the maximal expected displacement from the previous 3D location. If the single-camera tracking results are good and the estimated disparities from left to right and right to left are correct, they should be very close to each other. In that case, the disparities are averaged to get a more precise and stable estimate of the hand location. If the two results do not correspond, the result that is closest to the previous 3D location of the hand is used. If the result is physically impossible (too far or too fast), it is ignored and the previous 3D location and templates are retained. The refined 3D hand locations are projected back to camera coordinates to facilitate tracking in the next frame.

4　Feature Extraction

Feature extraction for each sign consists of two steps: converting the measured data into relevant feature types and time warping to obtain fixed-length synchronized feature vectors.

4.1　Feature Types

The measurements and feature types obtained for each video frame are shown in table 1, where X, Y, Z are horizontal, vertical and depth co-ordinates respectively

Table 1. Feature types extracted for classification

left/right hand coordinates	$\mathbf{h}_{l/r}(t) = [X_{l/r}(t), Y_{l/r}(t), Z_{l/r}(t)]^T$
left/right hand motion	$\tilde{h}_{l/r}(t) = S\{\|d\mathbf{h}_{l/r}(t)/dt\|, c_{\tilde{h}}\}$
left/right hand acceleration	$\tilde{\tilde{h}}_{l/r}(t) = S\{\|d^2\mathbf{h}_{l/r}(t)/dt^2\|, c_{\tilde{\tilde{h}}}\}$
left/right sideways orientation	$\theta_{Sl/r}(t) = \arcsin(dX_{l/r}(s)/ds)$
left/right upward orientation	$\theta_{Ul/r}(t) = \arcsin(dY_{l/r}(s)/ds)$
left/right forward orientation	$\theta_{Fl/r}(t) = \arcsin(dZ_{l/r}(s)/ds)$
left/right hand motion curvature	$\tilde{\kappa}_{l/r}(t) = S\{\kappa_{l/r}(t), c_\kappa\}$
left/right hand motion curvature change	$\tilde{\tilde{\kappa}}_{l/r}(t) = S\{d\tilde{\kappa}_{l/r}(t)/dt, c_{\tilde{\kappa}}\}$
left/right hand size change	$\tilde{B}_{l/r}(t) = S\{dB_{l/r}(t)/dt, c_{\tilde{B}}\}$

(the median face location was taken as the origin for the hand coordinates), t is the time frame number, s is arc length of the hand motion path, and B is hand blob size in pixels. No hand shape features other than size change could be robustly extracted from the skin blobs. Several features are mapped with a sigmoid function $S(f, c)$:

$$S(f, c) = \frac{1}{1 + \exp(-f/c)} \qquad (2)$$

where c is a scaling parameter that determines where the sigmoid flattens out. In the time derivative features, sigmoid mapping acts as a soft threshold to obtain invariance to signer speed. For curvature $\tilde{\kappa}$, it reduces a logarithmic infinite-range scale measurement into a limited feature range.

4.2 Time Warping

The features are aligned with a fixed-length feature model by a time warping procedure. This is done using 'Statistical Dynamic Time Warping' (SDTW), first introduced by Bahlmann and Burkhardt [18]. The difference of SDTW with normal DTW is that instead of comparing two signals using a fixed distance measure, SDTW compares a new signal $t = [\mathbf{t}_1, ..., \mathbf{t}_{N_t}]$ to a sequence of statistical feature models $R = [R_1, ..., R_{N_R}]$. The distance function for time frame i of a gesture t now depends on the time frame (or state) j of the model R. This makes SDTW more robust against variation than normal DTW. The applied distance function is the inverse log probability, based on a Gaussian model $R_j = \{\mu_j, \Sigma_j\}$:

$$d(\mathbf{t}_i, R_j) = \frac{1}{2}(\ln(|2\pi\Sigma_j|) + (\mathbf{t}_i - \mu_j)^T\Sigma_j^{-1}(\mathbf{t}_i - \mu_j)), \qquad (3)$$

where Σ_j is a covariance matrix and μ_j is the mean of model-frame j. The optimal time warping Φ^* is found by minimizing:

$$-\ln(p(t, \Phi|R)) = \sum_{n=1}^{N_\phi} d(\mathbf{t}_{\phi_t(n)}, R_{\phi_R(n)}). \qquad (4)$$

Where $\Phi = \{\phi_t(1), ..., \phi_t(N_\phi), \phi_\mathcal{R}(1), ..., \phi_\mathcal{R}(N_\phi)\}$ are the steps of the path through the 2D correspondence matrix of the time frames of t and $\mathcal{R}$, constrained by transitions $[(\phi_t(n+1) - \phi_t(n)), (\phi_\mathcal{R}(n+1) - \phi_\mathcal{R}(n))] \in \{[0,1], [1,0], [1,1]\}$, corresponding to horizontal, vertical and diagonal steps, respectively. Note that we have left out transition probabilities as they did not improve the result. Equation 4 is minimized efficiently using the Viterbi algorithm. The SDTW model $\mathcal{R}$ is trained on a set of examples by iteratively warping all training samples and recomputing each μ_j and Σ_j from the aligned observations, until convergence, starting with an initial model $\mathcal{R}_0$. When multiple frames of t are mapped onto the same frame of $\mathcal{R}$ the respective feature vectors are averaged in the final warped signal. Figure 4(a) gives an example of synchronisation through SDTW. 4(b) shows examples of $\mathcal{R}_j = \{\mu_j, \Sigma_j\}$ at three time points in $\mathcal{R}$.

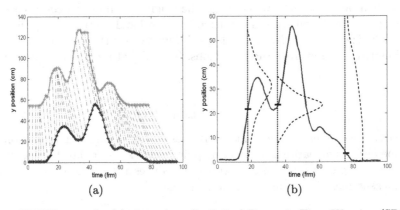

(a)   (b)

Fig. 4. SDTW example. (a) shows how Statistical Dynamic Time Warping (SDTW) maps a gesture *(upper)* onto the feature model *(lower)*. The signals have been shifted vertically for visualization. (b) When mapping is done for all signs, we get a distribution of values *(dashed lines)* for each time instance of the feature model. Three distributions are shown. This example shows only one feature type (y-position of the right hand), but the SDTW match is made using all properties combined, and distributions are modeled for all features types at all model-frames.

5   Sign Classification

Since not all features of a time-warped sign are relevant for classification, a feature selection procedure determines which features to use. The selected set of features is classified with a classifier that assumes that all features have been perfectly aligned.

5.1   Feature Selection

A feature $f_j(m)$ of type m (see table 1) corresponding to the normalized time frame j is selected for classification only if the middle 50% of its distribution over the training examples of the correct sign (positive examples) has an overlap of less than 25% with the distribution of the training examples of incorrect signs (negative examples).

5.2   Feature Classifier

After feature selection, a relatively large number of features still remains (around 500), and it is difficulty to obtain a large multi-signer training set (variation of a single signer does not generalize well to others). Because of the curse of dimensionality, we assume independence between features. The classification is based on the same measure as equation 3, but with a warped signal $\hat{t}$ and an independent variance per feature type:

$$\ln\left\{p(\hat{t}_j(m)|\mathcal{R}_j(m))\right\} = -\frac{1}{2}\left(\ln(2\pi\sigma_j^2(m)) + \frac{(\hat{t}_j(m) - \mu_j(m))^2}{\sigma_j^2(m)}\right), \qquad (5)$$

However, instead of computing a total log likelihood by the sum of feature log likelihoods, the feature likelihood distributions are first converted into partial uniform functions:

$$q(\hat{t}_j(m), \mathcal{R}_j(m)) = \begin{cases} 1, \ln\left\{p(\hat{t}_j(m)|\mathcal{R}_j(m))\right\} \geq T_j(m) - T_g \\ 0, \ln\left\{p(\hat{t}_j(m)|\mathcal{R}_j(m))\right\} < T_j(m) - T_g \end{cases} \qquad (6)$$

where T_g is the gauge parameter that will determine the operating point of the final classifier and $T_j(m)$ is the threshold that accepts 90% of the positive training data for a particular feature at $T_g = 0$. By using a piece-wise uniform likelihood function, all outliers are penalized equally, no matter how great their distance to the mean feature value. Furthermore, the flat top makes it possible to accept sloppy but completely correct signs, while rejecting incorrect signs that are very similar to a subset of the feature models (e.g. incomplete signs). The classifier output is generated by:

$$Q(t, \mathcal{R}) = \sum_{j=1}^{N_\mathcal{R}} \sum_{m=1}^{N_m} s_j(m) q(\hat{t}_j(m), \mathcal{R}_j(m)). \qquad (7)$$

Where $s_j(m)$ is 1 for selected features and 0 otherwise, and N_m is the number of feature types, equal to 25 (see table 1). A sign is classified by:

$$C(t, \mathcal{R}) = \begin{cases} correct, & Q(t, \mathcal{R}) >= T_C \\ incorrect, & Q(t, \mathcal{R}) < T_C \end{cases} \qquad (8)$$

where T_C is fixed to the value that classifies 50% of the positive training set correctly at $T_g = 0$ (median of Q).

6   Results

Our vocabulary consisted of 120 signs from the standard lexicon of Dutch Sign Language. We recorded these signs from 75 different adult persons (all right-handed), giving us 75 examples per class, a total of 9,000 signs. We trained and

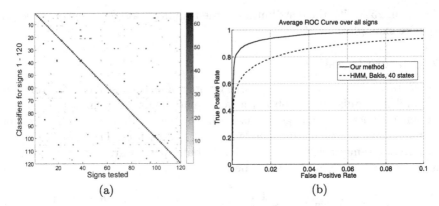

Fig. 5. (a) Confusion matrix of the sign recognition. Rows represent the one-class classifiers for each sign, columns are the classes of the test signs. The colour of the cells indicates the number of times a detector judged a test sign of that class as correct. (b) Average ROC curve of the sign recognition at varying tolerance levels. At an operating point of 96% true positives, about 3% of false positives will occur. For comparison, a standard HMM approach (whole word HMMs with Bakis topology and 40 states) was also used. The HMM ROC curve was created by varying the recognition threshold.

tested our system using 5-fold cross-validation. In each cycle, we used 60 positive examples for training, and 15 others for testing. As for the negative examples, in each cycle we used 96 signs (of all 75 persons) for training, and the other 23 (also of all 75 persons) in the test set. This to ensure that the negative (incorrect) examples in the test set had not been seen in training, so that we could test our ability to reject movements we had never seen before. Figure 5(a) shows the results in the form of a confusion matrix. The rows are the 120 detectors, the columns the 120 classes of test sign. The intensity of the cells shows how often the detector judged the test sign 'correct'. Ideally, this figure would be black along the diagonal and white everywhere else.

We tested the system at different settings of the tolerance T_g (as opposed to T_C). We made an ROC curve for each individual detector and averaged them. The result is shown in figure 5(b). If we want our recognizer to detect e.g. 96.5% of the correct signs, then 3.5% of incorrect signs will also be detected. For comparison, we included the ROC curve of a standard HMM approach on our dataset (whole word HMMs with 40 states, comparable to those used by [14]). Our system clearly outperforms the HMM approach.

The recognizer was also tested in a real world situation as part of ELo. ELo was set up at a school for deaf and hard-of-hearing children and ten children worked with it in eight 15-minute sessions over a period of four weeks. During the test the recognizer processed the children's signs real time and judged their correctness. The movies of three children were also shown to a sign language instructor experienced in working with young children. She was asked to give an evaluation of the correctness of the children's signs. Her judgement was then compared to the judgement of the recognizer. 78 signs were tested this way. The instructor judged 66 signs correct; of these, the recognizer judged 60 correct. Of the 12 signs found incorrect by the instructor, the recognizer judged 6 incorrect.

7 Discussion

In this paper, we presented a person-independent sign recognition system. Because we want the system to judge the correctness of a sign, we built a set of one-class classifiers, one for each class. Tests show that the system not only works well for adults, scoring significantly better than a standard HMM approach, but also for the target group, young deaf children, even though it was trained on adults only. Confusion between signs often arises when signs only differ in hand-shape. To deal with such pairs, we need to collect more detailed information on the handshape.

Compared to a human expert, the recognizer appears to be too strict for correct signs. Because of the small number of incorrect signs in the test, it is difficult to draw general conclusions about these. However, the instructor will reject some signs based on incorrect handshape, and this is information the recognizer does not have, which may explain the incorrect acceptances. Larger tests are necessary to draw reliable conclusions about the recognizer's performance on incorrect signs.

By changing the tolerance parameter T_g, the recognizer can be made less strict, so that its judgement of correct signs conforms to that of a human expert. However, it is possible that human experts are too accepting in some cases, as a form of positive reinforcement (rewarding the attempt instead of judging the result). In these circumstances, it may be preferable to let the recognition device retain its own, consistent measures of acceptability, not copy human teachers too much. The recognizer can of course maintain different tolerance settings for different age groups. Within the group, however, it would maintain a fixed threshold, against which progress can be measured accurately. To achieve this, however, the recognizer's 'blind spot' for handshapes must be remedied.

References

1. Schermer, G., Fortgens, C., Harder, R., De Nobel, E.: De Nederlandse Gebarentaal. Van Tricht, Twello (1991)
2. Spaai, G.W.G., Fortgens, C., Elzenaar, M., Wenners, E., Lichtenauer, J.F., Hendriks, E.A., de Ridder, H., Arendsen, J., Ten Holt, G.A.: A computerprogram for teaching active and passive sign language vocabulary to severely hearing-impaired and deaf children (in Dutch). Logopedie en Foniatrie 80, 42–50 (2004)
3. Grobel, K., Assam, M.: Isolated sign language recognition using hidden markov models. In: IEEE Int. Conf. on Systems, Man and Cybernetics, pp. 162–167. IEEE, Los Alamitos (1997)
4. Liang, R.H., Ouhyoung, M.: A real-time continuous gesture recognition system for sign language. In: 3rd Int. Conf. on Face & Gesture Recognition, pp. 558–565. IEEE Computer Society, Los Alamitos (1998)

5. Starner, T., Weaver, J., Pentland, A.: Real-time American sign language recognition using desk and wearable computer based video. IEEE TPAMI 20, 1271–1375 (1998)
6. Waldron, M., Kim, S.: Isolated ASL sign recognition system for deaf persons. IEEE Transactions on Rehabilitation Engineering 3, 261–271 (1995)
7. Kadous, W.: Machine recognition of auslan signs using powergloves: Towards large-lexicon recognition of sign language. In: Workshop on the Integration of Gesture in Language and Speech, pp. 165–174 (1996)
8. Holden, E.J., Owens, R., Roy, G.: Adaptive fuzzy expert system for sign recognition. In: Int. Conf. on Signal and Image Processing, pp. 141–146 (1999)
9. Zieren, J., Kraiss, K.F.: Non-intrusive sign language recognition for human-computer interaction. In: IFAC-HMS Symposium (2004)
10. Bauer, B., Kraiss, K.F.: Towards an automatic sign language recognition system using subunits. In: Wachsmuth, I., Sowa, T. (eds.) GW 2001. LNCS, vol. 2298, pp. 123–173. Springer, Heidelberg (2002)
11. Vogler, C., Metaxas, D.: Handshapes and movements: Multiple-channel American sign language recognition. In: Camurri, A., Volpe, G. (eds.) GW 2003. LNCS, vol. 2915, pp. 247–258. Springer, Heidelberg (2004)
12. Bowden, R., Windridge, D., Kadir, T., Zisserman, A., Brady, M.: A linguistic feature vector for the visual interpretation of sign language. In: Pajdla, T., Matas, J(G.) (eds.) ECCV 2004. LNCS, vol. 3021, pp. 390–401. Springer, Heidelberg (2004)
13. Chen, Y., Gao, W., Fang, G., Yang, C., Wang, Z.: Cslds: Chinese sign language dialog system. In: IEEE Int. Workshop on Analysis and Modeling of Faces and Gestures, pp. 236–237. IEEE, Los Alamitos (2003)
14. von Agris, U., Schneider, D., Zieren, J., Kraiss, K.F.: Rapid signer adaptation for isolated sign language recognition. In: Conf. on Comp. Vision and Pattern Recognition Workshop, p. 159. IEEE Computer Society, Los Alamitos (2006)
15. Wang, C., Chen, C., Gao, W.: Generating data for signer adaptation. In: Int. Workshop on Gesture and Sign Language based Human-Computer Interaction (2007)
16. von Agris, U., Kraiss, K.F.: Towards a video corpus for signer-independent continuous sign language recognition. In: Int. Workshop on Gesture and Sign Language based Human-Computer Interaction (2007)
17. Lichtenauer, J., Hendriks, E., Reinders, M.: A self-calibrating chrominance model applied to skin color detection. In: Int. Conf. on Computer Vision Theory and Applications (2007)
18. Bahlmann, C., Burkhardt, H.: The writer independent online handwriting recognition system frog on hand and cluster generative statistical dynamic time warping. IEEE TPAMI 26, 299–310 (2004)

Skin Color Profile Capture for Scale and Rotation Invariant Hand Gesture Recognition

Rafael Bastos[1] and Miguel Sales Dias[1,2]

[1] ADETTI Av. das Forças Armadas, Edifício ISCTE 1600-082 Lisboa, Portugal
Tel.: (+351) 21 782 64 80
[2] MLDC - Microsoft Language Development Center, Edifício Qualidade C1-C2,
Av. Prof. Doutor Aníbal Cavaco Silva, Tagus Park, 2744-010 Porto Salvo, Portugal
Tel.: (+351) 96 2093324

Abstract. This paper presents a new approach to real-time scale and rotation invariant hand pose detection, which is based on a technique for computing the best hand skin color segmentation map. This segmentation map, a vector entity referred to as a "skin profile", is used during an online hand gesture calibration stage to enable correct classification of skin regions. Subsequently, we construct efficient and reliable scale and rotation invariant hand pose gesture descriptors, by introducing an innovative technique, referred to as "oriented gesture descriptors". Finally, hand pose gesture recognition is computed using a template matching technique which is luminance invariant.

Keywords: Gesture Tracking, Skin Color Tracking, Image Processing, Feature Matching, Scale and Rotation Invariant Template.

1 Introduction

In this paper we present a new approach to real-time and rotation invariant hand pose detection, which is based on a technique for computing the best hand skin profile. This skin profile is used to classify each pixel in the current video frame as belonging to the skin color or to the background. The skin profile data correspond to a group of 3D line segments (vectors), where the control points are important HSV 3D coordinates extracted during the skin capture stage. The runtime pixel classification is accomplished by measuring the distance of each pixel's HSV 3D coordinates to each one of formed vectors of the current skin profile. The HSV 3D coordinates are the 3D representation of each color in the HSV cone. This space transformation is needed to avoid the Hue component discontinuity around the 360°, since it disables any direct arithmetic comparison between Hue values. After skin/background segmentation, we construct efficient and reliable scale and rotation invariant hand pose gesture descriptors, by introducing an innovative technique, referred to as "oriented gesture descriptors". These descriptors correspond to grayscale image representations of the hand gesture captured during gesture acquisition. Finally, hand pose recognition is computed using a template matching technique, which is luminance invariant [1], between the acquired gestures/descriptors and the current tracking gesture. The paper presents

M. Sales Dias et al. (Eds.): GW 2007, LNAI 5085, pp. 81–92, 2009.

some results of efficient hand pose gesture recognition, with examples taken from the recognition of Portuguese Sign language signs in use cases of spelled language recognition. The presented work discusses also the development of multimodal human-computer interaction, based on hand pose gesture recognition, to be applied in other interaction scenarios, such as in industrial augmented reality frameworks.

2 Related Work

The methods for face and gesture recognition which use skin color as a detection cue, have gained strong popularity, since color is highly robust to geometric variations of the skin pattern and allows fast processing. The human skin has a distinguishing color tone, which can be easily recognized by humans. Three main problems appear when building a system which uses skin color as a feature for gesture detection. The first one is "what colorspace to chose?", the second one is "how should we model the skin color distribution?", and the third one is "how will we process the segmentation results?". This paper addresses the pixel-based skin color detection based on the creation of a skin color profile, which provides an answer to the first two questions. For the third question we propose a solution based on scale and rotation invariant hand gesture recognition. Several methods were proposed to accomplish these goals, namely region-based methods [2], [3], [4], which try to take the spatial arrangement of skin pixels into account during the detection stage, to enhance the methods' performance. Some surveys issuing several colorspaces can be found in works of [5] and [6]. Several skin modeling strategies have been addressed by [7] and [8]. Other approaches, such as MoG (Gaussian Mixture Modeling) [9] have been also proposed, where the descriptor is obtained by learning a reduced model from several corresponding images in the category.

In our work we propose the use of HSV colorspace for skin color segmentation and modeling, and the use of template matching in luminance space, based on a robust correlation metric, and using scale and rotation invariant templates. We also address the performance enhancement issue, using gesture clustering, based on an in-house developed binary identifier algorithm, which we describe in detail.

3 Calibration: Skin Profile Capture

Our real-time hand detection technique requires the evaluation of the best skin color segmentation map, which enables us to correctly classify current video frame pixels as belonging or not to the captured user's skin in motion. When calibrating, the user selects a square region of his/her hand skin (see Figure 1). By using the selected region, the system is able to construct a skin profile, using the various skin-tones presented in the acquired sample. Since there are considerable differences between the spectrum present in the palm of the hand and the one existent in the back of the hand [10], the user may select skin regions, to be added to the profile, from both faces. Since a moving hand, in a dynamic light environment can present several variations of the predominant skin-tone, the system must be able to take this fact in to consideration, instead of just using a single color tone as a reference, such as in [11]. Our technique uses the HSV (Hue-Saturation-Value) colorspace as a basis, because the color information is the most important component when dealing with skin segmentation.

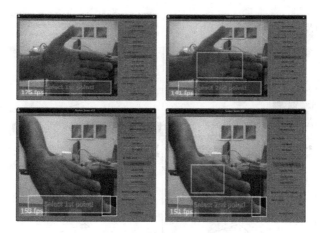

Fig. 1. User selecting the desired skin region

Assuming a general conversion from RGB colorspace to HSV colorspace, we compute HSV 3D coordinates for every pixel in the captured region of interest, using the HSV 3D cone representation as a basis, to avoid Hue discontinuities while comparing colors. The value's interval used for each HSV component is [0-255]. We can obtain the 3D cone HSV corresponding coordinates (x, y, z), by applying the following transformations for each (h, s, v) triplet:

$$x = \frac{v\,s\,\sin\left(360h/255\right)}{255}, \quad y = \frac{v\,s\,\cos\left(360h/255\right)}{255}, \quad z = v \tag{1}$$

The start vector of our skin profile corresponds to the HSV 3D coordinates of the pixels which have the minimum and maximum z values. This model is improved iteratively with additional points by computing the distance of every other pixel's 3D coordinates, which lie in the calibration region, to each one of the formed vectors of our growing profile. We can compute the distance d from a 3D point (P) to a 3D line segment (AB) as:

$$AB = B - A,$$

$$AP = P - A,$$

$$d = \| AB \times AP \| \, / \, \| AB \| \tag{2}$$

For each pixel and for each profile vector, the resulting distance is compared to a predetermined threshold value ε, which will allow us to specify the level of discrimination for each one of the compared coordinates. If distance d is above the predetermined threshold ε, then the newly evaluated point is added to our profile, being placed between the points of the compared profile vector, forming a new vector. As a final step of our skin profile creation algorithm, we use the Douglas-Peucker [12] simplification algorithm, using the same ε threshold value, in order to reduce the number of 3D points of the vector profile, for efficiency purposes (see Figure 2). We have heuristically determined that a good value for ε is 15% of the profile length.

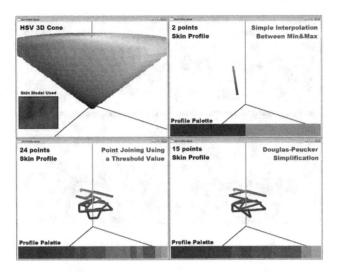

Fig. 2. Skin profile example (stages of profile creation)

4 Skin Color Classification

At runtime, we must evaluate each pixel in the current video frame, aiming at identifying and classifying skin color pixels. Assuming that the forearm is covered with a non skin colored cloth, we proceed to pixel classification by computing the minimum distance between the corresponding 3D coordinates of each pixel and each one of the formed vectors of the current skin profile. This process is similar to the one executed during the profile creation (Eq. 2). When this process is completed, we obtain a binary mask of the current video frame, where **1** corresponds to skin areas and **0** to background areas.

In order to fill small disconnected areas and eliminate some segmentation noise, we apply an erosion filter and subsequently a dilation filter to the binary mask image. By applying a recursive filter based on connected components evaluation, we are able to track connected areas (see Figure 3). We assume that the object which outlines the largest area corresponds to the hand we want to track. The retained area bounding rectangle is computed as well as its center of mass.

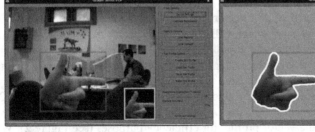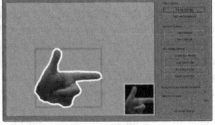

Fig. 3. Pixel classification and contour extraction example

5 Gestures Descriptors

To make the descriptors invariant to scale, we rescale each gesture patch (its gray-scale version) to a maximum value of $n \times n$ *pixel*, without discarding the aspect ratio (see Figure 4), where n is an odd fixed parameter which corresponds to the gesture patch size. A good value for n is 15, since we have heuristically determined that it maintains a high degree of gesture discrimination without compromising the system's performance. Higher values for n can be used when similar gesture patches are being tracked, in order to increase the gesture matching distinctiveness.

Fig. 4. Scale invariant transformation (left: original gesture patch marked at red; right: rescaled n x n gesture patch)

The descriptor's data is the $n \times n$ grayscale image patch (g_i) centered at (x_c, y_c). The descriptor's information is extracted using an in-plane rotation invariant method. We introduce now the concept of oriented gesture descriptors. Similar techniques have already been proposed, either as directionality textures [13], gesture recognition using orientation histograms and similar [14][15], image comparison [16], and Principal Components Analysis (PCA) [17]. For this purpose we have designed a function θ (g_i) which finds the main orientation angle of the patch descriptor g_i, in the form:

$$\theta\,(g_i) = b \max\left(\mathrm{H}(g_i)\right) \tag{3}$$

In the previous equation, *max* corresponds to the function which determines the vector index of $H(g_i)$ which contains the highest value of the orientation of g_i, that is, the main orientation of image patch g_i. The $H(g_i)$ function computes the orientation histogram (a vector) of a given grayscale patch descriptor g_i. This histogram vector is composed by b elements (b is the total number of histogram bins), where each element corresponds to a $360°/b$ degrees interval. We can define an indexing function $\kappa(g_i, x, y)$ for the histogram vector $H(g_i)$ as:

$$\kappa(g_i, x, y) = \arctan\left(\frac{\partial(g_i(x,y))/\partial y}{\partial(g_i(x,y))/\partial x}\right) \times \frac{b}{360} \tag{4}$$

The $H(g_i)$ histogram vector at index $\kappa(g_i, x, y)$ accumulates in the following manner:

$$\mathrm{H}(g_i)[\,\kappa(g_i, x, y)\,] = \sqrt{\left(\frac{\partial(g_i(x,y))}{\partial x}\right)^2 + \left(\frac{\partial(g_i(x,y))}{\partial y}\right)^2} + \mathrm{H}(g_i)[\,\kappa(g_i, x, y)\,] \tag{5}$$

After finding $\theta(g_i)$ – the grayscale patch main orientation – we create the final rotation invariant descriptor (g_r), which can be found by performing a rigid body transformation (a rotation of $-\theta(g_i)$ degrees) to the g_i grayscale patch. This rigid body transformation, which finds g_r from g_i, is:

$$g_r(x,y)=g_i\begin{pmatrix}(x-x_c)\cos(-\theta(g_i))-(y-y_c)\sin(-\theta(g_i))+x_c,\\(x-x_c)\sin(-\theta(g_i))+(y-y_c)\cos(-\theta(g_i))+y_c\end{pmatrix} \tag{6}$$

In the previous equation, although the signal of the normalizing rotation angle $\theta(g_i)$ applied is not significant (as long as it is the same for all analogous operations) we choose a negative sign in order to accomplish a simple off-centered (x_c, y_c) rotation towards 0°. Irrespective to the orientation of patch descriptor g_i, the gesture descriptor g_r is the version of the former always oriented towards the patch main direction (see Figure 5).

In Figure 6 we present 2 histogram representations corresponding to the examples shown in Figure 5. We can see the local maximum corresponding to example A (210°) and example B (80°).

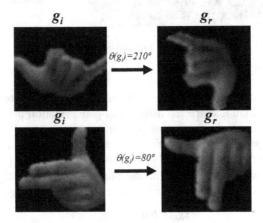

Fig. 5. Rotation invariant transformation (example A – top, B - bottom)

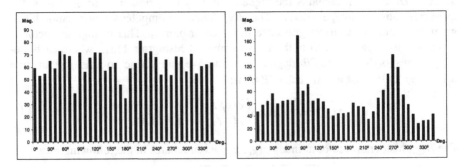

Fig. 6. Orientation histograms (example A – left, B - right)

6 Hand Pose Gesture Matching

Given two scale and rotation invariant gesture descriptors, gesture matching is accomplished using Normalized Cross Correlation, which is a near-luminance invariant [1] technique using the grayscale templates patches. This technique uses the image average and standard deviation to obtain a correlation value between the current gesture tracked and the ones in the gesture database. For two descriptors (I and P), we compute their mean value (μ_I and μ_P) and their standard deviation (σ_I and σ_P), allowing us to find the correlation factor ρ using the following equations:

$$\begin{cases} \mu_I = \dfrac{1}{xy}\sum_x\sum_y I(x,y) \\ \mu_P = \dfrac{1}{xy}\sum_x\sum_y P(x,y) \end{cases}, \begin{cases} \sigma_I = \left(\sum_x\sum_y (I(x,y)-\mu_I)^2\right)^{\frac{1}{2}} \\ \sigma_P = \left(\sum_x\sum_y (P(x,y)-\mu_P)^2\right)^{\frac{1}{2}} \end{cases}$$

(7)

$$\rho = \frac{\sum_x\sum_y (I(x,y)-\mu_I)(P(x,y)-\mu_P)}{\sigma_I\sigma_P}$$

A value above 0.7 (70%) is a satisfying correlation factor in terms of classification error rate. To enable efficient gesture matching, in terms of search/matching time, the hand pose gesture database is organized in containers, each one aggregating the corresponding possible gestures. These containers possess a binary identification value (a kind of simple and efficient hand pose gesture signature), that is obtained by evaluating certain regions of the image in relation to its average.

By dividing the image into 8 different regions (left, right, top, bottom, top-right diagonal, down-left diagonal, top-left diagonal and bottom-right diagonal), and by comparing these areas average pixel value with the image's global average value, we obtain an 8 digit binary result. For each one of these areas we obtain a **0** value if the patch average is smaller than the global average, otherwise we obtain a value of **1**. For the sake of clarity, we exemplify this procedure in Figure 7. When a gesture descriptor is processed and created, this evaluation is performed, and this descriptor is inserted in the corresponding container using the obtained binary identification. While matching a gesture, we also compute the binary identification of the candidate hand pose gesture, which allow us to only match with potential candidates instead of matching with all gestures in the database. To obtain a final result in what concerns the tracked gesture, we have used a histogram approach based on a fixed time window. This time window can be adjusted by the user, since it is related to the system's response time in what concerns gesture transitions.

A good value for the time window length is 1 second, which is also the maximum transition time between two consecutive gestures. For each frame of this time window, we construct a statistical vector, where each position corresponds to each one of the loaded gestures in the database. In this vector, we have an accumulated sum of correlation values obtained for a given descriptor, as well as the number of occurrences for this descriptor. We compute the current matched gesture by finding the

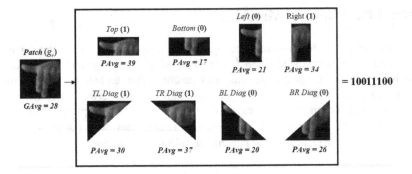

Fig. 7. Binary identifier creation example

descriptor which possesses the highest value in this histogram, taking also into consideration the number of occurrences.

7 Results and Discussion

In this section we present some performance and recognition results, in respect to the processing speed at various capture resolutions, as well as the success rate using the same gestures database. Although we only use a number of 12 gestures as reference (see Figure 8), the overhead imposed by a richer database is not significant, since all gestures are clustered using our binary identification algorithm. In these tests we have used a Pentium IV laptop featuring a 2.66 GHz CPU.

As shown in Table 1, the use of a background subtraction algorithm improves the processing speed, since the number of pixels to be tested for skin color is reduced significantly. Even with a capture resolution of 640x480 pixels and not using background subtraction, the system achieves real-time performance (25 FPS).

The use of a higher capture resolution for gesture creation and matching increases the classification rate, since: a) high definition contours increase the alignment of the gesture descriptor being matched, with the ones stored in the database; b) the gesture descriptor sensibility (failure rate) to the rotation invariant method increases when working with lower resolutions, since derivatives may be miscalculated due to CCD

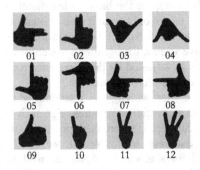

Fig. 8. Hand pose gestures used for the performance and recognition tests

Table 1. Performance results of the hand pose runtime matching algorithm

Resolution (pixel)	W/Background Sub	WO/Background Sub
160 x 120	225 FPS	220 FPS
176 x 144	190 FPS	185 FPS
240 x 180	140 FPS	130 FPS
320 x 240	90 FPS	85 FPS
352 x 288	70 FPS	60 FPS
640 x 480	30 FPS	25 FPS

Table 2. Performance results for each one of the stages which comprise the descriptor creation and matching algorithms

Scale Transform Operation	Rotation Invariant Operation	Template Matching Opertaion	TOTAL
0,006 ms	0,019 ms	0,002 ms	0,027 ms

Table 3. Performance results comparison between matching one descriptor either using clustering or full database matching

No. Gestures in Database	Without Clustering	With Clustering
12	0,024 ms	0,0038 ms
25	0,05 ms	0,007 ms
50	0,1 ms	0,017 ms
100	0,2 ms	0,03 ms

interpolation constraints; c) the hand's centre of mass can be extracted with much more precision when using higher definition contours (superior resolution).

In Table 2 we evaluate the descriptors creation and matching performance. These results cover the 3 main operations while creating and matching a gesture descriptor: Scale Transform, Rotation Invariant and Template Matching.

Although our work is focused in the 12 set of gestures depicted in Figure 8, we present further performance tests while using larger gesture databases, namely with 25, 50 and 100 gesture descriptors (see Table 3). We have concluded that our clustering algorithm may reduce the matching time with a full gesture database up to ~15%.

In what concerns to the results for gesture descriptor classification, we conclude that our developed algorithm achieves a success rate of ~90% (see Table 4). These tests were performed using a full set of 240 evaluations, where each on of the gesture descriptors was submitted 20 times to classification, varying hand position, rotation (small degrees) and proximity to the camera.

In Figure 9 we present two random examples of hand pose gesture recognition while performing the Recognition/Classification Tests. The gestures are identified even if they show rotations changes (to some tolerance degree variation, specified by the user) in contrast with the ones in the gesture database (see Figure 8). A typical value for this degree of variation factor (ϖ) is 20°. By applying this factor, a gesture descriptor g_i, is only eligible for a classification test against a gesture descriptor g_j in the database, if $(\theta(g_j) - \varpi) \leq \theta(g_i) \leq (\theta(g_j) + \varpi)$. We have included gesture 01 and

Table 4. Recognition test results for the hand pose runtime matching algorithm

Gesture ID	No. Tests	Outliers	Inliers	Failure Rate	Success Rate
01	20	3	17	15,00%	85,00%
02	20	4	16	20,00%	80,00%
03	20	3	17	15,00%	85,00%
04	20	2	18	10,00%	90,00%
05	20	0	20	0,00%	100,00%
06	20	5	15	25,00%	75,00%
07	20	2	18	10,00%	90,00%
08	20	0	20	0,00%	100,00%
09	20	0	20	0,00%	100,00%
10	20	5	15	25,00%	75,00%
11	20	2	18	10,00%	90,00%
12	20	1	19	5,00%	95,00%
TOTAL	**240**	**27**	**213**	**11,25%**	**88,75%**

Fig. 9. Gesture detection and matching

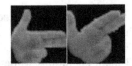

Fig. 10. Gesture templates

02 in the full set of gestures to illustrate this issue, since they are equal if we apply a 90° in plane rotation.

In these examples (Figure 9 and Figure 10), we explore the scale invariant and rotation invariant property of our gesture recognition algorithm. Figure 9 shows two examples of hand gesture matching/classification. The gesture is signed in the video frame by a white contour. At the bottom right of the application window, we present the database gesture template (leftmost) and the extracted template (rightmost). At the top of these two templates, a certainty value is also presented. In Figure 10 we depict the two groups of gesture templates used in Figure 9. In each group, the left template is the one belonging to the gestures database and the right one is the current extracted gesture template.

For the first group (leftmost) we have obtained a similarity of 70%, as for the second group (rightmost) we have obtained 79%. The hand gesture classification algorithm has revealed to be robust (~90% of success rate) and efficient (25 FPS using a 640x480 video capture resolution). Nevertheless, the algorithm in restricted to some

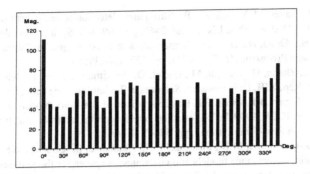

Fig. 11. Example of a gesture descriptor orientation histogram not showing a defined orientation

conditions, since it won't achieve satisfying results or stability if: a) the skin color being tracked is not similar to the one acquired during skin color profile creation; b) the background elements or cloth are very similar to the predominant skin color that was used during the color profile creation; c) the gesture descriptors that are being used don't have a well defined orientation (see Figure 11).

In Figure 11 we depict an orientation histogram with 2 local maximums, which increases the probability of classification error. This issue can be further solved by inserting 2 or more instances of the same gesture identifier in the database, each one processed with a distinct main orientation.

8   Conclusions and Future Work

In this paper we have addressed the problem that can be expressed in the following question: "how should we model the skin color distribution and what colorspace to chose, in the framework of robust hand gesture recognition?". We have proposed the use of HSV colorspace for skin color segmentation and modeling, and an approach for hand pose gesture recognition, based on template matching in luminance space, using a robust correlation metric and scale and rotation invariant templates. We have also addressed the performance enhancement issue, using gesture clustering, based on a binary identifier algorithm, which we have described in detail. The system has presented promising results in what concerns accuracy (~90%) and performance, revealing a processing frame rate of 25 FPS when using a capture resolution of 640x480, thus maintaining the real-time. As future work we intend to use this technique as a component of a broader hand pose gesture interface server, capable of providing the gesture modality in Human-Computer Interface to the multimodal interaction requirements of augmented and virtual reality systems, to be used in design authoring, industrial and architectural use cases.

References

1. Bastos, R., Dias, J.M.S.: Fully Automated Texture Tracking Based on Natural Features Extraction and Template Matching. In: ACM SIGCHI International Conference on Advances in Computer Entertainment Technology, Valencia, Spain (2005)

2. Kruppa, H., Bauer, M.A., Schiele, B.: Skin patch detection in real-world images. In: Van Gool, L. (ed.) DAGM 2002. LNCS, vol. 2449, pp. 109–117. Springer, Heidelberg (2002)
3. Yang, M.-H., Ahuja, N.: Detecting human faces in color images. In: International Conference on Image Processing (ICIP), vol. 1, pp. 127–130 (1998)
4. Jedynak, B., Zheng, H., Daoudi, M., Barret, D.: Maximum entropy models for skin detection., Tech. Rep. XIII, Universite des Sciences et Technologies de Lille, France (2002)
5. Zarit, B.D., Super, B.J., Quek, F.K.H.: Comparison of five color models in skin pixel classification. In: ICCV 1999 Int'l Workshop on recognition, analysis and tracking of faces and gestures in Real-Time systems, pp. 58–63 (1999)
6. Terrillon, J.-C., Shirazi, M.N., Fukamachi, H., Akamatsu, S.: Comparative performance of different skin chrominance models and chrominance spaces for the automatic detection of human faces in color images. In: Proc. of the Int. Conference on Face and Gesture Recognition, pp. 54–61 (2000)
7. Brand, J., Mason, J.: A comparative assessment of three approaches to pixel level human skin-detection. In: Proc. of the International Conference on Pattern Recognition, vol. 1, pp. 1056–1059 (2000)
8. Lee, J.Y., Yoo, S.I.: An elliptical boundary model for skin color detection. In: Proc. of the 2002 International Conference on Imaging Science, Systems, and Technology (2002)
9. Smith, P., Lobo, N.V., Shah, M.: Resolving Hand over Face Occlusion. In: Sebe, N., Lew, M., Huang, T.S. (eds.) HCI/ICCV 2005. LNCS, vol. 3766, pp. 160–169. Springer, Heidelberg (2005)
10. Angelopoulou, E., Molana, R., Daniilidis, K.: Multispectral skin color modeling. In: IEEE CVPR 2001, conference on Computer Vision and Pattern Recognition, pp. 635–642 (2001)
11. Malima, A., Ozgur, E., Cetin, M., Peucker, T. K.: A Fast Algorithm for Vision-Based Hand Gesture Recognition for Robot Control. In: IEEE 14th Signal Processing and Communications Applications (2006)
12. Douglas, D.H., Peucker, T.K.: Algorithms for the reduction of the number of points required to represent a digitised line or its caricature. The Canadian Cartographer 10(2), 112–122 (1973)
13. Tamura, H., Mori, S., Yamawaki, T.: Textural features corresponding to visual perception. IEEE Transactions on Systems, Man and Cybernetics 8, 460–473 (1978)
14. Freeman, W.T., Roth, M.: Orientation Histograms for Hand Gesture Recognition. In: IEEE International Workshop on Automatic Face and Gesture Recognition, Zürich (June 1995)
15. Kölsch, M., Turk, M.: Analysis of Rotational Robustness of Hand Detection with Viola&Jones' Method. In: Proceedings of ICPR 2004 (2004)
16. Dreuw, P., Keysers, D., Deselaers, T., Ney, H.: Gesture Recognition Using Image Comparison Methods. In: Gibet, S., Courty, N., Kamp, J.-F. (eds.) GW 2005. LNCS, vol. 3881, pp. 124–128. Springer, Heidelberg (2006)
17. Birk, H., Moeslund, T.B., Madsen, C.B.: Real-Time Recognition of Hand Alphabet Gestures Using Principal Component Analysis. In: 10th Scandinavian Conference on Image Analysis, Lappeenranta, Finland (1997)

Robust Tracking for Processing of Videos of Communication's Gestures

Frédérick Gianni, Christophe Collet, and Patrice Dalle

Institut de Recherche en Informatique de Toulouse,
Université Paul Sabatier, Toulouse, France
{gianni,collet,dalle}@irit.fr

Abstract. This paper presents a method of image processing used in a mono-vision system in order to study semiotic gestures. We present a robust method to track the hands and face of a person performing gestural communication and the Signs' language communication. A model of skin is used to compute the observation density as a skin colour distribution in the image. Three particle filter trackers are implemented, with re-sampling and annealed update steps to increase their robustness to occultation and high acceleration variations of body parts'. Evaluations of the trackers with and without these enhancements, show the improvement that they bring.

Keywords: Hands and Head Tracking, Skin Colour Segmentation, Particle Filter, Sign Languages, Video Analysis.

1 Introduction

In the context of the research undertaken on gestural man machine communication and on signs language's (SL), we are interested in the study of image processing tools able to automate part of the video annotation and then to build gestures recognition systems. In these contexts, the gestures should be performed naturally, without of any constraints. Hands' movements are thus very fast in particular in SL, and one of the major problems is to find a robust tracking method. In this paper, we present an enhanced tracking method using particle filtering. First we present the realisation context of the gestures studied and the parts of the body involved : hands and face. Next, we detail the method used to model and to track body parts. In the last section we present results of robustness of the tracking method.

2 Communication Gestures

During a communication such as a dialogue, work presentation, lot of gestures are emitted by numerous body parts. Each ones having their own meaning. According to Cadoz [1] the functionalities of the gestures are epistemic, ergotic and semiotic. We are here focus on the semiotic function, the semantic information

M. Sales Dias et al. (Eds.): GW 2007, LNAI 5085, pp. 93–101, 2009.

convey by the gesture. McNeil [2] gives a classification of those kinds of gestures: iconic, metaphoric, deictic or relative to the beat of the given information. If one wants to analyse gestures according to this classification, there is a need to retrieve, qualify and quantify the information given by the body parts to interpret the whole meaning of a communication. Those informations are useful in order to build interactive gesture systems for man-machine communication [3] and for linguistic's analysis in the studies of SL.

3   Tracking of Body Parts

Human motion tracking needs accurate features detection and features correspondence between frames using position, velocity and intensity information. In our approach, the feature correspondence is achieved using statistical estimators via a particle filter for the head and the two hands. As the particle filter models the uncertainty, it will provide a robuste framework for the tracking of the hands of a person communicating in french sign language.

Particle Filter

The particle filter (PF) aims at estimating a sequence of hidden parameters x_t from only the observed data z_t. The idea is to approximate the probability distribution by a weighted sample set :

$$\{(s_t^{(0)}, \pi_t^{(0)}) \ldots (s_t^{(n)}, \pi_t^{(n)})\}$$

with $n = 1, \ldots, N$ numbers of samples used. Each sample s represents one state of the tracked object with a corresponding discrete sampling probability π.

The state is modelled as:

$$s_t = [x, y, \dot{x}, \dot{y}, \ddot{x}, \ddot{y}]^t$$

the position, velocity and acceleration of the sample s in the observation at time t. Three states are maintained during the tracking, one for each body part tracked. We track the head and the hands separately, each of those areas is represented by one sample set. In the prediction phase, the samples are propagated throught a dynamic model : a first order auto-regressive process model $x_t = Sx_{t-1} + \eta$, where η is a multivariate Gausian random variable and S a transition matrix.

We use the particle filter defined in [4] applied in a color based context to achieve robustness against non rigidity and rotation. The observation density $p(z_t|x_t)$ is modelled as a skin colour distribution using the histogram backprojection method (fig.1).

In the particle filter, a resampling step is used to avoid the problem of degeneracy of the algorithm, that is, avoiding the situation that all but one of the importance weights are close to zero. The stratified resampling proposed by Kitagawa [5] is used, because it is optimal in terms of variance.

Fig. 1. Observation densities as a skin colour for head, right hand and left hand

Particle filter with annealed update step (APF). To maintain a good representation of the posterior probability, one may iterate the algorithm a certain amount of time. But this leads to an over-representation of the possible local maximum. This is caused by the weighting function applied at each iteration. The annealed effect proposed by [6] and with a more generic formulation [4] provides a mean to apply the weighting function to the sample set smoothly.

Update with simulated annealing

For $m = M, \ldots, 1$

    For $i = 0, \ldots, N$, $\pi_{t,m}^{(i)} \leftarrow p(z_t | \tilde{x}_{t,m} = \tilde{s}_{t,m}^{(i)})^{\beta_m}$

    For $i = 0, \ldots, N$, $\pi_{t,m}^{(i)} \leftarrow \dfrac{\pi_{t,m}^{(i)}}{\sum_{j=1}^{n} \pi_{t,m}^{(j)}}$

    For $i = 0, \ldots, N$, $x_{t,m}^{(i)} \leftarrow \tilde{x}_{t,m}^{(j)}$ with likelihood $\pi_{t,m}^{(j)}$

    For $i = 0, \ldots, N$, $\tilde{x}_{t,m-1}^{(i)} \leftarrow \tilde{s}_{t,m-1}^{(i)} \leftarrow \tilde{s}_{t,m}^{(i)} + \mathbf{B}_m$

    For $i = 0, \ldots, N$ $\pi_{t,0}^{(i)} \leftarrow p(z_t | x_t = \tilde{s}_t^{(i)})$

    For $i = 0, \ldots, N$ $\pi_{t,0}^{(i)} \leftarrow \dfrac{\pi_{t,0}^{(i)}}{\sum_{j=1}^{n} \pi_{t,0}^{(j)}}$

The value of β_m will determine the rate of annealling. The value of this parameter is chosen following the recommandations of Deutscher *et al.* [6]. From the survival diagnostic :

$$D = \left(\sum_{n=1}^{N} (\pi^{(n)})^2 \right)^{-1}$$

MacCormick [7] provides the particle survival rate $\alpha = \frac{D}{N}$. The annealing rate can be computed as follow: for each iteration an annealing rate α_m is given and using a gradient descent we can find the corresponding β^m :

$$\alpha_{i-1} = \left(N \sum_{i=0}^{N} ((\pi^{(i)})^{\beta_{m-1}})^2 \right)^{-1}$$

$$\alpha_i = \left(N \sum_{i=0}^{N} ((\pi^{(i)})^{\beta_m})^2 \right)^{-1} \text{ with } \beta_m = \tfrac{1}{2}\beta_{m-1}$$

while $\alpha_i - \alpha_{desired} > \varepsilon$

$$\Delta_\alpha = \frac{\alpha_i - \alpha_{i-1}}{\beta_m - \beta_{m-1}}$$

$$\beta_{m-1} = \beta_m$$

$$\beta_m = \beta_m + \frac{\alpha_{desired} - \alpha_i}{\Delta_\alpha}$$

$$\alpha_{i-1} = \alpha_i$$

$$\alpha_i = \left(N \sum_{i=0}^{N} ((\pi^{(i)})^{\beta_m})^2 \right)^{-1}$$

$\mathbf{B}_m$ is a multi-variate gaussian random variable with mean $\mathbf{0}$ and variance $\mathbf{P}_m$. The diffusion variance vector has been set as $\mathbf{P}_m = (\alpha_M \alpha_{M-1} \ldots \alpha_m)$ [6].

Multiple-object tracking. Here arise the problem of data association which makes the problem harder than single object tracking. Multiple object tracking and data association techniques have been extensively studied in [8] and a number of statistical data association techniques such as probabilistic data association filter, joint probabilistic data association filter, multiple hypothesis tracking filter have been developed. These generally employ a combination of "blob" identification and some assumption on the target motion. One may think of avoiding this problem in a way of interpreting the target as "blob" which merge and split again [9]. A "blob" interpretation does not maintain the identity of the targets, and it's difficult to implement for target which are not easily separable.

What is needed is an "exclusion principle" such as the one provide by Mac-Cormick [10]. This way we do not allow two targets to merge when their configuration become similar. First we compute the posterior density for each tracker, then we use it to penalize the measurement of the other trackers in a second computation of the posterior density.

4   Evaluations

Evaluations were conduct on a sequence of a person signing a story in the french sign language. We are here interested in testing the robustness of our approach against high dynamics motion variation and body part occlusions. Such a language is a tracking challenge as the tracked targets are very similar, the performed gestures have got a lot of dynamic variations (fig. 2), the targets are relatively often occluded and it's a long sequence (3 000 frames).

As expected the APF achieves a better robustness against strong dynamic variations than the PF and in the same way against local maxima (fig. 3).

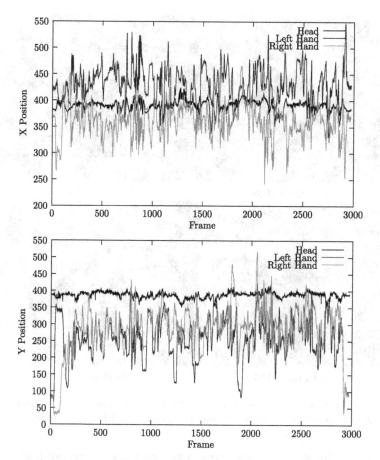

Fig. 2. The ground truth trajectories of the head and the two hands, (x,y) coordinates

We have estimated the frame to frame tracking that is to say if a link between two physical objects detected at two consecutive time instants is correctly computed or not. The metric uses the following comparison information:

1. Detected object at time t and $t + 1$ are related to the same reference data using the euclidean distance and a threshold.
2. A link exists between detected objects at time t and $t + 1$ and a link exists also in reference data

If there are several links between detected objects related to the same reference data, the one which maximize the overlap with reference data is kept as the good link and is removed for further association. Using this we compute four metrics (fig.4):

- **Good tracking.** *GT*, reference data link matching a link between two physical objects.

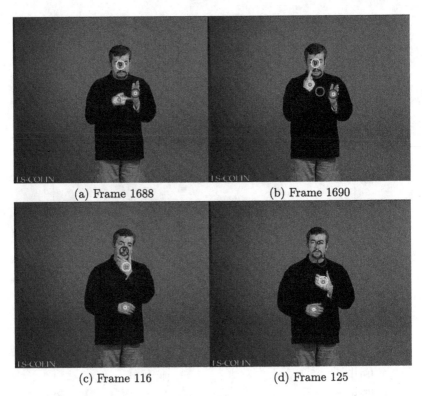

(a) Frame 1688   (b) Frame 1690

(c) Frame 116   (d) Frame 125

Fig. 3. The APF (small circles) achieve a better robustness against strong dynamic variations (a,b) and against local maxima (c,d) than the PF (large circle)

- **False tracking.** FT, a link between two physical objects not matching any reference data.
- **Miss tracking 1.** $MT1$, reference data link not found due to frame-to-frame tracking shortcomings, reject of case (1)
- **Miss tracking 2.** $MT2$, reference data link not found due to frame-to-frame tracking shortcomings, reject of case (1) and (2).

and then:

$$\text{Precision } \frac{GT}{GT + FT}, \quad \text{Sensitivity1 } \frac{GT}{GT + MT1} \quad \text{and} \quad \text{Sensitivity2 } \frac{GT}{GT + MT2}$$

We have performed evaluations with a different particle number 2000, 3000 and 6000 to outline the behavior of the filter (fig. 5). The optimal number of particles is around 3000 for the hands and around 6000 for the head, numbers that correspond to the size (in pixels) of those areas (table 1). For each filter the survival diagnostic has been evaluated and reflects those results.

The error in position has been computed from the euclidean distance between the computed position and the ground truth (fig. 5). Error peaks are caused by

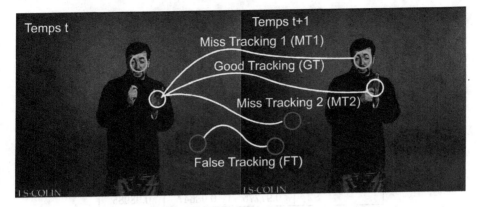

Fig. 4. Metrics used for frame-to-frame evaluation

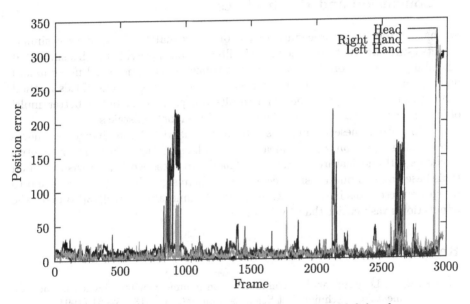

Fig. 5. Position error for the head, right hand and left hand

situations where the hands and head are very close to each others or merely occluding each other and move away under heavy acceleration. However the trackers do not miss their target a long time, they re-find them quickly. With a threshold of 50 pixels of distance (the tracker miss the target), one counts 224 errors for the head (7,4%), 25 and 79 for each hand (1,7%) on the 3000 images. The program is written in C++ and it can treat up to two frames per seconde without of any optimisation on a 1.86GHz Pentium M processor powered laptop.

Table 1. Precision and sensitivity results of the tracking with different particle numbers

Number of particles		Head	Right Hand	Left Hand
2000	P	0.90393	0.85489	0.90024
	S1	0.94091	0.98491	0.91875
	S2	0.95833	0.86624	0.97810
3000	P	0.92912	0.96708	0.98589
	S1	0.93890	0.97428	0.99323
	S2	0.98892	0.99242	0.99256
6000	P	0.93013	0.95532	0.94995
	S1	0.95024	0.96801	0.95929
	S2	0.97775	0.98647	0.98985

5   Conclusion and Perspectives

We have presented a procedure to perform a visual tracking of very similar objects using particle filter. The particle filter has been provided with a simulated annealing update in order to improve the robustness against local maxima and high dynamics variations. An evaluation shows the improvement of this method compared to the original one. The results are promising, but a better multi object framework has to be developed to reduce labels mistakes.

Starting from these results, a study on the hands' shape changes is undertaken, being based on various measurements like, motion, Cartesian geometric moments [11] and features of texture. Thanks to these works, we wish to build tools based on computer vision techniques to help signs' langage analysis and to integrate these tools in our software of video's annotation's [12][13] to make the annotation's task easier than by hand.

References

1. Cadoz, C.: Le geste canal de communication homme/machine. La communication "instrumentale". Techniques et Sciences Informatiques (13), 32–61 (1994)
2. McNeill, D.: Hand and mind: What gestures reveal about thought. University of Chicago Press (1992)
3. Carbini, S., Viallet, J.E., Bernier, O., Bascle, B.: Tracking body parts of multiple people for multi-person multimodal interface. In: IEEE International Workshop on Human-Computer Interaction, Beijing, China, October 21 (2005)
4. Gall, J., Potthoff, J., Schnoerr, C., Rosenhahn, B., Seidel, H.: Interacting and annealing particle filters: Mathematics and a recipe for applications. Technical Report MPI-I-2006-4-009, Max-Planck Institute for Computer Science (2006)
5. Kitagawa, G.: Monte carlo filter and smoother for non-gaussian nonlinear state space models. Journal of Computational and Graphical Statistics 5(1), 1–25 (1996)
6. Deutscher, J., Blake, A., Reid, I.: Articulated body motion capture by annealed particle filtering. In: Computer Vision and Pattern Recognition (2000)

7. MacCormick, J., Isard, M.: Partitioned sampling, articulated objects, and interface-quality hand tracking. In: Vernon, D. (ed.) ECCV 2000. LNCS, vol. 1843, pp. 3–19. Springer, Heidelberg (2000)
8. Bar-Shalom, Y.: Tracking and data association. Academic Press Professional, Inc, San Diego (1987)
9. Haritaoglu, I., Harwood, D., Davis, L.S.: Ghost: a human body part labelling system using silhouette. In: Proc. of IEEE Conf. on Pattern Recognition (1), pp. 77–82 (1998)
10. MacCormick, J., Blake, A.: A probabilistic exclusion principle for tracking multiple objects. Int. Journal on Computer Vision 39(1) (2000)
11. Cassel, R., Collet, C., Gherbi, R.: Real-time acrobatic gesture analysis. In: Gibet, S., Courty, N., Kamp, J.-F. (eds.) GW 2005. LNCS, vol. 3881, pp. 88–99. Springer, Heidelberg (2006)
12. Braffort, A., Choisier, A., Collet, C., Dalle, P., Gianni, F., Lenseigne, B., Segouat, J.: Toward an annotation software for video of sign language, including image processing tools and signing space modelling. In: Proc. of 4th International Conference on Language Resources and Evaluation - LREC 2004, Lisbon, Portugal, May 26–28, 2004, vol. 1, pp. 201–203 (2004)
13. Lenseigne, B., Dalle, P.: Using Signing Space as a Representation for Sign Language Processing . In: Gibet, S., Courty, N., Kamp, J.-F. (eds.) GW 2005. LNCS, vol. 3881, pp. 25–36. Springer, Heidelberg (2006)

Representation of Human Postures for Vision-Based Gesture Recognition in Real-Time

Antoni Jaume-i-Capó, Javier Varona, and Francisco J. Perales

Unitat de Gràfics i Visió per Ordinador
Departament de Ciències Matemàtiques i Informàtica
Universitat de les Illes Balears
{antoni.jaume,xavi.varona,paco.perales}@uib.es
http://dmi.uib.es/~ugiv/

Abstract. Using computer vision to sense and perceive the user and his/her actions in a Human-Computer Interaction context is often referred to as Vision-Based Interfaces. In this paper, we present a Vision-Based Interface guided by the user gestures. Previously to recognition, the user's movements are obtained through a real-time vision-based motion capture system. This motion capture system is capable to estimate the user 3D body joints position in real-time. By means of an appropriate representation of limbs orientations based on temporal histograms, we present a scheme of gesture recognition that also works in real-time. This scheme of recognition has been tested through control of a classical computer videogame showing an excellent performance in on-line classification and it allows the possibility to achieve a learning phase in real-time due to its computational simplicity.

Keywords: Vision-Based Gesture Recognition.

1 Introduction

Nonverbal communication is usually understood as the process of sending and receiving wordless messages [1]. Specifically, a gesture is a form of non-verbal communication made with a part of the body, used instead of or in combination with verbal communication. The language of gestures is rich in ways for individuals to express a variety of feelings and thoughts. Usually, the meaning of a gesture depends of the origin of the transmitter. On the other hand, some gestures are decided by the society and its meaning is regulated, as the sign language, although one exists for each spoken language.

Using computer vision to sense and perceive the user and his/her actions in an Human-Computer Interaction context is often referred to as Vision-Based Interfaces [2]. In this sense, the idea of using body gestures as a means of interacting with computers is not new. The first notable system was Bolt's *Put That There* multimodal interface [3]. Bolt combined speech recognition and pointing to move objects within the scene.

In this paper, we present a Vision-Based Interface guided by the user gestures that takes into account all body limbs, involved in the considered gestures. The

M. Sales Dias et al. (Eds.): GW 2007, LNAI 5085, pp. 102–107, 2009.

advantage of our system is that it is built over a motion capture system that recovers the body joints positions of the user's upper body in real-time.

This paper is organized as follows. The used real-time full-body motion capture system to obtain the user motions is presented in section 2. Next, in section 3, our gesture representation is described. How the gestures are recognized, is explained in section 4. The application of our system in a real-time interactive application and the obtained results are described in section 5. The obtained results are discussed in the last section to demonstrate the viability of this approach.

2   The Real-Time Vision-Based Motion Capture System

In this work, the real-time constraint is very important due to our goal of using the captured motions as input for gesture recognition in a vision-based interface (VBI). In this sense, the motions of the user's limbs are extracted through a real-time vision-based motion capture system. Usually, locating all the user body joints in order to recover the user's posture is not possible with computer vision algorithms only. This is mainly due to the fact that most of the joints are occluded by clothes. Inverse Kinematic (IK) approaches can solve the body posture from their 3D position if we can clearly locate visible body parts such as face and hands. Therefore, these visible body parts (hereafter referred to as end-effectors) are automatically located in real-time and fed into an IK module, which in turn can provide a 3D feedback to the vision system. Detailed technical information on this system can be found in [4].

3   Gesture Representation

Using the computed 3D positions of the involved body joints, we address the main problems in the gesture recognition challenge: temporal, spatial and style variations between gestures. Temporal variations are due to different gesture speed between different users. Spatial variations are due to physical constraints of the human body such as different body sizes. Style variations are due to the personal way in which a user makes its movements.

3.1   Posture Representation

An appropriate posture representation for gesture recognition must cope spatial variations. We propose a representation of each body limb by means of a unit vector, which represents the limb orientation. In this way, depending on the desired gesture alphabet, it is only necessary to compute the unit vector for the involved body limbs. This representation causes data to be independent from the user's size and it solves the spatial variations.

Once the motion capture data is spatially invariant, the next step is to represent the human posture. We build the posture representation by using unit vectors of the limbs involved in the gesture set. The idea is to represent the user's body posture as a feature vector composed by all the unit vectors of the user's limbs. Formally, the representation of the orientation of a limb, l, is

$$\mathbf{q}^l = (u_x^+, u_x^-, u_y^+, u_y^-, u_z^+, u_z^-), \tag{1}$$

where u_x^+ and u_x^- are respectively the positive and negative magnitudes of the x-component of unit vector, u_x, note that $u_x = u_x^+ - u_x^-$ and $u_x^+, u_x^- \geq 0$. The same applies for components u_y and u_z. In this way, the orientation components of the limb unit vector are half-wave rectified into six non-negative channels. Therefore, we build a histogram of limbs orientations which represents the complete user's limbs orientations. We propose two forms to build the histogram.

The first one is by cumulative limbs orientations, see Equation 2,

$$\mathbf{q} = \sum_{l=1}^{n} \mathbf{q}^l, \tag{2}$$

and the second one is by linking limbs poses, see Equation 3,

$$\mathbf{q} = \{\mathbf{q}^l\}_{l=1..n}, \tag{3}$$

where n, in both cases, is the number of limbs involved in the gestures to recognize.

The main difference between the two representations depends on the considered gesture set. The cumulative representation is more robust to tracking errors, but the set of recognized gestures is much reduced. For example, the same movements of different limbs can not be distinguished. On the other hand, the linked representation allows the definition of more gestures, although it is more sensible to errors in the estimation of the limbs orientations.

3.2   Making Data Temporally Invariant

Our approach represents gestures by means of a temporal representation of the user's postures. The reason for using posture information is that the postures directly define the gestures, even, in several cases, with only one posture it is possible to recognize a gesture. If we consider that a gesture is composed by several body postures, the gesture representation feature vector is composed by the cumulative postures involved in the gesture, that is

$$\hat{\mathbf{q}}_t = \frac{1}{T} \sum_{i=t-T}^{t} \mathbf{q}_i, \tag{4}$$

where t is the current frame and T is the gesture periodicity, and could be interpreted as a temporal window of cumulative postures. This process resumes the temporal variations of gestures by means of a detection of the periodicity of each user's gesture performance in order to fix the T value, that is, its temporal extent.

4   Gestures to Recognize

An important goal of this work is that the human-computer interaction should be performed using natural gestures. As it has been shown in several experiments with children[5], a gesture is natural depending on the user experience. The key is to take advantage of the system overall possibility of working in real-time. For these reasons, before the recognition process starts the system asks the user to perform several of the allowable gestures in order to build a training set in real-time. Performing several times the gestures in random order, the gesture models consider styles variations. This is a way to automatically build the training set. This fact reinforces the idea of making user's specific gestures models. In order to complete the process, it is necessary to choose a distance for comparison between the current gesture, $\hat{\mathbf{q}}_t$, and a gesture model, $\hat{\mathbf{p}}$. If we interpret the gesture representation as a distribution of the posture variations that occur when the user performs a gesture, we can use the next distance between two discrete distributions

$$d = \sqrt{1 - \rho[\hat{\mathbf{p}}, \hat{\mathbf{q}}_t]}, \tag{5}$$

where

$$\rho[\hat{\mathbf{p}}, \hat{\mathbf{q}}_t] = \sum_{j=1}^{M} \sqrt{p_j q_{t,j}}, \tag{6}$$

is the sample estimate of the Bhattacharyya coefficient between the exemplar and the current gesture, and M is the number of vector elements and depends on the chosen representation. In our case, the Bhattacharyya coefficient has the meaning of a correlation score between gestures. Distance of Eq. 5 has been applied in visual tracking obtaining excellent results [6].

5   Results

In order to test our gesture recognition approach, we have proposed playing a computer videogame interacting by means of body gestures with different users. In this case, the proposed game, a modified version of Tetris, allows users to use four different forms of control: *left*, *right*, *down* and *rotate*.

To test the real-time, we have calculated the time used to recognize a gesture once the joints positions of the user have been obtained. The real time of the vision-based motion capture system was tested in [4]. Including the gesture recognition step the frame rate is 21 frames per second. Therefore, we can conclude that our approach works near real-time.

For testing purposes, we acquired different sessions of different users while producing all the gestures during videogame. The game is manually controlled by a user in order to provide the immersive experience of really playing the game with its own gestures. This is the classical Wizard of Oz experiment [5].

Fig. 1. Some visual results of gesture recognition. In the case of the rotate gesture, a sequence gesture is shown.

Table 1. Comparative results between the proposed posture representations

Posture Representation	Gestures	Correct	Wrong	Non Recognized	False Possitive
cumulated	73	**84.95%**	4.10%	10.95%	7.20%
linked	73	**87.69%**	2.73%	9.58%	4.18%

At the moment, our dataset contains a training set where each user performs three times each form of control. After the training of the system, we evaluate its performance by testing the real behaviour of the recognition system. Specifically, the testing set is composed by 73 different gesture performances of the command set by three different users.

The results presented in Table 1 and in Figure 1 show that both representations obtain good results with a reasonable rate of correct recognition. Although, it should be considered that in this application the gesture set is reduced. Note that the linked representation is more accurate because the number of false positives is smaller than the cumulated representation, considering a false positive when the system recognizes a gesture although the user does not perform any gesture.

In addition, the majority of misclassifications and not recognized gestures are due to errors on the Vision-PIK estimation of the user's body joints. In this case, in Table 1 it can be seen that the linked representation is again more robust to these feature extraction errors than the cumulated one.

6 Conclusions

The most important contribution of this work is that we have defined two gesture representations, capable to cope with variations between gestures in different users and performances, making also possible the recognition in real-time. Our approach is original and it could be extended for representing more complex gestures and human activities. In fact, hand-based gesture recognition can be approached with the presented representation by substituting the user's body posture by the finger's poses.

The key idea is use a scheme for building specific user's models in real-time for on-line learning. Experiments have shown that the system adapts itself to each particular user's way of performing the gestures, avoiding a previous user's off-line training for learning the gestures that can be recognized by the system.

The complete system has been tested in a real-time application, a gesture-based videogame control, and the results obtained state that the presented approach for gesture recognition performs well. From these experiments, we can conclude that for the control of interactive applications with a reduced alphabet, the linked representation could alleviate the errors of the feature extraction step making the interface more robust. On the other hand, this approach can be extended by means of the linked representation to more complex gestures than the ones shown in the presented application.

Acknowledgements

This work has been supported by the Spanish M.E.C. under projects TIN2007-67993 and TIN2007-67896 and the Ramon y Cajal fellowship of Dr. J. Varona.

References

1. Knapp, M.L., Hall, J.A.: Nonverbal Communication in Human Interaction, 6th edn. Wadsworth Publishing (2005)
2. Turk, M., Kolsch, M.: Perceptual interfaces. In: Emerging Topics in Computer Vision. Prentice-Hall, Englewood Cliffs (2004)
3. Bolt, R.A.: 'put-that-there': Voice and gesture at the graphics interface. In: SIG-GRAPH 1980: Proceedings of the 7th annual conference on Computer graphics and interactive techniques, pp. 262–270. ACM Press, New York (1980)
4. Boulic, R., Varona, J., Unzueta, L., Peinado, M., Suescun, A., Perales, F.: Evaluation of on-line analytic and numeric inverse kinematics approaches driven by partial vision input. Virtual Reality (online) 10 (1), 48–61 (2006)
5. Höysniemi, J., Hämäläinen, P., Turkki, L., Rouvi, T.: Children's intuitive gestures in vision-based action games. Commun. ACM 48(1), 44–50 (2005)
6. Comaniciu, D., Ramesh, V., Meer, P.: Kernel-based object tracking. IEEE Transactions on Pattern Analysis and Machine Intelligence 25(5), 564–577 (2003)

Enhancing a Sign Language Translation System with Vision-Based Features

Philippe Dreuw, Daniel Stein, and Hermann Ney

Human Language Technology and Pattern Recognition, RWTH Aachen University
surname@cs.rwth-aachen.de

Abstract. In automatic sign language translation, one of the main problems is the usage of spatial information in sign language and its proper representation and translation, e.g. the handling of spatial reference points in the signing space. Such locations are encoded at static points in signing space as spatial references for motion events.

We present a new approach starting from a large vocabulary speech recognition system which is able to recognize sentences of continuous sign language speaker independently. The manual features obtained from the tracking are passed to the statistical machine translation system to improve its accuracy. On a publicly available benchmark database, we achieve a competitive recognition performance and can similarly improve the translation performance by integrating the tracking features.

1   Introduction

Most of the current sign language recognition systems use specialized hardware [14] and are very person dependent [11]. Furthermore, most approaches focus on the recognition of isolated signs only [12], or on the simpler case of isolated gesture recognition [13] which often can be characterized just by their movement direction. In [8] a review on recent research in sign language and gesture recognition is presented.

In statistical machine translation for sign language, only a few groups reported works on corpus-based approaches. In [7], an example-based approach is used for the translation. A statistical phrase-based translation model for the translation of weather forecasting news is presented in [10], which uses additional morphosyntactic linguistic knowledge derived from a parser to improve the translation performance. In [2], a novel approach is proposed to translate Chinese to Taiwanese sign language and to synthesize sign videos based on joint optimization of two-pass word alignment and intersign epenthesis generation.

Although deaf, hard of hearing and hearing signers can fully communicate among themselves by sign language, there is a large communication barrier between signers and hearing people without signing skills.

We use a vision-based approach for automatic continuous sign language recognition [5], which does not require special data acquisition devices (e.g. data gloves or motion capturing systems), and a statistical machine translation framework

M. Sales Dias et al. (Eds.): GW 2007, LNAI 5085, pp. 108–113, 2009.

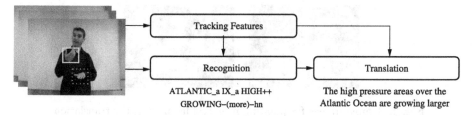

Fig. 1. Complete system setup with an example sentence: After automatically recognizing the input sign language video, the translation module has to convert the intermediate text format (glosses) into written text. We propose to use tracking based features also during translation.

for sign language translation [6]. Here, we propose to enhance a sign-to-text communication system with vision-based features. The system can aid the signing community with their everyday communication problems with the non-signing community. Fig. 1 illustrates the various components necessary for such a system.

2   Translation System: Overview

As mentioned above, recognition is only the first step of a sign-language to spoken-language system. The intermediate representation of the recognized signs is further processed to create a spoken language translation.

Statistical machine translation (SMT) is a data-based translation method that was initially inspired by the so-called noisy-channel approach: the source language is interpreted as an encryption of the target language, and thus the translation algorithm is typically called a decoder. In practice, statistical machine translation often outperforms rule-based translation significantly on international translation challenges, given a sufficient amount of training data.

A statistical machine translation system is used here to automatically transfer the meaning of a source language sentence into a target language sentence. Following the notation convention, we denote the source language with J words as $f_1^J = f_1 \dots f_J$, a target language sentence, with I words, as $e_1^I = e_1 \dots e_I$ and their correspondence as the a-posteriori probability $\Pr(e_1^I | f_1^J)$. The sentence $\hat{e}_1^I$ that maximizes this probability is chosen as the translation sentence as shown in Eq. 1. The machine translation system accounts for the different grammar and vocabulary of the sign language.

$$\hat{e}_1^I = \arg\max_{e_1^I} \left\{ \Pr(e_1^I) \cdot \Pr(f_1^J | e_1^J) \right\} \tag{1}$$

This classical source-channel model is generalized into a log-linear model, which allows the easy integration of additional models into the system. Each model's weighting factors are trained according to the maximum entropy principle. For a complete overview of the translation system, see [6].

To enhance translation quality, we propose to use visual features from the recognition process and include them into the translation as an additional

Fig. 2. Sample frames for pointing near and far used in the translation

knowledge source. The tracking positions of the 161 training sentences of the RWTH-Boston-104 database were clustered and their mean calculated. Then, for deictic signs, the nearest cluster according to the Euclidean distance was added as additional word information for the translation model (see Fig. 2).

3   Tracking System: Overview

For feature extraction, relevant body parts such as the head and the hands have to be found. To extract features which describe manual components of a sign, the dominant hand is tracked in each image sequence. Therefore, a robust tracking algorithm is required as the signing hand frequently moves in front of the face, may temporarily disappear, or cross the other hand. Our head and hand tracking framework is based on the algorithm described in [3,4]. This tracking algorithm is based on dynamic programming and is inspired by the time alignment algorithm in speech recognition and which guarantees to find the optimal path w.r.t. a given criterion and prevents taking possibly wrong local decisions.

These hand features, which are usually used within the recognition framework, can also be used within the translation framework, in order to decrease the translation error rate, too.

4   Experimental Results

All recognition experiments are measured similar to that done for speech recognition in terms of word error rates (WER) which is composed of errors that are due to deletion, insertion, or substitution of words.

To overcome the problem of incorrect WER due to the dependency on the perfect word order, we use the position independent word error rate (PER) as an additional measure in the translation experiments, which ignores the order of the words when comparing the words of the produced translation and the reference translation.

Sign Language Recognition: Some results concerning the recognition performance of our sign language recognition system on the RWTH-Boston-104 database and detailed information about the database itself are presented in [5]. A WER of 17.9% (i.e. 17 del., 3 ins., and 12 subst.) is achieved for a log-linear combination of two independently trained models accounting for long words and

Table 1. Recognition examples

Recognition reference	JOHN IX GIVE MAN IX NEW COAT
Recognition recognized as	JOHN ___ GIVE ___ IX NEW COAT

Fig. 3. Sample frames of the RWTH-Boston-Hands database with annotated hand positions. Left and right hand are marked with red and blue circles respectively. The last image shows different tolerance radii for $\tau = 15$ and $\tau = 20$ pixels.

short words respectively. The model weights have been optimized empirically. An example of a recognition result is shown in Tab. 1.

Tracking: A database for the evaluation of hand tracking methods in sign language recognition systems has been prepared. The RWTH-Boston-Hands database[1], which is freely available for further research, consists of a subset of the RWTH-Boston-104 videos. The positions of both hands have been annotated manually in 15 videos. A total of 1119 frames have been annotated.

For an image sequence $X_1^T = X_1, \ldots, X_T$ and corresponding annotated hand positions $u_1^T = u_1, \ldots, u_T$, the tracking error rate (TER) of tracked positions $\hat{u}_1^T$ is defined as the relative number of frames where the Euclidean distance between the tracked and the annotated position is larger than or equal to a tolerance τ:

$$TER = \frac{1}{T} \sum_{t=1}^{T} \delta_\tau(u_t, \hat{u}_t) \quad \text{with} \quad \delta_\tau(u, v) := \begin{cases} 0 & \|u - v\| < \tau \\ 1 & \text{otherwise} \end{cases} \quad (2)$$

For $\tau = 20$, we achieve 2.30% TER for a 20×20 search window, where frames, in which the hands are not visible, are disregarded. Examples of annotated frames and the tolerance τ are shown in Fig. 3.

Sign-To-Text Translation: On the best recognition result of the 40 test sentences presented in [5], we achieve an overall system baseline performance of a signed-video-to-written-English translation of 27.6% WER, and 23.6% PER (computed on the written language) which is a very reasonable quality and, in spite of glosses, is intelligible for most people.

In another set of experiments, for incorporation of the tracking data, the tracking positions of the dominant-hand were clustered and their mean calculated. Then, for deictic signs, the nearest cluster according to the Euclidean distance

---

[1] http://www-i6.informatik.rwth-aachen.de/~dreuw/database.php

Table 2. Examples for different translation output while integrating hand tracking features from the sign language recognition system

Translation without tracking features	Translation with tracking features
John gives that man a coat .	John gives the man over there a coat .
John buy a car in the future .	John will buy a car soon .
Sue buys the blue car .	the blue car over there .

was added as additional word information for the translation model. The reference point was taken from the average positions in the training material, and so far only from the frontal perspective, thus without including 3-dimensional distance information. For example, the sentence JOHN GIVE WOMAN IX COAT might be translated into *John gives the woman the coat* or *John gives the woman over there the coat* depending on the nature of the pointing gesture IX. For temporal signs, we also measured the velocity, for example for the sign FUTURE, where it depends on the speed of the movement if it just marks future tense, refers to some event in the very near future ("soon") or in the general future. In Tab. 2, the first sentence corrects the meaning of the deictic sign from a distinctive article, "that", to a location reference "over there". For the second sentence, the temporal sign is refering to the very near future, "soon", instead of the more general "in the future", and is also corrected with the additional input. The last example corrects the deictic sign, but the overall translation deteriorates since the subject was not translated – it seems that, with different alignments in the training phase, some errors are possible. In general, however, the newly introduced words derived from the tracking feature, which affect roughly 18% of all sentences, helped the translation system to discriminate between deixis as distinctive article, locative or discourse entity reference function, and improved translation quality by 3% in WER and 2.2% PER.

5   Summary and Conclusions

We presented an approach to improve an automatic sign language translation system using visual features which is strongly inspired by state-of-the-art approaches in automatic sign language recognition. The used tracking system achieves a very good TER of 2.30% on the publicly available RWTH-Boston-Hands database.

For the translation step, preliminary experiments have shown that the incorporation of the tracking data for deixis words helps to properly interpret the meaning of the deictic gestures. By combining different data sources, the translation error rate decreases about 3% in WER and 2.2% PER.

The results suggest that hand tracking information is an important feature for sign language translation, especially for grammatically complex sentences where discourse entities and deixis occur a lot in signing space.

Other features that are likely to improve the error rates include tilt of the head, shifts of the upper body, or features describing the hand and body configuration as e.g. in [1,9]. These features should be analyzed and combined with the existing feature set in the recognition and translation framework.

Furthermore, a thorough analysis of the entities used in a discourse is required to properly handle pronouns.

References

1. Agarwal, A., Triggs, B.: Recovering 3D Human Pose from Monocular Images. IEEE Trans. PAMI 28(1), 44–58 (2006)
2. Chiu, Y.-H., Wu, C.-H., Su, H.-Y., Cheng, C.-J.: Joint Optimization of Word Alignment and Epenthesis Generation for Chinese to Taiwanese Sign Synthesis. IEEE Trans. PAMI 29(1), 28–39 (2007)
3. Dreuw, P., Deselaers, T., Rybach, D., Keysers, D., Ney, H.: Tracking Using Dynamic Programming for Appearance-Based Sign Language Recognition. In: 7th Intl. Conference on Automatic Face and Gesture Recognition, pp. 293–298. IEEE, Southampton (2006)
4. Dreuw, P., Forster, J., Deselaers, T., Ney, H.: Efficient Approximations to Model-based Joint Tracking and Recognition of Continuous Sign Language. In: IEEE Face and Gesture Recognition, Amsterdam, The Netherlands (September 2008)
5. Dreuw, P., Rybach, D., Deselaers, T., Zahedi, M., Ney, H.: Speech Recognition Techniques for a Sign Language Recognition System. In: Interspeech 2007 - Eurospeech, Antwerp, Belgium, August 2007, pp. 2513–2516 (2007)
6. Mauser, A., Zens, R., Matusov, E., Hasan, S., Ney, H.: The RWTH Statistical Machine Translation System for the IWSLT 2006 Evaluation. In: IWSLT, Kyoto, Japan, November 2006, pp. 103–110 (2006) (Best paper award)
7. Morrissey, S., Way, A.: An Example-Based Approach to Translating Sign Language. In: Workshop Example-Based Machine Translation (MT X 2005), Phuket, Thailand, September 2005, pp. 109–116 (2005)
8. Ong, S.C., Ranganath, S.: Automatic Sign Language Analysis: A Survey and the Future beyond Lexical Meaning. IEEE Trans. PAMI 27(6), 873–891 (2005)
9. Ramanan, D., Forsyth, D.A., Zisserman, A.: Tracking People by Learning Their Appearance. IEEE Trans. PAMI 29(1), 65–81 (2007)
10. Stein, D., Bungeroth, J., Ney, H.: Morpho-Syntax Based Statistical Methods for Sign Language Translation. In: 11th Annual conference of the European Association for Machine Translation, Oslo, Norway, June 2006, pp. 169–177 (2006)
11. Vogler, C., Metaxas, D.: A Framework for Recognizing the Simultaneous Aspects of ASL. CVIU 81(3), 358–384 (2001)
12. von Agris, U., Schneider, D., Zieren, J., Kraiss, K.-F.: Rapid Signer Adaptation for Isolated Sign Language Recognition. In: CVPR Workshop V4HCI, New York, USA, June 2006, p. 159 (2006)
13. Wang, S.B., Quattoni, A., Morency, L.-P., Demirdjian, D., Darrell, T.: Hidden Conditional Random Fields for Gesture Recognition. In: CVPR, June 2006, vol. 2, pp. 1521–1527 (2006)
14. Yao, G., Yao, H., Liu, X., Jiang, F.: Real Time Large Vocabulary Continuous Sign Language Recognition Based on OP/Viterbi Algorithm. In: 18th ICPR, August 2006, vol. 3, pp. 312–315 (2006)

Generating Data for Signer Adaptation

Chunli Wang[1], Xilin Chen[2], and Wen Gao[3]

[1] School of Computer Science and Technology, Dalian Maritime University, 116026, Dalian, China
[2] Institute of Computing Technology, Chinese Academy of Science,100080, Beijing, China
[3] School of Electronics Engineering and Computer Science, Peking University, China
clwang@dl.cn

Abstract. In sign language recognition (SLR), one of the problems is signer adaptation. Different from spoken language, there are lots of "phonemes" in sign language. It is not convenient to collect enough data to adapt the system to a new signer. A method of signer adaptation with little data for continuous density hidden Markov models (HMMs) is presented. Firstly, hand shapes, positions and orientations that compose all sign words are extracted with clustering algorithm. They are regarded as basic units. Based on a small number of sign words that include these basic units, the adaptation data of all sign words are generated. Statistics are gathered from the generated data and used to calculate a linear regression-based transformation for the mean vectors. To verify the effectiveness of the proposed method, some experiments are carried out on a vocabulary with 350 sign words in Chinese Sign Language (CSL). All basic units of hand shape, position and orientation are found. With these units, we generate the adaptation data of 350 sign words. Experimental results demonstrate that the proposed method has similar performance compared with that using the original samples of 350 sign words as adaptation data.

Keywords: Sign Language Recognition, Adaptation, MLLR.

1 Introduction

Sign language is one of the most natural means of exchanging information for the hearing impaired. It is a kind of visual language via hand and arm movements accompanying facial expressions and lip motions. In China, there are more than 20 million people with hearing disability. Whereas most hearing people cannot understand sign language, it is appealing to direct efforts toward electronic sign language translators. The aim of sign language recognition is to provide an efficient and accurate mechanism to translate sign language into text or speech.

Moreover, humans use gestures in their everyday communication with other humans. Therefore, to make human-computer interaction truly natural, computer must be able to recognize gestures in addition to speech. Gestures are destined to play an increasing role in human-computer interaction in the future. Closely related to the field of gesture recognition is that of sign language recognition. Therefore, sign language recognition provides a research platform for Human-Computer interaction (HCI).

M. Sales Dias et al. (Eds.): GW 2007, LNAI 5085, pp. 114–121, 2009.

2 Related Work

The reports about sign language recognition began to appear at the end of 80's. T.Starner [1] used HMM to recognize American Sign Language sentences from video images. By imposing a strict grammar on this system, the accuracy rates in excess of 99% were possible with real-time performance. Fels and Hinton [2][3] developed a system using a VPL DataGlove Mark II with a Polhemus tracker as input devices. Neural network was employed for classifying hand gestures. Y. Nam and K.Y. Wohn [4] used three–dimensional data as input to HMMs for continuous recognition of a very small set of gestures. R.H.Liang and M. Ouhyoung[5] used HMM for continuous recognition of Tainwan Sign language with a vocabulary between 71 and 250 signs by using Dataglove as input devices. Kisti Grobel and Marcell Assan also adopted HMMs to recognize isolated signs collected from video recordings of signers wearing colored gloves, and 91.3% accuracy out of a 262-sign vocabulary was reported [6]. C.Vogler and D.Metaxas[7] described an approach to continuous, whole-sentence ASL recognition, in which Etymons instead of whole signs were used as the basic units. They experimented with 22 words and achieved similar recognition rates with Etyma-based and word-based approaches. Wen Gao[8] proposed a Chinese Sign language recognition system with a vocabulary of 1064 sign words. The recognition accuracy is about 93.2%. C. Wang[9] realized a Chinese Sign Language (CSL) recognition system with a vocabulary of 5100 sign words.

For signer-independent sign language recognition, Vamplew [11] reported the SLARTI sign language recognition system with an accuracy of around 94% on the signers used in training, and about 85% for other signers. It used a modular architecture consisting of multiple feature-recognition neural networks and a nearest-neighbor classifier to recognize 52 Australian sign language hand gestures. All of the feature-extraction networks were trained on examples gathered from 4 signers, and tested on both fresh examples from the same signers and examples from 3 other signers. Akyol and Canzler [12] proposed an information terminal that can recognize 16 signs of German Sign Language from video sequences. 7 persons were taken for training the HMMs and the other three for testing. The recognition rate is 94%. R. Martin McGuire [10] reported a mobile one-way American Sign Language translator. The recognition results of 94% accuracy on 141 sign vocabulary are gotten. But the vocabularies of these researches are limited.

Up to now, one of the problems in Sign Language recognition is to collect enough data. Data collection for both training and testing is a laborious but necessary step. All of the statistical methods used in Sign Language Recognition suffer from this problem. Furthermore, in order to realize signer-independent recognition system, the self-adaptation is an effective technique. But there are too many sign words in sign language, so it is impossible to request a new signer perform so many signs to adapt the system to him. The lack of the data makes the research, especially the large vocabulary signer-independent recognition, very formidable. This paper focuses on this problem.

We try to extract the basic units in Chinese Sign Language. The number of basic units is less than that of sign words in CSL. Each sign word is composed of limited types of components, such as hand shape, position and orientation. In this paper, we find the basic units of each component by clustering algorithm, and then generate the codebook that records which units each sign word is composed of. A set of sign words that includes all basic units is found. The data of these units are combined to generate all sign words. With these data, Maximum Likelihood Linear Regression (MLLR) transforms the mean parameters of HMMs.

The rest of this paper is organized as follows. In Section 3, basic units are extracted. In Section 4, the procedure of generating data is given. And MLLR is introduced in Section 5. Experimental results are reported in Section 6. Finally in Section 7, we give the conclusions.

3 Extracting Basic Units

First, we extract the basic units in Chinese Sign Language. In order to get the "phonemes" of the sign words in CSL, we respectively cluster different component of the sign word, namely hand shape, position and orientation.

3.1 Representing Sign Words

Two CyberGlove and a Pohelmus 3-D tracker with three receivers positioned on the wrist of CyberGlove and the back are used as input device in this system. A frame of raw gesture data is formed as 48-dimensional vector, which includes hand postures, positions and orientations. An algorithm based on geometrical analysis for the purpose of extracting invariant feature to signer position is employed. Each element value is normalized to ensure its dynamic range 0-1.

3.2 Clustering

There are not ready-made basic units in Chinese Sign Language. We must find them by ourselves. It is difficult to look up in the dictionary directly, so we employ the method of clustering.

Firstly, one CHMM is built for each sign word. Secondly, we cluster all the states of these CHMMs. Because the means on the states is abstracted from the samples and describe the features of one sign word exactly, only means on the states are clustered. In order to reduce the number of the classes, we split one mean vector into three parts, namely position & orientation (P&O), left hand shape (LH) and right hand shape (RH). Because the number of the classes is not known, the clustering algorithm must be able to find the appropriate number automatically. We implement this procedure based on the modified k-means algorithm. The steps are given as follows.

1. $n = 1$, where n denotes the current number of the classes;
2. Set the center of the class as the average of all samples;
3. Compute the centers of all classes by k-means and dispatch each sample to its corresponding class;
4. Compute the intra-distance of each class according to the expression:

$$D_i = \max_{j,k=1}^{N_i}\{d_{j,k}\} \quad i = 1,\ldots,n \tag{1}$$

In which N_i denotes the number of samples belongs to class i. $d_{j,k}$ is the Euclidian distance between two samples.

5. We record the maximum D_i as *MaxD*, and that class is recorded as i.

   If *MaxD > threshold* Then
       Divide the class i into two parts:
       $Center_i = Center_i + Cov_i/2$;
       $Center_{n+1} = Center_i - Cov_i/2$;
       $n = n + 1$;
       Goto step 2;
   End

   Here $Center_i$ denotes the center of class i, and Cov_i denotes the square root of the variance in class i. The value of *threshold* is set by experiments.

6. Output the centers of all classes and stop.

Each class is regarded as a basic unit. According to these units of each part gotten by the above method, we record the labels of the class that each part of each sign word belongs to. Then we get a codebook.

3.3   Subset of Sign Words

Because all sign words are composed by these basic units gotten by the above method, we can find a subset of sign words that includes all basic units of three parts based on the codebook. Then the data of the signs excluded in this subset can be generated.

In order to reduce the amount of data that a new signer must provide, the number of sign words in this subset should be as small as possible. Therefore, a scoring method to select the most suitable sign words is defined as follows:

$$S(S_i) = \sum_{U^i_j \in S_i} \frac{1}{F(U^i_j)} \qquad (2)$$

Where S_i represents a sign word; U^i_j represents the unit which belongs to s_i and is not included in the set; $F(U^i_j)$ represents the frequency of U^i_j in all sign words. Large score of $S(S_i)$ indicates that the sign word S_i can provide more new and special units therefore has higher priority to be selected.

The data of each component of the sign words in the subset are used as the basic units, based on which we can generate the samples of other sign words.

4   Generating New Samples

Each sign word is composed of limited types of components, namely hand shape, position and orientation, which are independent of each other. We collect the samples of the signs in the set we find. Each component of these samples is used as a basic unit. According to the codebook, we can combine the new samples based on the data of these units.

If the lengths of these three parts are same, we can combine them at each frame directly. The procedure is shown in Figure 1.

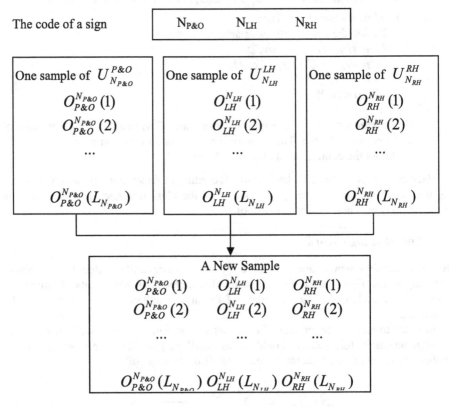

Fig. 1. Generate a new sample. Each frame is composed by three parts, which are gotten from the units. $U_{N_{P\&O}}^{P\&O}$ denotes one sample of class $N_{P\&O}$. $O_{P\&O}^{N_{P\&O}}(i)$ denotes the ith frame of observation in $U_{N_{P\&O}}^{P\&O}$. $L_{N_{P\&O}}$ denotes the length of $U_{N_{P\&O}}^{P\&O}$.

If the lengths of the three samples are different, we select the mean length as the length of the new sample and the other two samples are warped according to this length. Dynamic Time Warping algorithm is applied for this job. The generated new samples are used as the adaptation data to modify HMMs.

5 MLLR

The Maximum likelihood linear regression (MLLR) approach to signer adaptation requires an initial signer independent continuous density HMM system. MLLR takes some adaptation data from a new signer and updates the model mean parameters to maximize the likelihood of the adaptation data. The other HMM parameters are not adapted since the main differences between signers are assumed to be characterized by the means [13].

MLLR computes a set of transformations that will reduce the mismatch between an initial model set and the adaptation data. The effect of these transformations is to shift the component means in the initial system so that each state in the HMM system is more likely to generate the adaptation data [14].

Let W denote the $n \times (n+1)$ transformation matrix (where n is the dimensionality of the data) and μ denotes the mean vector to be adapted. The adapted mean vector $\hat{\mu}$ can be expressed as follows:

$$\hat{\mu} = W\xi \qquad (3)$$

here ξ is the augmented original mean vector,

$$\xi = [\omega\, \mu_1\, \mu_2 \cdots \mu_n]^T$$

where ω represents a bias offset whose value is fixed at 1.

The transformation matrix W is obtained by solving a maximization problem using the Expectation-Maximization (EM) technique [14].

To enable robust transformations to be trained, the transform matrices are tied across a number of Gaussians. The set of Gaussians which share a transform is referred to as a regression class. For a particular transform case W_m, the R Gaussian components $\{m_1, m_2, \ldots, m_R\}$ will be tied together, as determined by the regression class tree. By formulating the standard auxiliary function, and then maximizing it with respect to the transformed mean, and considering only these tied Gaussian components, the following is obtained,

$$\sum_{t=1}^{T}\sum_{r=1}^{R} L_{m_r}(t)\Sigma_{m_r}^{-1}o(t)\xi_{m_r}^{T} = \sum_{t=1}^{T}\sum_{r=1}^{R} L_{m_r}(t)\Sigma_{m_r}^{-1}W_m\xi_{m_r}\xi_{m_r}^{T} \qquad (4)$$

and $L_{m_r}(t)$, the occupation likelihood, is defined as,

$$L_{m_r}(t) = p(q_{m_r}(t) \mid M, O_T)$$

where $q_{m_r}(t)$ indicates the Gaussian component m_r at time t, and $O_T = \{o(1), \ldots, o(T)\}$ is the adaptation data. The occupation likelihood is obtained from the forward-backward process.

By solving equation (4), we can get the transformation matrix W_m [14].

6 Experiments

To verify the generalization capability of the proposed method, some experiments are performed based on a vocabulary with 350 sign words. Experimental data are collected from 4 signers represented by A-F. Each signer performs 350 isolated words for 4 times. Using the approach of cross validation test, 20 groups' data samples from five signers are used as the training samples.

One CHMM is built for each sign word. In our system, CHMM is left-to-right model allowing possible skips. The number of states is set to be 3, and the number of mixture components is set to be 2. We fix the values of variances of covariance matrix. The variances of the feature data in the dimensions representing Position and Orientation are set to be 0.2 and those in the dimensions representing Hand Shape are set to be 0.1. These above values are obtained by experiments.

With the clustering method introduced in Section 3, we get 107 basic units of P&O, 69 basic units of LH and 95 basic units of RH. All these units are included in 136 sign words.

For each new signer, we generate one group of adaptation data of 350 sign words (Generate) with the data of these 136 sign words. One group original data of 350 sign words from the new signer are used as training data (Regist). And another group data from the same signer are referred to as the unregistered test set. The recognition results are shown in Table 1.

Table 1. The recognition results of 350 sign words with different methods

New Signer	Without MLLR	Regist	MLLR (Generate)
A	59.4%	66.9%	72.6%
B	64.9%	70.8%	77.1%
C	60.1%	64.3%	66.9%
D	61.1%	61.1%	70.5%
E	61.7%	68.9%	67.7%
F	62.6%	68.3%	68.9%
Average	61.6%	66.7%	71.8%

7   Conclusions and Future Work

In this paper, an approach is proposed to generate adaptation data for the new signer from a small number of signs. These generated data are used to switch the means of CHMMs with MLLR. Experiments are carried out on a sign language database containing 350 sign words. The results show that the generated data are effective. By this method it is applicable to realize the self-adaptation of sign language recognition system.

This idea can be used for dynamic gestures, too. But the procedure of generation will be much more complicated. How to describe and cluster the movement is difficult. We will focus on this problem in the future. Moreover, this idea will be used in visual sign language recognition.

Acknowledgment

This research is sponsored in part by the National Natural Science Foundation of China under Contract 60603023 and Contract 60533030, in part by the Natural

Science Foundation of Beijing municipal under Contract 4061001, and in part by open project of Beijing Multimedia and Intelligent Software Key laboratory in Beijing University of Technology.

References

1. Starner, T.: Visual recognition of American Sign Language using hidden Markov models. Master's thesis, MIT Media Laboratory (1995)
2. Fels, S.S., Hinton, G.: GloveTalk: A neural network interface between a DataDlove and a speech synthesizer. IEEE Transactions on Neural Networks 4, 2–8 (1993)
3. Sidney Fels, S.: Glove –TalkII: Mapping hand gestures to speech using neural networks-An approach to building adaptive interfaces. PhD thesis, Computer Science Department, University of Torono (1994)
4. Nam, Y., Wohn, K.Y.: Recognition of space-time hand-gestures using hidden Markov model. In: ACM Symposium on Virtual Reality Software and Technology, Hong Kong, pp. 51–58 (1996)
5. Liang, R.-H., Ouhyoung, M.: A real-time continuous gesture recognition system for sign language. In: 3rd Proceeding of International Conference on Automatic Face and Gesture Recognition, Nara, Japan, pp. 558–565. IEEE Press, Los Alamitos (1998)
6. Grobel, K., Assan, M.: Isolated sign language recognition using hidden Markov models. In: Proceedings of the International Conference of System, Man and Cybernetics, Orlando, USA, pp. 162–167. IEEE Press, Los Alamitos (1996)
7. ChristianVogler, D.M.: Toward scalability in ASL Recognition: Breaking Down Signs into Phonemes. In: Braffort, A., Gibet, S., Teil, D., Gherbi, R., Richardson, J. (eds.) GW 1999. LNCS, vol. 1739, pp. 400–404. Springer, Heidelberg (2000)
8. Gao, W., Ma, J., Wu, J., Wang, C.: Large Vocabulary Sign Language Recognition Based on HMM/ANN/DP. International Journal of Pattern Recognition and Artificial Intelligence 14(5), 587–602 (2000)
9. Wang, C., Gao, W., Ma, J.: A Real-time Large Vocabulary Recognition System for Chinese Sign Language. In: Gesture and Sign Language in Human-Computer Interaction, London, UK, pp. 86–95. Springer, Heidelberg (2001)
10. McGuire, R., Hernandez-Rebollar, J., Starner, T., Henderson, V., Brashear, H.: Towards a One Way American Sign Language Translator. In: 6th IEEE International Conference on Face and Gesture Recognition, Seoul, Korea, pp. 620–625. IEEE Press, Los Alamitos (2004)
11. Vamplew, P., Adams, A.: Recognition of Sign Language Gestures Using Neural Networks. Australian Journal of Intelligent Information Processing Systems 5(2), 94–102 (1998)
12. Akyol, S., Canzler, U.: An information terminal using vision based sign language recognition. In: ITEA Workshop on Virtual Home Environments, Paderborn, Germany, pp. 61–68 (2002)
13. Leggetter, C., Woodland, P.: Maximum likelihood linear regression for speaker adaptation of HMMs. Computer Speech and Language 9, 171–186 (1995)
14. Microsoft Corporation, Cambridge University Engineering Department.: The HTK Book, Version 3.2 (2002)

A Qualitative and Quantitative Characterisation of Style in Sign Language Gestures

Alexis Heloir and Sylvie Gibet

Laboratoire Valoria, Université de Bretagne Sud.
Vannes, France
alexis.heloir@dfki.de,
sylvie.gibet@univ-ubs.fr

Abstract. This paper addresses the identification and representation of the variations induced by style for the synthesis of realistic and convincing expressive sign language gesture sequences. A qualitative and quantitative comparison of styled gesture sequences is made. This comparison leads to the identification of temporal, spatial, and stuctural processes that are described in a theoritical model of sign language phonology. Insights raised by this study are then considered in the more general framework of gesture synthesis in order to enhance existing gesture specification systems.

1 Introduction

Embodying a virtual humanoid with expressive gestures requires the taking into account of the properties that influence the perception of convincing movements. One of these properties is style. Style, on the one hand, enhances, augments and colours the inherent meaning of a message. On the other hand, style carries information about the speaker's age, gender, cultural background, and emotional state. As a consequence, style contributes to making a virtual humanoid more convincing and may increase its acceptance by human users.

This paper presents both a qualitative and quantitative analysis of styled motion gesture data. The temporal, spatial and structural differences between styled gestures are confronted with the phenomenons described in the literature dedicated to sign language phonology [1].

It is already well-known that gesture style modifies the temporal and the spatial aspects of gestures. In this paper, we address how style may also influence the structure organisation of some lexical units.

We then briefly present new insights for taking into account both the spatio-temporal and structural variations induced by style in existing gesture specification frameworks.

This paper is organised as follows: related work is reviewed in section 2, section 3 presents the gesture data upon which the study was performed and the manual segmentation scheme we applied. Section 4 presents the temporal variations that have been identified while section 5 deals with the spatial and structural variations that have been observed. Section 6 raises insights towards

M. Sales Dias et al. (Eds.): GW 2007, LNAI 5085, pp. 122–133, 2009.

the enhancement of existing expressive gesture specification models. Section 7 concludes and presents pointers to future work.

2   Related Works

Studies on sign language which have been carried out since the 1960's have lead to dedicated description/transcription systems [2,3]. Several gestural generation systems inspired by those works have appeared since. The eSign project [4] designed and set up a communicative gesture synthesis system inspired by phonological description of sign language. Gibet & al. [5] propose an expressive gesture synthesis system where the task is expressed as a discrete sequence of targets in the euclidian space around the virtual signer. Projects dedicated to geometrically based modelling of sign language [6,7,8] have appeared more recently.

Style and emotion centric studies around human motion appeared by the end of the XIXe century and have been continued and enhanced until today [9]. The underlying theory derived from those works served as a base for procedural motion synthesis systems [10]. Other procedural systems deal with psycho-cognitive studies [11] in order to convey emotional content [12]. Finally, inter-subject variability of style has been addressed in [13].

Recent studies dedicated to expressive gesture rely on segmentation and annotation of gesture. Those studies and are aimed at characterising the spatial structure of a Sign Language phrase [8], investigating the systematic synchrony between modalities [14] or transcribing and modelling gestures with the goal of further resynthesis [15].

In this paper, we rely on a slightly modified version of the transcription scheme proposed by Kita et al. [16]. This transcription scheme provides a description of the temporal structure of gesture by identifying basic movement phases. The goal of the segmentation is to confront styled gesture sequences with the timing description, enhancement and surfacing processes described by Brentari [1]. The subsequent section presents the segmentation process more thoroughly.

3   Motion Acquisition and Segmentation

This section presents the motion data on which we relied for this study. We then present our gesture segmentation scheme that is inspired by previous work dedicated to the segmentation of expressive gestures.

3.1   Motion Data

The motion data on which we conducted the study has been obtained thanks to an original motion capture process [17]. This process relies on two complementary techniques. The first technique aims at capturing facial and body motions thanks to a set of reflective markers placed on standardized anatomical landmarks and a network of 12 *Vicon-MX*[1] infrared cameras located all around the

---

[1] http://www.vicon.com/products/viconmx.html

subject. The second technique aims at capturing finger motion thanks to a pair of *Cybergloves*[2] measuring finger abduction and flexion. This technique is well suited for finger motion, as it is robust to visual occlusions of fingers that may appear too often during acquisition. The two devices are synchronised together and the data acquired is made available in a single file after postprocessing. By the more, a video stream is used for manual annotation of the sequences while three dimentional data serves as a base for numerical computation and comparison on the motion.

The capture sequences have been performed by a professional deaf instructor. The sequences are mainly composed of a succession of lexical units. These sequences depict the same weather forecast presentation. The difference among the sequences is in the emotional content the signer was asked to mimic during the gesture performance. No perceptive validation has been performed over the signer's performance. Three gesture sequences have been used in this study: in the first one, the signer was asked to be neutral, for the second one, the signer was asked to mimic anger, and for the third one, weariness. The gesture sequence can be depicted as the following gloss sequences:

{ HELLO, PLEASE, LOOK_AT_ME, TODAY, SIX, JULY, WEATHER, BRIT-TANY, MORNING, CLOUDS_CROSSING, AFTERNOON, RAIN, TOMOR-ROW, SUN, SWIM, GO, MUST, FRIDAY, CLOUDS, EVENING, CLOUDS, MORNING, FOG, SEE_YOU_SOON, GOOD_BYE }

The following table depicts the main characteristics of the gesture sequences:

Table 1. Gesture sequences details

Sequence	style	Duration (s)	number of glosses
1	neutral	45	25
2	angry	33	25
3	weary	52	25

3.2 Segmentation Scheme

In order to highlight the succession of gesture phases occurring during a gesture sequence, we relied on the segmentation method proposed by Kita [16]. This method was originally applied to manual annotation of gesture recorded as video streams. However, in our case it makes sence to take advantage of the extra information that is provided by the three dimensional reconstruction of the motion. Although Kita's model has already been adapted to automatic segmentation of three dimensional motion data in [18]. This method did not provide us with relevant segmentation over sign language gesture sequences, we thus prefered to rely on automated analysis only to provide hints that could help a human annotator to take a decision during a manual segmentation process.

---

[2] http://www.immersion.com/3d/products/cyberglove.php

According to [16], movement phases are characterised by either an abrupt change in the direction in the hand *movement* and discontinuity in the velocity profile of the hand *movement* before and after the abrupt direction change. As it may be challenging for a human annotator to precisely detect hand configuration change, the original segmentation process was enhanced by introducing information obtained from the three dimentional gesture representation of the motion into two supplementary annotation channels. Those supplementary channels are dedicated to represent how hand configuration change along a gesture sequence. It is computed for both hands, along the entire sequence. For each frame i in the sequence, a distance D_i is computed over two consecutive hand configuration (A_i, A_{i+1}) aligned in the Cartesian space [19]. The sum of squared distances between the corresponding joint positions ($\overrightarrow{P_j}$ and $\overrightarrow{P_j'}$) gives the distance between two consecutive frames: $D(A_i, A_{i+1}) = \sum_j \|(\overrightarrow{P_j} - \overrightarrow{P_j'})\|$ We assume that a hand configuration change occurs when $D(A_i, A_{i+1})$ exceeds two standard deviation from the mean distance value computed over the entire sequence.

The remaining of the segmentation proccess was manually performed over the video recording of the gesture sequences and segmented thanks to the Anvil software [15]. The segmentation was performed througouth the three styled gesture sequences and lead to the identification of the movement phases described in [16] and summarized in the following.

- **stroke:** A phase characterised by a lexical-internal movement;
- **preparation:** A phase with a moving limb between two strokes;
- **retraction:** A phase that happens during the resting position;
- **partial retraction:** An interrupted retraction phase followed by a preparation phase;
- **hold:** A phase in which the hand is held "still".

Both a qualitative and quantitative comparison of the gesture sequences is presented in the next section.

4   Temporal Variations and Gesture Phases Differences between Styles

This section presents the temporal characterization of style among the gesture sequences that have been segmented in the previous section. The results focus on the coordination between articulators and the temporal variations between simple gestures performed according to different styles.

4.1   Coordination between Channels

A study was conducted on the coordination between the channels involed in gesture movements. In order to identify coordination characteristics, the channels dedicated to the identification of hand motion were confronted to the channel dedicated to gesture phase identification.

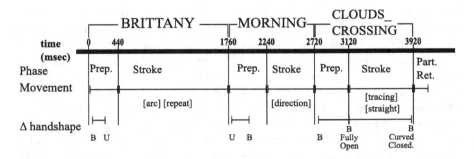

Fig. 1. Segmentation of gesture phases and temporal relations between hand and arm movement, from [1]

By making comparisons between the channels dedicated to handshape change and gesture phase, we are able to compare the *handshape change duration / movement duration (HSΔ/Mov Ratio)*. This measure represents the amount of time a subject takes to execute a given handshape change simultaneously with a given movement [1]. This measure reveals relations about the coordination between arm and hand in the production of expressive gesture. We compared the *HSΔ/Mov* Ratio between two types of gesture phases where a handshape change was observed: preparation phases and stroke phases (see Fig. 1 for details). The comparison was driven for each of the three captured gesture sequences. Results are summarised in table 2.

Table 2 highlights on the one hand the similarities between handshape and motion coordination regarding style and on the other hand, the differences in the coupling of handshapes and movement between gesture phases. It appears that word-internal movements present high coupling while non-meaningful gesture phases present low coupling. Existing studies dedicated to sign language phonology state that the coupling and decoupling of handshape changes and movements constitutes evidence on the representation of word-internal movements around global timing units [1]. Considering gesture specification, these facts suggest that gesture phases should take into account different coordination schemes regarding their type: whereas word internal gesture phases should be specifed according to timing units and should reveal strong coordination between articulators involved in motion, non-meaningful gestures like preparation or retraction should reveal a loose temporal coupling between articulators.

Table 2. *HSΔ/Mov* Ratio regarding gesture phase and style of gesture sequence

	preparation (mean, std. deviation)	stroke (mean, std. deviation)
neutral	38%, 19	93%, 5
angry	43%, 16	95%, 8
weary	37%, 12	86%, 8

4.2   Timing Variations between Single Path Signs

According to the literature dedicated to sign language linguistics, timing variation may occur at several levels. In this subsection, we focus on the temporal variation which occurs between simple gesture movements. In order to highlight the temporal variations induced by style between simple gesture units, a non-linear distance evaluation was performed on each lexical unit containing a single movement path (identified as a non-repetitive, non-alternating stroke phase). According to Brentari [1], such movements contain two timing units[3]. The timing distance evaluation was performed thanks to a dynamic time warping algorithm, described in detail in [20]. Dynamic Time Warping finds a non-linear timing adjustment between two time series that minimizes their global distance. The warp paths presented in Fig. 2 were computed by taking into account the preparation phase to the strokes, as it is difficult to identify precisely the separation between preparation phase and stroke phase in a lexical unit.

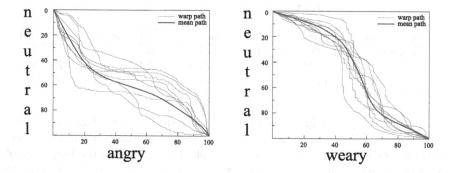

Fig. 2. In-sign temporal alignement between styles

Fig. 2 highlights the non-linear relationship that links styled gestures. The light curves represent warp paths that were obtained by the DTW algorithm between a styled lexical unit and its neutral equivalent. The lexical unit contains a preparation phase plus a single movement path, segmented as a stroke phase. The bold curve represents a cubic regression of the average path over the actual computed paths. The DTW calculation was performed over 9 motion sequences. All composed of a preparation phase and a stroke phase. The comparison was done between the neutral and angry style Fig. 2.a, then between the neutral and weary style Fig. 2.b.

Those paths highlight three distinct phases occuring along the lexical unit. The first one represents the preparation phase and is subject to a linear timing deformation. The second phase represents the first timing unit of the simple movement in the lexical unit and the third phase stands for the second timing

---

[3] Timing units can be referred as segments in the literature dedicated to sign language phonology [1].

unit of the lexical unit. On the one hand it seems that the maximum timing deformation is observed during the first timing unit of the simple movement. On the other hand, timing deformation induced by style may be generalized, at a word level by a temporal variation profile that may be characterized according to a simple analytical formulation, like cubic Hermite splines.

4.3 Phase Repartition

Table 3 presents the number and the distribution of the annotated phases along the gesture sequences according to gesturing style. This table reveals that there is a very small difference between the number of preparation phases and the number of stroke phases. According to [16], retraction phases occur at the end of movement phrases or movement units. Thus, retraction phases highlights the end of an *idea unit*. Finally hold phases seems to occur more frequently in the *weary* sequence and less frequently in the *angry* sequence.

Table 3. Frequency of phase types

gesture sequence	preparation	stroke	retraction	partial retraction	hold	total
neutral	27 (40%)	27 (40%)	2 (3%)	6 (9%)	5 (7%)	67
angry	26 (39%)	27 (40%)	8 (12%)	2 (3%)	4 (6%)	67
weary	26 (37%)	27 (38%)	9 (13%)	2 (3%)	7 (10%)	71

The results depicted in Table 3 suggest that the election of gesture phases involded in a gesture phrase vary according to style. The most noticeable difference concerned retraction phases. For example, the increase of the frequency of complete retraction phases, in the angry-styled gesture tends to convey a more perceptive rythm [21] in the gesture sequence.

5 Spatial and Structural Features

This section highlights the Spatial and structural variations that have been observed between styled elementary gestures. The described phenomenons have been depicted in the sign language phonology litterature [1].

5.1 Proximalisation/Distalisation

A sign gesture may undergo variations in its spatial extend. In other words, the trajectory described by the signers wrist may be dilated or contracted in the signers signing space. This phenomenon is described in the context of enhancement as proximalisation/distalisation [1]. Thus, a sign may surface in a way that the initial joints mainly involved in the execution of the movement migrate to a more proximal (closer to the body) or distal (closer to the fingers) joint. One example of proximalisation/distalisation is expressed in Fig. 3.a , where an initial movement, WIND (Fig. 3.a center) may surface as distalised (fig. 3.a left)

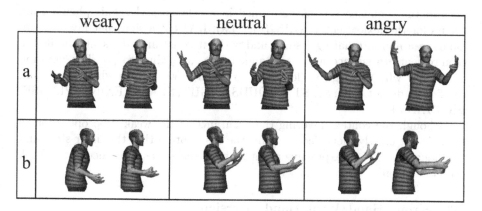

	weary	neutral	angry
a			
b			

Fig. 3. Proximalisation and distalisation examples performed by a synthetic agent

(the movement is mainly performed by the wrist) or may surface as proximalised (Fig. 3.a right): In this other example, the movement is performed by both the shoulders and the elbows. Another example is given in Fig. 3.b where the initial movement (YOU_MUST), originally performed mainly by the elbow (Fig. 3.b center) may surface as distalised (Fig. 3.b left) where the movement is mainly performed by the wrists. Finally, the movement may surface as proximalised (Fig. 3.b right), with the shoulder joints participating in the movement.

These phenomenons may convey, as highlighted in the examples, insights about the internal and emotional state of the signer, but, as stated in [12,13], they may also provide information about the personnality, cultural and social background of the performer.

5.2   Weak Drop

The weak drop phenomenon is an optional operation in which a two-handed sign is actually realised as a one handed sign. The weak drop phenomenon is observed

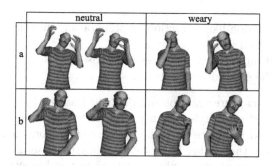

	neutral	weary
a		
b		

Fig. 4. Example of Weak Drop and Hand Inversion performed by a synthetic agent

once in the sequence that is performed in a relaxed style. This phenomenon occurs for the lexical entry RAIN (Fig. 4.a). RAIN is a sign that involves two hands in a non-alternating fashion and without constraint. This sign fulfils the requirements to surface as a one-handed sign, according to [1]. The question is to know why this sign is elected to to undergo weak drop while other valid candidates do not {GO, MUST, CLOUDS, NIGHT, SEA, EVENING, PLEASE, BRITTANY}.

Although the context favoring the occurance of the weak drop operation to occur is not clearly identified, we emit the assumption that the inner state and emotional state of an expressive agent may influence the occurence of the weak drop operation.

5.3   Strong Hand/Weak Hand Inversion

Along the gesture sequences, we were able to identify one occurence of the hand inversion phenomenon. This phenomenon consists of performing a one-handed sign thanks to the weak hand (H2) rather than the strong hand (H1). The operation is depicted in Fig. 4.b, for the sign word TOMORROW, successively performed according to neutral and weary style. This sign is a one-handed sign that is (in weary style), surrounded by two other one-handed signs : RAIN, surfaced as a one handed sign (see above pararaph) and SUN, which is a one handed sign. Thus, the migration of the path movement in rain from H1 to H2 leads to an alternation of Right-Left-Right arm movements. This phenomenon illustrates an important change in the structure of gesture.

6   Gesture Specification and Generation Framework

Our goal is to propose a framework dedicated to the specification and the generation of convincing expressive gestures. In order to take into account the variability induced by style, we choose to rely on the qualitative and quantitative study presented in previous sections. We thus plan to extend the Lebourque et al. gesture specification system [5], by introducing new features in order to take into account:

– Parts of the motion like retraction or preparation phases;
– Features observed in gesture phases;
– Spatial variation between styles gesture phases;
– Changes in the structure of gestures.

The analysis of captured motion data should lead to the creation of gesture libraries taking gesturing style into account. The generation of expressive gesture phrases should therefore be realised thanks to a concatenation of elected gesture phases from the gesture libraries according to a specified style. The style should be dependant on the Agent's characteristics and emotional state, which is in accordance with the style dictionary paradigm proposed in [13]. We briefly present the main insights introduced by the gesture analysis presented in this

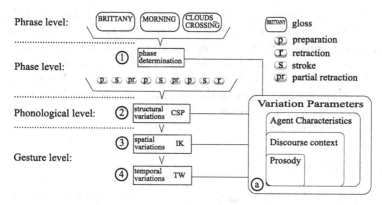

Fig. 5. Overview of the styled gesture gesneration process "clouds are crossing brittany in the morning"

paper and how they fit in our gesture specification and generation framework. Fig. 5 depicts the overall organisation of the framework.

1. At the phrase level, by introducing gesture phases and specifying different classes of gestures { *preparation, retraction, partial retraction, stroke and hold* }, we are able to represent gesture phases in a more accurate and realistic fashion;
2. At a phonological level, phenomenons presented in section 5, such as weak drop or hand inversion could be taken into account by considering the surfacing process as a constraint satisfaction problem (CSP);
3. Proximalisation/distalisation is handled at a gesture level by expanding or shrinking the trajectories of end effectors involved in a gesture. This operation rely on inverse kinematics (IK) algorithms;
4. By specifying explicit timing relations between timing units and gesture articulators, we are able to specify faithful descriptions of gestures. In addition, the correspondence between timing profiles highlighted in 4.1 leads to time warp patterns that provide realistic timing deformations between styles.

The variation parameters are the result of the combination of several variational layers. These layers are ordered according to their temporal extend (fig. 5.a) : for instance, agent inners characteristics (sex, culture) are permanent, while discourse context stands for the duration of a discourse and prosody has even shorter temporal resolution. The combination of these attributes leads to a set of variational attributes that parameterize the transformation steps described above.

7   Conclusion and Future Works

We have presented both a qualitative and quantitative study of the influence of style over expressive gesture sequences. We have highlighted how gesture may be modified by style at a structural, temporal and spatial level. This study leads to the design of an original framework dedicated to the specification and generation of styled sign language utterances. The way gestures are modified is taken into account by a set of variational parameters. These parameters are influenced by agent inner characteristics, discourse context and prosody. We are currently working on validating each block of the generative framework by implementing relevant demonstrators. a future step will consist into arranging every block in a consistent general demonstrator.

Acknowlegdements

This work is part of the Signe projet, funded by the regional council of Brittany (Ref. B/1042/2004/SIGNE). Motion capture has been performed by Alain Cahut, deaf instructor from the Brittany based organization Polycom. Authors would like to thank the reviewers and Loïc kervajan for their constructive remarks and Joanna Roppers for having read the manuscript.

References

1. Brentari, D.: A prosodic model of sign language phonology. Bradford Book (1998)
2. Stokoe, W.: Sign language structure: An outline of the visual communication systems of the american deaf. In: Studies in Linguistic, Occasional Papers, vol. 8 (1960)
3. Prillwitz, S.L., Leven, R., Zienert, H., Zienert, R.: T.Hanke, Henning, J.: Ham-NoSys. Version 2.0. International Studies on Sign Language and Communication of the Deaf (1989)
4. Zwiterslood, I., Verlinden, M., Ros, J., van der Schoot, S.: Synthetic signing for the deaf: Esign. In: Conference and Workshop on Assistive Technologies for Vision and Hearing Impairment, Granada, Spain (July 2004)
5. Gibet, S., Lebourque, T., Marteau, P.F.: High level specification and animation of communicative gestures. Journal of Visual Languages and Computing 12(6), 657–687 (2001)
6. Filhol, M., Braffort, A.: A sequential approach to lexical sign description. In: LREC 2006 - Workshop on Sign Languages, Genova, Italy (2006)
7. Braffort, A., Lejeune, F.: Spatialized semantic relations in french sign language: Towards a computational modelling. In: Proc. of Int. Gesture Workshop (2006)
8. Lenseigne, B., Dalle, P.: Using signing space as a representation for sign language processing. Gesture in Human-Computer Interaction and Simulation 6, 25–36 (2006)
9. Laban, R.: The Mastery of Movement. Northcote House (1988)
10. Chi, D.M., Costa, M., Zhao, L., Badler, N.I.: Emote. In: Akeley, K. (ed.) Siggraph 2000, Computer Graphics Proceedings, pp. 173–182. ACM Press / ACM SIGGRAPH / Addison Wesley Longman (2000)
11. Wallbot, H.: Bodily expression of emotion. European journal of social psychology 28, 879–796 (1998)
12. Hartmann, B., Mancini, M., Pelachaud, C.: Implementing expressive gesture synthesis for embodied conversational agents. In: Gesture in human-Computer Interaction and Simulation (2006)

13. Ruttkay, Z., Noot, H.: Variations in gesturing and speech by gestyle. International Journal of Human-Computer Studies. International Journal of Human-Computer Studies 62, 211–229 (2005) (Special Issue on Subtle Expressivity for Characters and Robots)
14. Attina, V., Cathiard, M.-A., Beautemps, D.: Temporal measures of hand and speech coordination during french cued speech production. In: Gibet, S., Courty, N., Kamp, J.-F. (eds.) GW 2005. LNCS, vol. 3881, pp. 13–24. Springer, Heidelberg (2006)
15. Boca Raton, F. (ed.): Gesture Generation by Imitation - From Human Behavior to Computer Character Animation (2004), http://Dissertation.com
16. Kita, S., van Gijn, I., van der Hulst, H.: Movement phasers in signs and co-speech gestures, and their transcription by human coders. In: Wachsmuth, I., Fröhlich, M. (eds.) GW 1997. LNCS, vol. 1371, pp. 23–35. Springer, Heidelberg (1998)
17. Heloir, A., Gibet, S., Multon, F., Courty, N.: Captured motion data processing for real time synthesis of sign language. In: Gibet, S., Courty, N., Kamp, J.-F. (eds.) GW 2005. LNCS, vol. 3881, pp. 168–171. Springer, Heidelberg (2006)
18. Majkowska, A., Zordan, V.B., Faloutsos, P.: Automatic splicing for hand and body animations. In: ACM SIGGRAPH / Eurographics Symposium on Computer Animation, pp. 309–316 (2006)
19. Kovar, L., Gleicher, M., Pighin, F.: Motion graphs. In: Proceedings of the 29th Annual Conference on Computer Graphics and InteractiveTechniques, pp. 473–482. ACM Press, New York (2002)
20. Heloir, A., Courty, N., Gibet, S., Multon, F.: Temporal alignment of communicative gesture sequences. Computer Animation and Virtual Worlds 17, 347–357 (2006)
21. Wachsmuth, I.: Communicative rhythm in gesture and speech. In: Braffort, A., Gibet, S., Teil, D., Gherbi, R., Richardson, J. (eds.) GW 1999. LNCS, vol. 1739, pp. 277–289. Springer, Heidelberg (2000)

Sequential Belief-Based Fusion of Manual and Non-manual Information for Recognizing Isolated Signs

Oya Aran[1], Thomas Burger[2], Alice Caplier[3], and Lale Akarun[1]

[1] Dep. of Computer Engineering, Bogazici University 34342 Istanbul, Turkey
aranoya@boun.edu.tr, akarun@boun.edu.tr
[2] France Telecom R&D, 28 ch. Vieux Chêne, Meylan, France
thomas.burger@orange-ftgroup.com
[3] GIPSA-lab, 46 avenue Félix Viallet, 38031 Grenoble cedex 1, France
alice.caplier@lis.inpg.fr

Abstract. This work aims to recognize signs which have both manual and non-manual components by providing a sequential belief-based fusion mechanism. We propose a methodology based on belief functions for fusing extracted manual and non-manual features in a sequential two-step approach. The belief functions based on the likelihoods of the hidden Markov models are used to decide whether there is an uncertainty in the decision of the first step and also to identify the uncertainty clusters. Then we proceed to the second step which utilizes only the non-manual features within the identified cluster, only if there is an uncertainty.

Keywords: Sign language recognition, hand gestures, head gestures, non-manual signals, hidden Markov models, belief functions.

1 Introduction

Sign language (SL) is the natural communication medium of hearing impaired people. Similar to the evolution of spoken languages, many sign languages have evolved in different regions of the world. American Sign Language (ASL), British Sign Language, Turkish Sign Language, French Sign Language are different sign languages used by corresponding communities of hearing impaired people. These are visual languages and the whole message is contained not only in hand motion and shapes (manual signs - MS) but also in facial expressions, head/shoulder motion and body posture (non-manual signals - NMS).

Sign language recognition (SLR) is a very complex task: a task that uses hand shape recognition, gesture recognition, face and body parts detection, facial expression recognition as basic building blocks. For an extensive survey on SLR, interested readers may refer to [1]. Most of the SLR systems concentrate on MS and perform hand gesture analysis only [2]. As a state of the art, Hidden Markov models (HMM) and several variants are used successfully to model the signs [3]. In [4], a parallel HMM architecture is used to recognize ASL signs where each HMM models

M. Sales Dias et al. (Eds.): GW 2007, LNAI 5085, pp. 134–144, 2009.

the gesture of left and right hands respectively. A similar approach is applied to integrate the hand shape and movement [5].

However, without integrating NMS, it is not possible to extract the whole meaning of the sign. In almost all of the sign languages, the meaning of a sign can be changed drastically with the facial expression or body posture while the hand gesture remains the same. Moreover, the NMS can be used alone, for example to indicate negation in many SLs. Current multimodal SLR systems either integrate lip motion and hand gestures, or only classify either the facial expression or the head movement. There are only a couple of studies that integrate non-manual and manual cues for SLR [1]. NMS in sign language have only recently drawn attention for recognition purposes. Most of those studies attempt to recognize only non-manual information independently, discarding the manual information. Some works only use facial expressions [6], and some use only the head motion [7].

We propose a methodology for integrating MS and NMS in a sequential approach. The methodology is based on (1) identifying the level of uncertainty of a classification decision, (2) identifying sign clusters, and (3) identifying the correct sign based on MS and NMS. Our sequential belief-based fusion methodology is explained in Section 2 and our automatic sign cluster identification is explained in Section 3. In Section 4, we give the results of our experiments.

2   Sequential Belief Based Fusion

In a SLR problem, where a generative model such as an HMM is used to model the signs, the classification can be done via the maximum likelihood (ML) approach. In the ML approach, for a test sign, the sign class is selected as the class of the HMM that gives the maximum likelihood. The problem of the ML approach is that it does not consider the situations where the likelihoods of two or more HMMs are very close to each other. The decisions made in these kinds of cases are error-prone and further analysis must be made. We propose to use belief functions to consider such situations. Belief function formalism provides a way to represent hesitation and ignorance in different ways. This formalism is especially useful when the collected data is noisy or semi-reliable. Interested readers may refer to [8], [9] for more information on belief theories.

In HMM based SLR, each HMM typically models a different class for the sign to be recognized [10]. Our purpose is to associate a belief function with these likelihoods. Then, it is possible to model these error-prone cases by associating high belief into the union of classes. By analyzing the proportion of belief which is associated with the union of classes, it is possible to decide whether the classification decision is certain or error-prone [11]: when the decision is certain, a single class is selected, whereas, when it is uncertain or error-prone, a subset of classes among which the good decision is likely to be found is selected. In this latter case, the decision is incomplete.

We propose the following SLR process: (1) Sign clusters are defined based on the similarity of the classes. (2) A first classification step is made. If the analysis of this classification indicates no uncertainty, then, a decision is made and the classification process is over. On the contrary, if there is significant uncertainty, (3) a second

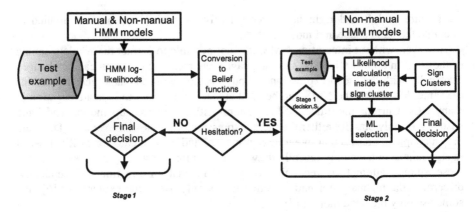

Fig. 1. Sequential belief-based fusion flowchart

classification step must be applied. This second step is applied to classes among which the uncertainty is detected.

The two-stage sequential belief based fusion technique is illustrated in Fig. 1. In this setup, the assumption is that the HMMs of the first bank are more general models which are capable of discriminating all the classes up to some degree. The HMMs of the second bank are specialized models and can only be used to discriminate between a subset of classes, among which there is an uncertainty.

3 Automatic Sign Cluster Identification

What we define as a sign cluster is a group of signs which are similar and the differences are either based on the non-manual component or variations of the manual component. In SLR point of view, a sign cluster indicates signs that are hard to discriminate. This can be a result of performance differences or systematic differences such as usage of NMS, or variations of MS. In linguistic point of view, a semantic interpretation of the signs may lead to totally different clusters. In a recognition task, although one can utilize prior knowledge such as the sign clusters based on semantic information, this has some disadvantages. First, it is not guaranteed that these semantic clusters are suitable for the recognition task, and second, the trained model will be database dependent and extending the database with new signs will require the re-definition of the cluster information. Thus, an automatic clustering method that depends on the data and considers the capabilities of the classifier would be preferable.

A first classical method is to use the confusion matrix of the HMM based classifier to automatically identify sign clusters. The confusion matrix is converted to a sign cluster matrix by considering the confusions for each sign. Signs that are confused form a cluster. For example, assume that sign i is confused with sign j half of the time. Then the sign cluster of class i is $\{i,j\}$. The sign cluster of class j is separately calculated from its confusions in the estimation process. The disadvantage of this method is its sensitivity to odd mistakes which may result from the errors in the feature vector calculation as a result of bad segmentation or tracking.

We propose a more robust alternative which evaluates the decisions of the classifier and only consider the uncertainties of the classifier to form the sign clusters. For this purpose, we define a hesitation matrix. Its purpose is close to the classical confusion matrix, but it contains only the results of the uncertain decisions, regardless of their correctness. Then, when a decision is certain, either true or false, it is not taken into account in the calculation of the hesitation matrix. On the other hand, when a decision is uncertain between sign i and sign j, it is counted in the hesitation matrix regardless of the ground truth of the sign being, i, j or even k. As a matter of fact, the confusion between a decision (partial or not) and the ground truth can be due to any other mistake (segmentation, threshold effect, etc...) whereas, the hesitation on the classification process depends on the ambiguity at the feature level with respect to the class borders. Our method of determining clusters only based on the hesitation is more robust. In addition, it is not necessary to know the ground truth on the validation set on which the clusters are defined. This is a distinctive advantage in case of semi-supervised learning, to adapt the system to the signer's specificity.

4 Methodology and Experiments

In order to assess the appropriateness of our belief-based method, we have performed experiments on a sign language database which has been collected during the eNTERFACE'06 workshop. In the following section, we give details about this database.

4.1 eNTERFACE'06 ASL Database

The signs in the eNTERFACE'06 American Sign Language (ASL) Database [12] are selected such that they include both manual and non-manual components. There are

Table 1. Signs in eNTERFACE'06 Database

Base Sign	Variant	Variation on hand motion	Head Motion (NMS)	Base Sign	Variant	Variation on hand motion	Head Motion (NMS)
Clean	Clean			Here	[smbdy] is here		✓
	Very clean		✓		Is [smbdy] here?		✓
Afraid	Afraid				[smbdy] is not here		✓
	Very afraid	✓	✓	Study	Study		
Fast	Fast				Study continuously	✓	✓
	Very fast		✓		Study regularly	✓	✓
drink	To drink		✓	Look at	Look at		
	Drink (noun)	✓			Look at continuously	✓	✓
open (door)	To open				Look at regularly		
	door (noun)	✓				✓	✓

Fig. 2. Sign CLEAN and VERY CLEAN. The main difference between these two signs is the existence of NMS, motion of the head.

eight base signs that represent words and a total of 19 variants which include the systematic variations of the base signs in the form of NMS, or inflections in the signing of the same MS. A base sign and its variants will be called as a *"base sign cluster"* for the rest of this paper. Table 1 lists the signs in the database. As seen from Table 1, some signs are differentiated only by the head motion; some only by hand motion variation and some by both.

A single web camera with 640x480 resolution and 25 frames per second rate is used for the recordings. The camera is placed in front of the subject. The database is collected from eight subjects, each performing five repetitions of each sign. Fig. 2 shows example signs form the database.

The dataset is divided to training and test set pairs where 532 examples are used for training (28 examples per sign) and 228 examples for reporting the test results (12 examples per sign). The distributions of sign classes are equal both in training and test sets. For the cases where a validation set is needed, we apply a stratified 7-fold cross validation (CV) on the training set.

Since we concentrate on the fusion step in this paper, we have directly used the processed data from [13] where the features of hand shape, hand motion and head motion are extracted. In the following sections, we summarize the detection and feature extraction methodology. Further details can be found in [13].

4.2 Hand and Face Detection

To ease the hand and face detection, subjects in the eNTERFACE'06 ASL database wear gloves with different colors when performing the signs. We use the motion cue and the color cue of the gloves for hand segmentation. Although skin color detection can be applied in restricted illumination and lighting conditions, segmentation becomes problematic when two skin regions, such as hands and face, overlap and occlude each other. For the signs in the eNTERFACE ASL database, the hand position is often near the face and sometimes, in front of the face.

Hands are segmented by using trained histograms for each glove color using HSV color space [14]. The connectivity within the hands is ensured by double thresholding and the largest connected component over the detected pixels is considered as the hand. A bounding box around the face is found by applying the Viola and Jones face detection algorithm [15], using the MPI toolbox [16].

4.3 Feature Extraction

Sign features are extracted both for MS (hand motion, hand shape, hand position with respect to face) and NMS (head motion). The resulting feature vector, for two hands and the head, is composed of 61 features per frame.

The system tracks the center of mass of the hand and calculates the coordinates and velocity of each segmented hand at each frame. Two independent Kalman filters, one for each hand, are used to obtain smoothed trajectories. This is required since the original calculations are corrupted by segmentation noise and occlusion. The motion of each hand is approximated by a constant velocity motion model, in which the acceleration is neglected. We calculate the hand motion features for each hand from the posterior states of each Kalman filter: x, y coordinates of the hand center of mass and velocity. The hand motion features in each trajectory are further normalized to the range [0,1] by min-max normalization.

Hand shape features are appearance-based shape features calculated on the binary hand images. These features include the parameters of an ellipse fitted to the binary hand and statistics from a rectangular mask placed on top of the binary hand [13]. Most of the features are scale invariant. The recordings are with a single camera and the features do not have depth information; except for the foreshortening due to perspective. In order to keep this depth information, some features were not normalized. Prior to the calculation of the hand shape features, we take the mirror reflection of the right hand so that we analyze both hands in the same geometry; with thumb to the right.

Hand position is calculated with respect to the face center of mass. The distance between the hand and the face is calculated by the x and y coordinates and normalized by the face width and height respectively.

For head motion analysis, the system detects rigid head motions such as head rotations and head nods working in a way close to the human visual system [17]. By analyzing the head motion, two features are extracted: the quantity of motion and motion event alerts. Only on the motion events alerts, with an optic flow algorithm, both the orientation and velocity information are provided. As head motion features, we use the quantity of motion and the vertical, horizontal velocity of the head at each frame.

4.4 Clustering for Sequential Fusion

As explained in Section 4, we propose a belief based method for automatic identification of the clusters via the hesitation matrix: The clusters are defined by transforming the hesitation matrix so that it is closed, transitive and reflexive. The cluster identification is done by applying 7-fold CV on the training data. The hesitation matrices of each fold are combined to create a joint matrix, which is used to identify the clusters.

Fig. 3 shows the sign clusters identified by the uncertainties provided by the belief functions. The automatically identified sign clusters are the same as the base sign clusters except for the base signs LOOK AT and STUDY.

For the LOOK AT sign, the differentiation is provided by both non-manual information and variations in signing. However, the hands can be in front of the head

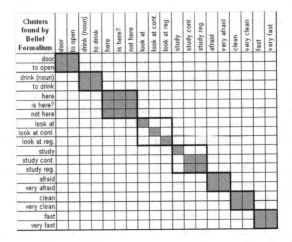

Fig. 3. Sign clusters identified by the uncertainties between the classes in 7-fold cross validation. Clusters are shown row-wise, where for each sign row, the shaded blocks show the signs in its cluster.

for many of the frames. For those frames, the face detector may fail to detect the face and may provide wrong feature values which can mislead the recognizer.

It is interesting to observe that the base STUDY sign is clustered into two sub-clusters. This separation agrees with the nature of these signs: In the sign STUDY, the hand is stationary and this property directly differentiates this sign from the other variations. The confusion between STUDY REGULARLY and STUDY CONTINUOUSLY can stem from a deficiency of the 2D capture system. These two signs differ mainly in the third dimension. However a detailed analysis of the non-manual components can be used at the second stage to resolve the confusion.

4.5 Results

To model the MS and NMS and perform classification, we trained three different HMMs. The first one is trained for comparison purposes and the last two are for the first and second steps of our fusion method:

(1) HMM_M uses only *manual* features;
(2) $HMM_{M\&N}$ uses both *manual and non-manual* features
(3) HMM_N uses only *non-manual* features

The classification of a sign is performed by the maximum likelihood approach. We train HMMs for each sign and classify a test example by selecting the sign class whose HMM has the maximum log-likelihood. The HMM models are selected as left-to-right 4-state HMMs with continuous observations where Gaussian distributions with full covariance are used to model the observations at each state. Baum-Welch algorithm is used for HMM training. Initial parameters of transition and prior probabilities and initial parameters of Gaussians are randomly selected.

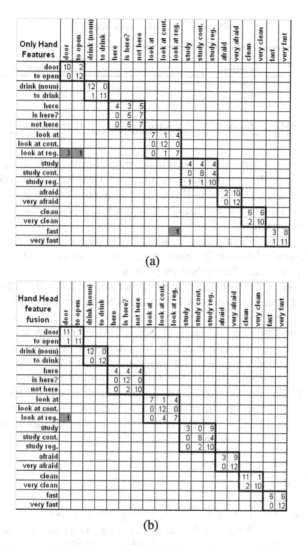

Fig. 4. (a) Confusion matrix of HMM_M, 97.8% base sign accuracy, 67.1% total accuracy (b) Confusion matrix of $HMM_{M\&N}$, 99.5% base sign accuracy, 75.9% total accuracy. Rows indicate the true class and columns indicate the estimated class. Base sign and its variations are shown in bold squares. The classification errors are mainly between variations of a base sign.

We compared the classification performance of HMM_M and $HMM_{M\&N}$ to see the information added by the non-manual features via feature level fusion. The classification results of these two models should show us the degree of effective utilization of the non-manual features when combined into a single feature vector with manual features. Although there is no direct synchronization between the manual and non-manual components, the second model, $HMM_{M\&N}$, models the dependency of the two components for sign identification.

Table 2. Classification performance

Models Used	Fusion method	Cluster identification	Test Accuracy
HMM_M	No fusion	-	67.1 %
$HMM_{M\&N}$	Feature fusion	-	75.9 %
$HMM_{M\&N} \rightarrow HMM_N$	Sequential *belief-based* fusion	Hesitation matrix	**81.6 %**

The classification results and confusion matrices for the two techniques are shown in Fig. 4. Although the classification accuracy of $HMM_{M\&N}$ is slightly better than HMM_M, total accuracy is still low. However, it is worth noting that the classification errors in both of the models are mainly between variants of a base sign and out of cluster errors are very few.

From these confusion matrices, it appears that some mistakes occur between signs which are completely different. It illustrates that the use of such matrices to define the clusters is less robust than the method we propose.

The accuracies of the techniques are summarized in Table 2. Although the time dependency and synchronization of MS and NMS are not that high, feature fusion ($HMM_{M\&N}$) still improves the classification performance (13% improvement over HMM_M) by providing extra features of NMS. However, NMS are not effectively utilized by $HMM_{M\&N}$. Nevertheless, it is important that the classification errors are mainly between variants of a base sign and out of cluster errors are very few, with 99.5% base sign accuracy (Fig. 4). We further improve the accuracy by sequential-belief based fusion: up to 81.6%. The improvement is mainly based on (1) the possibility of accepting the first stage classification decision thanks to belief formalism and the robustness of the belief-based cluster identification, and (2) the robustness of the method to define the clusters.

5 Conclusions

We have proposed a technique for integrating MS and NMS in an isolated sign recognition system. A dedicated fusion methodology is needed to accommodate the nature of MS and NMS in sign languages. Although NMS can also be used alone, we concentrated on the signs in which MS and NMS used in parallel, to complement or emphasize the meaning of the MS. Our fusion technique makes use of the fact that the manual information gives the main meaning of the sign and the non-manual information complements or modifies the meaning. The sequential fusion method processes the signs accordingly. The key novelties of our fusion approach are two-fold. The first novelty is the two stage decision mechanism which ensures that if the decision at the first step is without hesitation, the decision is made immediately. This would speed up the system, since the system can understand that there is no need for further analysis. Even in the case of a hesitation, the decision of the first step identifies the cluster which the test sign belongs to, if not the exact sign class. The second novelty is the clustering mechanism: the sign clusters are identified automatically at the training phase and this makes the system flexible for adding new signs to the database by just providing new training data. Our results show that automatic belief based clustering outperforms the feature fusion and increases the accuracy of the classifier.

Acknowledgments. This work is a result of a cooperation supported by SIMILAR 6FP European Network of Excellence (www.similar.cc). This work has also been supported by TUBITAK project 107E021 and Bogazici University project BAP-03S106.

References

1. Ong, S.C.W., Ranganath, S.: Automatic Sign Language Analysis: A survey and the Future beyond Lexical Meaning. IEEE Transactions on Pattern Analysis and Machine Intelligence 27(6), 873–891 (2005)
2. Wu, Y., Huang, T.S.: Hand modeling, analysis, and recognition for vision based human computer interaction. IEEE Signal Processing Magazine 21, 51–60 (2001)
3. Vogler, C., Metaxas, D.: Adapting Hidden Markov models for ASL recognition by using three-dimensional computer vision methods. In: IEEE International Conference on Systems, Man and Cybernetics (SMC), pp. 156–161 (1997)
4. Vogler, C., Metaxas, D.: Parallel Hidden Markov Models for American Sign Language Recognition. In: International Conference on Computer Vision, Kerkyra, Greece, pp. 116–122 (1999)
5. Vogler, C., Metaxas, D.: Handshapes and Movements: Multiple-Channel American Sign Language Recognition. In: Camurri, A., Volpe, G. (eds.) GW 2003. LNCS, vol. 2915, pp. 247–258. Springer, Heidelberg (2004)
6. Ming, K.W., Ranganath, S.: Representations for Facial Expressions. In: Proceedings of International Conference on Control Automation, Robotics and Vision, vol. 2, pp. 716–721 (2002)
7. Erdem, U.M., Sclaroff, S., Automatic Detection, S.: of Relevant Head Gestures in American Sign Language Communication. In: International Conference on Pattern Recognition, vol. 1, pp. 460–463 (2002)
8. Shafer, G.: A Mathematical Theory of Evidence. Princeton University Press, Princeton (1976)
9. Smets, P., Kennes, R.: The transferable belief model. Artificial Intelligence 66(2), 191–234 (1994)
10. Rabiner, L.R.: A tutorial on Hidden Markov Models and Selected Applications in Speech Recognition. Proceedings of IEEE 77, 257–285 (1989)
11. Burger, T., Aran, O., Caplier, A.: Modeling hesitation and conflict: A belief-based approach. In: International Conference of Machine Learning and Applications (ICMLA), pp. 95–100 (2006)
12. eNTERFACE06 ASL Database, http://www.enterface.net/enterface06/docs/results/databases/eNTERFACE06_ASL.zip
13. Aran, O., Ari, I., Benoit, A., Campr, P., Carrillo, A.H., Fanard, F., Akarun, L., Caplier, A., Sankur, B.: SignTutor: An Interactive System for Sign Language Tutoring. IEEE Multimedia 16(1) (2009)

14. Jayaram, S., Schmugge, S., Shin, M.C., Tsap, L.V.: Effect of Color space Transformation, the Illuminance Component, and Color Modeling on Skin Detection. In: IEEE Conference on Computer Vision and Pattern Recognition (CVPR 2004), vol. 2, pp. 813–818 (2004)
15. Viola, P., Jones, J.: Robust real time face detection. International Journal of Computer Vision 57(2), 137–154 (2004)
16. Machine Perception Toolbox (MPT), http://mplab.ucsd.edu/grants/project1/free-software/MPTWebSite/API/
17. Benoit, A., Caplier, A.: Head Nods Analysis: Interpretation of Non Verbal Communication Gestures. In: IEEE International Conference of Image Processing (2005)

Gesture Modelling for Linguistic Purposes

Guillaume J.-L. Olivrin

Meraka Institute*, City of Tshwane, RSA
golivrin@meraka.org.za

Abstract. The study of sign languages attempts to create a coherent model that describes the expressive nature of signs conveyed in gestures with a linguistic framework. 3D gesture modelling offers a precise annotation and representation of linguistic constructs and can become an entry mechanism for sign languages. This paper presents the requirements to build an input method editor for sign languages and the initial experiments using signing avatars input interfaces. The system currently saves and annotates 3D gestures on humanoid models with linguistic labels. Results show that the annotating prototype can be used in turn to ease and guide the task of 3D gesture modelling.

1 Introduction

Information systems are not well suited to store, represent and process information in sign language. Digital video with emerging description standards such as MPEG annotation tools have not yet been applied to provide linguistic descriptions of sign language media on computers. Modelling sign language in 3D with traditional controls and 2D views is not always intuitive. To generate sign language animations, computational representations of sign languages have been proposed but are difficult to learn. Utilizing these notations to constrain and guide the modelling of sign languages gestures with 3D signing avatar would both ease 3D modelling and provide visualization capabilities for the notation systems. Our prototype estimates 3D avatar poses according to existing notation systems and derives additional linguistic knowledge from the modelling context.

1.1 Related Work

The study of linguistic constructs of sign languages is generally performed on annotated video corpora ([4]). Because signs need to be timely and spatially located, it has become necessary to go beyond gloss and word categorization [5, 6, 7]. Hence beyond most recent video corpus there is a quest for modelling sign languages virtually based on signing space [8] and classifier predicates [9]. Sign languages notations have been used as points of departure to describe, document and even animate sign languages. Project *eSign* [10] uses a central

---

* With StellenboschUniversity [1, 2] and Thibologa Sign Language Institution [3].

M. Sales Dias et al. (Eds.): GW 2007, LNAI 5085, pp. 145–150, 2009.

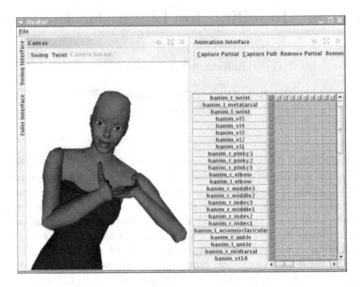

Fig. 1. H-anim compliant Signing avatar [2] for direct gesture modelling

phonetic notation, HamNoSys, to produce animation scripts. Part of speech tagging, fingerspelling, types of quantities and body sites localisation on 2D avatars makes working with HamNoSys easier but learning the phonological notation still presents a steep learning curve. [11]'s approach offers to generate sign languages animations from Sutton sign writing descriptions. The notation is more graphically representative of sign languages because of its non-linearity but at the cost of a loss of precision in 3D positioning.

Instead of scripting and generating 3D animations, other approaches have been found more intuitive to model sign language directly in 3D. With all the challenges that 3D modelling imposes on the user, efforts have been concentrating on easing the positioning of body parts. VSign [12] for example provided indirect controls to the avatar body parts via *slider* controls, implicitly capturing joint limits. Because all possible gestures within joint limits are not humanly achievable, [13] modelled joint's limit with interdependency constraints to guide 3D gesture editions. The direct 3D modelling interface of *GestureBuilder* [14] introduced virtual controls and artifacts to help create virtual signs. Building sign libraries with *GestureBuilder* [14] and then composing sign language animations with *SignSmithStudio* is a two-step process. But taking pre-made signs and concatenating the gestures makes sign language composition a staggered process which results in robotic animations. Because gestures in sign languages obey linguistic rules, further control for 3D gesture composition can be provided by discretizing the domain with phonetic and symbolic notations and using these notations as constraining features for gesture editing processes within specific sign language linguistic constructs.

1.2   Requirements

A linguistically driven approach to gesture modelling is characterized by the introduction of specific expert knowledge during the language acquisition process. What linguistic knowledge is captured when composing in sign language? Primitive phonological and morphological information are captured and linked together to create syntactic constructs such as classifiers, agreements, co-reference and eye gaze agreements. 3D models of signing space for deictic and co-reference phenomena in [6] and for classifiers predicates in [9] exemplify how linguistic constructs could be used to edit sign languages in 3D.

Sign language end-users are not experts in linguistics. Adapting information systems to their needs also incites to capture and document sign languages as directly and intuitively as possible. Interacting directly with the avatar seems preferrable to using indirect controls whose effects often vary depending on orientations and contextual elements. Adjusting articulations and body parts one by one is inefficient, time consuming and the system should seek to shortcut redundant editing operations without necessarily relying on libraries of signs. Browsing libraries is an expensive cognitive task which interferes with the creative process. Although sign language notations are at the heart of the system, the symbols are not necessarily visible to the user. The current interface is designed to focus on the signing avatar and gestures themselves and is progressively being stripped of English concepts, names and writings which are external to sign languages.

The current prototype makes it possible to interact directly with the signing avatar but minimalist controls have also been provided. In addition to graphical and mechanical constraints, the system could also use simple linguistic constraints. With various notation systems available —Stokoe, HamNoSys, Berkley Transcription System, SLIPA [15], Sutton SignWriting, Szczepankowski to cite a few, there are many candidates to build descriptive models of sign languages. The current prototype used a complementary approach and defined predicates necessary for descriptive reasoning based on HamNoSys [10] and SLIPA [15].

2   Sign Language Modelling

The descriptive models of gestures produced by *VSign* [12] and *gEditor*(Fig.1) [1,2] are presented. The process of deriving linguistic knowledge from these 3D models is then explored.

2.1   Describing Gestures with Humanoid Joint Model

The early annotation prototype used *VSign* to model signs in 3D because ① *VSign* didn't require knowledge of sign language notation systems; ② raw joints angles values could be exported with the model and ③ the model was close to H-anim. Subsequently *gEditor* [2] was developed and could use any H-anim compliant avatar to export instances of modelled gestures. The current annotating prototype labels the H-anim hierarchical joint structure with SLIPA [15] and HamNoSys [10] labels.

Because VRML97 H-anim models are based on body joints and articulations rather than on muscles, only basic facial expressions can be modelled. Reasoning over simple facial features such as eye lids, eye brows and jaw to infer basic expressions is however possible and was implemented for 3 generic facial expressions : questionning, negative expressions and expressions of surprise.

2.2 Inferring Linguistic Annotations

The annotation prototype uses the avatar joint values to label a H-anim model at each time frame and across multiple time frames. The annotation process follows a bottom-up approach which starts by tagging single joint values and then goes on to labelling combinations of body parts and joints, progressively forming linguistic constructs. The final output of the system is an annotated model of predicates that establish relations between 3D body parts and joints in time and space.

The inference engine is implemented in Prolog which provides the following advantages: ① Prolog is an efficient framework for constraints satisfaction problems and linguistic rules; ② dynamic dependencies and constraints in gestures and signs are easily unified in a Prolog database; ③ predicate logic is appropriate for agent embodiment as in [16] and ④ Prolog has generative abilities for scripting animations just as STEP [17] does as well as inductive and backtracking capabilities.

Experiments have been conducted on static gesture models exported from the gesture editors *Vsign* and *gEditor*. The annotation procedure is as follow : ① An H-anim compliant avatar model is loaded and the system calibrated according to joints limits and goniometric specifications (limb metrics, skin thickness). A fuzzy logic is initialised which associates linguistic notations to ranges of joints angles values. ② When modelled gestures are committed to the Prolog database, a bottom-up process starts tagging simple joint angles and labelling pre-defined linguistic constructs. ③ The system can be queried to see what linguistic constructs may apply over certain body parts over certain time-ranges. It is also possible to manually specify linguistic tags to affect certain body parts. These linguistic interactions informs the 3D modelling process. ④ At any instant and interaction with the system, the state of the Prolog database represents all the modelled and annotated gestures and can be exported as a descriptive model of sign language.

3   Evaluation and Future Work

The annotating prototype currently performs a labelling task by estimating poses and gestures. There are presently 90 primitive tags associated to different articulations, sites, orientations and local movements. From these primitive tags are built 60 labels representing final handshapes, contacts and symmetries. The

60 labels are currently used to describe 40 signs and 3 *higher order* linguistic constructs, i.e. circular movements, eye gaze and body sites agreements and 3 facial expressions.

Three Deaf SASL users [3] assisted in modelling 40 test signs. Each sign was modelled multiple times on *VSign* and on *gEditor* to record internal variations due to the choice of 3D modelling controls. These modelling experiments were carried out on closely related handshapes, 10 in total. These 10 handshapes had to be annotated and would lead to either an intermediary handshape, or yield one of the 50 final handshapes described in the system. Labelling fingers and inferring handshapes performed a 94% precision and an 86% recall. The system generalizes well over handshapes and returns many *intermediary* handshape, a sign of robustness hence the low recall. The labelling task performs worse when wrist, elbow and shoulders joints tags are introduced to identify a sign. The precision dropped to 88% with a higher recall. Introducing additional features made the system more confident at identifying the correct poses, but it failed more often because of modelling inconsistencies. Amongst inconsistencies in gesture modelling, incorrectly articulated gestures are treated as mal-formed sign language. To prevent these 3D modelling problems, the annotating prototype may dynamically constrain the degrees of freedom in the controls when editing a certain sign for a particular linguistic context and in a special *editing modes*. In the future it will become possible to interact with the annotation system and to anticipate and correct the effects of modelling interactions. This principle, composing sign language through modelling and annotating cycles, is illustrated in figure 2.

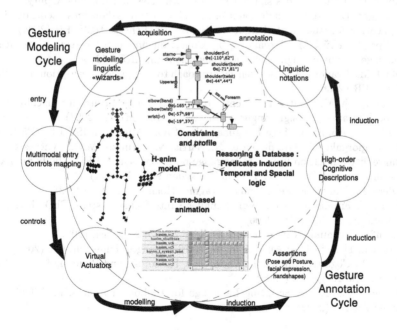

Fig. 2. Gesture modelling and annotation life cycles

The annotation of gestures can remain flexible and unobtrusive since it is also part of the modelling process. The induction cycle does a lot of guesswork when tagging the model. When the system offers many alternatives, the user can disambiguate the linguistic context to gain graphical guidance in modelling sign languages.

4 Conclusion

An original approach to capturing and annotating sign language has been presented. Our annotating prototype works on H-anim compliant avatar models and produces linguistic descriptions of sign languages. This linguistically driven approach suggests new gesture modelling strategies which combine user interactions with annotation cycles to make 3D gesture modelling easier.

References

1. Van Zijl, L., Fourie, J.: Design and development of a generic signing avatar. In: Graphics and Visualization in Eng., Florida, USA, Uni. Stellenbosch (2007)
2. Potgieter, D.: Signing avatar: Sign editor. Master's thesis, Uni. Stellenbosch (2006)
3. Mohlamme, I.: Thibologa Sign Language Institution (2007), http://www.thibologa.co.za
4. Hanke, T., Storz, J.: Ilex a database tool for integrating sign language corpus linguistics and sign language lexicography. In: LREC (2008)
5. Cuxac, C.: La langue des signes française - les voies de l'iconicité. Ophrys (2000)
6. Lenseigne, B.: Intégration de connaissances linguistiques dans un système de vision, application à l'étude de la langue des Signes. PhD thesis, IRIT, FR (2004)
7. Campr, P., Hrúz, M., Trojanová, J.: Collection and preprocessing of czech sign language corpus for sign language recognition. In: LREC (2008)
8. Filhol, M., Braffort, A.: A sequential approach to lexical sign description. In: LREC, Orsay, FR (2006)
9. Huenerfauth, M.: Spatial representation of classifier predicates for machine translation into american sign language. In: LREC, Lisbon, PT (2004)
10. Hanke, T.: Animating Sign Language: the eSIGN Approach. IST EU FP5 (2003)
11. Papadogiorgaki, M., Grammalidis, N., Sarris, N., Strintzis, M.G.: Synthesis of virtual reality animation from sign language notation using MPEG-4 body animation parameters. In: ICDVRAT, Thermi-Thessaloniki, GR (2004)
12. Pyfers, L.: VSign Builder Manual. Pragma, Hoensbroek, NL (2002)
13. Yi, B.: A Framework for a Sign Language Interfacing System. PhD thesis, Uni. Nevada, Reno, NV (May 2006)
14. Vcom3D: Vcommunicator Gesture Builder 2.0, Orlando, FL (2007)
15. Peterson, D.J.: SLIPA: An IPA for Signed Languages, Fullerton, CA (2007)
16. Funge, J.: Cognitive Modeling: Knowledge, Reasoning and Planning for Intelligent Characters. AI games (1999)
17. Huang, Z.: STEP: A Scripting Language for Embodied Agents. In: Lifelike Animated Agents (2002)

Automatic Classification of Expressive Hand Gestures on Tangible Acoustic Interfaces According to Laban's Theory of Effort

Antonio Camurri, Corrado Canepa, Simone Ghisio, and Gualtiero Volpe

InfoMus Lab, DIST – University of Genova
Viale Causa 13, I-16145 Genova, Italy
{toni,corrado,ghisio,volpe}@infomus.org
http://www.infomus.org

Abstract. Tangible Acoustic Interfaces (TAIs) exploit the propagation of sound in physical objects in order to localize touching positions and to analyse user's gesture on the object. Designing and developing TAIs consists of exploring how physical objects, augmented surfaces, and spaces can be transformed into tangible-acoustic embodiments of natural seamless unrestricted interfaces. Our research focuses on *Expressive TAIs*, i.e., TAIs able at processing expressive user's gesture and providing users with natural multimodal interfaces that fully exploit expressive, emotional content. This paper presents a concrete example of analysis of expressive gesture in TAIs: hand gestures on a TAI surface are classified according to the Space and Time dimensions of Rudolf Laban's Theory of Effort. Research started in the EU-IST Project TAI-CHI (Tangible Acoustic Interfaces for Computer-Human Interaction) and is currently going on in the EU-ICT Project SAME (Sound and Music for Everyone, Everyday, Everywhere, Every way, www.sameproject.eu). Expressive gesture analysis and multimodal and cross-modal processing are achieved in the new EyesWeb XMI open platform (available at www.eyesweb.org) by means of a new version of the EyesWeb Expressive Gesture Processing Library.

Keywords: expressive gesture, tangible acoustic interfaces, natural interfaces, multimodal interactive systems, multimodal analysis of expressive movement.

1 Introduction

The EU-IST Project TAI-CHI (Tangible Acoustic Interfaces for Computer Human Interaction) investigated a new generation of tangible interfaces, Tangible Acoustic Interfaces (TAIs). TAIs exploit the propagation of sound in physical objects in order to localize touching positions and to analyze user's gesture on the object, both from a low-level, quantitative point of view and from a high-level qualitative one. Designing TAIs consists of exploring how physical objects, augmented surfaces, and spaces can be transformed into tangible-acoustic embodiments of natural seamless unrestricted interfaces. The goal of TAI-CHI was therefore to design TAIs employing physical objects (also including complex-shaped everyday objects) as media to bridge the gap

M. Sales Dias et al. (Eds.): GW 2007, LNAI 5085, pp. 151–162, 2009.

between the virtual and physical worlds and to make information accessible through large size touchable objects as well as through ambient media.

In this framework, a relevant aspect for the success of TAI-based interactive systems is their ability of processing expressive information, i.e., information related to the affective, emotional sphere conveyed by users through non-verbal channels [1][2]. Such information is what Cowie et al. call "implicit messages" [3] or what Hashimoto calls KANSEI [4], and it is often conveyed through expressive gesture [5].

We call *Expressive TAIs* a subset of TAIs endowed with the special ability of extracting, analysing, and processing such emotional, affective, expressive content. Expressive TAIs are based on high-level multimodal analysis of users' gesture on or approaching the TAI. Consider for example a dragging gesture on a TAI: it can be qualitatively characterized along several different dimensions: e.g., it may be hesitant or fluent, soft or hard, smooth or rigid. The way in which a TAI is approached can also be qualitatively different: e.g., a direct and determined approach versus a hesitant and undecided one. Expressive TAIs are thus a novel generation of human-computer interfaces combining the naturalness of vision and touching gesture with the power and the impact of human non-verbal expressive communication in experience-centric tasks and collaborative applications. Research on Expressive TAIs needs to address models and algorithms for multimodal and cross-modal high-level analysis and interpretation of integrated data from video images and tangible acoustic interfaces.

This paper presents and discusses a concrete example of high-level analysis of expressive gesture on Expressive TAIs: hand gestures on a TAI surface are analysed and classified according to two major dimensions of Rudolf Laban's Theory of Effort [6][7], the Space and Time dimensions. According to these dimensions an expressive gesture can be direct or flexible, quick or sustained. Expressive gestures are thus mapped on a 2D abstract space, and further analysed with respect to the occupation of such space along time. Such a classification is a preliminary step toward further higher-level analyses. For example, according to psychological research (e.g., [8]), indirect and hesitant gestures can be associated with negative emotional states, e.g., difficulties in handling the interface, fear, feeling of lack of control over the interface.

Results have been exploited in public events in which the developed techniques have been applied and evaluated with experiments involving both experts and the general audience. In particular, the high-level expressive gesture processing models and algorithms discussed in this paper have been exploited in prototypes for the IST2006 Convention, Helsinki, November 2006 (grand prize as best booth of the Convention), and for the science exhibitions "Cimenti di Invenzione e Armonia", held in the framework of Festival della Scienza (International Festival of Science), at Casa Paganini, Genova, Italy, Oct. – Nov. 2006 and 2007 (more than 4000 visitors).

The techniques introduced in this paper have been implemented as software modules for the new EyesWeb XMI platform [9] (freely available at the EyesWeb website www.eyesweb.org). The new EyesWeb XMI platform (i.e., EyesWeb for eXtended Multimodal Interaction) explicitly supports extended multimodal and cross-modal processing, especially for high-level gesture analysis, by providing users with transparent synchronization of different data streams (e.g., audio, video, data from sensors at different sampling rates) from different channels. Software modules are included in a new version of the EyesWeb Expressive Gesture Processing (see [10] for a summary of a previous version) and Machine Learning Libraries.

2 Rudolf's Laban Theory of Effort

In his Theory of Effort [6][7], choreographer Rudolf Laban points out the dynamic nature of movement and the relationship among movement, space and time. Laban's approach is an attempt to describe, in a formalized way, the main features of human movement without focusing on a particular kind of movement or dance expression. In fact, it should be noticed that while being a choreographer, Laban did not focused only on dance, but rather he envisaged in his theory the whole complexity of human movement including dance expression, but also extended to everyday movements like the ones performed by workers in their usual activities.

The basic concept of Laban's theory is Effort considered as a property of movement. From an engineering point of view it can be considered as a vector of parameters identifying the qualities of a movement performance. The effort vector can be regarded as having four components generating a four-dimensional "effort space" whose axes are Space, Time, Weight, and Flow. During a movement performance such effort vector moves in the effort space. Laban investigates the possible paths followed by the vector and the expressive intentions that may be associated with them. Each effort component is measured on a bipolar scale, the extreme values of which represent opposite qualities along each axis. In the work described in this paper, we mainly focused on two of the four Laban's dimensions: Space and Time. Such dimensions were selected since (i) they have been successfully used in previous studies on analysis of human full-body movement and (ii) they demonstrated to be particular suitable in representing key features of common users' gestures on TAIs.

Space refers to the direction of a motion stroke and to the path followed by a sequence of strokes (i.e., a sequence of directions). If the movement follows these directions smoothly the space component is considered to be "flexible", whereas if it follows them along a straight trajectory the space component is "direct".

Time is also considered with respect to a bipolar representation: an action can be "quick" or "sustained", which allows the binary description of the time component of the effort space. Moreover, in a sequence of movements, each of them has a given duration in time: the ratio of the durations of subsequent movements gives the time-rhythm, as in a music score and performance.

In a recent study [11] by Zhao, four neural networks were trained to recognize the two extreme qualities for each effort component. The training set consisted of a collection of arm movements whose features were extracted by using both motion capture and video camera based systems.

Laban did never explicitly associate any Effort component or quality to higher-level expressive intentions or emotional states, though he considered this plausible. Thus, investigation of Effort qualities should be considered as a first step toward a higher-level characterization of gesture. In other words, the Effort theory provides an intermediate-level description of gesture qualities that can be used as the basis for a further classification e.g., in terms of emotions or expressive intentions, grounded on results and models from psychological research (e.g., [8]). Nevertheless, such Effort qualities can already provide a characterization of expressiveness of 2D gesture e.g., in terms of hesitation, that can be fruitfully exploited in concrete applications.

3   High-Level Gesture Analysis in Expressive TAIs

For this study we selected a simple vocabulary of hand gestures performed on a tangible acoustic surface. The selected gestures are related to everyday actions and to common tasks with computer interfaces, e.g., dragging, tapping, pushing, and pulling. A major reason is that being the focus on a qualitative analysis of how the gesture is performed, we preferred to rely on simple gestures that are easy and straightforward for users to perform and to expressively modulate. Nevertheless, such gestures are important, since they are the most common gestures performed by users while interacting with TAIs, and therefore they can be fruitfully employed in the interaction design process. Moreover, expressive arm and hand gestures have already been studied from a psychological point of view (e.g., see the studies by psychologist Frank Pollick on expressive movement in everyday actions [12]).

Our approach to high-level gesture analysis in Expressive TAIs is grounded on the multi-layered framework for expressive gesture processing we developed in the EU-IST MEGA Project (Multisensory Expressive Gesture Applications)[1][2][5]. Such a framework has been adapted and extended for application to Expressive TAIs.

3.1   Expressive TAI Technical Set-Up

The set-up (Figure 1) consists of an MDF (Medium-density fibreboard) rectangular surface sensorized with four Knowles BU-1771 accelerometers, placed at the four corners. A panel of phonoabsorbent material is introduced below the tangible surface in order to reduce vibrations along the depth of the material, thus emphasizing vibrations along the surface. Accelerometers are connected through a custom audio front-end to a Firepod PreSonus audio interface, so that data is received as audio signals. A b&w video camera is hung on the top of the surface, the major axis of the video camera normal with respect to the surface. The video camera is endowed with an infrared filter and the tangible surface is enlightened with infrared light, so that possible video-projections on the surface are filtered out. A PC (Dell Precision 380, 2

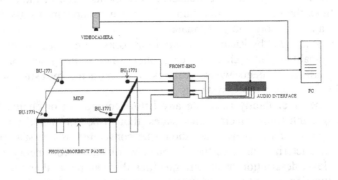

Fig. 1. Expressive TAI set-up consisting of a common table covered with a phonoabsorbent surface and an MDF board. Four accelerometers detect acoustic vibrations in the material and send data as audio streams to a computer, which performs high-level gesture analysis. A video camera, placed in a normal position above the table is also connected to the same computer.

Pentium 4 3.2 GHz CPUs, 1 GB RAM, Windows XP Professional) receives and processes audio and video signals and performs analysis.

3.2 Localization of Touch Positions and Tracking of Motion Trajectories

Localization of touch position is performed with techniques based on the Time Delay of Arrival (TDOA) of the acoustical waves to the sensors [13]. Another technique by the Laboratoire Ondes et Acoustique at the Institut pour le Developement de la Science, l'Education et la Technologie, Paris, France, employs just one sensor and is based on pattern matching of the sound patterns generated by the touching action against a collection of stored patterns. In order to increase reliability of localization we developed an EyesWeb application integrating the two methods and compensating possible weakness of one method with the outcomes of the other one.

Continuous tracking of motion trajectories on the surface is performed by means of multimodal integration of visual and acoustical techniques. Video-based tracking supports audio based tracking in case of noisy audio signal. At the same time, audio-based tracking supports video-based tracking in case of occlusions (e.g., the head of the user occludes the hand positioned on the table). The acoustical techniques developed by the Image and Sound Processing Group at Politecnico di Milano, allow for robust and continuous localisation and tracking of touching position on TAI solely based on real-time analysis of acoustic propagation patterns. The output of such techniques is the trajectory of the touching positions along time. The TAI surface can be of any shape (e.g., rectangular or circular) and can be positioned in different ways (e.g., horizontal, vertical, inclined like a painting on a stand).

3.3 Extraction of Expressive Features from TAIs

The trajectories provided by the combined acoustic and visual continuous tracking algorithms and the video frames obtained from the video camera are both processed by the EyesWeb Expressive Processing Library, in order to extract expressive gesture qualities. Trajectory points and video frames are provided at a sampling rate of 25 Hz.

As a first step, segmentation of hand movements on the tangible surface in single gestures is performed. Segmentation is obtained by thresholding the audio input from the TAI. In this first prototype we simply set a fixed threshold operating over the sum of the four audio channels. In a more refined prototype, an adaptive threshold will be applied to a weighted sum of the audio channels, so that, for example, a sequence of soft movements would lower the threshold, whereas a sequence of movements performed near one accelerometer would raise the weight associated to that sensor.

Extracted features include consolidated kinematical features, as well as expressive qualities such as directness, impulsiveness, fluidity, symmetry, contraction/expansion. We performed a preliminary analysis on a wider set of expressive features aiming at isolating the most suited ones. Preliminary analysis was carried out by means of computation of statistical descriptors over the whole set of features. As a result, we identified the following expressive features: eccentricity of a gesture, time duration, peak velocity, impulsiveness, spatial length, and directness index. Whereas such features are sometimes partially overlapping and are not completely orthogonal, they however proved to provide enough information for reliably distinguishing among the bipolar extremes of Laban's Effort Space and Time dimensions.

Eccentricity of gesture trajectories
In order to compute eccentricity (EC) for a gesture trajectory, the trajectory is
integrated over time, obtaining for each gesture a bitmap summarizing the trajectory
followed during the whole gesture. An elliptical approximation of the shape of the
trajectory is then computed [14]. The eccentricity of such ellipse is taken as the
eccentricity of the gesture trajectory. Intuitively, a trajectory spread over a circular
area gets low eccentricity values (being the approximating ellipse almost a circle),
whereas an elongated trajectory gets high eccentricity values. Figure 2 shows an
example of trajectory characterized by low eccentricity (a) and an example of
trajectory characterized by high eccentricity (b).

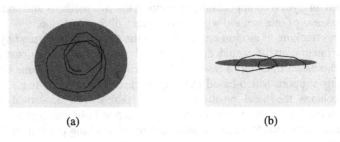

(a)   (b)

Fig. 2. Two gesture trajectories and their approximating ellipse. The first trajectory (a) is
characterized by low eccentricity, whereas the eccentricity of the second one (b) is high.

Peak velocity in a gesture
Given the sequence of velocity vectors in the motion trajectory corresponding to a
single gesture $v_1, v_2, ..., v_N, v_k = (v_{xk}, v_{yk})$, peak velocity (PV) is computed as the
maximum module of velocity in the gesture:

$$PV = \max_k \sqrt{v_{xk}^2 + v_{yk}^2}$$

Time duration of a gesture
If N is the number of points in the motion trajectory corresponding to a single gesture
after segmentation and ΔT is the sampling period (40 ms in this prototype), the overall
time duration of a gesture (TD) is simply computed as $TD = N \cdot \Delta T$.

Impulsiveness
Impulsiveness (IM) is computed from the shape of the profile of the module of
velocity. For each segmented gesture IM is calculated as the ratio between the peak of
the module of velocity in the gesture and the overall time duration of the gesture, that
is $IM = PV / TD$. Intuitively, impulsive movements are characterized by short gesture
duration with high velocity peaks, while sustained movements are characterized by
longer duration of gesture with low variance of the velocity.

Spatial length of a gesture
Given a gesture trajectory as a sequence of 2D points $p_1, p_2, ..., p_N, p_k = (x_k, y_k)$, the
overall spatial length of the gesture (SL) is computed as:

$$SL = \sum_{k=1}^{N-1} d(p_k, p_{k+1})$$

where $d(p_i, p_j)$ is the Euclidean distance between the i-th and the j-th point.

Directness Index

Directness Index (DI) is an expressive feature related to the geometric shape of a movement trajectory. It is a measure of how much a trajectory is approximately direct or flexible. It is strongly related to the Space dimension of Laban's Theory of Effort, and therefore it was selected for this study. In the current implementation DI is computed as the ratio between the length of the straight line connecting the first and last point of a given trajectory and the sum of the lengths of each segment composing the trajectory (the spatial length). That is, given the sequence of 2D points of a motion trajectory $p_1, p_2, \ldots, p_N, p_k = (x_k, y_k)$, Directness Index is computed as follow:

$$DI = \frac{d(p_1, p_N)}{SL}$$

where $d(p_1, p_N)$ is the Euclidean distance between the first and the last point in the trajectory. The more DI is near to one, the more direct is the trajectory.

3.4   Classification of Gestures According to Laban's Effort Dimensions

In order to classify gesture according to Laban's dimensions, we adopted a machine learning approach. SVM classifiers with probability estimation were used for real-time bipolar classification of gesture as Direct or Flexible, Quick or Sustained.

Analysis is performed on the whole gesture, from its beginning to its end. Such analysis provides a global overview of the expressive qualities of the whole gesture but it might be less significant if the gesture is not characterized by a single over-standing quality, but rather its expressive qualities change during execution.

Four subjects were asked to perform hand gestures on the Expressive TAI according to the 4 bipolar qualities Direct, Flexible, Quick, and Sustained. A training set built up from multiple subjects makes it easier to generalize the results beyond the personal moving style of the single subject. Each subject was asked to perform 20 gestures for each class. After a filtering step for removal of possible outliers, the training set consisted of 64 Quick gestures, 51 Sustained gestures (for a total of 115 gestures for the Time dimension), 65 Direct gestures, and 39 Flexible gestures (for a total of 104 gestures for the Space dimension).

Two distinct SVMs were trained, one for the Time dimension and one for the Space dimension. Both SVMs were set to use a radial basis function kernel. The Time SVM received as input the following expressive features: IM, SL, TD. The Space SVM the following ones: EC, DI, SL. Such choice is the results of repetitive training with different sets of features for both Space and Time. Peak Velocity that seemed significant at a preliminary analysis does not appear instead to bring a significant amount of information to the classifier. This may due to the fact that the acoustic continuous tracking algorithm does not allow very fast movements.

10-folds cross-validation produced the following results (chance level 50%):

- Time dimension: 77.39% accuracy
- Space dimension: 81.73% accuracy.

3.5 Representation of Gestures in a 2D Laban's Space

A decisive step for high-level gesture interpretation and analysis is accomplished through the representation of gestures as trajectories in abstract multidimensional spaces whose dimensions are relevant for expressive characterization. In this study, we mapped expressive gestures in a 2D space whose dimensions are Laban's Space and Time dimensions. Both dimensions are normalized in the range [-1, 1].

Probability estimations from the SVM classifiers are used for positioning a gesture in the 2D space. As a first step probability estimations p_S and p_T for the Space and Time components (where p_S is the probability that a direct gesture was recognized and p_T is the probability that a quick gesture was recognized) are quantized in three ranges: $[0, p_{Xl})$, $[p_{Xl}, p_{Xh})$, and $[p_{Xh}, 1]$, being p_{Xl} and p_{Xh} two thresholds on the probability estimations ($X = S$ or $X = T$), set by default to 0.33 and 0.66. As a result from such quantization the space of probability estimations for Space and Time is divided in 9 regions as shown in Figure 3a.

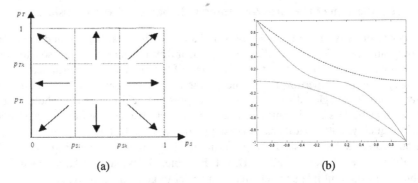

(a)   (b)

Fig. 3. The probability estimation space (a) and the quadratic curves (b) used for computing the position of the current classified expressive gesture in the Laban's 2D space

Mapping on the 2D Laban's space depends on the position of the last classified gesture in the probability estimation space and on the current position in the 2D Laban's space. The components of the displacement along Space and Time, ΔS and ΔT, are computed each time a new gesture is classified.

The direction of the displacement depends on the region in the probability estimation space where the last classified gesture is located. For example, if the last classified gesture was recognized as direct with a probability of 0.8 and quick with a probability of 0.7, the direction of the displacement would be North East. Arrows in Figure 3a show the direction of the displacement.

The module of the displacement depends on the position of the last classified gesture in the probability estimation space (e.g., the stronger the probability of a direct gesture, the wider the displacement toward the right side of the space) and on the current position in the 2D Laban's space (the nearer is the current position to the borders of the 2D space, the smaller the displacement).

A quadratic model is used for computing the components of the displacement. Consider ΔS. If the probability estimation of the last classified gesture is greater than p_{Sh} an increment of the Space component is expected and it is computed as follows:

$$\Delta S = p_S \left[\frac{1}{4}(s^2 + 1) - \frac{1}{2}s \right]$$

where s is the Space component of the current position in the Laban's space. That is, the farther is the current value of the Space component from its upper limit ($s_{max} = 1$) the bigger is the increment (dashed curve in Figure 3b).

If the probability estimation of the last classified gesture is lower than p_{Sl} a decrement of the Space component is expected and it is computed as follows:

$$\Delta S = p_S \left[-\frac{1}{4}(s^2 + 1) - \frac{1}{2}s \right]$$

That is, the farther is the current value of the Space component in the 2D space from its lower limit ($s_{min} = -1$) the bigger is the decrement (dotted curve in Figure 3b). A saturation effect is obtained, so that if the current Space component value is near to its upper limit, further direct gestures do not produce further significant big increments.

If the probability estimation of the last classified gesture is in between p_{Sl} and p_{Sh}, the Space component is expected to be not very significant and its value should be almost zero. The displacement component ΔS is computed as follows:

$$\Delta S = \begin{cases} -p_S s^2 & \text{if } s \geq 0 \\ p_S s^2 & \text{if } s < 0 \end{cases}$$

That is, the model works as an attractor for the Space component toward 0 (see the continuous curve in Figure 3b): if the current value of the Space component is negative an increment is computed, whereas if it is positive a decrement is obtained. The same quadratic model is used for computing the Time component ΔT.

3.6 Analysis of Trajectories in the 2D Laban's Space

A further step consists in analyzing the trajectories generated by classified gestures in the 2D Laban's space. For example, concentration of trajectories in the Quick and Direct quarter of the space may be interpreted as a preference of the user for fast, direct, targeted movements with a high degree of confidence and decision. At the opposite quarter of the space, a prevalence of sustained, smooth, and flexible movement may account for a calmer and more relaxed interaction style. Besides the high-level interpretation of users' gestures, this information could provide useful insights on users' attitudes and behavior and could be employed for assessment and evaluation of Expressive TAIs as well as for user profiling.

In order to estimate how much gestures are concentrated in a portion of the space we quantized it in 20×20 square regions $R_1, R_2, ..., R_N$ ($N = 400$) and we computed occupations rates for each region. If q_1, q_2, ..., q_M, $q_k = (s_k, t_k)$ is a trajectory in the 2D Laban's space, the set of gestures falling in the n-th region of the space is defined as

$$Q_n = \{q_k = (s_k, t_k) : q_k \in R_n\}, \; n = 1...N.$$

The occupation rate (OR) for the n-th region is therefore computed as

$$OR_n = \frac{|Q_n|}{M}, \; n = 1...N$$

The value for M depends on how long a user interacts with the interface. Typical values for quite short sessions may range from 10 to 30. Figure 4 shows the running EyesWeb XMI application performing real-time classification and mapping on the 2D Laban's space: on the right the space is represented. The blue squares are the 400 regions in which the space has been divided. The saturation of the colour is proportional to the occupation rate for that region, light blue corresponding to low occupation rates and dark blue to high ones. In the case of the figure, some preponderance of sustained gestures can be observed. Starting from occupation rates we are currently investigating further aspects of Laban's Effort Theory (e.g., basic effort, stressed effort, incomplete effort).

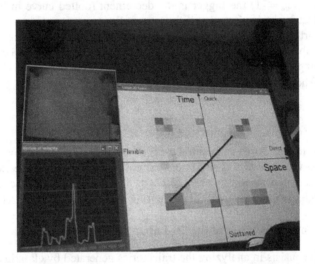

Fig. 4. Gestures represented as trajectories in the Laban's Space/Time space. The occupation rate of a region of the space provides further qualitative information on how the interaction is going on (e.g., whether the user is determined or hesitant).

4 Conclusions

This paper presented a concrete example of high-level analysis of expressive gesture on TAIs. The techniques here discussed were used for TAI prototypes at the IST2006 Convention, Helsinki, Nov. 2006 (grand prize as best booth), and for the science exhibitions "Cimenti di Invenzione e Armonia", held in the framework of Festival della Scienza (International Festival of Science), at Casa Paganini, Genova, Italy,

Oct. – Nov. 2006 and 2007 (more than 4000 visitors). We presented a TAI installation consisting of an interface to the Google Earth application allowing for use of the two hands for rotating and zooming in and out satellite images. High-level gesture processing techniques were used to improve feedback to the user (e.g., direct and quick gestures associated to faster navigation and to auditory feedback).

Feedback from users allowed for a preliminary qualitative evaluation of the TAI. Whereas feedback was generally positive, some aspects emerged that need further work. For example, in the current prototype gesture classification is performed at the end of the gesture. This is sometimes confusing for the user who, especially in the Google Earth installation, would expect a faster and more reactive system. Also, observation of users interacting with the system suggests to expand the gesture vocabulary, to move toward prototypes able to process gestures performed with both hands, and to consider collaborative scenarios. The results of a first psychological study aiming at evaluating TAIs in general are reported in [15]. A formal evaluation of Expressive TAIs is planned as future work. Further ongoing work includes:

(i)   Analysis of the preparation phase of a gesture (anticipation). This is obtained from the video-camera images and is triggered by the detection of a touching event. That is, once the touching gesture is detected through acoustic techniques, analysis is performed on a collection of expressive features previously computed on the video frames and stored by the system. Such features are computed on a time window whose duration is between 0.5 s and 3 s before the start of touch.

(ii) Continuous analysis of gestures on a running time window. This analysis aims at providing a continuous estimate on a small-scale time window of the expressive qualities while the gesture is executed. As such, this analysis can account for punctual variation of gesture qualities and can be used for providing a more reactive feedback. The duration of the time window is between 0.5 s and 3 s and can be dynamically adapted to the kinematical features of the gesture.

(iii) Extension of the analysis to the Weight component of Laban's Theory of Effort, based on expressive features extracted from acoustic signals. As a result gestures are represented in a 3D Laban's space and it is possible to classify them in terms of Laban's gesture categories (e.g., pushing, gliding, slashing, etc.).

(iv) Extension to mobile devices in collaborative frameworks. Future mobile devices will include various sensors, significantly increased wireless communication and computational power. Specific TAIs can be integrated in the mobile device to be able (i) to sense the surrounding space, (ii) to recognize the objects touched by the mobile, (iii) to perform a qualitative (including expressive) and quantitative analysis of user's actions. Moreover, integration with emerging context-aware technologies will enable the user to become participative and socially engaged. Research on these topics is currently carried out in the framework of the EU-ICT Project SAME (www.sameproject.eu).

Acknowledgements

We thank our colleagues at DIST-InfoMus Lab for the useful discussions. This work has been partially supported by the EU-IST Project TAI-CHI. The work is continuing with the partial supported of the EU-ICT Project SAME.

References

1. Camurri, A., De Poli, G., Leman, M., Volpe, G.: Toward Communicating Expressiveness and Affect in Multimodal Interactive Systems for Performing Art and Cultural Applications. IEEE Multimedia Magazine 12(1), 43–53 (2005)
2. Camurri, A., Mazzarino, B., Volpe, G.: Expressive interfaces. Cognition, Technology and Work. 6(1), 15–22 (2004)
3. Cowie, R., Douglas-Cowie, E., Tsapatsoulis, N., Votsis, G., Kollias, S., Fellenz, W., Taylor, J.: Emotion Recognition in Human-Computer Interaction. IEEE Signal Processing Magazine 18(1), 32–80 (2001)
4. Hashimoto, S.: KANSEI as the Third Target of Information Processing and Related Topics in Japan. In: Proc. International Workshop on KANSEI: The technology of emotion, Genova, pp. 101–104 (1997)
5. Camurri, A., Mazzarino, B., Ricchetti, M., Timmers, R., Volpe, G.: Multimodal analysis of expressive gesture in music and dance performances. In: Camurri, A., Volpe, G. (eds.) GW 2003. LNCS, vol. 2915, pp. 20–39. Springer, Heidelberg (2004)
6. Laban, R., Lawrence, F.C.: Effort. Macdonald & Evans Ltd., London (1947)
7. Laban, R.: Modern Educational Dance. Macdonald & Evans Ltd., London (1963)
8. Wallbott, H.G.: Bodily expression of emotion. European Journal of Social Psychology 28(6), 879–896 (1998)
9. Camurri, A., Coletta, P., Drioli, C., Massari, A., Volpe, G.: Audio Processing in a Multimodal Framework. In: Proc. 118th AES Convention, Barcelona (2005)
10. Camurri, A., Mazzarino, B., Volpe, G.: Analysis of Expressive Gesture: The EyesWeb Expressive Gesture Processing Library. In: Camurri, A., Volpe, G. (eds.) GW 2003. LNCS, vol. 2915, pp. 460–467. Springer, Heidelberg (2004)
11. Zhao, L.: Synthesis and Acquisition of Laban Movement Analysis Qualitative Parameters for Communicative Gestures, Ph.D. Dissertation, University of Pennsylvania (2001)
12. Pollick, F.E., Paterson, H., Bruderlin, A., Sanford, A.J.: Perceiving affect from arm movement. Cognition 82, B51--B61 (2001)
13. Polotti, P., Sampietro, M., Sarti, A., Tubaro, S., Crevoisier, A.: Acoustic Localization of Tactile Interactions for the Development of Novel Tangible Interfaces. In: Proc. 8th Intl. Conference on Digital Audio Effects (DAFX 2005), Madrid (2005)
14. Kilian, J.: Simple Image Analysis By Moments, Open Computer Vision (OpenCV) Library documentation (2001)
15. Bornand, C., Camurri, A., Castellano, G., Catheline, S., Crevoisier, A., Roesch, E., Scherer, K., Volpe, G.: Usability evaluation and comparison of prototypes of tangible acoustic interfaces. In: Proc. Intl. Conference Enactive 2005, Genova, Italy (2005)

Implementing Distinctive Behavior for Conversational Agents

Maurizio Mancini[1] and Catherine Pelachaud[2]

[1] University of Paris 8
and
DIST Lab, University of Genova, Italy
[2] INRIA - France
and
CNRS, TELECOM - ParisTech, Paris, France

Abstract. We aim to define conversational agents exhibiting distinctive behavior. To this aim we provide a small set of parameters to allow one to define behavior profiles and then leave to the system the task of animating the agents. Our approach is to manipulate the behavior tendency of the agents depending on their communicative intention and emotional state. In this paper we define the concepts of *Baseline* and *Dynamicline*. The Baseline of an agent is defined as a set of fixed parameters that represent the personalized agent behavior, while the Dynamicline is a set of parameters that derive both from the Baseline and the current communicative intention and emotional state.

1 Introduction

We present a model for the definition of conversational agents exhibiting *distinctive behavior*. It means that even if the communicative intentions or emotional states of two agents are exactly the same they behave in a different way according to their global behavior tendencies. Differences are noticeable both in the signals chosen by the agents to communicate and in the quality of their behaviors.

Human communication involves verbal and non-verbal behaviors. People communicate through several modalities like face, gestures, posture. The same beliefs and goals can be communicated in different personalized ways, and the interaction with other people is always influenced by personal behavior tendencies. For example we are able to give a quick but usually precise definition of the global behavior tendency of a person: we say "this person *never* moves, she is expressiveless" or "she is very expansive and gestures a lot while talking" and so on. Some people may tend to use one modality more than the others, other people may use more than one modality at the same time and so on. For example let us consider a person that gestures a lot while speaking. This is a basic trait of that person, we can expect that in most circumstances she prefers to convey non-verbal signals more on the gesture modality than with other modalities. That is the idea we want to capture with the concept of *Baseline* for virtual agents. On the other hand there can be some events or situations in which one's basic tendencies change, and one gestures in a greatly different way. For example

M. Sales Dias et al. (Eds.): GW 2007, LNAI 5085, pp. 163–174, 2009.

a person that never does hand/body gestures while she talks may change her behavior if she is very angry at someone. We embody the current tendency of behavior with the concept of *Dynamicline* of a virtual agent.

In the next Section we briefly describe other systems that have implemented agents exhibiting distinctive behavior. In Section 3 we illustrate the definition of the modality preference and the expressivity parameters. In Sections 4 and 5 we explain how Baseline and Dynamicline are used to generate the final agent's behavior. Then we give an example of our system and we conclude the paper.

2   State of the Art

Several researchers addressed the problem of defining conversational agents exhibiting distinctive behavior. Some of them applied psychological theories to the creation of models that simulate personality, mood and emotion [3]. Others defined parameters that aim to modify the quality of movement dynamically to increase the expressivity of the agent [4,12,14]. In other systems, the agent's behavior, previously stored in script files manually or statistically computed, is selected during the interaction with the user [2,10].

Ruttkay et al. [15,18] propose the idea of behavior style, defined in terms of *when* and *how* the agent uses certain gestures. Styles are implemented by selecting gestures from a *style dictionary* that defines both which gestures an agent has in its repertoire and its habits in using them. The style dictionaries are written in GESTYLE. This language specifies which modalities should be used to display non-verbal behaviors and is also used to annotate the text that the agent has to utter. Ball and Breese [3] propose a model for individualization for virtual agents in which the final behavior is computed depending on the agent's current emotional state and personality by choosing the most appropriate style. The PAR model of Allbeck et al. [1] offers a parameterization of actions. The actions that the agent is able to carry out are defined together with the conditions that need to be true in order to perform the actions. Conditions can refer to the state of other agents or objects in the agent's environment. EMOTE [4] is a system for creating differentiated gestures. Starting from Laban's annotation scheme, gestures are defined in terms of *Effort* and *Shape*. Effort gives information about the sense of impact (delicate vs strong), speed (indulging vs urgent/sudden) and control (uncontrolled/abandoned vs controlled/tense) of movement. space, weight, time and flow. Shape defines the movement path in the 3D space. Neff et al. [14] found out some key movement properties by reviewing arts and literature, for example from theater and dance. They found that body and movement characteristics such as balance, body silhouette (contour of the body), position of torso and shoulder, etc. influence the way in which people perceive the others. They implemented three motion properties into animated characters: the pose of the character, the timing of movements and the transition from one pose to another. In this model physical constraints are also considered, for example gravity and body balance, to obtain a very realistic animation. In André et al. [2] the agent's behavior depends both on a script that describes what the agent has to communicate to the user (for example how to do a reservation for a room in a hotel's website) and its personalized behavior. The last one includes idle movements like for example tapping with its foot while the user does nothing or jumping when the mouse passes over the agent's figure. Maya et al. [12] define a taxonomy to classify the influences on people's behavior. Intrinsic influences are personal habits that derive from personality, culture, gender, etc. Contextual influences come from the physical environment in which the person is acting. Finally dynamic influences represent the person's emotional states, beliefs and goals during the conversation. In our model we also use the notion of dynamic influence but we look at how these influences can be computed in term of movement quality and modalities preference without looking at the factors that could have caused them. In Michael Kipp's work [9] the author presents a gesture animation system based on statistical models of human speaker's gestures. Videos of interviewed people have been manually annotated in terms of gestures types (iconic, deictic, etc. [13]), together with their frequency of occurrence and timing (that is the synchronization between the gesture stroke and the most emphasized syllable of the sentence). The statistics on the speaker's gestures are then used to model the agent's set of preferred gestures (the probability of their occurrence is computed from the annotated gesture frequency) and synchronization tendency (for example an agent can perform gesture strokes always synchronized with speech emphasis). In a more recent work [10], the agent's gestures selection can be human authored or automatically learned using machine learning algorithms on the basis of previously annotated scripts. In our work we look at behavior qualitative differences rather than gesture types differences. Kipp's approach and ours are thus complementary. Similarly to our work, Kipp does not model the possible causes of visible variations in behavior.

3   Modality Preference and Behavior Expressivity

Conversational agents are graphical representations of humans that are increasingly used in a large variety of applications to help, assist or direct the user in performing a wide range of tasks. They can communicate to the user multimodally, that is by using many modalities at the same time. In our work, agents produce signals on the following modalities:

- face (eyebrows/eyelids/mouth/cheek movements)
- head movement (head direction and rotation, such as nods and shakes)
- gestures (arms and hands movements)
- body posture (upper part of the body movements)

People differ in the way they use their modalities: one can be very expressive on the face, another can gesture a lot. The concept of *Modality preference* encompasses this variability in the modalities use. People can also differ in the quality of their behavior. For example, one can have the tendency to do large hand gestures at a fast pace. Thus behavior expressivity is also a characteristic of an agent.

3.1   Modality Preference

People can communicate by being more or less expressive in the different modalities. The *modality preference* represents the agent's degree of preference for each available modality. If for example we want to specify that the agent has the tendency to mainly use hand gestures during communication we assign a high degree of preference to the *gesture* modality, if it uses mainly the face, the face modality is set to a higher value, and so on. For every available modality (face, head movement, gesture, posture), we define a value between 0 and 1 which represents its degree of preferability. Agents can also use two or more modalities with the same degree of preference. This means that the agent communicates with these modalities equally.

3.2   Behavior Expressivity

Behavior expressivity is an integral part of the communication process as it can provide information on the current emotional state, mood, and personality of the agent [20]. We consider it as the manner the physical behavior is executed. Starting from the results reported in [20], we defined and implemented [7,8] a set of parameters that affect the qualities of the agent's behavior such as its speed, spatial volume, energy, fluidity. Thus, the same gestures or facial expressions are performed by the agent in a qualitatively different way depending on the following parameters:

- *Overall activation (OAC)*: amount of activity (quantity of movement) across several modalities during a conversational turn (e.g., simultaneous use of facial expression, gaze, gesture to visualize communicative intentions passive/static or animated/engaged).
- *Spatial extent (SPC)*: amplitude of movements (e.g., extension of the arms; amplitude of eyebrow raise)
- *Temporal (TMP)*: duration of movements (e.g., quick versus sustained actions)
- *Fluidity (FLD)*: smoothness and continuity of overall movement (e.g., smooth, graceful versus sudden, jerky)
- *Power (PWR)*: dynamic properties of the movement (e.g., weak/relaxed versus strong/tense)
- *Repetitivity (REP)*: tendency to rhythmic repeats of specific movements.

4   Baseline and Dynamicline

In our model for conversational agents exhibiting distinctive behavior we want to capture the idea that people have tendencies that characterise globally their behavior, but these tendencies can change in situations arising after some particular events. We introduce the concepts of *Baseline* and *Dynamicline*, which both contain information on the agent's modalities preferences and expressivity but with different time span: while the Baseline is the *global* definition of how the agent behaves in most situations, the Dynamicline is the *local* specification of the agent's behavior (for example during a given agent's emotional state).

In our model, Baseline and Dynamicline do not only differ by their meaning (global vs local behavior tendency) but also by the fact that the Baseline is an input parameter, that is, it is used to define some characteristics of an agent, while the Dynamicline is automatically computed by the system at runtime, depending on the agent's current communicative intention or emotional state.

4.1 Baseline

We define the Baseline by the couple *(Mod,Expr)* where:

- *Mod*: is the modality preference. As described in Section 3.1 this is the agent's tendency to use its modalities during communication. The modality preference is defined by assigning a real value between 0 and 1 to each modality.
- *Expr*: is the behavior expressivity. It is a set of expressivity values (see Section 3.2) that represents the base behavior tendency of the agent. An agent could for example tend to do slow and smooth gestures while another agent could tend to move in a fast and jerky manner. Note that we implemented expressivity separately for each modality, that is there is a set of expressivity parameters for each modality.

4.2 Behavior Quality Computation

Figure 1 outlines the module called *Behavior Quality Computation*, or *BQC*, which computes the agent's Dynamicline at runtime. The data provided as input is the agent's Baseline, which is a constant, and its current communicative intention or emotional state. Each time the communicative intention or emotional state varies the module computes a new Dynamicline for the agent.

During the execution of the BQC module, the modality preference and the expressivity parameters contained in the Baseline are modulated depending on the agent's actual communicative intention and the resulting values are stored in the Dynamicline. It means that communicative intention has a different impact on the Dynamiclines of two agents having different Baselines. For example, if an agent has a general tendency (Baseline) to perform movements with average speed/amplitude and to use hand gestures moderately then in a sad state it does very few hand gestures with very low amplitude and speed. On the other hand, an agent with a general tendency of gesturing a lot with fast and large movements even when being sad continues making gestures that would be fewer in number and with a lower expressivity (average speed and amplitude).

As shown in Figure 1, the computation of the agent's Dynamicline consists in "applying" some *behavior qualifiers* to the agent's Baseline. The behavior qualifiers allow us to define mathematical operations to be performed over the parameters contained in the agent's Baseline each time a certain intention must be communicated.

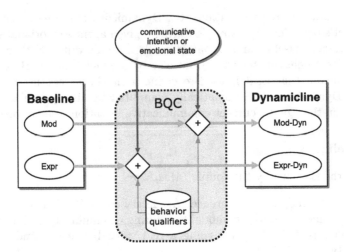

Fig. 1. The agent's Baseline, communicative intention or emotional state determine the computation of the agent's Dynamicline

For example, we could define a behavior qualifier that represents the following description:

"a angry state (i) increases the degree of bodily activation and at the same time (ii) the speed, amplitude and energy of movements are very high".

To implement such qualifiers we defined an XML-based language in which we could represent:

- the name of the parameter of the Dynamicline affected by the qualifier;
- the mathematical operator that is used in the qualifier (addition, subtraction, maximum and so on);
- the name of the parameter of the Baseline involved in the computation specified by the qualifier;

So the qualifier in the above example could be described with the following pseudo-code:

```
behavior qualifier for anger:
    affects body OAC by multiplying by a factor;
    affects TMP, SPC and PWR of all modalities by setting them to
    high values;
```

In the BQC module (see Figure 1), a repository of behavior qualifiers is stored, that is, a behavior qualifier for each possible agent's communicative intention or emotional state is defined. For every variation of one of these two data in input the module computes the agent's Dynamicline by selecting the corresponding behavior qualifier from the repository. The modulations induced by the behavior sets on the agent's Baseline to compute the Dynamicline have been defined starting from the studies of Wallbott [19] and Gallaher [6] and have been tested in previous works [7,11].

4.3 Dynamicline

The output of the BQC module (see Figure 1) is the agent's current Dynamicline. Structurally the Dynamicline is identical to the Baseline and is modeled by the couple *(Mod-Dyn,Expr-Dyn)* where:

- *Mod-Dyn*: The agent's current modality preference. It represents the agent's tendency to use its modalities given a certain communicative intention or emotional state. It is obtained by modulating the modality preference *Mod* contained in the Baseline depending on the current communicative intention or emotional state.
- *Expr-Dyn*: The agent's current expressivity parameters. It represents the agent's expressivity of movements given a certain communicative intention or emotional state. It is obtained by modulating the expressivity parameters *Expr* contained in the Baseline depending on the current communicative intention or emotional state.

5   Distinctive Behavior Generation

The presented work has been implemented within the Greta conversational agent framework [16]. The input of such a system is a text file in which both text to be spoken and the associated communicative intentions and emotional states are written. The text is translated into a speech file by a speech synthesizer while another process computes the animation of a virtual human that performs facial, arm and body gestures. Figure 2 represents the architecture of our system, showing how the modules are connected.

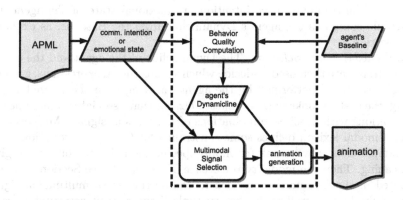

Fig. 2. The architecture of our system for distinctive behavior

```
01 <apml>
02
03 <rheme affect="anger">
04 <emphasis deictic="point">
05 what are you doing
06 </emphasis>
07 </rheme>
08
09 <performative type="warn">
10 Did you
11 <emphasis>
12 pay
13 </emphasis>
14 attention to what I said or
15 <emphasis deictic="self">
16 not
17 </emphasis>
18 </performative>
19
20 </apml>
```

Fig. 3. An APML file

Here is a description of each system component:

- *APML*: The input of our system is a file with a high-level description of the communicative intentions that the agent aims to communicate. It is written in APML [5], an XML-based language whose tags represent the communicative intentions [17]. For example in Figure 3 the APML tags surrounding the text specify that the agent is going to *warn* the user, see the *performative* tag from line 09 to line 18. The emotional state of the agent is also specified with the *affect* attribute of the *rheme* tag, from line 03 to line 07.

  The input APML file is read sequentially, and the contained tags are sent one by one to the behavior generation module. In Figure 2 the block called *communicative intention or emotional state* contains one APML tag at a time.

- *Behavior Quality Computation*: Depending on the current APML tag which can be the communicative intention or emotional state of the agent, this module computes the agent's Dynamicline from the Baseline, as explained in Section 4.

- *Multimodal Signal Selection*: The Dynamicline of the agent and the current APML tag are then used to decide which signals (facial expressions, gestures, etc) have to be performed by the agent. Starting from the current APML tag, the system looks in a *multimodal lexicon* that associates communicative intentions with possible combinations of multimodal signals. Moreover, the multimodal lexicon defines some constraints for the signals selection, as for example using always one (or more) specific modality to convey the given meaning. Then the modality preference of the agent (see Section 3.1) computed in the Dynamicline is used to choose the set of multimodal signals with the highest preference. For example if the current communicative intention contained in the APML file can be communicated with two or more groups of signals, the system chooses to generate the signals that are from the modalities with the highest preference. If these modalities cannot be instantiated (because, for example, the modalities are already in use) other signals with lower preference is used.

- *animation generation*: This is the last step of the generation process. Once all the signals corresponding to a given APML tag have been instantiated, this module computes the animation of the agent. The set of expressivity parameters contained in the agent's Dynamicline are now applied to the agent's movements [8].

6   A Working Example

We aim to define conversational agents that, even if they have the same communicative intention and emotional state, they would exhibit different multimodal behavior. We saw how the Baseline can be instantiated into the Dynamicline and how the contained data could influence the selection of the agent's communicative modalities and the expressivity of behaviors.

Let us see an example of how the proposed system works in practice. We want to model two conversational agents, *agent1* and *agent2*, with different behavior Baselines (reported in Figure 4). To simplify the explanation, we consider only two communication modalities: facial expressions and arm/hand gestures.

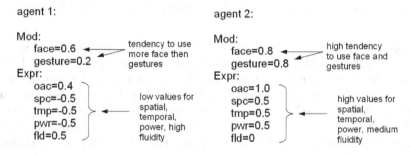

Fig. 4. Examples of Baseline: an *indolent*-type agent on the left; an *exuberant*-type agent on the right

Agent 1 is defined by a Baseline with a very low preference for doing gestures. It prefers communicating through facial expressions. It is not very expressive and its overall behavior is slow, powerless and low in amplitude. On the other hand, agent 2 uses equally its face and gestures. It is very expressive and uses a lot of non-verbal behaviors during communication. Its overall behavior is expansive, rapid and powerful.

Let us see how agent 1 and agent 2 differ in communicating the utterances of the APML example reported in Figure 3.

For the tag *affect= "anger"* the system looks in the multimodal lexicon and finds that the tag corresponds to a facial expression (frown + tense lips). The tag spans from lines 3 to 7 and contains an *emphasis* tag (lines 4-6) that can be

agent 1	agent 2
start Baseline: • Emo: neutral • Mod: face=0.6, gesture=0.2 • Expr: oac=0.4, spc=-0.5, tmp=-0.5, pwr=-0.5, fld=0.5	Baseline: • Emo: neutral • Mod: face=0.8, gesture=0.8 • Expr: oac=1.0, spc=0.5, tmp=0.5, pwr=0.5, fld=0
tag: affect+emphasis	*tag: affect+emphasis*
step 1 Dynamicline: • Mod: face=0.7, gesture=0.4 • Expr: oac=0.6, spc=-0.1, tmp=-0.1, pwr=-0.1, fld=0.1 Selected signals: • face=anger, gesture=nothing	Dynamicline: • Mod: face=0.9, gesture=1.0 • Expr: oac=1.0, spc=1.0, tmp=1.0, pwr=0.9, fld=-0.4 Seleced signals: • face=anger, gesture=beat
tag: performative	*tag: performative*
step 2 Dynamicline: • Mod: face=0.7, gesture=0.6 • Expr: oac=0.6, spc=-0.1, tmp=-0.1, pwr=-0.1, fld=0.1 Selecetd signals: • gesture=deictic(single)	Dynamicline: • Mod: face=0.9, gesture=1.0 • Expr: oac=1.0, spc=1.0, tmp=1.0, pwr=0.9, fld=-0.4 Selected signals: • gesture=deictic(with repetition)

Fig. 5. Evolution of the Baselines of an *indolent* and an *exuberant* agent. There are differences in the values of the expressivity parameters and the chosen signals.

performed by a combination of signals on the face (raised eyebrows) and gesture (beat). At this point the Dynamiclines of the two agents are computed by the system. The current communicative intention (emphasis) and emotional state (anger) are used to modulate the agents' Baselines (see Figure 5, line *start*) and to obtain the corresponding Dynamiclines (see Figure 5, line *step 1*). Based on the computed Dynamiclines, agent 1 assumes an angry facial expression, doing no gesture (the gesture modality in the agent's modality preference is still low). Moreover, the angry face is not very intense (spatial parameter). Instead agent 2 performs both an angry facial expression and a beat gesture, because the two modalities are high in its Dynamicline. Both the signals are intensified (spatially expanded, fast, powerful) by the agent's expressivity parameters.

The same computation is repeated for each communicative intention in the APML file. As shown in Figure 5 (see line *step 2*), for the *performative* tag (lines 9-18 of Figure 3) the Dynamicline of agent 1 has a quite high degree of preference for the gesture modality, so the agent performs a deictic gesture, even if globally (due to its Baseline) it prefers to do no gesture.

7   Conclusion and Future Work

We have presented a system for creating agents exhibiting *distinctive behavior*. We define the concept of Baseline as the agent's global expressivity and tendency in using communicative modalities. Depending on the agent's Baseline, communicative intention and emotional state, our system computes the agent's Dynamicline, which is then used in the process of behavior selection and generation. The consequence is that we are able to distinguish the behavior of two agents that have been defined with different Baselines, even if their communicative intentions and emotional states are the same.

One of the main limitations of our system concerns the definition of the behavior qualifiers needed to compute the Dynamicline from the Baseline. Defining these qualifiers is neither obvious nor simple, because only few experimental data is available about the variation of human nonverbal behavior depending on the communicative and emotional context. Further research direction we foresee is to automatically extract these behavior qualifiers from videos.

We also aim to add the layering of the effects of communicative intentions and emotional states that happen at the same time. How could we consider the effects of, for example, a communicative intention of "helping the user" happening at the same time of an emotional state of anger? In the future we could allow one to configure these superpositions of communicative intentions and emotional states.

Finally we need to further evaluate the agent's behavior resulting from the computation performed by our system. We need to verify that we can characterize an agent with its behavior tendencies, by investigating if users could recognize a certain agent just by watching its behavior. Another evaluation of the system could consist in comparing the quality of the interaction between users and agents exhibiting or not distinctive behavior.

References

1. Allbeck, J., Badler, N.: Toward representing agent behaviors modified by personality and emotion. In: Workshop on Embodied Conversational Agents - Let's specify and evaluate them! ACM Press, New York (2002)
2. André, E., Rist, T., Müller, J.: Integrating reactive and scripted behaviors in a life-like presentation agent. In: Second International Conference on Autonomous Agents, pp. 261–268 (1998)
3. Ball, G., Breese, J.: Emotion and personality in a conversational agent. In: Prevost, S., Cassell, J., Sullivan, J., Churchill, E. (eds.) Embodied Conversational Characters. MIT Press, Cambridge (2000)
4. Chi, D., Costa, M., Zhao, L., Badler, N.: The EMOTE model for effort and shape. In: Proceedings of the 27th annual conference on Computer graphics and interactive techniques, pp. 173–182. ACM Press/Addison-Wesley (2000)
5. DeCarolis, B., Pelachaud, C., Poggi, I., Steedman, M.: APML, a mark-up language for believable behavior generation. In: Prendinger, H., Ishizuka, M. (eds.) Life-Like Characters. Cognitive Technologies, pp. 65–86. Springer, Heidelberg (2004)
6. Gallaher, P.E.: Individual differences in nonverbal behavior: Dimensions of style. Journal of Personality and Social Psychology 63(1), 133–145 (1992)
7. Hartmann, B., Mancini, M., Buisine, S., Pelachaud, C.: Design and evaluation of expressive gesture synthesis for embodied conversational agents. In: Third International Joint Conference on Autonomous Agents & Multi-Agent Systems, Utretch (July 2005)

8. Hartmann, B., Mancini, M., Pelachaud, C.: Towards affective agent action: Modelling expressive ECA gestures. In: International conference on Intelligent User Interfaces - Workshop on Affective Interaction, San Diego, CA (2005)

9. Kipp, M.: Gesture Generation by Imitation (2005), http://Dissertation.com

10. Kipp, M.: Creativity meets automation: Combining nonverbal action authoring with rules and machine learning. In: Gratch, J., Young, M., Aylett, R.S., Ballin, D., Olivier, P. (eds.) IVA 2006. LNCS, vol. 4133, pp. 230–242. Springer, Heidelberg (2006)

11. Mancini, M., Bresin, R., Pelachaud, C.: From acoustic cues to an expressive agent. In: Gibet, S., Courty, N., Kamp, J.-F. (eds.) GW 2005. LNCS, vol. 3881, pp. 280–291. Springer, Heidelberg (2006)

12. Maya, V., Lamolle, M., Pelachaud, C.: Influences on embodied conversational agent's expressivity: Towards an individualization of the ecas. In: Proceedings of the Artificial Intelligence and the Simulation of Behaviour, Leeds, UK (2004)

13. McNeill, D.: Hand and Mind: What Gestures Reveal about Thought. University Of Chicago Press (1992)

14. Neff, M., Fiume, E.: AER: Aesthetic Exploration and Refinement for Expressive Character Animation. In: Proceedings of the 2005 ACM SIGGRAPH/Eurographics symposium on Computer animation, pp. 161–170. ACM Press, New York (2005)

15. Noot, H., Ruttkay, Z.: Gesture in style. In: Camurri, A., Volpe, G. (eds.) GW 2003. LNCS (LNAI), vol. 2915, pp. 324–337. Springer, Heidelberg (2004)

16. Pelachaud, C.: Multimodal expressive embodied conversational agents. In: MULTIMEDIA 2005: Proceedings of the 13th annual ACM international conference on Multimedia, pp. 683–689. ACM Press, New York (2005)

17. Poggi, I.: Mind markers. In: Trigo, N., Rector, M., Poggi, I. (eds.) Gestures. Meaning and use, University Fernando Pessoa Press, Oporto (2003)

18. Ruttkay, Z., Pelachaud, C., Poggi, I., Noot, H.: Exercises of style for virtual humans. In: Canamero, L., Aylett, R. (eds.) Animating Expressive Characters for Social Interactions, J. Benjamins Publishing(to appear)

19. Wallbott, H.G.: Bodily expression of emotion. European Journal of Social Psychology 28, 879–896 (1998)

20. Wallbott, H.G., Scherer, K.R.: Cues and channels in emotion recognition. Journal of Personality and Social Psychology 51(4), 690–699 (1986)

Using Hand Gesture and Speech in a Multimodal Augmented Reality Environment

Miguel Sales Dias[1,2], Rafael Bastos[1], João Fernandes[1],
João Tavares[1], and Pedro Santos[2]

[1] ADETTI Av. das Forças Armadas, Edifício ISCTE 1600-082 Lisboa, Portugal
Tel.: (+351) 21 782 64 80
[2] MLDC - Microsoft Language Development Center, Edifício Qualidade C1-C2,
Av. Prof. Doutor Aníbal Cavaco Silva, Tagus Park, 2744-010 Porto Salvo, Portugal
Tel.: (+351) 96 2093324

Abstract. In this work we describe a 3D authoring tool which takes advantage of multimodal interfaces such as gestures and speech. This tool allows real-time Augmented Reality aimed to aid the tasks of interior architects and designers. This approach intends to be an alternative to traditional techniques. The main benefit of using a multimodal based augmented reality system is the provision of a more transparent, flexible, efficient and expressive means of human-computer interaction.

Keywords: Gesture Tracking, Augmented Reality, 3D Authoring Tool, Speech, Multimodal interfaces.

1 Introduction

Information Technologies (IT) use is now spread out through the world in several areas, such as medicine, communications, industry, media and many others. IT professionals require new ways of interacting with computers using more natural approaches. Computer Vision, as an example, has enabled these professionals to explore new ways for humans to interact with machines and computers [1][2]. The adoption of multimodal interfaces in the framework of augmented reality, is one way to address these requirements [3]. Our main goal was to develop a multimodal augmented reality application to explore the integration of gestures and speech, and could provide a valuable aid for interior design professionals in their work. Gesture interfaces generally involve cumbersome tethered devices and gloves based on joint angles. One alternative is by using computer vision gesture recognition techniques [4], such as multi-scale color feature detection, view based hierarchical hand models, particle filtering and other techniques. In this paper we have used O.G.R.E - Open Gesture Recognition Engine, a framework previously developed by some of the authors [5], in order to track and recognize hand gestures, which is part of the in-house MX Toolkit library [6]. Although there are other viable computing environments to track hand gestures [7], we have chosen this computer vision-based engine, since it has been extensively tested in our group and has proven to accomplish good results, especially

M. Sales Dias et al. (Eds.): GW 2007, LNAI 5085, pp. 175–180, 2009.

for static hand poses which could fit our requirements. The use of gesture and speech in an augmented reality authoring framework is the main contribution of this paper.

2 Previous Work

Our research group has been interested in the fields of Computer Vision, Augmented Reality and Gesture Recognition for the past nine years, therefore developing a variety of work in these areas. This paper exploits some previously obtained knowledge, namely the MX Toolkit library [6]. One of the relevant modules used in this work is O.G.R.E.. This module uses background detection and subtraction, color segmentation and contour tracking for detecting the human hand pose. The result is then compared with a pre-defined hand poses library to obtain the final recognition result. This module also includes several algorithms for testing static hand poses - discrete cosine transform (DCT), pair-wise geometrical histogram (PWGH), template matching (TM) and others. For this paper we decided to use the latter, since it's the one which presents better pose recognition results [5].

3 User Requirements

Traditionally interior design has been done using the "paper and pencil" metaphor. However, this method is slow for the designer and sometimes hard to communicate for the client. Recently, a set of computational applications for interior design through the use of 3D models, both for rooms and for furniture elements, has become standard in the industry and retail. If on one hand these tools make the design task easier, on the other hand the creation of 3D models is still time consuming. The inclusion of furniture elements into scenes implies searching large databases. Another problem is the visualization of results. Although the presentation of the solution is better than before, these systems continue to show a small, limited and hard to navigate virtual model, without the notion of the real dimensions. Our work envisages the creation of a tool for architects and interior designers which allows, via multimodal interaction (gestures and speech), the designers or the clients, to visualize the implementation of real size furniture using augmented reality. The tool has to be capable of importing, disposing, moving and rotating virtual furniture objects in a real scenario. The users should be able to take control of all actions with gestures and speech, and should be able to walk into the augmented scene, seeing it from a variety of angles and distances. The tool has also to address a common problem in this kind of authoring tools, which is the large variety of objects available, making the navigation and selection of the desired object difficult. One of our primary objectives was also to create "familiar" interfaces so that no training to use this software was needed, making it attractive to everyone.

4 System Architecture

The proposed logical architecture of the system is depicted in Fig. 1 and can be divided in two modules: Plaza, responsible for Augmented Reality authoring and

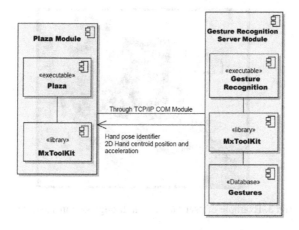

Fig. 1. System Architecture Diagram

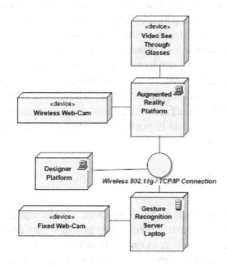

Fig. 2. Hardware block diagram

Speech Recognition and the Gesture Recognition Server, responsible for Hand Gesture recognition. Both modules use the MX Toolkit library and communicate through the TCP/IP COM module. The Gesture Recognition Server also maintains a Gesture Database, which will be used at runtime for gesture matching.

The system hardware (Fig. 2) or deployment architecture can be also divided in two distinct modules: Gesture Recognition Server and Plaza. The Gesture Recognition Server is connected to a fixed webcam device. The Plaza module is connected to a wireless webcam device and to a video see-through glasses device. Both modules have Wireless 802.11g interfaces and communicate using TCP/IP protocol. The fixed webcam device is only used for gestures recognition, while the wireless webcam provides an augmented reality image of the room, which can be perceived in the video see through glasses.

Fig. 3. Example of user interaction through gestures and voice

The processes sequence and data flows of the system are straightforward:
a) Launch the Gesture Recognition Server; b) Launch Plaza (it also launches Speech Recognition and selects the applicable language); c) Plaza registers the gestures for notification, sending information to the Gesture Server; d) At each frame, the Gesture Server sends Plaza relevant information (in a non null case), about the detected gesture (hand pose identifier) and the hand´s position (2D centroid coordinates) and acceleration; e) Plaza, at each frame, receives a gesture identifier (in a non null case), as well as other gesture information (position, acceleration); f) Plaza uses the received information as multimodal interface and authors the Augmented Reality environment.

The user's gesture interaction is performed using a fixed camera near the Gesture Recognition Server (see Fig. 3).

5   User Study and Discussion

In order to associate commands to hand gestures, a predefined gesture database must be created. The system supports several user profiles that can be created using the Gesture Recognition Server, either in online or offline modes.

Each profile corresponds to different gesture templates, since segmentation conditions may vary from one user to another (skin tone, hand size, etc.). For each command there is an associated hand pose gesture. Each one of these commands can be also invoked using the Speech Recognition Module, which is always running in background performing speech recognition. This ensures the possibility for the user to choose between issuing a command from gesture or speech. Every time the user activates an action (being a hand pose gesture or a speech command), this action is associated with a timestamp, so the system can synchronize the received instructions from the two interfaces, speech and gesture. This way the user can choose freely between the two interfaces.

Every time a valid gesture identifier is sent to Plaza from the Gesture Recognition Server, the user will view, in the Video See-Through rendered augmented reality image, some type of feedback (circles, point paths, text, etc.) depending on the performed action. The user may select the desired object by choosing the object from the

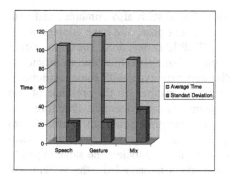

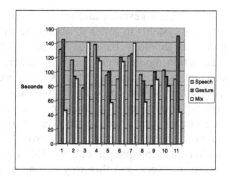

Fig. 4. Average time for the test (time unit in seconds)

Fig. 5. Time consumed by each subject during the test

Plaza interface. The user can perform two types of transformations on the object: translate, or rotate. Each one of these operations may be activated by a gesture or a speech command. To determine the usability of the system we developed a test, based on simple geometric transformations applied to virtual models using gesturing and voice interfaces. Our objective was to determine which interface the user would prefer and why. We applied the same test 3 times to each subject, using each time a different interface (Voice, Gestures and the two together). The usability experiment was run on 11 unpaid users, which were students in their early 20's from the undergraduate course of ISCTE, Instituto Superior de Ciências do Trabalho e da Empresa in Lisbon, Portugal and some developers with computer graphics experience from our laboratory (see Fig. 3). First, a 10 minute briefing, was given to each tester, explaining the project and features, showing what could be done with the system. After this briefing, each subject was given 2 minutes to play freely with the system and expose any doubt. Then the users performed the 3 tests, first using only voice, then using only gestures and finally using the two interfaces freely. After all the tests, each subject was given 5 minutes to fill a questionnaire related to the tests and their feedback. It was revealed that the use of the two interfaces was definitively the best way to interact with the system reducing in 20% (average) the time to complete the test. Most of the users used voice to activate simple commands like "Mover[1]" and "Rodar[2]" or to modify the speed (see Fig. 4 and Fig. 5). The use of gestures was preferred to move the objects, after the corresponding action has been selected using speech. The subjects provided valuable feedback during and after the experiment.

Several subjects said that the three velocity factors should be refined, because there was a much larger difference between fast and normal than the difference between normal and slow.

6 Conclusions and Future Work

In this paper we have presented an application developed to help interior design professionals using multimodal interaction in augmented reality. The HCI modalities

---

[1] "Move".
[2] "Rotate".

used are hand gestures and speech commands. The system also combines different tracking systems in order to obtain the virtual camera pose. We have adopted a client/server topology, based on Wireless 802.11g TCP/IP connections, since the gesture recognition module must be separated from the authoring module, due to efficiency constraints. The created system is still a preliminary prototype, with some restrictions. The system shows some difficulties when tracking gestures, in the presence of bad lighting conditions. The shadows turn color segmentation inaccurate, therefore gesture matching may fail. In the near future, we will integrate some other technologies on this system, in order to improve the performance and usability. Using multimarkers, a technique present in X3M, we will be able to associate the same object to several markers, and this way, if one of the markers is occluded , the system will continue to track the object, as long as one of the markers remains visible. We also would like to integrate the ARTIC module, as another multimodal interface, giving the user other alternatives to interact with the system and expanding the way tasks are accomplished. Searching a 3D object database for an item, can be difficult and inefficient. To solve this issue, we want to implement a system based on the CaLi [8] library. This library is based on fuzzy logic and it was developed for recognizing drawn forms in calligraphic interfaces.

References

1. Abowd, G.D., Mynatt, E.D.: Charting Past, Present, and Future Research in Ubiquitous Computing. ACM Transactions on Computer-Human Interaction (TOCHI) 7, 29–58 (2000)
2. Segen, J., Kumar, S.: Look Ma, No Mouse! – Simplifying human-computer interaction by using hand gestures. Communications of the ACM 43(7), 102–109 (2000)
3. Oviatt, S.L.: Multimodal interfaces. In: Jacko And, J., Sears, A. (eds.) The Human-Computer Interaction Handbook: Fundamentals, Evolving Technologies and Emerging Applications, vol. 14, pp. 286–304. Lawrence Erlbaum Assoc., Mahwah (2003)
4. Elgammal, A., Shet, V., Yacoob, Y., Davis, L.: Learning dynamics for exemplar-based gesture recognition. In: IEEE Conference on Computer Vision and Pattern Recognition, pp. 571–578 (2003)
5. Dias, J.M.S., Nande, P., Barata, N., Correia, N.: O.G.R.E. – open gestures recognition engine, a platform for gesture-based communication and interaction. In: Gibet, S., Courty, N., Kamp, J.-F. (eds.) GW 2005. LNCS, vol. 3881, pp. 129–132. Springer, Heidelberg (2006)
6. Dias, J.M.S., Bastos, R., Santos, P., Monteiro, L., Silvestre, R.: Developing and Authoring Mixed Reality with MX Toolkit. In: ART 2003, Toki, Japan (2003)
7. Camurri, A., Mazzarino, A., Volpe, G.: Analysis of Expressive Gesture: The EyesWeb Expressive Gesture Processing Library. In: Camurri, A., Volpe, G. (eds.) GW 2003. LNCS (LNAI), vol. 2915. Springer, Heidelberg (2004)
8. Jorge, J.A., Fonseca, M.: Using Fuzzy Logic to Recognize Gestures Interactively. In: FUZZ-IEEE 2000, vol. 1941, pp. 265–275 (2000)

A Virtual Reality-Based Framework for Experiments on Perception of Manual Gestures

Sebastian Ullrich[1], Jakob T. Valvoda[1], Marc Wolter[1],
Gisela Fehrmann[2], Isa Werth[2], Ludwig Jaeger[2], and Torsten Kuhlen[1]

[1] Virtual Reality Group
[2] Deaf & Sign Language Research Team Aachen
[1,2] RWTH Aachen University, Germany
s.ullrich@ieee.org

Abstract. This work contributes an integrated and flexible approach to sign language processing in virtual environments that allows for interactive experimental evaluations with high ecological validity. Initial steps deal with real-time tracking and processing of manual gestures. Motion data is stereoscopically rendered in immersive virtual environments with varying spatial and representational configurations. Besides flexibility, the most important aspect is the seamless integration within a VR-based neuropsychological experiment software. Ongoing studies facilitated with this system contribute to the understanding of the cognition of sign language. The system is beneficial for experimenters because of the controlled and immersive three-dimensional environment enabling experiments with visual depth perception that can not be achieved with video presentations.

1 Introduction

Experimental evaluation of sign language is of major interest in the areas of linguistics, media theory, psycholinguistics and psychology. However, most times conventional presentations of manual gestures and facial expressions by video or mirrors are used. Virtual Reality (VR) is one of the most sophisticated interactive media capable of closely resembling reality and has been therefore increasingly used for neuropsychological experiments. The methods proposed are used in current projects focusing on spatial cognition of manual gestures in hearing and deaf [1]. In these experiments we concentrate on the fact that in contrast to hearing speakers, who receive a constant auditory feedback of their own voice while speaking, the visual perception of a manual sign is different for the signer and the addressee. Even though the described toolkit is the enabling technology for our experiments, its application is not limited to one specific paradigm.

The remainder is structured as follows. Section 2 presents current computer-based systems for acquisition, processing, and presentation of sign language and discusses open issues. The proposed approach is detailed in section 3 and technical details are described in section 4. Its applications for gesture acquisition and experimental evaluations are presented in section 5. Section 6 provides a conclusion and an outlook on future work.

M. Sales Dias et al. (Eds.): GW 2007, LNAI 5085, pp. 181–186, 2009.

2   Related Work

There are many contributions to the simulation of sign language gestures. We focus on systems that deal with 3D motion data and visual representation of sign language by the use of virtual humanoids. In order to create a corpus with manual gestures, there are three common approaches: manual modeling and animation, semi-automatic generation, and motion capturing. The software of Vcom3D[1] is the "gold standard" for producing American Sign Language animations. Although it provides a very sophisticated GUI and features 3D characters, the output can be only rendered into 2D movie-clips. Synthetic generation is often done based on semantic input from specialized description languages and merges basic components to complete gestures [2,3]. Motion capturing approaches deal with calibration issues of data gloves [4] and retargeting of motion data to different models. Some recent systems focus on real-time communication with embodied conversational agents. One of the first such systems is called TESSA [5]. It has been developed to translate speech to sign language for transactions in a Post Office. Motion capture techniques have been used to create a corpus with typical phrases. The research project ViSiCAST is focused on automatic translation into sign language [6]. The main contribution is an animation synthesizer that combines input sequences in HamNoSys (a gesture description language) with items from a static hand shape database to generate animation data. Most recently, the research project HuGEx introduced expressiveness to virtual gesture communication [7]. From a motion database significant features are extracted, labeled with semantics and applied with different executional styles to synthesize varying expressiveness.

The aforementioned systems are all showing promising results. Although, 3D computer graphics are employed, VR-techniques to immerse the user (like stereoscopic displays and head tracking) are not utilized, which is essential for depth perception. In addition, they do not facilitate controlled virtual environments dedicated for experiments.

3   Flexible Architecture

The requirements for interactive experimental evaluations of sign language processing cover a broad field of different disciplines. Four distinct tasks have been identified (data input, model, representation and experimental platform) and integrated into a shared framework (cp Fig. 1).

The first component consists of an arbitrary hardware or software source producing **data input** (e. g., output from modeling, motion capturing, kinematic algorithms or synthesized gestures). This includes automatic or manual post-processing and mapping of the data to a model. The **model** consists of a complete description of a time-varying hierarchical structure based on human anatomy. It combines the data from an arbitrary number of data inputs to provide a consistent and complete model. For the **representation** to a human user

---

[1] http://www.vcom3d.com

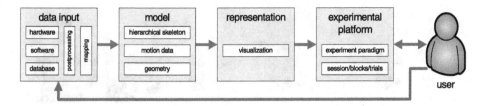

Fig. 1. Flexible pipeline with extenible components

the structural model must be visualized in a stereoscopic 3D environment. Several techniques can be chosen to vary the degree of realism or to change the appearance. Thus, the same structural model can be visualized differently, e. g., as puristic dots, as stick-figure or as realistic human model. The **experimental platform** adds the semantic context for sign language experiments. Here, the representations are integrated into interactive virtual environments according to a user-defined experimental design. This includes the specification of a chain of events structured into sessions, blocks, and trials, of analysis parameters and the interaction possibilities of the human user. The last step of the workflow is the **user**, who is able to interact with the experimental platform (e. g., reacting to stimuli) or with the data inputs directly.

4   Implementation

Within this section we describe technical details of the components from the previous section.

The **data input** covers a broad range of sources. Different types of gloves are supported, each with device specific calibration techniques and mapping functions, which are responsible for production of data compliant with our model. The calibration can be modified on-the-fly with a LUA script to adjust for difficult hand postures. In addition, motion capturing of body parts or a full body is realized with either electro-magnetic tracking or optical markers. This motion data is processed and mapped to an articulated structure (model). Retargeting allows to transfer data from one structural model to another. Motion sequences can be cut, merged or blended together. Because the synthesized motion data uses pointers and time markers to refer to the original data, these operations are performed interactively in real-time. Also, modeling of movement is supported through forward and inverse kinematics. Forward kinematics enables direct joint manipulation and affects all subsequent joints. Combined with a picking metaphor it is used to create specific postures interactively. The implementation of inverse kinematics solutions includes analytical solutions for human limbs and algorithms based on the Jacobian matrix for longer kinematic chains. Our toolkit contains multiple readers and writers, e.g., the H-Anim format for articulated humanoids and the BVH format for motion data are supported.

The **model** consists of several extendible systems that are grouping functional anatomic data structures [8]. An articulated hierarchical joint structure (based

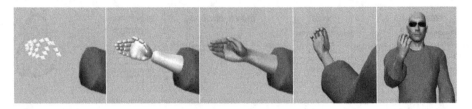

Fig. 2. Different degrees of realism (joints only, robot and realistic hand) and variation of perspective (egocentric, addressee) for intuitive interaction and experiments in VR

on the H-Anim standard) is defined within the skeletal system that is mainly used for motion data. A joint has among other properties a local quaternion, a rotation center, optional references to segments and sites. Additionally, realistic degrees of freedom are enforced with joint limits. Motion is stored by using discrete samples that contain quaternions, which represent local orientations of the joints. Another important system is the integumentary system that represents the outermost layer of the human body. It contains the representational data of the virtual humanoid, e. g., skin geometries with vertex weights that are linked to the skeletal system.

Our implementation of **representational** components places emphasis on different interactive visualizations (cp. Fig. 2). Thus, the joints, segments and sites of the skeletal system can be visualized, as well as the skin from the integumentary system. In particular, state-of-the art methods for rigid skin visualization, stitching, blendshapes (i. e., for facial animation), and vertex blending are integrated. GPU-optimizations have been applied to ensure interactive frame rates for skin visualizations with complex geometries. Through the usage of the Model-View-Controller design pattern the representational algorithms can be flexibly exchanged or extended without changes to the data input or model. This enables the creation of multiple views for one humanoid, that can be shown concurrently or can be switched instantly [9].

ReactorMan serves as the **experiment platform** to define and conduct experiments [10]. Recorded or synthesized gestures are visualized in ReactorMan by applying the representational component of the pipeline. The experimental paradigm is defined by the sign language linguist. The ReactorMan software is also used to record several experiment-related variables, for example user movement, user interaction, and reaction times. In particular, ReactorMan provides special hardware for accurate (i. e., error < 1 ms), software-independent reaction time measurements. All recorded values are integrated into a single consistent timeline and can be evaluated by common tools (e. g., SPSS or MatLab).

5   Results

The framework and components described in the previous two sections have already been successfully utilized in different setups to build a motion database for perception experiments. In addition first experiments on spatial perception of manual gestures have been conducted with it already.

A CyberGlove is used in conjunction with an electromagnetically tracked sensor to capture hand posture and trajectory. Due to the pipeline, real-time visualization is possible during recording, which allows to adjust calibration errors instantly. In a post-processing session the recorded items are edited and cut. Inverse kinematics (IK) is used to animate the upper limbs from shoulder to the hand. The signing space is adjusted interactively within our software by moving the hand position of the looping gestures whilst the arm automatically aligns accordingly. After these steps the items are stored in the database for subsequent experiments, although they may be used for other purposes as well. Over 100 items from the German Sign Language (GSL) have been recorded, categorized and adjusted. In addition, over 100 non-signs have been conceived and created accordingly (by new recordings, as well as, edited from GSL signs). Non-signs are phonologically possible but non-occuring GSL signs, analogous to German nonsense words like "Rakane" and "mieren" or English nonsense words "raner" and "marg". That is, non-signs were recombined out of separate existing phonological components (i. e., handshape and movement). All items are balanced in length and movement manner. The recording sessions took about 2 weeks with two deaf signers performing the signs. The post-processing was done by a deaf signer iteratively with review sessions by deaf signers and linguists in-between to evaluate and categorize the items. The average adjustment time for one item was about 10 minutes to half an hour.

In a first experiment all subjects run a lexical decision task to decide whether the presented item is a lexical sign taken from German Sign Language or not. Participants view randomized meaningful signs and meaningless non-signs displayed in 3D on a stereoscopic desktop-VR screen from varied perspectives (lateral, egocentric and addressee). They are instructed to react as soon and as correctly as possible by pressing designated keys for 'Yes' or 'No'. Responses are scored for the number of correct items and for reaction time. This experiment design has been implemented in the scripting language of ReactorMan.

The system is interactive, i. e., it allows for on-line recording and immediate representation of hand gestures in virtual environments. It combines several processing stages in one framework. The ease of use has been proven by the fact that the deaf signers did most of the post-processing on their own and were pleased about the direct manipulation with the tools. Especially, the seamless integration into a neuropsychological experiment platform in combination with VR closes a gap in current approaches.

6 Conclusion and Future Work

Th presented system is for the experimental evaluation of sign language processing in virtual environments. A pipeline has been developed to reach flexibility in terms of data input during acquisition of signs. It allows for multimodal and immersive representation of the signs and adds an integrated platform for controlled experiments. Possible scenarios include: interactive studies on online-monitoring (i. e., monitoring of kinesthetic feedback processes), studies of monitoring processes with delayed visual feedback and studies on morphing of discrete hand forms to distinguish spatial and linguistic borders. The system has proven its capability in first studies and enables a large variety of experiments in VR that will contribute to the understanding of the cognition of sign language.

Acknowledgment

This work was funded by the German Research Foundation (DFG) SFB/FK 427. The authors would like to thank Babak Modjtabavi, Michael König and Horst Sieprath for their support during acquisition of hand gestures.

References

1. Fehrmann, G., Jäger, L.: Sprachbewegung und Raumerinnerung. Zur topographischen Medialität der Gebärdensprachen. In: der Bewegung, K. Kinästhetische Wahrnehmung und Probehandeln in virtuellen Welten. Publikationen zur Zeitschrift für Germanistik, vol. 8, pp. 311–341. Peter Lang, Bern (2004)
2. Lee, J., Kunii, T.L.: Visual translation: from native language to sign language. In: Proc. of IEEE Workshop on Visual Languages, USA, pp. 103–109 (1992)
3. Lebourque, T., Gibet, S.: High level specification and control of communication gestures: the GESSYCA system. In: Proc. of IEEE Computer Animation, Switzerland, pp. 24–35 (1999)
4. Heloir, A., Gibet, S., Multon, F., Courty, N.: Captured Motion Data Processing for Real Time Synthesis of Sign Language. In: Gibet, S., Courty, N., Kamp, J.-F. (eds.) GW 2005. LNCS, vol. 3881, pp. 168–171. Springer, Heidelberg (2006)
5. Cox, S., Lincoln, M., Tryggvason, J., Nakisa, M., Wells, M., Tutt, M., Abbott, S.: TESSA, a system to aid communication with deaf people. In: Proc. of ASSETS 2002, Fifth International ACM SIGCAPH Conference on Assistive Technologies, Scotland, pp. 205–212 (2002)
6. Kennaway, R.: Synthetic Animation of Deaf Signing Gestures. In: Wachsmuth, I., Sowa, T. (eds.) GW 2001. LNCS, vol. 2298, pp. 146–157. Springer, Heidelberg (2002)
7. Rezzoug, N., Gorce, P., Héloir, A., Gibet, S., Courty, N., Kamp, J.F., Multon, F., Pelachaud, C.: Virtual humanoids endowed with expressive communication gestures: The HuGEx project. In: Proc. of IEEE International Conference on Systems, Man, and Cybernetics, Taiwan (2006)
8. Ullrich, S., Valvoda, J.T., Prescher, A., Kuhlen, T.: Comprehensive Architecture for Simulation of the Human Body based on Functional Anatomy. In: Proc. of BVM 2007, Germany (2007)
9. Valvoda, J.T., Kuhlen, T., Bischof, C.: Interactive Virtual Humanoids for Virtual Environments. In: Short Paper Proc. of Eurographics Symposium on Virtual Environments, Portugal, pp. 9–12 (2006)
10. Valvoda, J.T., Kuhlen, T., Wolter, M., et al.: NeuroMan: A Comprehensive Software System for Neuropsychological Experiments. CyberPsychology and Behaviour 8(4), 366–367 (2005)

Processing Iconic Gestures in a Multimodal Virtual Construction Environment

Christian Fröhlich, Peter Biermann, Marc E. Latoschik, and Ipke Wachsmuth

Artificial Intelligence Group
Faculty of Technology, University of Bielefeld
D-33594 Bielefeld, Germany
{cfroehli,pbierman,marcl,ipke}@techfak.uni-bielefeld.de

Abstract. In this paper we describe how coverbal iconic gestures can be used to express shape-related references to objects in a Virtual Construction Environment. Shape information is represented using Imagistic Description Trees (IDTs), an extended semantic representation which includes relational information (as well as numerical data) about the objects' spatial features. The IDTs are generated online according to the trajectory of the user's hand movements when the system is instructed to select an existing or to create a new object. A tight integration of the semantic information into the objects' data structures allows to access this information via so-called semantic entities as interfaces during the multimodal analysis and integration process.

Keywords: Gesture Representation, Iconic Gestures, Virtual Construction, Multimodal Human-Computer Interaction.

1 Introduction

In the description of object shapes, humans usually perform iconic gestures that coincide with speech (are coverbal). Marked by a similarity between the gestural sign and the described object, iconic gestures may easily depict content difficult to describe using words alone. Though the expressive potential of iconic gestures in human-computer communication is generally acknowledged, few applications of non-verbal modalities go beyond pointing and symbolic gestures, one of the first to mention is [7].

Using iconic gestures in virtual construction scenarios can be very useful when it comes to the description of shape-related aspects of certain construction parts. The processing of iconic gestures enables the user to specify the shape of a new object and to reference objects by their shape. To be able to do so, the system needs to have an internal representation formalism for shape-related information of the construction parts.

The next section introduces the Imagistic Description Tree (IDT) formalism [6] as an appropriate representation for shape-related information in multimodal systems. Section 3 will then describe our application scenario and some technical details about the use of IDTs in virtual construction. Section 4 will conclude with a brief outline of possible future work.

M. Sales Dias et al. (Eds.): GW 2007, LNAI 5085, pp. 187–192, 2009.
© Springer-Verlag Berlin Heidelberg 2009

2   Defining Shape through Iconic Gestures

Based on a comprehensive corpus of speech-gesture shape descriptions acquired from an empirical study [6], the Imagistic Tree was proposed as a representation for the semantics of multimodal shape-related expressions, to the end of algorithmically interpretive operational shape descriptions from gesture and speech input modalities. It extends an earlier approach [5], which models the two factors of extent and (partial) profile information in gestures, but which has not included structured spatial organization of gesture and accompanying speech reflecting this factor.

The IDT models object extent, profile, and structure, as the salient semantic elements contained in iconic gestures. The basic level of IDT representations are object schemes, in which each object is described by a collection of up to three axes which represent the objects extents in one, two, or three spatial dimensions. Using different combinations of axes in an object schema, several basic objects can be represented, such as cubes, cylinders, etc.

Structural aspects of an object are represented in an imagistic description which can recursively embed further imagistic descriptions for object parts, to result in a tree-like structure similar to the hierarchical structure used in the Marr and Nishihara [3] model. For each such description of an object part, an object schema is used to define its overall proportions, a spatial anchor flag which signals whether the description is spatially anchored in a parent coordinate system, and a transformation matrix defining the position, orientation, and size of the object or part in relation to the parent description. The complete tree describing an object including all parts, parts of parts, etc. is called Imagistic Description Tree. A more detailed description of the formal structure can be found in [4].

Initially, the IDT model was developed as the conceptual basis to represent shape-related information acquired via gesture and speech for usage in an operational gesture understanding system. Capturing gesture (motion) data via data-gloves and motion trackers, the system is able to recognize and to conceptualize shape-related gestures and verbal expressions in a unified spatial representation of an object description and to determine target objects which most closely match the input. In our application system–called the Virtuelle Werkstatt [2]–this procedure has been used to make reference or select objects for further manipulation in the virtual environment. More information on the technical approach will be given in Section 3.

3   Technical Approach

Our application system is concerned with the processing of multimodal user input – natural language as well as deictic, symbolic and iconic gestures – to drive the modifications of a 3D-visualized virtual construction scene. The 3D-visualization is done inside a three-sided CAVE environment to give the user a high degree of immersion. The trajectories of the gestural movements are detected with the help of an optical tracking system, which uses 9 infrared cameras in conjunction with retroreflective markers. The number of cameras is sufficient to ensure that the gestures are visible to the system at most times. Hand postures and handshapes are detected using data gloves.

The application domain is a virtual construction scenario. The user is able to create virtual construction parts and to modify them via gestures and speech, e.g. scale a part using a two-handed gesture. The parts are semantically enriched with necessary information about properties (e.g. shape or color) and capabilities (e.g. connection ports). This information is stored using a knowledge representation layer, which is accessed by the multimodal interpretation and analysis modules via semantic entities – virtual placeholders for the semantically enriched parts, which offer a standardized knowledge access interface. The trial task of the application is the creation of a "city mobile", which is a scooter car for handicapped and elderly people, though the general ideas and principles can be applied to a variety of virtual construction scenarios.

In this application IDTs are used to represent shape-related information about the virtual construction parts. Creation and referencing of objects is always done by speech and can be multimodally augmented by adding a gesture, which contains additional information. To create an object the user would for example say something like *"Give me a tube"*. Alternatively the user can interact multimodally with the system by specifying an object's shape with the help of an iconic gesture, e.g. *"Give me such a tube"* + *iconic gesture*. The same works for selecting an object. The user can instruct the system in natural language, e.g. by saying *"Take that tube"*, and issue a gesture (deictic as well as iconic) describing the object to be selected.

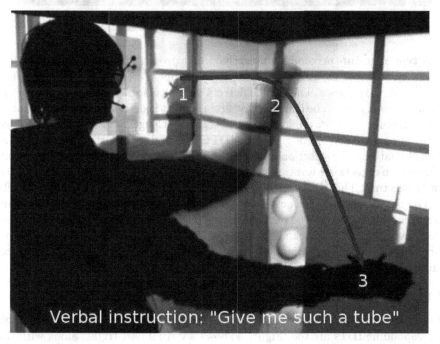

Verbal instruction: "Give me such a tube"

Fig. 1. Defining an object's shape via an iconic gesture, in this case a bent tube

Fig. 2. Newly created construction part resulting from an iconic gesture

A typical gesture accompanying verbal input processed to create a bent object in virtual reality is shown in Figure 1. The bent tube is created by making two linear gesture movements. The system detects the linear segments and computes the angle between them. The length of the first segment is determined by the distance between points *1* and *2*, while the second segment's length is given by the distance between points *2* and *3*. The generated IDT is assigned to the virtual part as semantic information. The selection of a tube by its shape works similar to its creation. The system detects the linear segments, computes the angle and generates an IDT for the gesture. This IDT gets then compared to the IDTs of all available objects and finally the one with the best match is selected. The resulting construction part can be seen in Figure 2. The part consists of two segments and a parametrized angle between them, which can be adjusted after the part was created (for more information on the parametrization of virtual construction parts, see [1]). The next subsection illustrates the IDT structure of such a construction part.

3.1   Example: IDT Structure of a Virtual Construction Part

As our basic construction parts are rather simple in their spatial structure, their corresponding IDTs are too. Figure 3 shows a virtual part (right) along with the structural outline of its IDT (left).

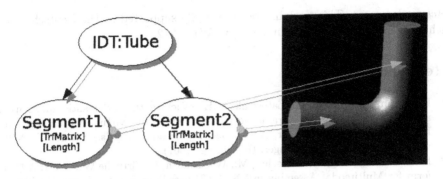

Fig. 3. Simplified IDT structure of a virtual construction part

The bent tube in the figure has a simple tree structure. It has an imagistic description for the whole part, which contains information about the shape of the complete tube itself. Shape meaning in this case extent, position (relative position of the segements towards each other) and also possible verbal descriptions of the object. It also contains two child imagistic descriptions, one for each segment of the bent tube. The segment descriptions have object schemes themselves, which again contain information about their shape. The relevant information which is needed for interacting with them are their relative position towards each other (their transformation matrices) together with their lengths. The angle between the two segments is computed through their transformation matrices. It is parametrized and can be adjusted through speech or gesture later on. The angle itself is not explicitly expressed in the IDT, but it is implicitly contained in the relative transformation matrices of both subparts.

4   Conclusion and Future Work

In this paper we have presented a way to utilize iconic gestures inside virtual reality environments. We showed how to make use of the Imagistic Description Tree formalism to enhance virtual construction parts with shape-related information. This enables the user to specify and reference construction parts with the help of iconic gestures. The IDT formalism has turned out to be a very powerful way to represent shapes for virtual construction parts, and we expect that further exploration of the formalism and the use of more of its features will introduce a broader range of interaction capabilities.

Future work consists of integrating more general shape-related concepts like properties such as longish or thin, so the user can for example instruct the system to create an abstract thin object with its corresponding IDT. Furthermore we plan to model and also automatically generate IDT structures for more complex construction parts – like tires or car-seats – to be able to interact with them using iconic gestures as well. It would also be possible to exploit information derived from the handshape when it comes to specifying and referencing of an object.

Acknowledgment. This work has been partially supported by the Deutsche Forschungsgemeinschaft (DFG) under grant Wa 815/2.

References

1. Biermann, P., Fröhlich, C., Latoschik, M.E., Wachsmuth, I.: Semantic information and local constraints for parametric parts in interactive virtual construction. In: Butz, A., Fisher, B., Krüger, A., Olivier, P., Owada, S. (eds.) SG 2007. LNCS, vol. 4569, pp. 124–134. Springer, Heidelberg (2007)
2. Biermann, P., Jung, B., Latoschik, M., Wachsmuth, I.: Virtuelle Werkstatt: A Platform for Multimodal Assembly in VR. In: Proceedings Fourth Virtual Reality International Conference (VRIC 2002), Laval, France, June 2002, pp. 53–62 (2002)
3. Marr, H., Nishihara, D.: Representation and recognition of the spatial organization of three-dimensional shapes. In: Proceedings of the Royal Society. B 200, pp. 269–294 (1978)
4. Sowa, T.: Towards the integration of shape-related information in 3-D gestures and speech. In: Proceedings of the Eighth International Conference on Multimodal Interfaces, pp. 92–99. ACM Press, New York (2006)
5. Sowa, T., Wachsmuth, I.: Interpretation of Shape-Related Iconic Gestures in Virtual Environments. In: Wachsmuth, I., Sowa, T. (eds.) GW 2001. LNCS (LNAI), vol. 2298, pp. 21–33. Springer, Heidelberg (2002)
6. Sowa, T., Wachsmuth, I.: Coverbal Iconic Gestures for Object Descriptions in Virtual Environments: An Empirical Study. In: Rector, M., Poggi, I., Trigo, N. (eds.) Proceedings of the Conference Gestures. Meaning and Use, Porto, Portugal, pp. 365–376. Edições Universidade Fernando Pessoa (2003)
7. Sparrell, C.J., Koons, D.B.: Interpretation of coverbal depictive gestures. In: AAAI Spring Symposium Series, March 1994, pp. 8–12. Stanford University (1994)

Analysis of Emotional Gestures for the Generation of Expressive Copying Behaviour in an Embodied Agent

Ginevra Castellano[1,2] and Maurizio Mancini[2,3]

[1] Department of Computer Science, Queen Mary,
University of London, UK
[2] InfoMus Lab, DIST - University of Genova
Viale Causa 13, I-16145, Genova, Italy
ginevra@dcs.qmul.ac.uk
[3] LINC, IUT de Montreuil, University of Paris8, France
maurizio@infomus.org

Abstract. This paper presents a system capable of acquiring input from a video camera, processing information related to the expressivity of human movement and generating expressive copying behaviour of an Embodied Agent. We model a bi-directional communication between user and agent based on real-time analysis of movement expressivity and generation of expressive copying behaviour: while the user is moving, the agent responds with a gesture that exhibits the same expressive characteristics. An evaluation study based on a perceptual experiment with participants showed the effectiveness of the designed interaction.

Keywords: gesture expressivity; emotion; embodied agent.

1 Introduction

In human-computer interaction the ability for systems to understand users' behaviour and to respond with appropriate feedback is an important requirement for generating an affective interaction [1]. Systems must be able to create a bi-directional communication with users: analysing their verbal and non-verbal behaviour to infer their emotional states and using this information to make decisions and/or plan an empathic response.

Virtual agent systems represent a powerful human-computer interface, as they can embody characteristics that a human may identify with [2]. The ability for virtual agents to display a social, affective behaviour may encourage users to engage in a natural interaction and establish bonds with them [3]. In this paper we focus on modelling a bi-directional communication between an embodied conversational agent and human users based on the non-verbal channel of the communication involving movement and gesture. Specifically, our research considers movement and gesture expressivity as a key element both in understanding and responding to users' behaviour.

We present a system capable of acquiring input from a video camera, processing information related to the expressivity of human movement and generating expressive copying behaviour in real-time. Our system has been formed by the integration of two different software platforms: EyesWeb [4] for video tracking and analysis of human

M. Sales Dias et al. (Eds.): GW 2007, LNAI 5085, pp. 193–198, 2009.

movement and the Greta embodied agent for behaviour generation [5]. In this context, we model a bi-directional communication between user and agent: for each gesture performed by the user, the agent responds with a gesture that exhibits the same expressive characteristics. We describe a mapping between the expressive cues analysed in human users and the corresponding expressive parameters of the agent. Moreover, movement expressivity is mapped onto emotions, which are used to select the type of gesture performed by the agent.

In the following sections we report some examples of related work and a description of the system. Finally, we provide an evaluation study based on a perceptual experiment with participants and show results and conclusions.

2   Related Work

Several systems have been proposed in the literature in which virtual agents provide visual feedback or response by analysing some characteristics of users' behaviour. In these systems the input data can be obtained from dedicated hardware (joysticks, hand gloves, etc), audio and video sources. SenToy [6] is a doll with sensors in the arms, legs and body. According to how users manipulate the doll, they can influence the emotions of characters in a virtual game. Kopp et al. [7] designed a virtual agent able to imitate natural gestures performed by humans using motion-tracked data. Reidsma and colleagues [8] designed a virtual rap dancer that invites users to join him in a dancing activity. In a previous study the Greta agent was animated off-line based on the motor behaviour of users extracted from visual data [9].

Previous works [10] introduced the notion of expressivity for virtual agents. The expressivity of the Greta agent is defined over a set of six dimensions, which qualitatively modify the gestures performed by the agent. For the purposes of the presented work, we only focus on four of these parameters: *Spatial Extent*, that changes the amplitude of movements (e.g., expanded versus contracted); *Temporal Extent*, that modifies the duration of movements (e.g., quick versus sustained actions); *Fluidity*, that determines the smoothness and continuity of movement (e.g., smooth, graceful versus sudden, jerky); and *Power*, that alters the dynamic properties of the movement (e.g., weak/relaxed versus strong/tense). In this paper we describe the first application on which the Greta agent responds to users' motor behaviour analysed in real-time.

3   Description of the System

In Figure 1 we present a system that allows for the real-time analysis of human movement and gesture expressivity and the generation of expressive copying behaviour in an agent. The system integrates two different platforms: EyesWeb [4] for video tracking and movement analysis and the Greta agent for behaviour generation [5]. We designed an application in which data is exchanged between these two components through a blackboard structure, implemented with Psyclone [11]. The system modules are connected to the same Psyclone blackboard via a TCP/IP socket. Further details about how the modules work are provided by the following Sections.

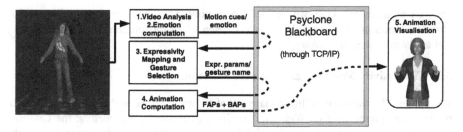

Fig. 1. Overview of the system architecture

3.1 Video Analysis

The automatic extraction of the expressive motion cues is done with EyesWeb [4] and the EyesWeb Expressive Gesture Processing Library. Based on previous studies on emotion and bodily expressions [12]:

- *Contraction Index* (CI) is a measure of the degree of contraction or expansion of the user's body. CI can be computed using a technique related to the bounding region, i.e., the minimum rectangle surrounding the body: the algorithm compares the area covered by this rectangle with the area currently covered by the silhouette.
- *Velocity* and *Acceleration* are computed on the trajectory of the user's left or right hand in the 2D plane of the video image provided as input to EyesWeb. We extract the 2D coordinates of the hand and we compute the module of velocity and acceleration.
- *Fluidity* is considered as a measure of the uniformity of motion, so that fluidity is maximal when, in the movement between two specific points in the space, the acceleration is equal to zero.

3.1.1 Time Window

The expressive motion cues extracted by EyesWeb in real-time are *continuous*: that is, we do not segment the user's movement by looking for example for the occurrence of a gesture or posture change. Instead, the output of our system is an agent that performs a sequence of *discrete* gestures, each of them with its own expressivity and shape. So, in order to use continuous values (the movement cues) to drive discrete events (the agent's gestures) we defined a *time window*, an interval of time at the end of which we send the computed motion cues from EyesWeb to the rest of the system.

The duration of the time window corresponds to the duration of a gesture performed by the agent. Inside the time window we continuously extract the motion cues from the user's movement, but we consider the following *local* indicators: the *maximum* for Velocity and Acceleration, the *minimum* of the Contraction and the *average* value of the Fluidity. At the end of the time window we send these indicators to the rest of the system.

3.2 Emotion Computation

After extracting expressive motion cues in real-time, the system associates them with one of the following emotion states: *anger, joy, sadness*. Based on previous studies on emotion expressivity [12] we defined correspondences between expressive motion cues and emotions: for example anger is chosen when movements are expanded, very fast and accelerates, and so on.

3.3 Expressivity Mapping and Gesture Selection

We defined the one-to-one linear mapping of Figure 2 between the motion cues automatically extracted by EyesWeb and the Greta expressivity parameters: the *Contraction Index* is mapped onto the *Spatial Extent*, since they provide a measure on the amplitude of movements; the *Velocity* onto the *Temporal Extent*, as they refer to the velocity of movements; the *Acceleration* onto the *Power*, as both are indicators of the acceleration of the movements; the *Fluidity* onto the *Fluidity*, as they refer to the degree of the smoothness of movements.

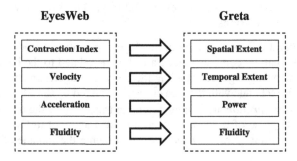

Fig. 2. One-to-one mapping between EyesWeb motion cues and Greta expressivity parameters

Moreover, we select of the gesture to be performed by the agent depending on the emotion determined by our system, as explained in 3.2. If *anger* is detected, the agent performs a deictic gesture; if the detected emotion is *joy*, the agent performs a gesture by opening its arms; if the user's expresses *sadness*, the agent raises and lowers its arms.

3.4 Animation Computation and Animation Visualization

These modules receive the expressivity parameters and the information about the gesture to be performed from the blackboard and compute the animation data needed to animate the agent. Then the Greta graphical engine, given the animation data in input, creates a graphical representation of the virtual agent.

4 Evaluation

In order to evaluate the mapping between the expressive motion cues extracted with EyesWeb and the Greta expressivity parameters, we performed an evaluation study. We selected a set of videos from the GEMEP corpus of acted emotional expressions [13] and we provided these videos as input to our system. More specifically, we focused on six videos of the corpus, with three different emotions (anger, joy, sadness) expressed by two different actors, observed by a frontal camera. For each video provided as input we recorded the video synthesized by our system. That is, we obtained videos in which the Greta agent performs emotion-specific gestures (see the end of Section 3.3) by modulating expressivity. We performed a perceptual experiment to verify how participants perceived the emotions communicated by the agent. Both the actors and the generated videos were modified so as to hide the face of the actor/agent in order not to influence the participants' perception of emotions by the facial expression of the actor/agent.

4.1 Perceptual Experiment

Twelve students and researchers in computer science and computer engineering (8 male and 4 female, from 26 to 38 years old, average age: 31.4) participated in the experiment. Twelve videos were evaluated by each participant: the six videos of the real actors and the six videos of Greta. Participants were asked to observe the actor/agent movements and to choose an emotional label (anger, joy or sadness) using a slider: each emotion could be rated from a minimum of 0 to a maximum of 10. Participants were allowed to watch each video as many times as they wanted and to select and rate all the emotions they wanted. Table 1 shows the recognition rates of each emotion. Results show that emotions expressed by the actors are always recognized with a high percentage, except joy, which is confused with anger. As far as it concerns the gestures performed by the Greta agent, emotion recognition rates are high for sadness (70.8%) and reach the 83.37% for anger and joy.

Table 1. From left to right: recognition rates for anger, joy and sadness when gestures are performed by actors and by Greta

	Recognition rates for ANGER		Recognition rates for JOY		Recognition rates for SADNESS	
	Actors	Greta	Actors	Greta	Actors	Greta
Anger	**95.8%**	**83.3%**	**58.3%**	8.3%	20.8%	20.8%
Joy	0%	16.7%	33.3%	**83.3%**	4.2%	8.3%
Sadness	4.2%	0%	8.3%	8.3%	**70.8%**	**70.8%**
None	0%	0%	0%	0%	4.2%	0%

5 Conclusion

In this paper we modelled a bi-directional communication between human users and an agent based on movement and gesture. We designed a system capable of processing information related to the expressivity of the user's movement, associating an emotion with the expressivity communicated by it and generating the agent's expressive behaviour in real-time. This system represents a first step towards the design of an empathic agent. Movement expressivity can increase the effectiveness of the affective interaction between user and agent by generating an affective loop: it can be used to recognize the user's emotions and to increase the user's sense of engagement when the agent generates a copying behaviour. The evaluation study showed the effectiveness of the designed interaction between user and agent, demonstrating that the analysis and synthesis processes were successful, as well as the choice of the indicators of movement expressivity to communicate emotions.

Acknowledgements. This research was supported by the EU-IST Project HUMAINE (Human-Machine Interaction Network on Emotion) (IST-2002-507422). We thank Tanja Bänziger and Klaus Scherer for the concession of videos of the GEMEP corpus.

References

1. Picard, R.W.: Affective Computing. MIT Press, Cambridge (1997)
2. Reeves, B., Nass, C.: The media equation: How people treat computers, television and new media like real people and places. CLSI Publications, Stanford (1996)
3. Gratch, J., Wang, N., Gerten, J., Fast, E., Duffy, R.: Creating Rapport with Virtual Agents. In: Pelachaud, C., Martin, J.-C., André, E., Chollet, G., Karpouzis, K., Pelé, D. (eds.) IVA 2007. LNCS, vol. 4722, pp. 125–138. Springer, Heidelberg (2007)
4. Camurri, A., Coletta, P., Massari, A., Mazzarino, B., Peri, M., Ricchetti, M., Ricci, A., Volpe, G.: Toward real-time multimodal processing: EyesWeb 4.0. In: Proc. AISB 2004 Convention: Motion, Emotion and Cognition, Leeds, UK (March 2004)
5. Pelachaud, C.: Multimodal expressive embodied conversational agents. In: MULTIMEDIA 2005: Proceedings of the 13th annual ACM international conference on Multimedia, pp. 683–689. ACM Press, New York (2005)
6. Paiva, A., Chaves, R., Piedade, M., Bullock, A., Andersson, G., Höök, K.: Sentoy: a tangible interface to control the emotions of a synthetic character. In: AAMAS 2003: Proceedings of the second international joint conference on Autonomous agents and multiagent systems, pp. 1088–1089. ACM Press, New York (2003)
7. Kopp, S., Sowa, T., Wachsmuth, I.: Imitation games with an artificial agent: From mimicking to understanding shape- related iconic gestures. In: Camurri, A., Volpe, G. (eds.) GW 2003. LNCS, vol. 2915, pp. 436–447. Springer, Heidelberg (2004)
8. Reidsma, D., Nijholt, A., Poppe, R.W., Rienks, R.J., Hondorp, G.H.W.: Virtual Rap Dancer: Invitation to Dance. In: Olson, G., Jeffries, R. (eds.) CHI 2006, Conference on Human Factors in Computing Systems, Montréal, Québec, Canada, April 25, 2006, pp. 263–266. ACM, New York (2006)
9. Mancini, M., Castellano, G., Bevacqua, E., Peters, C.: Copying behaviour of espressive motion. In: Proc. of the the Mirage Conference (2007)
10. Hartmann, B., Mancini, M., Pelachaud, C.: Implementing expressive gesture synthesis for embodied conversational agents. In: Gibet, S., Courty, N., Kamp, J.-F. (eds.) GW 2005. LNCS, vol. 3881, pp. 188–199. Springer, Heidelberg (2006)
11. Thórisson, K.R., List, T., Pennock, C., DiPirro, J.: Whiteboards: Scheduling Blackboards for Interactive Robots. In: The AAAI 2005 Workshop On Modular Construction of Human-Like Intelligence, AAAI 2005, Pittsburgh, PA, July 9-13 (2005)
12. Wallbott, H.G.: Bodily expression of emotion. European Journal of Social Psychology 28, 879–896 (1998)
13. Bänziger, T., Pirker, H., Scherer, K.: GEMEP – GEneva Multimodal Emotion Portrayals: A corpus for the study of multimodal emotional expressions. In: 5th International Conference on Language Resources and Evaluation (LREC 2006), Genova, Italy (2006)

Gestures to Intuitively Control Large Displays

Wim Fikkert[1], Paul van der Vet[1], Han Rauwerda[2],
Timo Breit[2], and Anton Nijholt[1]

[1,*]Human Media Interaction, University of Twente, The Netherlands
{f.w.fikkert,p.e.vandervet,a.nijholt}@ewi.utwente.nl
[2] Microarray Department, University of Amsterdam, The Netherlands
{j.rauwerda,t.m.breit}@uva.nl

Abstract. Large displays are highly suited to support discussions in empirical science. Such displays can display project results on a large digital surface to feed the discussion. This paper describes our approach to closely involve multidisciplinary omics scientists in the design of an intuitive display control through hand gestures. This interface is based upon a gesture repertoire. This paper describes how this repertoire is designed based on observations of, and scripted task experiments with, omics scientists.

1 Introduction

A large display is highly suited to support discussions. Such a large digital surface is a valuable resource that can display various pieces of information to feed the discussion. Especially discussions that involve numerous complex visualizations can benefit from such a resource, for example, in empirical science.

Controlling such a large display with a mouse and keyboard is tedious at best. Hand gestures are a powerful means to control the a large display directly. However, display control through hand gestures is not obvious by itself because the large display is an altogether new resource in the discussion. A gesture repertoire is needed that discussants can both understand intuitively and learn easily. We aim to design such a gesture repertoire to control a large display directly through touch and free-handed gesturing. Our gesture repertoire will consist of (using gesture types as defined by Kipp [1]): *deictics* to point to display contents, *iconics* to directly refer to display contents and *beats* to indicate something important. We focus on gestures that are meant to directly control the display; by addressing it explicitly. The goal of this work is to design such a repertoire in close collaboration with its intended users: empirical scientists.

This paper is structured as follows. In Section 2 we introduce omics research as our use case. Section 3 then describes three consecutive experiments in which the gesture repertoire is designed with close involvement of the end-users. Our preliminary results are reported in Section 4. Section 5 discusses the extent to which this repertoire can be applied in other fields.

---

* We thank our reviewers for their input. This work is part of the BioRange program carried out by the Netherlands Bioinformatics Centre (NBIC), which is supported by a BSIK grant through the Netherlands Genomics Initiative (NGI).

M. Sales Dias et al. (Eds.): GW 2007, LNAI 5085, pp. 199–204, 2009.

2 Use Case: Omics

A use case in empirical science is highly suited for our study due to complex problems, processes and results. Moreover, diverse expertise is needed to address these problems. Omics is an empirical science in which multidisciplinary research teams address complex biological problems, for example, improving medicines for breast cancer based on genetic expressions in a patient. 'Omics' is a suffix that is commonly attached to biological research into the 'whole' make-up of an organism on a certain biological level, for example, proteomics on the protein level, and by which huge datasets are produced. An example topic—microarrays—easily generates hunderds of scans that can each contain information about more than 50.000 transcripts. Hence millions of separate measurements have to be analysed. The expertise from all involved disciplines is needed when biological meaning is sought in the experiments' results. Interviews with these researchers indicated that 'strange' results that stand out in the whole can be identified based purely on the result overview. This then leads to a closer analysis.

Fig. 1. The large display in use as a discussion resource

Facilities that support multidisciplinary teams in validating and analysing project results are found in so called dry labs. Such facilities mainly consist of a large amount of computing power and multiple (large) displays. One such dry lab, the e-BioLab, is being developed at the University of Amsterdam [2]. One aim of the e-BioLab is to enrich omics meetings with more on-demand information to improve their efficiency. Our efforts in the design of a gesture repertoire are aimed at the large display in the e-BioLab, see Figure 1. In the e-BioLab, we can observe and get involved with scientific discussions that are supported by the large display.

3 Designing the Gesture Repertoire

Large displays have great potential as a discussion resource in face-to-face cooperation. However, such displays are a new phenomenon in discussions; therefore, interacting with them will be a novelty for the participants. An interaction scheme should be designed with close involvement of our end-users. By studying the behaviour of omics researchers in discussions, an understanding is gained that helps to characterise a gesture repertoire that is tuned to them. We propose three consecutive user studies that gradually build up this repertoire: 1) observing display control in omics research meetings, 2) verifying behaviour cue interpretation through scripted sessions with users and 3) implementing the gesture repertoire in an automated recognition system.

3.1   Experiment 1: Observations in the *e*-BioLab

In the first experiment, we observe discussants using the large display as a discussion resource. The discussions are recorded by four video cameras in addition to the display contents. We then annotate these recordings, focusing on hand gesturing. We aim to identify the minimum information needed for an automated computer vision based system to recognize and interpret these gestures. The following highlights some decisions in our approach.

Recordings in our corpus are reduced to scenes where a discussion between two or more discussants are within arms-length of the display. Gill [3] defines three interaction zones: reflection, negotiation and action. These zones are based on activities in a discussion with a large display resource. Fikkert et al. [4] defined these zones based on the physical distance to the screen: hand-held (action), at arms-length (negotiation) and distal (reflection). The nature of these zones excludes reflection from our annotations, focusing on 'active' discussions where discussants react to and interact with the display contents. Discussions in three distinct projects are recorded. We focus on discussions that address the validation and analysis of project results.

Differences in the gestures that are made by users with varying background will mostly be mitigated by the fact that a single chairman heads all of the meetings in the *e*-BioLab. He demonstrates the capabilities of the large display as a discussion resource. We have observed that discussants pick up on these possibilities easily.

Annotations of our recordings consist of transcriptions of person identified speech, body posture, location, gaze direction and hand gestures. We use the Nite XML Toolkit (NXT) [5]. NXT provides annotation tracks in which each modality can be transcribed completely separately and can be synchronised to a common timeline. As such, we are not restricted by a schema that, for example, arrays gestures parallel to speech.

Transcription of hand gesturing requires a notation for written sign language. HamNoSys transcribes body posture, gaze direction and both hand shapes and movements [6]. Languages designed for behaviour synthesis such as MURML [7] and BML [8] do not offer the abstraction capabilities that HamNoSys does. We have used SiGML which is based upon the XML and HamNoSys standards [9]. SiGML can describe scenes on multiple levels: phonology, phonetics and physical articulation. Its XML structure also allows easy incorporation into NXT.

Deictics includes a target on the display. This target is found using both the display's snapshots and speech annotation [10]. Krandstedt, Kühnlein and

Wachsmuth [7] used a pointing game to study the co-occurence of speech and pointing. They found that pointing to objects within arms-length was disambiguated through simultaneously occurring speech. We transcribed speech with a focus on specific deictic keywords such as: 'this', 'your' and 'it'. These keywords are linked explicitly to gesturing [7,10]. Both body posture and gaze direction are included in the hand gesturing annotations [1]. User location and orientation are found and indicated on a map of the e-BioLab using the 4 camera views.

To further classify behaviour, we annotate interaction context and tasks orthogonally based on time occurrences. We distinguish distinct phases in the omics research process: data interpretation, cleaning and quality control. This distinction is based on a previous task analysis in the e-BioLab [11].

(Semi-) automated annotation is currently being studied to enrich and speed up the tedious, slow annotation process. Consider computer vision algorithms that (partially) extract body postures or hand positions [12].

Analysis of our annotations aims to identify gestures that the scientists typically make when performing a certain task. Gestures are linked to the orthogonal framework of interaction tasks and context based on their occurrence in time. The difference between the gestures is determined by defining a distance measure, for example, based on the motions and shape of the hands. An unsupervised learning algorithm might be capable of deriving these.

3.2   Experiment 2: Scripted User Sessions

The gestures and their interpretation for controlling the display that were found in the previous experiment are verified here. We ask our end-users to complete a scripted task. These scripted tasks are rooted both in the first experiment and in the task analysis [11]. We examine settings that include one and two users. In the latter case, the users are given roles that suit their experiences.

During this experiment, an operator is in actual control of the system. He has a list of action-reaction cases that was defined in our first experiment. Gestures on this list are described using the annotation scheme from the first experiment. Whenever a participant tries an action that is not on this list, no system response follows which may be confusing to the participant. He then either tries a different action to complete his goal, for example, using a different gesture, or—after some idle time—he is asked explicitly by the operator what his intention is.

These sessions are both recorded and annotated in the same manner as in the first experiment. We aim to verify our basic repertoire by comparing the gesture occurrence and type in similar interaction tasks and context. At this stage, we can add new gestures to, and adjust existing gestures in our repertoire. Interviews with our end-users result give us an appreciation of this new way of large display control.

3.3   Experiment 3: Automated System

This experiment introduces an automated behaviour detection, recognition and tracking system. The operator's interpretation of a scene may have influenced the second experiment slightly and it has been removed here. Such an automated system consolidates the gesture repertoire because it cannot profit from human – operator – interpretation of scenes. The aim of this experiment is to polish all previous findings and to arrive at a robust, stable system. Such a system is ideally based on unobtrusive sensing using, for example, computer vision analysis.

A somewhat unobtrusive solution for human behaviour analysis is the best that can be expected in the coming years given the current state of the art in this field [12]. Therefore, we are currently exploring the use of data gloves and a motion capturing system that provide highly accurate behaviour measurements. In the literature it is often argued that obtrusive solutions impose restrictions that influence user behaviour. The extent of this influence, in this setting, remains to be determined.

The result of this last experiment will have confirmed our gesture repertoire. The repertoire will then define the interpretation of gestures in a rule-based manner so that it can be incorporated in an automated system for display control. It can possibly linked to other modalities as well [12].

4   Preliminary Results

Currently, our first experiment is ongoing and we are engaged in our second experiment. Some observations that support and encourage our approach are worth mentioning here. From the start of a meeting, users intuitively move between reflection, negotiation and actions zones as identified by [3]. The reflection zone is used roughly half of the time. Our scientists use the large display actively as a resource in their discussions. When asked, these omics researchers find this resource an 'indispensable' asset in their discussions. The fact that other life science groups as well as academic hospitals are building their own e-BioLabs supports this opinion. However, our end-users repeatedly indicated that a direct and easy means of controlling the display is needed.

Figure 1 shows end-users using the large display as a discussion resource. Scientists point to pieces of data. They correlate various results that are simultaneously depicted on the display by sequentially 'grasping' and walking up to these results whilst arguing their case. Users typically select an object by pointing towards it and then grabbing it. The grabbing gesture varies per user; some use their whole hand, others just linger on the target for a short amount of time. Repositioning an object is done by dragging it to its new location in all cases. Enlarging or shrinking a target does differ to a significant extent; some users use just one hand close to the display by moving their fingers apart, others use their whole arms at arms-length and yet other users grab an object in one hand and resize it by moving their other hand as a virtual slidebar.

5   Discussion

We have described a method to arrive at a gesture repertoire for large display control. Even without the third experiment, we will have constructed a gesture repertoire that omics researchers can use to operate a large display. Porting our gesture repertoire to other user communities will require further investigation. It seems plausible that, due to the nature of scientific work, this repertoire can be ported to other empirical scientific disciplines. However, generalisation to other user groups may be less easy. Empirical scientists carry out tasks that are highly constrained by both their task environment and their explorative research approach.

References

1. Kipp, M.: Gesture Generation by Imitation - From Human Behavior to Computer Character Animation. PhD thesis, Saarland University, Saarbruecken, Germany, Boca Raton, Florida (2004)
2. Rauwerda, H., Roos, M., Hertzberger, B., Breit, T.: The promise of a virtual lab in drug discovery. Drug Discovery Today 11, 228–236 (2006)
3. Gill, S., Borchers, J.: Knowledge in co-action: social intelligence in collaborative design activity. AI and Society 17(3), 322–339 (2003)
4. Fikkert, W., D'Ambros, M., Bierz, T., Jankun-Kelly, T.: Interacting with visualizations. In: Kerren, A., Ebert, A., Meyer, J. (eds.) GI-Dagstuhl Research Seminar 2007. LNCS, vol. 4417, pp. 77–162. Springer, Heidelberg (2007)
5. Carletta, J., Evert, S., Heid, U., Kilgour, J., Robertson, J., Voormann, H.: The NITE XML toolkit: Flexible annotation for multimodal language data. Behavior Research Methods, Instruments, and Computers 35(3), 353–363 (2003)
6. Prillwitz, S., Leven, R., Zienert, H., Hanke, T., Henning, J.: Hamburg Notation System for Sign Languages - An introductory guide, vol. 5. Signum, Hamburg (1989)
7. Kranstedt, A., Kühnlein, P., Wachsmuth, I.: Deixis in multimodal Human Computer Interaction: An interdisciplinary approach. In: Camurri, A., Volpe, G. (eds.) GW 2003. LNCS, vol. 2915, pp. 112–123. Springer, Heidelberg (2004)
8. Vilhjálmsson, H., Cantelmo, N., Cassell, J., Chafai, N., Kipp, M., Kopp, S., Mancini, M., Marsella, S., Marshall, A., Pelachaud, C., Ruttkay, Z., Thórisson, K., van Welbergen, H., van der Werf, R.: The behavior markup language: Recent developments and challenges (2007)
9. Elliott, R., Glauert, J., Kennaway, R., Parsons, K.: Sigml definition. Technical Report ViSiCAST Deliverable D5-2, University of East Anglia (2001)
10. Kranstedt, A., Lücking, A., Pfeiffer, T., Rieser, H., Wachsmuth, I.: Deixis: How to determine demonstrated objects using a pointing cone. In: Gibet, S., Courty, N., Kamp, J.-F. (eds.) GW 2005. LNCS, vol. 3881, pp. 300–311. Springer, Heidelberg (2006)
11. Kulyk, O., Wassink, I.: Getting to know bioinformaticians: Results of an exploratory user study. In: Workshop on Combining Visualisation and Interaction to Facilitate Scientific Exploration and Discovery in conjunction with British HCI 2006, pp. 30–38. ACM Press, New York (2006)
12. Pantic, M., Pentland, A., Nijholt, A., Huang, T.: Human computing and machine understanding of human behavior: A survey. In: ICMI 2006: Proceedings of the 8th international conference on Multimodal interfaces, vol. 8, pp. 239–248. ACM Press, New York (2006)

Geometry and Effort in Gestural Renderings of Musical Sound

Rolf Inge Godøy

Department of Musicology, University of Oslo, P.B. 1017 Blindern,
N-0315 Oslo, Norway
r.i.godoy@imv.uio.no

Abstract. As may be seen at concerts and in various everyday listening situations, people often make spontaneous gestures when listening to music. We believe these gestures are interesting to study because they may reveal important
features of musical experience. In particular, hand movements may give us information on what features are perceived as salient by listeners. Based on various current ideas on embodied cognition, the aim of this paper is to argue that
gestures are integral to music perception, and to present research in support of
this. A conceptual model of separating geometry and effort is presented in order
to better understand the variety of music-related gestures we may observe, leading up to some ideas on how to apply this conceptual model in present and future research.

Keywords: Music, perception, gestures, geometry, effort, perception-action,
key-postures, movement.

1 Introduction

In our research on music-related gestures [1] we have had a particular focus on the
spontaneous gestures that listeners make to musical sound. This has been motivated
by the belief that perception and cognition of musical sound is intimately linked with
mental images of movement, and that a process of incessant motor imagery is running
in parallel with listening to, or even just imagining, musical sound. We have called
this *motormimetic cognition* of musical sound [2], and see evidence for this in a number of research findings as well as in our own observation studies. Furthermore, we
believe *hand movements* have a privileged role in motormimetic cognition of musical
sound, and that these hand movements may trace the *geometry* (i.e. elements such as
pitch contours, pitch spread, rhythmical patterns, textures, and even timbral features),
as well as convey sensations of *effort*, of musical sound, hence the focus in this paper
on *geometry and effort in the gestural renderings of musical sound*.

There are many different gestures that may be associated with music (see [3] and
[4] for overviews). Using the Gibsonian concept of *affordance* [5], we can thus speak
of rich *gestural affordances* of musical sound. For practical purposes we can in this
paper think of two main categories of music-related gestures, namely *sound-
producing* gestures (such as hitting, stoking, bowing, etc.) and *sound-accompanying*

M. Sales Dias et al. (Eds.): GW 2007, LNAI 5085, pp. 205–215, 2009.

gestures (such as dancing, marching, or making various movements to the music), as well as several sub-categories of these. The distinction between these two main categories as well as their sub-categories may not always be so clear, e.g. musicians may make gestures in performance that are probably not strictly necessary for producing sound, but may be useful for reasons of motor control or physiological comfort, or may have communicative functions towards other musicians or the audience.

In order to know more about gestural renderings of musical sounds by listeners, we have carried out a series of observation studies where we have asked listeners with different levels of musical training to make spontaneous hand movements to musical excerpts. In these studies we have proceeded from giving the listeners rather well defined tasks with limited gestural affordances onto progressively more open tasks with quite rich gestural affordances. This was done by proceeding from studies of *air-instrument performances* where listeners were asked to make sound-producing movements [6], onto what we have called *sound-tracing* studies where listeners were asked to draw (on a digital tablet) the gestures they spontaneously associated with the musical excerpts and where the musical excerpts were quite restricted as to their number of salient features [7], and finally onto what we have called *free dance gestures* with more complex, multi-feature musical excerpts and rather general instructions to listeners about making spontaneous gestural renderings based on what they perceived as the most salient features of the musical excerpts [8].

The idea of gestural rendering of musical sound is based on a large body of research ranging from classical motor theory of perception [9] to more recent theories of motor involvement in perception in general [10], and more specifically in audio perception [11], as well as in music-related tasks in particular [12], research that converge in an understanding of motor cognition as integral to most areas of perception and cognition.

Obviously, auditory-motor couplings as well as the capacity to render and/or imitate sound is not restricted to hand movements, as is evident from vocal imitation of both non-musical and musical sound (e.g. so-called *beat-boxing* in hip-hop and other music and *scat singing* in jazz). But the focus on hand movements in our case is based not only on innumerable informal observations of listeners making hand movements to musical sound, but also on the belief that hand movements have a privileged role from an evolutionary point of view [13] and from a general gesture-cognitive point of view [14]. Furthermore, we believe that a listener through a process of translation by the principle of *motor equivalence* [15] may switch from one set of effectors to another, translating various sound features to gestures and hence revealing more amodal gestural images of musical sound.

It seems quite clear that even novices can make gestures that reflect reasonably well what is going on in the music when asked to imitate sound-producing actions, although experts tend to make more detailed renderings as reported in [6]. Also when listeners were asked to draw gestures they felt reflected the musical excerpt they heard, i.e. in what we have called *sound-tracing* studies, there was reasonable agreements as long as the excerpts did not have more than one or two prominent features, e.g. an ascending pitch contour or an ascending pitch contour combined with various ornamental ripples, and greater disagreement when the number of concurrent prominent features was increased, e.g. excerpts with several concurrent textural elements [7]. A subsequent so-called interrater study (i.e. a study of agreement/disagreement in judgment) of the resultant sound-tracings seems to have confirmed these agreements and/or disagreements [16]. In the case of 3-dimensional bi-manual movements to sounds, i.e. *free dance gestures*, we got even more varied results, something that we would expect given the greater choice of movement trajectories and feature focus [8, 16].

Rather than despair because of these increasingly divergent and also often rather approximate gestural renderings of musical sound, we shall in the following see how the elements of geometry and effort may be understood as intrinsic to the *perception-action cycle* spontaneously at work in musical experience, and furthermore try to see how gestural renderings of musical sound may be understood as a means for intentional focus in listening, and may even be put to active use in the exploration of musical sound.

It is generally accepted that music is a multidimensional phenomenon in the sense that music has elements such as rhythm, tempo, intensity (often referred to as dynamics), pitch, melody, accompaniment, harmony, timbre, texture, etc., and that these elements in turn may be differentiated into a number of sub-elements. This is one of the reasons for the abovementioned rich gestural affordances of musical sound, as listeners may attend to, and gesturally render, any single or any selection of such musical elements. Also, elements that from a music theory perspective may be thought of as separate, may be fused in actual perception, such as in the well known interdependence of perceived intensity and timbre. This dimensional fusion may even extend to dimensions that 'are not really there', i.e. we may see what the authors of [17] have termed a 'spill over' effect, e.g. that a *crescendo* may also be perceived as an *accelerando* by some listeners even though the tempo was constant.

Although the elements of geometry and effort are inseparable in the sense that we can not have images of geometry (e.g. pitch change, timbre change, etc.) without some image of movement and hence of effort, and conversely, can hardly have images of effort in music without images of movement in space and hence of geometry, it is strategically convenient to separate these elements here in order to be able to better differentiate what features listeners focus on in various gestural renderings of musical sound, as well as to be able to appreciate the sometimes seemingly divergent gestural renderings of musical sound that we may observe: Music is complex and multi-faceted and listeners' attention to features will often vary, so it goes without saying that we may observe seemingly divergent gestural renderings, and our task here is to try to summarize which features are most commonly shared by listeners and which features seem to be more variably rendered by listeners.

It should also be noted that we have initially had a qualitative approach in our studies of gestural renderings of musical sound, meaning that we have proceeded in a top-down manner from overall features to progressively finer sub-features, when analyzing our video material. However, we have also used various sensor technologies and software tools in our studies, as for instance may be seen in figures 1 to 3. Currently we are using a multi-sensor setup for motion capture together with a multi-stream data storage and retrieval scheme for this motion capture data [18], something

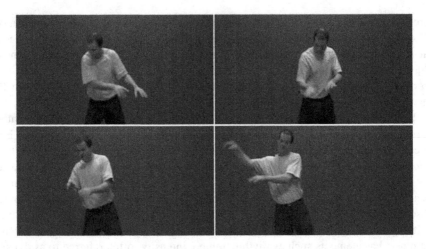

Fig. 1. Air-piano rendering of the opening of Scriabin's *5th Piano Sonata*, here with four key-frames running left to right, top to bottom

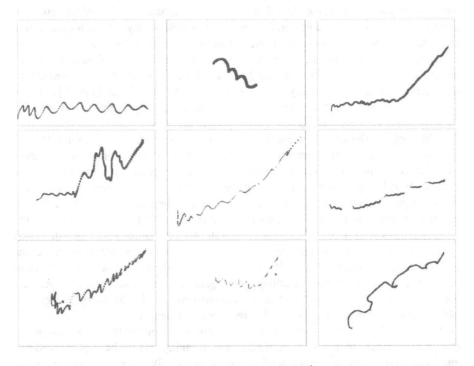

Fig. 2. Sound-tracing renderings of the opening of Scriabin's *5th Piano Sonata* by nine different subjects, time running from left to right in all tracings. Notice that with the exception of the left and middle rendering of the first row, there seems to be more or less agreement about the pitch contour.

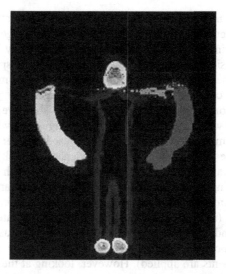

Fig. 3. Gestural rendering of five seconds of sustained sound at the opening of the Lento movement of Ligeti's *Ten Pieces for Wind Quintet*. The dancer makes a slow upward gesture with the arms, starting from arms aligned with the hips and ending up with the arms stretched out horizontally.

we believe in the future will give us more detail data on the various features in gestural renderings of musical sound. But as a point of method, we believe that we regardless technologies will need to have a conceptual apparatus for understanding what we are observing, something I shall try to present in the following sections of this paper.

2 Geometry

Musical sound seems to be a good transducer of various features related to the geometric layout of musical instruments, i.e. of real-world 3-D Euclidian space, such as the left-to-right, low-to-high pitch layout of the piano, or such as the spatial layout of drums. Notions of geometry for pitch-space or for relative-approximate pitch (in the case of non-tuned instruments) are probably learned, and to what extent this left-to-right scheme for pitch ordering is valid across different cultures is uncertain (see [17] for a discussion). In the case of air-piano playing, the gestural renderings seem to reflect quite well not only the pitch space of melodic movement on the piano, but also the relative position and spread of pitches, i.e. deep tones were rendered to the left, high pitches to the right, dense textures with both hands close together, and spread textures with hands spread out across the imaginary keyboard. An example of this may be seen in figure 1 where the subject is giving a gestural rendering of the opening passage of Scriabin's 5th *Piano Sonata* where there is a rapid and rather loud passage running from deep tones up to high tones, and where the texture is quite dense throughout the passage (see [6] for details on the setup and method of this study). The same musical excerpt may be seen rendered in a sound-tracing study in figure 2 where we can see a similar rendering of the pitch profile of this passage (see [7] for details).

In the subsequent interrater study of our sound-tracing study [16], 20 subjects with different levels of musical training were asked to rate the correspondences between 18 of the sounds and their respective sound-tracing images from the original sound-tracing study (which consisted of 50 sounds and images [7]) according to a forced choice task of match or mismatch. The subjects in this study were presented with displays of the nine drawings of the sounds (like in figure 2) while the sounds were played back, and the method of forced choice was used in order to collect the spontaneous reactions of the subjects to the correspondences (or lack thereof) between the sounds and the gestural trajectories. The nine drawings of each of these sounds were then arranged according to these match-mismatch judgments, and also the judgments of all the subjects were pairwise compared in order to see agreements/disagreements between the subjects (see [16] for details on this). Briefly stated, the overall agreement for all the sounds-images and subjects in this study was not very strong, although seems to be above chance (but this is open to discussion as to what criteria for above chance agreements are applied). However, looking at the results for individual sounds and their respective tracings, there seems to be some clear tendencies:

Pitch contours are generally more agreed on than single pitches, i.e. pitch-wise stationary, but otherwise (timbrally, dynamically) evolving sounds are not well agreed on. For instance, the sound of a single piano tone was by some of the original sound tracers variously rendered as a straight horizontal line, as a curve (perhaps alluding to the envelope of the tone) or as a single point (perhaps alluding to the singular impact of the finger on the key). Compared with this, a sequence of several piano tones (as in figure 2) resulted in a much higher degree of agreement. In a different study [19], there seems to be a similar agreement on the perception of pitch contours as long as they are fairly simple, i.e. as long as they do not have more than one or very few directions in their contours.

But also other musical elements such as intensity and timbral changes may be conceived as geometric features, something that partly seems to be reflected in the match-mismatch study [16]. Although we may assume that listeners have some experiences of physiological links with intensity and/or timbral changes, as in the case of a *crescendo* with increased amplitude in the hand movements, or in the case of timbral changes related to experiences of changing shape of the vocal tract, or experiences of seeing musicians move mutes, change bow positions, etc., the sound-tracing renderings of these intensity and/or timbral evolutions seem to vary a good deal more than those of pitch contours [7]. In the subsequent interrater study [16], the subjects seemed to agree more on tracings that depicted some kind of envelope or motion than on tracings that only suggested one attack point of the sounds, as in the case of a single cymbal sound or a single trumpet sound. This variety in the sound-tracings of timbral evolutions of sounds can probably be understood as a result of the limitations of a 2D rendering on the digital tablet, i.e. several participants in the original sound-tracing study expressed frustration at being asked to draw timbral evolutions of sounds on a flat surface [7], hence, this could be seen as a source of error both in the original sound-tracing and in the subsequent interrater study.

From all our studies, we believe we may conclude that the geometry of positions, spread, and trajectories in pitch-space is well rendered by hand movements, including elements such as pitch-contours and textural elements, although we may see differences in detail, or in what we could call frequential resolution of the gestures. Gestural renderings of musical excerpts with clearer textural-timbral fluctuations, such as the 'grainy' quality of iterative sounds, suggests that also 'micro features' of sounds are reflected in the gestures, something that has useful applications in sound research [20].

Naturally, with increasing richness of features, e.g. with musical excerpts with more composite textures, there was also increasing diversity in the geometry of the gestural renderings of the musical excerpts, something that we would understand as differences in focus of listening. However, in several detailed annotation analyses of our free dance studies in [16], it seems quite clear that we rarely found gestural renderings that did not at all correspond with some features or salient events in the music. In particular, there seemed in these free dance studies to be good agreements in the gestural renderings at the level of chunks, meaning the geometry of both the overall melodic and overall textural shape.

3 Effort

Musical sound also seems to be a good transducer of the overall activation level in sound-producing gestures: The density, speed, and force of events are well rendered, e.g. rapid passages are rapidly rendered, loud events are rendered by high amplitude gestures, etc., as evident both from quantity of motion estimations and detailed annotations. This seemed to be the case in all our observation studies [6, 7, 8, 16], and although we could see individual variations in the activation levels, we could not see gestural renderings that were clearly contradictory to the overall nature of the music, e.g. we could not see agitated movements to calm music, or calm movements to agitated music.

Furthermore, there seemed to be a fairly good discrimination between sounds with different types of excitatory actions, actions that we believe are based on biomechanical and neurocognitive constraints, and which we have classified as follows:

- *Sustained*, meaning protracted sounds requiring continuous excitatory effort such as in bowing or blowing. But whereas there is a more or less direct rendering of the events in the case of short, distinct sounds and rapid passages, for sustained sounds there was a tendency to 'fill in', i.e. to make long, slow, and curved gestures. This may be seen in figure 3 where the dancer makes a slow upward gesture with both hands to the sustained sound of the opening of the Lento movement of Ligeti's *Ten Pieces for Wind Quintet*. The sustained sound does not change in pitch or loudness so as to suggest an upward gesture, yet its sustained character does suggest a continuous movement, and we could very well imagine different directions of such continuous movement to this particular excerpt without any one of them being perceived as in conflict with the effort character of the music.
- *Impulsive*, meaning percussive or other discontinuously excited sounds, also including rapidly rendered groups of tones such as in short glissandi or ornaments.
- *Iterative*, meaning rapid repetition of onsets as well as rapid modulatory movements, e.g. rapid vibrato or tremolo.

These sound types and their associated modes of excitations are quite distinct, requiring quite distinct types of effort and attention. The sustained and impulsive actions seem to be mutually exclusive, but iterative actions may have elements of both sustained and impulsive actions, e.g. in the playing of washboard, maracas, and even drum rolls where the stream of individual strokes is so fast as to require effort quite distinct from singular drum strokes. It seems that we may observe so-called *phase-transitions* between singular impulsive actions and iterative actions, as in the case of the drum roll: With increasing speed there is a transition from singular to iterative actions, and conversely, with decreasing speed there is a transition from iterative to singular actions. Notably, this is valid for other tone repetitions as well, e.g. a rapid rush of tones on any instrument may be perceived as an iterative sound, but slowed down below a certain threshold, the tones may be perceived as sustained.

Furthermore, we may see multiple frequencies simultaneously at work in the gestural rendering of musical sound, e.g. see the combination of high-frequency finger movement with low-frequency hand/arm movement in the rendering of rapid passages of piano music. This subsumption of movements into more superordinate movements (e.g. finger movements as sub-movements of the hand/arm movements) can be understood as *coarticulation*. In coarticulation, the focus is typically shifted to a more superordinate trajectory, actually providing the basis for the parsing of music-related movements into chunks. This process of action chunking is important for understanding the process of auditory chunking as well, because we may often see that the overall trajectory of the chunk, e.g. its pitch contour or its textural spread, is more readily rendered, and thus presumably more robustly perceived, than the detail movements within the chunk.

4 The Perception-Action Cycle of Gestural Rendering

On the basis of our own observation studies and other research, it seems reasonable to conclude that listeners readily may make gestural renderings that reflect features of musical sound, but that these gestural renderings may be quite variable in resolution or acuity of detail. Seeing such variability in gestural renderings of musical sound, one of the main challenges in studying music-related gestures then becomes that of understanding and appreciating *approximate information*.

This can be done by trying to understand gestural renderings of musical sound as an instance of what has been called the *perception-action cycle* [21]. Various versions of this may be found in different domains of research, but in our context we can understand the perception-action cycle as an incessant process of trying to make sense of what we hear by covertly or overtly making gestures that simulate the generation of what we hear, or that trace the perceived contours (or what is often called envelopes) of what we hear. This means that perception is understood as an *active* process where the point is to proceed by sketches from initially rather coarse images to progressively more refined images. This could also be understood as a process of incessant production of hypotheses as to the causes and features of what we perceive [22], in other words, engaging in a feedback loop of an incessant process of top-down hypothesis-generation followed by bottom-up driven comparison with what we assumed in our hypothesis, successively adjusting and refining our top-down generated hypothesis by each period of the perception-action cycle as schematically illustrated in figure 4. One

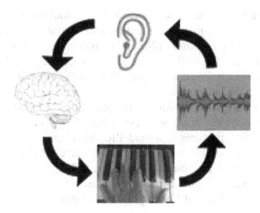

Fig. 4. Gestural rendering, overt or covert (as mental simulation), of musical sound as an instance of the *perception-action cycle* where the coupling of sound to action and action to sound enhances our perception of musical sound by this incessant circular activity of listening and rendering. Notably, the images of actions associated with the sounds may vary considerably with regards to specificity and/or expert knowledge, yet may still be an essential element in the embodied perception of music.

essential point of this perception-action cycle (as well as in motor theories of perception in general) is that the motor sensation may vary considerably in detail, i.e. may vary between very precise images of sound-production as is often the case with trained musicians [12] and more unspecific sensations of onset events as when listeners wave their hands to the rhythm of the music [8]. In both the expert/specific movements and the non-expert/unspecific movements there will be a coupling between the sounds and actions, a coupling that is one of the core elements of embodied music cognition (see [8] for a further discussion of this).

Accepting that such a perception-action cycle is at work, we can then appreciate the often quite approximate types of gestural renderings that we have seen, where initially rather coarse and sometimes even seemingly divergent gestural renderings may be seen as necessary in the perception and progressively finer discrimination of musical sound. Reminiscent of children's babbling, such approximate gestural renderings also indicate that the holistically perceived chunk of musical sound (e.g. a rhythmical motive, a textural fragment, a melodic fragment, etc.) may be primordial to the singular sound or tone. In other words, the gesture is primordial to the note in music, something that is not obvious in western musical thinking.

This capacity for perceiving chunks better than details remains to be better understood, as does also the time-scales at work here, i.e. how often and at what time-intervals our percepts are updated in such a perception-action cycle. Although we tend to think of both musical sound and music-related actions as continuous in time, there are also indications of an intermittent segmentation of sound and action into chunks in our minds. Briefly stated, both sound and action requires a certain minimum duration in order to be perceived as meaningful, something that is due to constraints of our perceptual-cognitive apparatus, and also actions need to be planned and initiated in advance (see [23] for an overview of recent research on chunking of sound and action).

One interesting idea here is to think of action as a combination of *key-postures* and *movement between these key-postures*, similar to the distinction in animation between so-called *keyframes* and *interframes* [24]. This distinction between key-postures and movements seems to fit quite well with the notion of geometry and effort in our case, in that the key-postures are the position and spread of the effectors (i.e. fingers, hands, arms, feet, etc.) at certain salient points in the music such as downbeats and other accents, and that there are gestures with distinct sensations of effort between these key-postures. In our present research, we have adopted this idea of key-postures and movements between key-postures as a model for both being able to make more well-founded chunkings of music-related gestures and to have better knowledge of the motion and effort features of music-related gestures [18, 23]. For this reason, we will also in our future research on music-related gestures make use of the conceptual separation of geometry and effort that I have presented in this paper.

5 Conclusion: Thinking Music with Hands

From various research on music-related gestures, our own as well as that of others, it seems reasonable to conclude that listeners' capacity for making spontaneous gestural renderings of musical sound seems solid and seems to reflect well the geometric layout and the sound-producing effort of musical sound. Actually, we could call this 'thinking music with hands', and we believe this is a phenomenon well worth studying further, as it attests to a spontaneous motor involvement that many (if not most) people have with music. Also, thinking music with hands is interesting in demonstrating how ephemeral and/or fleeting musical sound can become more solidly present as motor images and as visible trajectories and postures, giving us insights into the enigmatic issues of musical memory and capacity for anticipation, i.e. for thinking ahead in musical sound. Further research on this thinking music with hands could hopefully also lead to several practical applications in music education, musical composition, improvisation, performance, control of new musical instruments, and in multi-media arts, as well as interesting insights for gesture research in general.

Needless to say, we have so far just scratched the surface of this topic of gestural renderings of musical sound, and we have substantial challenges ahead. These include developing better means for motion capture, better representation of motion capture data, better design for observation studies of how people make hand movements in ecologically valid (i.e. non-laboratory) situations, and better methods for studying the relationship between movements that we can observe and covert, mental sensations of movement that we can not see directly.

References

1. http://musicalgestures.uio.no
2. Godøy, R.I.: Motor-mimetic Music Cognition. Leonardo 36(4), 317–319 (2003)
3. Gritten, A., King, E. (eds.): Music and Gesture. Ashgate, Aldershot (2006)
4. Wanderley, M., Battier, M. (eds.): Trends in Gestural Control of Music. Ircam, Paris (2000)
5. Gibson, J.J.: The Ecological Approach to Visual Perception. Lawrence Erlbaum Associates, Hillsdale (1979)

6. Godøy, R.I., Haga, E., Jensenius, A.: Playing 'Air Instruments': mimicry of sound-producing gestures by novices and experts. In: Gibet, S., Courty, N., Kamp, J.-F. (eds.) GW 2005. LNCS (LNAI), vol. 3881, pp. 256–267. Springer, Heidelberg (2006)
7. Godøy, R.I., Haga, E., Jensenius, A.R.: Exploring Music-Related Gestures by Sound-Tracing: A Preliminary Study. In: Ng, K. (ed.) Proceedings of the COST287-ConGAS 2nd International Symposium on Gesture Interfaces for Multimedia Systems, pp. 27–33 (2006)
8. Godøy, R. I.: Gestural affordances of musical sound (book chapter in preparation, 2008)
9. Liberman, A.M., Mattingly, I.G.: The Motor Theory of Speech Perception Revised. Cognition 21, 1–36 (1985)
10. Wilson, M., Knoblich, G.: The case for motor involvement in perceiving conspecifics. Psychological Bulletin 131(3), 460–473 (2005)
11. Kohler, E., Keysers, C., Umiltà, M.A., Fogassi, L., Gallese, V., Rizzolatti, G.: Hearing sounds, understanding actions: Action representation in mirror neurons. Science 297, 846–848 (2002)
12. Haueisen, J., Knösche, T.R.: Involuntary Motor Activity in Pianists Evoked by Music Perception. Journal of Cognitive Neuroscience 13(6), 786–792 (2001)
13. Rizzolatti, G., Arbib, M.A.: Language Within Our Grasp. Trends in Neuroscience 21, 188–194 (1998)
14. Goldin-Meadow, S.: Hearing Gesture: How Our Hands Help Us Think. The Belknap Press, Cambridge (2003)
15. Kelso, J.A.S., Fuchs, A., Lancaster, R., Holroyd, T., Cheyne, D., Weinberg, H.: Dynamic cortical activity in the human brain reveals motor equivalence. Nature 392(23), 814–818 (1998)
16. Haga, E.: Correspondences between Music and Body Movement (unpublished doctoral dissertation). University of Oslo, Oslo (2008)
17. Eitan, Z., Granot, R.Y.: How Music Moves: Musical Parameters and Listeners' Images of Motion. Music Perception 23(3), 221–247 (2006)
18. Jensenius, A.R., Nymoen, K., Godøy, R.I.: A multilayered GDIF-based setup for studying coarticulation in the movements of musicians. In: Proceedings of ICMC 2008, Belfast, UK, August 24 - 29 (2008)
19. Pirhonen, A.: Semantics Of Sounds And Images - Can they be Paralleled? In: Proceedings of the 2007 International Conference for Auditory Display, Montreal, Canada, June 26-29, pp. 319–325 (2007)
20. Godøy, R.I.: Gestural-Sonorous Objects: embodied extensions of Schaeffer's conceptual apparatus. Organised Sound 11(2), 149–157 (2006)
21. Neisser, U.: Cognition and Reality. W.H. Freeman, San Francisco (1976)
22. Berthoz, A.: Le sens du mouvement. Odile Jacob, Paris (1997)
23. Godøy, R.I.: Reflections on chunking in music. In: Schneider, A. (ed.) Systematic and Comparative Musicology: Concepts, Methods, Findings. Hamburger Jahrbuch für Musikwissenschaft, Band 24, pp. 117–132. Peter Lang, Vienna (2008)
24. Rosenbaum, D., Cohen, R.G., Jax, S.A., Weiss, D.J., van der Wel, R.: The problem of serial order in behavior: Lashley's legacy. Human Movement Science 26(4), 525–554 (2007)

String Bowing Gestures at Varying Bow Stroke Frequencies: A Case Study

Nicolas Rasamimanana[1], Delphine Bernardin[2],
Marcelo Wanderley[2], and Frédéric Bevilacqua[1]

[1] IRCAM, CNRS - UMR 9912, 1 Place Igor Stravinsky, 75004 Paris, France
{Nicolas.Rasamimanana,Frederic.Bevilacqua}@ircam.fr
[2] IDMIL/CIRMMT, McGill University, Montreal, QC, Canada
{Delphine.Bernardin,Marcelo.Wanderley}@mcgill.ca

Abstract. The understanding of different bowing strategies can provide key concepts for the modelling of music performance. We report here an exploratory study of bowing gestures for a viola player and a violin player in the case of bow strokes performed at different frequencies. Bow and arm movements as well as bow pressure on strings were measured respectively with a 3D optical motion capture system and a custom pressure sensor. While increasing bow stroke frequency, defined as the inverse time between two strokes, players did use different bowing movements as indicated from the measurement of bow velocity and arm joint angles. First, bow velocity profiles abruptly shift from a rectangle shape to a sinus shape. Second, while bow velocity is sinusoidal, an additional change is observed: the wrist and elbow relative phase shifts from out-of-phase to in-phase at the highest frequencies, indicating a possible change in the players coordinative pattern. We finally discuss the fact that only small differences are found in the sound while significant changes occur in the velocity / acceleration profiles.

1 Introduction

The understanding of different bowing strategies can provide key concepts for the modelling of music performance. Such model can be applied in music pedagogy [1] or in the design of novel musical interfaces [2]. We previously reported the study of three standard bowing techniques in violin playing [3]. In particular, we discussed issues on gesture "continuity". This concept relates to the fact that an expert violinist is able to play several and subtle variations between two bowing techniques, e.g. *Détaché* and *Martelé*. We showed in reference [3] that such subtle variations can be directly tracked in the bowing dynamics and described with features derived from bow acceleration profiles.

In this paper, we report complementary results on violin playing by studying bowing gestures, i.e. movements directly involved in sound production, at different stroke frequencies and further question the concept of gesture "continuity". Slow bowing generally requires a relaxed right arm. Nevertheless, it is usually recognized among bowed string players that rapid, repeated bow strokes can require the right arm to be tensed up. Such strategy is usually used to achieve a given

M. Sales Dias et al. (Eds.): GW 2007, LNAI 5085, pp. 216–226, 2009.

rhythm, for example four sixteenths, or to perform a *tremolo*. From the players' viewpoint, these are different arm movements to perform cyclic, repetitive bowings. We here test this hypothesis with the study of an *accelerando/decelerando*, i.e. bow strokes performed with an increasing/decreasing frequency, and investigate on the continuity between slow and fast bowing.

The paper is structured as follows. First we describe related works and our experimental method based on optical 3D motion capture technology combined with a bow pressure sensor. Second, we present and discuss results obtained by measuring arm and bow movements of two instrumentalists. Third, we investigate sound characteristics at different bow stroke frequencies. Finally, we present conclusions and directions for future work.

2   Related Works

When performing a *glissando*, it may happen that singers produce a discontinuity in pitch. It corresponds to the transition from one laryngeal mechanism to another, such as described in reference [4]. This drastic change in voice production enables singers to achieve the highest frequencies of the *glissando*. We hypothesize that a similar phenomenon occurs for bowed string instruments: players can change their bowing gestures to perform high bow stroke frequencies.

This configuration change in voice production relates to a well-known notion in motor control: the reorganisation of coordinative patterns, as occuring in gait shifting. In particular, Kelso studied the abrupt phase transitions in human hand movements according to the cycling frequency [5,6]: for example, a periodic out-of-phase movement of human's fingers, i.e. one finger up while the other is down, shifts to an in-phase movement, i.e. both fingers up or down at the same time, when increasing frequency. These results are especially insightful for our study as we are dealing with a cyclic movement with increasing frequency (*accelerando*), and involving the upper arm, the forearm and the hand.

Several studies report on the movement analysis of instrument performance [7,8], [9], [10] and in particular bowed string players [11]. Winold et al. [12] first studied coordination issues in bow arm movements in a musical context. They analyzed cellists' bowing coordinations while performing fragments by Brahms and Schubert at different tempi. They concluded that increasing tempi produced a proportional scaling of stroke amplitudes and durations. Nevertheless, they did not notice any change in within-limb coordinations. More recently, Baader et al. [13] studied coordination between fingering and bowing and showed anticipatory movements between the left hand and the right arm. While our approach is similar to Winold's, we here focus on bow, elbow and wrist movements on a simpler musical task: *accelerando/decelerando* on one single note.

3   Method

We used a Vicon System 460 optical motion capture system to measure the arm and bow movements. Six M2 cameras were placed around the instrumentalists providing a spatial resolution below 1mm with a frame rate of 500Hz. Markers were placed on the players' upper body, following the standard marker placement in the Vicon Plug-in Gait [14]. Six markers were placed on the instrument, four for the table and two for the strings. Three markers were placed on the bow. With this setup, the movement of the bow can be computed relatively to the instrument. The position of the contact point between the bow and the strings is calculated and is used as the center of an instrument-based frame of reference.

Bow pressure on string was measured with a custom sensor designed at Ircam [15], with a ±3% error. Bow pressure data were recorded separately from motion capture data. To ensure a post-recording synchronization between both sets of data, the sound was recorded simultaneously with each sensing system: we use the arg-maximum of the cross-correlation between the audio signal envelopes to align both sets of data.

Two students from McGill Schulich School of Music were recorded playing an *accelerando*, from medium paced *Détaché* to a "as fast as possible", tied with a *decelerando* back to medium paced *Détaché*. Musicians were asked to stay on a fixed note. One McGill student played the violin, the other student played the viola. Both McGill students were advanced level with more than ten years of instrument practice.

4   Results and Discussion

The presentation of results is structured as follows: first, we study bow movement and focus on a change in bowing gestures found on the velocity and acceleration profiles during an *accelerando/decelerando*. Second, we present the results relative to the arm joint angles providing additional insights on this change. Last, we show results of the sound characteristics at the moment of the bowing change.

4.1   Change in Bowing Gestures

Bow Movements: Figure 1 shows the position, velocity and acceleration of one point of the bow, for the viola player. For clarity, the bow stroke frequency is also plotted, showing the *accelerando/decelerando*. Bow stroke frequency is defined as the inverse of a stroke duration and is computed as the inverse of the time separating two successive zero crossings of the bow velocity curve. Due to the physics of bowed strings, the amplitude variations of velocity and acceleration are bounded within an interval that guarantees the production of an acceptable sound [16]. There is no such constrain on the distance, and thus tempo variation is achieved by reducing the length of bow, as already noticed in reference [12]. Biomechanics also imposes this reduction: the combination fast tempo - long strokes is indeed very difficult to achieve. Figure 1 shows that the absolute value of the acceleration amplitude remains relatively constant, while the observed dramatic decrease of the position amplitude is directly correlated with the increase of bow stroke frequency.

However, a zoomed view of bow velocity and bow acceleration reveals an interesting profile change in the middle part of the *accelerando / decelerando*.

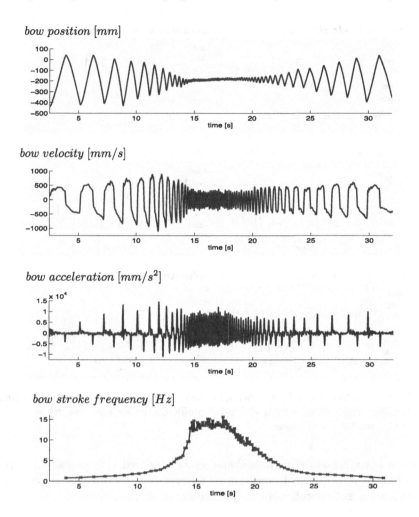

Fig. 1. From top to bottom: bow position, velocity, acceleration and bow stroke frequency for the *accelerando / decelerando* performed by the viola player

Figure 2 shows the two players' bow dynamics at this moment. The profile change is observable for both players. Two different patterns are clearly visible on the graphs: the acceleration profile drastically changes becoming smoother at times $t = 14s$ for the viola and $t = 11s$ for the violin. For both players, the reverse change occurs during the *decelerando*.

These two patterns allow us to section the *accelerando / decelerando* in three parts. In the first and third parts, denoted by $C1$ and $C3$, the velocity is close to a square signal, the acceleration profile is characterized by well defined short positive and negative peaks. Between these peaks, other smaller peaks are observable. In the second part, denoted $C2$, the velocity and acceleration profiles are smooth and close to sinusoidal. It is worth to notice that the change in bowing

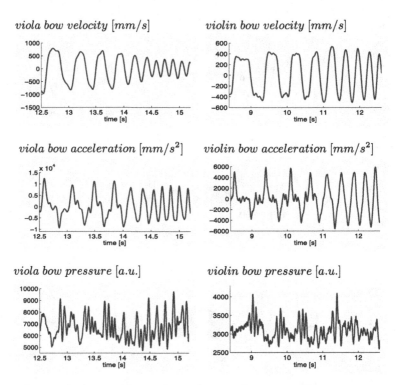

Fig. 2. From top to bottom: bow velocity, bow acceleration and bow pressure on strings. For both instrumentalists, a clear change in profile occurs for bow velocity and acceleration but not for bow pressure.

gesture is abrupt: no intermediate shape can be observed in the acceleration profile in Figure 2. It is also interesting to observe that no obvious, concomitant change occurs in the profile of bow pressure.

Profile Characterization: To quantitatively characterize this profile change, we perform a sinus non-linear fit on bow velocity. Bow velocity is segmented in individual strokes. Each segment is resampled to a fixed number of points: we chose 600 points, i.e. the length of the longest stroke in the measurements. Each segment is fitted to half period of a sinus fitting function, that allows for variable amplitude and phase, but with a fixed frequency. The estimation of the amplitude and phase parameters is performed with a non-linear least square regression. The mean square *fit error* therefore provides a measurement of the profile change.

Figure 3 shows the *fit error* parameter for the whole *accelerando* and *decelerando*. We can see a minimum plateau in the middle part for both players. Also, the value of the *error* is drastically higher at the beginning and at the end. This illustrates the change in profile observed in the previous section.

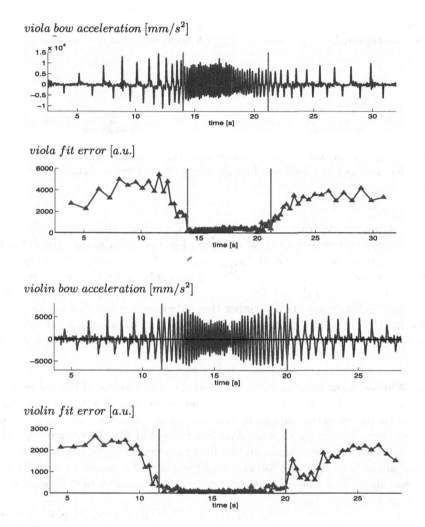

Fig. 3. Bow acceleration and the sinusoid *fit error*. The vertical bars were computed with a threshold based on *fit error* values.

In these figures, we can delimitate the $C1$, $C2$ and $C3$ parts by applying a threshold on the *fit error* parameter as shown by vertical bars in Figure 3. The profile changes in bow velocity and acceleration as seen in Figure 2 correspond approximately to a threshold of $560[a.u.]$ (value determined empirically).

Figure 4 plots the *fit error* along with the strokes period, defined as the time interval between up and down bows. For both players, we can see that while the period decreases and increases in a linear way, the *fit error* abruptly shifts from high to minimum values. This endorses our previous observation of abrupt transitions between the three parts $C1$, $C2$ and $C3$.

We can also observe an hysteresis between the *accelerando* and the *decelerando*: the transition $C2 \rightarrow C3$ takes more time than $C1 \rightarrow C2$ for the two

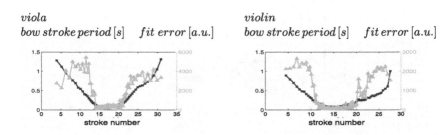

Fig. 4. In light color, the *fit error* and in dark color, the bow stroke period. While the period decreases and increases in a linear way, the *fit error* abruptly shifts from high to minimum values.

players. Moreover, we can notice that the frequency at which velocity profiles change is different between the two players. For the violin player, the $C2$ part comes early in the *accelerando*, at $f_{shift:C1\rightarrow C2} = 7Hz$, and the bowing frequency keeps on increasing up to $f_{max} = 15Hz$. On the contrary, for the viola player the $C2$ part coincides with the *accelerando* climax, at $f_{shift:C1\rightarrow C2} = f_{max} = 14Hz$. We cannot at this point know whether this difference is a function of the player or the instrument. More violin and viola players need to be considered to determine the typical frequencies for this profile change and their dependence on the instrument and the players' expertise.

Arm Angles: Bow movements result from the coordination of the upper arm, forearm and hand. The analysis of arm joint angles can therefore give further insights to the observed change in bowing gesture, described in the previous section. From the motion capture data, we computed the elbow angle, i.e. the angle between the upper arm and the forearm segments, and the wrist angle, i.e. the angle formed by the forearm and the hand. We therefore consider the wrist and elbow angles, main contributors to the bowing movement, in a periodic flexion-extension movement.

The angle derivatives provide interesting information. Figure 5 plots the second derivative of the elbow angle. First, contrary to bow movement, arm movement shows major differences between the two players, as shown on Figure 5. This is explained by the large number of degrees of freedom in the arm. These differences actually express the players' personal bowing technique. However, for both players, we can notice changes at the transition time we determined from bow movements ($C1 \rightarrow C2$ and $C2 \rightarrow C3$). In Figure 5, we can see that similarly to bow acceleration, the profile of the second derivative of the elbow angle shows a dramatic change for both players ($t = 14s$ and $t = 11s$): it becomes smoother and almost sinusoidal.

Moreover, three additional parts can be identified in the arm movement from the analysis of joints' relative phases. The first derivates for the wrist and elbow angles are plotted on Figure 6. Indeed, during the $C2$ part previously defined, we can see another clear change occuring at the climax of the *accelerando*: for the violin player, the wrist and elbow curves first are in anti-phase at $t = 12s$,

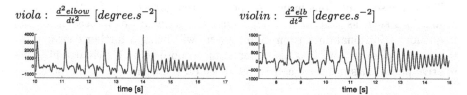

Fig. 5. Second derivative of the elbow angle. The vertical lines indicate the transition $C1 \rightarrow C2$. Similarly to bow acceleration, the profile of the second derivative of the elbow angle shows a dramatic change for both players.

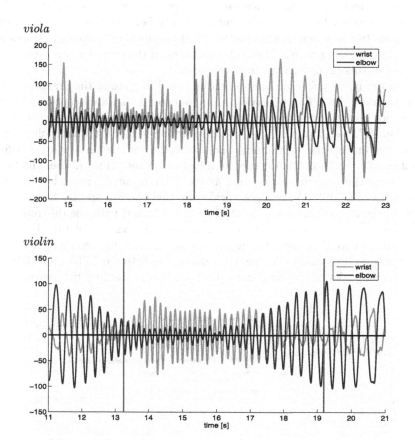

Fig. 6. First derivatives of elbow and wrist angles. Vertical bars indicate changes in the joints' relative phase.

suddenly shift to in-phase at $t = 13.2s$ and gradually shift back to anti-phase at $t = 19.2s$. This change occurs when the bowing frequency is the highest. A similar but less obvious change also occurs for the viola (changes at $t = 18.8s$ and $t = 22.2s$). For the viola player, the in-phase / anti-phase transition occurs in the reverse way, i.e. first in-phase, then anti-phase.

These phase transitions indicate a possible reorganisation of within-limb co-ordinations such as described in [5], under the influence of increasing bowing frequency. Additional data from more players will bring a further characterization of this observation. It is also interesting to note that this change in joints' relative phase does not have a clear influence on the dynamics of the bow.

4.2   Audio Comparison of the Two Bowing Gestures

In reference [3], we reported the relationships between bow acceleration curves and bowing techniques that correspond to specific sound characteristics. We particularly stressed the gesture-sound continuity between the different bowing techniques. In the previous sections, we identified different bowing gestures for slow and fast bowing with a brutal change between the two. We now investigate the effect of this change on the produced sound.

Interestingly, very few differences can be heard in spite of the drastic change previously described. This observation is supported by an audio spectrum comparison: for both players, there are indeed small differences in the spectra at the transitions ($C1 \rightarrow C2$ and $C2 \rightarrow C3$), as shown on Figure 7 for the viola player. We can see on top the mean audio spectrum $S1$ over the three strokes before transition $C1 \rightarrow C2$, in the middle the mean audio spectrum $S2$ over the three strokes after the same transition, and at the bottom the difference between the two spectra ($S1 - S2$). We can graphically see that the two spectra have similar peaks in frequencies and amplitudes. This is confirmed with the difference between the two spectra: mean of $1dB$ with a standard deviation of $4dB$. However, it is worth to note that the difference is not uniform among the frequencies but slightly more important in the medium range, i.e. between $100Hz$ and $600Hz$. The spectral peaks having similar amplitudes, this is due to a difference in the

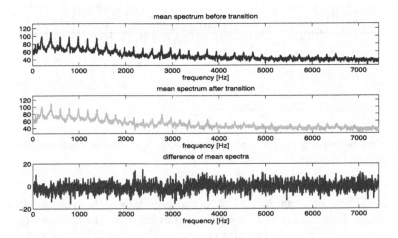

Fig. 7. Audio spectrum comparison for the viola player. Top: before $C1 \rightarrow C2$, Middle: after $C1 \rightarrow C2$, Bottom: spectrum difference.

noise level, which is lower in $C1$ than in $C2$. The origin of this last point will be further investigated with the help of physical models of bowed strings.

Further studies will also help to determine whether the sound similarities are actually due to an active, conscious or unconscious control of the musicians.

5   Conclusion and Future Directions

We present in this paper a study on the use of different bowing gestures by a violin player and a viola player to achieve different bow stroke frequencies. From the analysis of bow movement in an *accelerando/decelerando*, we showed the existence of two profiles in bow velocity and acceleration, therefore defining two bowing gestures. With a profile characterization based on a sinus non-linear fit, we noticed that the transition from one gesture to the other is abrupt with an hysteresis effect.

The study of arm joint angles also indicated the possible existence of a within-limb change of coordination for very fast bow strokes (15 Hz). In the case of the violin player, the elbow and the wrist first start in out-of-phase and shift to in-phase to achieve the fastest part of the *accelerando/decelerando*.

In the recorded performances of *accelerando/decelerando*, we could therefore clearly identify four parts in the players' movements: a square-shaped bow velocity, a sinus-shaped velocity with two possible arm coordinations, and a square-shaped bow velocity. Further studies must be performed to clarify the generalities of our findings.

Besides, an audio spectrum analysis does not reveal a clear concomitant change to the drastic change in bow velocity profiles. This might be due to the players being sufficiently experienced to smooth out the effects of changing bowing strategy. To test this hypothesis, new experiments with students of various levels, including beginners must be carried out. We can also hypothesize that the change in bowing gesture has an effect on finer timbre aspects like e.g. transitions between notes. These non obvious correspondances between gesture and sound and especially their evolutive aspect open interesting questions for the control of electronic sounds.

Acknowledgements

Nicolas Rasamimanana gratefully thanks funds from the Centre de Collaboration Interuniversitaire Franco Québécois. Thanks to Matthias Demoucron for his help and for lending us the pressure sensor he developed. We thank Florence Baschet, Christophe Desjardins, Serge Lemouton, Norbert Schnell and René Caussé for contributions, discussions and support.

This work was partly founded by the european project i-Maestro IST-026883. We also acknowledge the support of the project CONSONNES funded by the ANR (Agence Nationale de la Recherche, France).

The second and third authors are partially funded by the Natural Sciences and Engineering Council of Canada (Discovery and Special Research Opportunity grants) and by the Ministry of Economic Development of Quebec (Programme de soutien aux initiatives internationales de recherche et d'innovation). Thanks to support from the 6th Framework Project ENACTIVE Interfaces.

References

1. I-MAESTRO, http://www.i-maestro.org
2. Bevilacqua, F., Rasamimanana, N.H., Fléty, E., Lemouton, S., Baschet, F.: The augmented violin project: research, composition and performance report. In: NIME Proceedings, pp. 402–406 (2006)
3. Rasamimanana, N.H., Flety, E., Bevilacqua, F.: Gesture analysis of violin bow strokes. In: Gibet, S., Courty, N., Kamp, J.-F. (eds.) GW 2005. LNCS (LNAI), vol. 3881, pp. 145–155. Springer, Heidelberg (2006)
4. Henrich, N.: Mirroring the voice from garcia to the present day: Some insights into singing voice registers. Logopedics Phoniatrics Vocology 31, 3–14 (2006)
5. Haken, H., Kelso, J.A.S., Bunz, H.: A theoretical model of phase transitions in human hand movements. Biological cybernetics 51(5), 347–356 (1985)
6. Fuchs, A., Jirsa, V.K., Haken, H., Kelso, J.A.S.: Extending the hkb model of coordinated movement to oscillators with different eigenfrequencies. Biological cybernetics 74(1), 21–30 (1996)
7. Palmer, C.: Movement amplitude and tempo change in piano performance. Acoustical Society of America Journal 115, 2590–2590 (2001)
8. Dalla Bella, S., Palmer, C.: Tempo and dynamics in piano performance: the role of movement amplitude. In: Lipscomb, S.D., Ashley, R., Gjerdingen, R.O., Webster, P. (eds.) Proceedings of the International Conference on Music Perception and Cognition, pp. 256–257 (2004)
9. Wanderley, M.M., Vines, B.W., Middleton, N., McKay, C., Hatch, W.: The musical significance of clarinetists' ancillary gestures: An exploration of the field. Journal of New Music Research 34(1), 97–113 (2005)
10. Dahl, S.: Playing the accent - comparing striking velocity and timing in an ostinato rhythm performed by four drummers. Acta Acustica united with Acustica 90(4), 762–776 (2004)
11. Shan, G.B., Visentin, P.: A quantitative three-dimensional analysis of arm kinematics in violin performance. Medical Problems of Performing Artists 18(1), 3–10 (2003)
12. Winold, H., Thelen, E., Ulrich, B.D.: Coordination and control in the bow arm movements of highly skilled cellists. Ecological Psychology 6(1), 1–31 (1994)
13. Baader, A.P., Kazennikov, O., Wiesendanger, M.: Coordination of bowing and fingering in violin playing. Cognitive brain research 23(2-3), 436–443 (2005)
14. Vicon Plug-in-gait, http://www.vicon.com/applications/gait_analysis.html
15. Demoucron, M., Askenfelt, A., Caussé, R.: Mesure de la "pression d'archet" des instruments à cordes frottées: Application à la synthèse sonore. In: Actes du VIIIème Congrès Français d'Acoustique, Tours (2006)
16. Guettler, K.: Looking at starting transients and tone coloring of the bowed string. In: Proceedings of Frontiers of Research on Speech and Music (2004)

Gesture Control of Sound Spatialization for Live Musical Performance

Mark T. Marshall, Joseph Malloch, and Marcelo M. Wanderley

Input Devices and Music Interaction Laboratory
Centre for Interdisciplinary Research in Music Media and Technology
Music Technology Area - McGill University
Montreal, QC, Canada
{mark.marshall,joseph.malloch,marcelo.wanderley}@mcgill.ca
http://idmil.org

Abstract. This paper presents the development of methods for gesture control of sound spatialization. It provides a comparison of seven popular software spatialization systems from a control point of view, and examines human-factors issues relevant to gesture control. An effort is made to reconcile these two design- and parameter-spaces, and draw useful conclusions regarding likely successful mapping strategies. Lastly, examples are given using several different gesture-tracking and motion capture systems controlling various parameters of the spatialization system.

1 Introduction

Sound spatialization has been explored as a musical tool by a many composers (see [1] for a review) and a number of systems have been developed for controlling the spatialization of sound. These systems have offered control which has varied from simple multi-channel fader arrangements, to software-based mixer systems, to software containing graphical representations of the sound sources in space. Even in the simplest implementations, sound spatialization is a multidimensional system (the basic case being 2-dimensional position and volume for each sound source) and with the development of more complex systems incorporating modelling of sound source and room parameters the dimensionality of these systems has increased dramatically. Surprisingly, the interfaces for controlling these systems have remained generally unchanged, and so in most cases, the large numbers of spatialization parameters are handled by pre-programmed cues, envelopes, and trajectories. Using gesture[1] to control spatial parameters is generally restricted to low-dimensional tasks, such as placing a sound source in 2-dimensional space. Yet, gesture offers more interesting methods for control of sound spatialization, in which a performer may control large parameter-spaces in an intuitive manner. This paper describes ongoing development of a number

---

[1] There are a number of different definitions of the term gesture in the literature. For this work, we use the term to mean a separable segment of the continuous, multidimensional physical movements of the performer.

M. Sales Dias et al. (Eds.): GW 2007, LNAI 5085, pp. 227–238, 2009.

of examples of gesture control of sound spatialization. These include the development of standard gesture tracking systems, e.g. data gloves and position trackers, and also novel methods of control based on musical performance gestures. In addition to producing specific implementations, the final goal of this work is to develop general methods for gesture-controlled spatialization systems which can be used in real-time during concert performances. Since this work is taking place within the framework of a larger project on the compositional uses of gesture-controlled sound spatialization, much of the work is heavily influenced by the goals of the composer. We begin by examining the types of control parameters which are made available by existing spatialization systems, in order to determine the parameters of which we may wish to enable control using gesture. This is followed by a brief overview of control issues relevant to the task, and an examination of a number of systems which we have been developing that allow for different forms of gesture-controlled sound spatialization.

2   Related Work

Gesture control of sound spatialization for music has been investigated as early as 1951 with the development of the *potentiomètre d'espace* by Pierre Schaeffer in collaboration with composer Pierre Henry[2]. This system allowed the performer to route prerecorded audio signals through multiple speakers in a concert performance. This aim of positioning sounds in space has become the main focus of many works on gesture controlled spatialization.

The *Zirkonium* software described in [3] allows for the control of sound source positions in 3 dimensions, together with a control over the size of the sound source. Control of these parameters may be through a graphical interface using the mouse, using any HID (Human Interface Device) controller such as a joystick, or remotely from other software or hardware using messages sent by Open Sound Control (OSC).

One interesting implementation of gesture-controlled spatialization is given in [4]. In this case, the overall system is an immersive environment for the creation of sound and music. The system allows users to create, manipulate and position a large number of different sound objects (including audio files, real-time midi input, midi arpeggiators, synthesized rhythm loops, etc.) in a virtual environment. The sound objects are then spatialized through the audio system to match their position in the virtual environment. Manipulation of the object is performed by the user through a 6 degree-of-freedom hand tracking system along with handheld mice.

The idea of using gesture control together with immersive virtual environments and sound spatialization has been addressed in a number of other works also. [5] describes a system for collaborative spatial audio performance in a virtual environment. Multiple users may interact with the system at the same time to manipulate the position of objects in 3D space. Interaction is performed using hand gestures through tracked data gloves together with stereoscopic display projection.

A system is presented in [6] which offers a navigable 3D immersive virtual space which contains both sound sources and sound sinks. The sources and sinks can be combined and manipulated to create immersive soundscapes which are conveyed to the user using sound spatialization. Interaction can take place using a number of different devices for gesture control, including datagloves, cameras and HIDs.

In [7] the author proposes a hierarchical system for the control of sound source positions in space which allows a combination of different control methods at different levels. The use of small joysticks and graphics tablets is recommended for the control of 2-dimensional positions but thought is also given to the use of tracked datagloves and haptic devices for more complex control.

3   Comparing Spatialization System Control Parameters

In general, existing spatialization systems are considered to offer two groups of parameters which can be controlled, namely *sound source position and orientation parameters* and *room model parameters*. However, a number of newer systems allow for the control of sound source (and sink) characteristics, so it may be more intuitive to consider 3 levels of parameters:

- sound source/sink position and orientation
- sound source/sink characteristics
- environmental and room model parameters.

Table 1. Comparison of spatialization system control parameters

	VBAP[8]	Spat[9]	SSP[3]	audio TWIST[6]	Ambi- sonics[12]	WFS[11]	ViMiC[10]
Sound Source Position and Orientation							
Position (X,Y,Z)	√	√	(X,Y)	√	√	√	√
Azimuth, Elevation	-	√	-	√	-	√	√
Sound Source Characteristics							
Size	-	-	√	-	-	√	-
Directivity	-	√	-	√	-	√	√
Presence/Distance	-	√	-	-	-	-	-
Brilliance/Warmth	-	√	-	-	-	-	-
Room Parameters							
Size	-	√	-	√	-	√	√
Presence	-	√	-	-	-	√	-
Early Reflections	-	√	-	√	-	√	√
Reverberation	-	√	-	√	-	√	√
Reverb. Cutoff Freq.	-	-	-	-	-	-	√
Doppler Effect	-	√	-	√	-	-	-
Equalization/Filtering	-	√	-	√	-	-	-
Air Absorption	-	√	-	√	-	-	-
Distance Decay	-	√	-	√	-	-	√
Mic/Sink/Speaker Pos.	√	√	-	√	-	-	√
Mic/Sink Directivity	-	-	-	√	-	-	√
Heaviness/Liveness	-	-	-	-	-	-	√

The extra level (sound source/sink characteristics) includes aspects of the sound sources other than their position or orientation in space. Parameters such as source/sink size or directivity are important descriptors in some systems and cannot be accurately described as room model parameters. Environmental and room model parameters include room parameters such as the room size and amount of room reverberation, along with environmental parameters such as the energy absorption factor of the air or additional equalization.

In an attempt to include a broad range of possible parameters, we examined a number of available spatialization systems, including those which are currently most used and a number of more recently developed systems. These systems range in complexity from sound source panning systems such as VBAP [8], to complex positioning and room models such as Spat [9] and ViMiC [10]. Table 1 shows the results of this comparison of systems.

4   Control Issues

A number of issues are of crucial importance when using gesture to control sound spatialization parameters. Careful consideration of these issues, and carefully matching parameters in the mapping process, will allow not just intuitive and powerful control of sound spatialization, but yield rewarding performances for performer and audience alike. These issues must also inform choices in sensors, sampling rates, A/D converters, transmission bandwidth, and communication protocols.

Discrete vs. continuous parameters. Depending on the desired spatialization effects, some parameters, such as the number of sound sources, are usually approached as discrete values, while others, such as source volume, air absorption, or spatial position, usually require continuous control for common spatialization effects. In order to successfully map gestures for the control of these parameters, movement and sensing should match the discrete or continuous nature of the control. Discrete values can often be extracted from continuous signals, allowing the detection of discrete signs, but the opposite is not usually true: continuous parameters are best controlled by gestures that are continuously executed and sensed.

Resolution. The resolution required for controlling a given spatialization parameter depends on the desired spatialization effect and on the parameter's perceptual impact. Listeners are not likely to notice centimeter-scale changes in sound source location, especially for low-pitched sounds, but small changes in filter frequencies or air absorption parameters may be more easily perceived. On the gesture side, resolution can be limited by sensors or acquisition hardware, but is also naturally limited by human ability. As anyone who has tried to control musical pitch using finger pressure can attest, certain movements and certain body parts are unable to exert fine control, a problem that is compounded when the performer is not given adequate feedback regarding the state of the system they are controlling.

Control rates. The desired rate of change for the parameter must also be considered. Many spatialization parameters are typically considered to be static and are set only once before a performance, while others are constantly changing within a performance. Static parameters usually include room dimensions, wall reflectivity, and speaker positions; source position, orientation, and volume are usually changeable. Gestures used to control these parameters must obviously match or exceed the needed rate.

This description reflects a *current control* (or continuous control) approach to gesture control. However, another approach is familiar from percussion performance. A *ballistic* movement (such as a drum strike) may be used to determine the parameters of a sound spatialization event, after which no further control is exerted. In this case, all of the control information must be included in the launching gesture, or encoded in preparatory movements.

Integrality and separability. The relationships between spatialization parameters are also an essential consideration [13]. Certain parameters, such as the components of source position and orientation in each dimension, are closely related and deserve special attention during the mapping process. Similarly, the spatial position and orientation of the performers body, or parts thereof, are also related and should not be considered separately. In musical performance especially instrumental performance this is further complicated by the goal-directed manipulation of an external object (the instrument). In this way the posture and movement of individual body parts become integral to some extent.

Conscious vs. non-conscious control. An especially important issue when considering performance in the musical sense of gesture controlled sound spatialization is that of *cognitive load*, which is the total amount of mental activity imposed on working memory at an instance in time [14]. Considering that not all performers have spare bandwidth for controlling something other than their instrument [15], three main approaches may be taken: a separate performer may control *only* spatialization, a performer may be tasked with controlling spatial parameters in addition to their instrument, or spatialization parameters may be controlled by the performers gestures *without their conscious control*. If conscious control is desired, gestures must be chosen such that they can be performed without disturbing the instrumental performance, and it is assumed that the performer has spare attention for this task. For non-conscious control, mapping is more of a compositional process rather than performer interpretation, and raises some interesting questions: Will the performer feel that they are not in control of the sound? One partial solution is to attempt to map resting body states to neutral spatialization states.

5   Gesture for Control of Spatialization

In this section we describe our implementations of systems for gesture-controlled sound spatialization. In keeping with the three types of spatialization system parameters discussed in Sec. 3 we have identified three specific roles for control of spatialization. These roles are:

Spatial Performer - performs with sound objects in space by moving sound sources in real-time using gesture

Instrumental Performers - indirectly manipulate parameters of their own sound sources through their performance gestures on their own acoustic instrument

Spatial Conductor - directly controls large-scale (room and environment) parameters of the spatialization system using gesture

These roles derive from an examination of the types of parameters available to control, as well as the specific needs and goals of the composer for the musical portion of the project.

5.1   Manipulating Sound Source Positions: The Spatial Performer

One of the most obvious applications for gesture control of sound source position would be to make use of *direct manipulation*, or in this case *virtual direct manipulation*. In our specific implementation, we make use of a pair of custom-built datagloves, which allow measurement of the posture of the performer's hands using bend sensors mounted on the fingers. Along with a Polhemus Liberty magnetic position tracker to track the position and orientation of the hands, this system allows the performer to directly position multiple sound sources in space [16]. In order to take into account the integrated nature of the 3 positional parameters of the sound source objects, an integral 3-dimensional tracker is used to track the hand positions [13]. Tracking both hands (a bimanual system) allows for individual repositioning of two sources simultaneously.

To allow for a comparison between current control and ballistic control of sound sources, we have also implemented a ballistic sound source control system. This system allows the performer to launch sound sources by striking pads on a Roland V-Drum midi drumkit. Each pad provides a different angle of launch in the horizontal plane and the velocity of the strike controls the force of the launch. Multiple sound sources can be launched in this way and will move around the virtual room, pulled by gravity and potentially colliding with objects in its path. As can be imagined, this offers a much different form of interaction with the system than the more traditional direct manipulation-like system already described. Figure 1 shows this system in action.

Another example of a basic control system for sound source positioning uses the idea of "steering". In this case, "steering" forms a metaphor for interaction with the system [17]. It is possible to steer a single sound source around the space in a number of ways. For example, a joystick interface has been used to move the source in 2 dimensions, a task that could be performed similarly using a hand-held two-axis tilt sensor, allowing the user to steer by tilting their hand. In our implementation a weight-sensitive floor was developed, which allowed the user to steer a sound source in 2 dimensions by shifting their center of mass.

We have also implemented a simple system for concert use, in which a tilt sensor was mounted on the head of a percussionist to enable manipulation of a sound source position while playing vibraphone, a task which requires both

Fig. 1. A performer using our ballistic sound source control system to launch multiple sound sources in the virtual space

hands and feet and leaves few gestures for independent control. Both this system and the floor-based system allowed for a coarse level of control of sound source position but not surprisingly proved not to be well suited for fine positioning tasks (in direct contrast to the hand-tracking system). Also, both systems allow for only a 2-dimensional control of sound source position and so do not allow as much control as the hand-tracking system.

5.2   Control of Sound Source Parameters: Instrumental Performers

While controlling source location may seem obvious, the control of other sound source parameters offers further interesting possibilities. One method is to use existing musical performance gestures to control these parameters. Useful gestures include excitation and modification gestures involved in performance as well as ancillary gestures made by the performer while playing [18]. While using low-level gesture data from live performance can be interesting, they are often so closely correlated to the acoustic sound that higher level parameters may be more useful for mapping. For instance, when tracking a cellists bowing gestures, the energy of the gesture can prove to be a more useful control parameter than the physical position of the bow. This energy can be calculated using the amplitude and velocity of the bow movement and mapped to, for example, the volume or directivity of a sound source. As the performer plays more energetically the sound source could become louder (or perhaps for an unusual compositional effect the opposite could be true). This type of mapping allows us to give some control of the spatialized sound to the performers, but without having to give them any explicit instructions or increasing their cognitive load.

Control of spatialization using existing performance gestures is an area which we are actively investigating. In one approach we use a motion capture system to extract motion data from performances and use these data to design gesture control systems which are controlled indirectly by the performer. This means

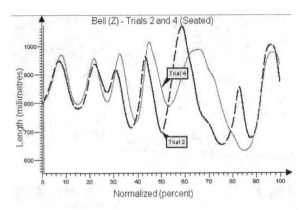

Fig. 2. Graph showing the vertical movement of the bell of a clarinet over two performances of the same piece by the same musician

that parameters which are extracted from the performer's movements are being used to control the system. For example, Fig. 2 shows a graph of the movement of the clarinet bell during two different performances of the same piece by a single performer. As can be seen from this graph, there is consistency between the performances, which would allow this data to be used to consistently control a parameter of the spatialization system, without requiring the performer to learn to use the system. As this movement is dependent on both the piece being played and the performer playing the piece, it allows for the control of spatialization parameters in a way which is directly tied to both the performer and the piece. The spatialization control becomes an intrinsic part of the performance. Similar consistancy of movement has also been found for changes in the center of mass of a clarinet performer and for the center of mass of a cello player, indicating that these could also be used to control the spatialization system in a similar way.

In order to allow us to make use of the performance gestures of instrumental performers, we have developed a wireless accelerometer-based system which can be either worn by the performer or directly attached to the instrument. The system tracks acceleration in 3 axes and can then be used to track a number of different gestures, including the clarinet bell movements discussed already. In particular we have found this system to be very useful in tracking aspects of cello performance gestures. When a cellist wears two of the accelerometer systems, one on each forearm, a number of interesting gesture parameters can be extracted. Thus far, we have managed to extract features such as bowing energy, relative position on the fingerboard and angle of bowing (which can allow us to determine which string is being bowed) [19]. Figure 3 gives some examples of these parameter signals. These gesture parameters can be used to subtly control sound source parameters allowing us to create interesting effects, such as mimicking changes in directivity which result from different playing techniques but which are lost when the sound is diffused using loudspeakers.

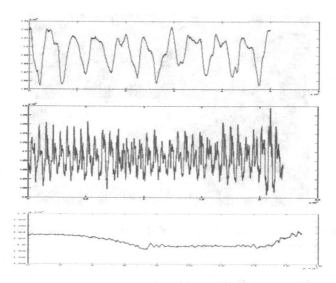

Fig. 3. Graphs of data captured from the accelerometer system worn by a cello performer. (a) bowing arm acceleration for regular bowing (b) bowing arm acceleration for tremolo bowing and (c) fingering arm rotation indicating relative position on the fingerboard.

5.3   Controlling Room and Environment Parameters: The Spatial Conductor

The control of room and environment model parameters offers scope for some unusual and large scale effects on the sound. By allowing the user in the role of spatial conductor to control these parameters, we allow them influence over the sound of the overall system and all the sounds within it. Simply by changing one parameter of the system, such as the virtual room size, the spatial conductor can make drastic changes to the overall system sound.

In order to implement a system for control of these parameters, we have once again used an instrumented data-glove system. Using a combination of bend sensors on the fingers and a 6 degree-of-freedom position tracker, we can recognize various hand gestures as a combination of hand postures (using the bend sensor signals) and movements (extracted from the position data). This allows us to evaluate the use of different gestures to control system parameters. Thus far, we have the ability to manipulate parameters such as room size (by grasping and stretching/shrinking the room), microphone ring diameter (through a measure of the openness of the hand) and reverb (through a hand posture together with a vertical position change). There remains some work in the evaluation of these gestures, along with the determination of an overall gesture vocabulary for these manipulations. Figure 4 shows a performer manipulating the size of the virtual room using an early prototype of the system.

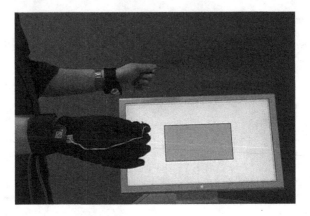

Fig. 4. A performer manipulating the size of the virtual room using simple hand postures and a stretching/shrinking motion

6   Discussion and Future Work

The primary aim of this work has been to investigate methods of gesture-based control of spatialization which have not so far seen much research. While systems such as our glove-based hand tracking system allow for a traditional direct manipulation-style interaction with a sound spatialization system, the other less traditional systems also offer some interesting forms of control.

Positioning sound sources using ballistic control methods or by steering using the performers center of mass offer a means in which a performers can spatialize sounds while still performing with their acoustic instruments. The spatialization becomes part of their performance. Using drum-pads for sound launching can allow a percussionist to both create and spatialize their own sounds, using gestures with which they are familiar. Similarly, a cello or clarinet performer can steer their own sound in the spatialization system while still playing their acoustic instrument. As has already been mentioned these systems offer a coarse level of control, rather than the fine level offered by the hand-tracking system. These systems could also place some extra level of cognitive load on the performer.

On the other hand, using data extracted from performers own gestures to control aspects of the spatialization system places less (in fact almost no) extra cognitive load on the performer. They can play their instrument and affect the spatialization system with little thought as to how the control is working. Choosing mappings such as one which increases the spatialized sounds brightness with increasing performer energy would mean that the performer would only have to play more or less energetically (and so think only in these terms rather than more complex ones) in order to affect the sound.

The division of the system control into the three primary roles already described also facilitates maximum control over the system. These roles also help distribute the cognitive load amongst the different performers based on the amount of work already placed on them by the performance. The roles themselves also inherit from the traditional roles of performer and conductor already present in orchestral performance.

While we have already been examining these roles and testing our systems in laboratory situations, there now remains the task of evaluating their use in actual concert spaces. As such we have planned to perform a number of experiments in concert halls to examine the control methods, both from the point of view of the performers and also of the audience. Also planned are a number of concerts which will make use of our interfaces, both singly for small pieces and together for larger performances. These tests, together with the performances, should allow us to examine in detail the usefulness of these systems as part of spatial musical performance.

7   Conclusion

This paper discussed our ongoing research into gesture control of sound spatialization. This work has involved the examination of a number of different existing spatialization systems in order to determine the types of parameters used in such a system which might be controlled using gesture. We have also examined a number of methods for gesture control from the human-computer interaction literature which might be useful in our project, as well as examining a number of mapping issues which impact the design of our systems.

Some examples of systems which we have developed and used for control of spatialization have also been discussed. We have been concentrating on three main roles for control of spatialization, which have been developed in conjunction with a composer to allow for good compositional use of gesture controlled spatialization. Results from informal use of the systems have been promising and now more formal evaluation is planned. Following on from this we will be holding a number of performances which will make use of these control interfaces to provide an aspect of gesture controlled sound spatialization.

Acknowledgements

This work has taken place with the support of the *Natural Science and Engineering Research Council of Canada* and the *Canada Council for the Arts*. Thanks to Chloe Dominguez for taking part in the motion capture sessions and to Nils Peters for feedback on the survey of spatialization systems.

References

1. Zvonar, R.: A history of spatial music (2006),
   http://cec.concordia.ca/econtact/Multichannel/spatial_music.html
2. Chadabe, J.: Electric Sound: The Past and Promise of Electronic Music. Prentice-Hall, Englewood Cliffs (1997)

3. Ramakrishnan, C., Goßmann, J., Brümmer, L.: The zkm klangdom. In: Proceedings of the 2006 Conference on New Interfaces for Musical Expression (2006)
4. Valbom, L., Marcos, A.: Wave: Sound and music in an immersive environment. Computers and Graphics 29, 871–881 (2005)
5. Naef, M., Collicott, D.: A vr interface for collaborative 3d audio performance. In: Proceedings of the 2006 International Conference on New Interfaces for Musical Expression (NIME 2006), pp. 57–60 (2006)
6. Wozniewski, M., Settel, Z., Cooperstock, J.: A system for immersive spatial audio performance. In: Proceedings of the 2006 Conference on New Interfaces for Musical Expression (2006)
7. Schacher, J.: Gesture control of sounds in 3d space. In: Proceedings of the 2007 Conference on New Interfaces for Musical Expression (NIME 2007), New York, USA, pp. 358–362 (2007)
8. Pulkki, V.: Spatial Sound Generation and Perception by Amplitude Panning Techniques. PhD thesis, Helsinki University of Technology (2001)
9. IRCAM: Spatializateur website, http://forumnet.ircam.fr/356.html
10. Braasch, J.: A loudspeaker based sound projection using virtual microphone control (vimic). In: 118th Convention of the AES, Barcelona, Spain (2005)
11. Spors, S., Teutsch, H., Rabenstein, R.: High-quality acoustic rendering with wave field synthesis. Vision, Modeling, and Visualization, 101–108 (2002)
12. Malham, D.: Spatial hearing mechanisms and sound reproduction. Technical report, Music Technology Group, University of York (1998)
13. Jacob, R.J.K., Sibert, L.E., McFarlane, D.C., Mullen, M.P.: Integrality and separability of input devices. ACM Transactions on Computer-Human Interaction 1(1), 3–26 (1994)
14. Cooper, G.: Research into cognitive load theory and instructional design at unsw (December 1998),
http://education.arts.unsw.edu.au/staff/sweller/clt/index.html
15. Cook, P.: Principles for designing computer music controllers. In: ACM CHI 2001 Workshop on New Interfaces for Musical Expression (2001)
16. Marshall, M.T., Peters, N., Jensenius, A.R., Boissinot, J., Wanderley, M.M., Braasch, J.: On the development of a system for the gesture control of spatialization. In: Proceedings of the International Computer Music Conference, pp. 260–266 (2006)
17. Baecker, R., Grudin, J., Buxton, W., Greenberg, S.: Readings in Human-Computer Interaction: Toward the Year 2000., 2nd edn. Morgan Kaufmann, San Francisco (1995)
18. Cadoz, C., Wanderley, M.: Gesture - music. Trends in Gesture Control of Music (2000)
19. Marshall, M., Malloch, J., Wanderley, M.: Using the 'energy' of performance gestures as a control for a spatialization system. Technical Report MUMT-IDMIL-07-08, Input Devices and Music Interaction Laboratory, McGill University (May 2007)

Validation of an Algorithm for Segmentation of Full-Body Movement Sequences by Perception: A Pilot Experiment

Donald Glowinski[1], Antonio Camurri[1], Carlo Chiorri[2], Barbara Mazzarino[1], and Gualtiero Volpe[1]

[1] InfoMus Lab-Casa Paganini- University of Genoa
Viale Causa 13, I-16145 Genoa, Italy
[2] Disa-Department of Anthropological Sciences/psychology unit- University of Genoa
Corso Andrea Podestà, 2 – 16128 –Genoa
{Donald.Glowinski,Antonio.Camurri,Carlo.Chiorri,
Barbara.Mazzarino,Gualtiero.Volpe}@unige.it

Abstract. This paper presents a pilot experiment for the perceptual validation by human subjects of a motion segmentation algorithm, i.e., an algorithm for automatically segmenting a motion sequence (e.g., a dance fragment) into a collection of pause and motion phases. Perceptual validation of motion and gesture analysis algorithms is an important issue in the development of multimodal interactive systems where human full-body movement and expressive gesture are a major input channel. The discussed experiment is part of a broader research at DIST-InfoMus Lab aiming at investigating the non-verbal mechanisms of communication involving human movement and gesture as primary conveyors of expressive emotional content.

Keywords: expressive gesture, motion segmentation, motion feature.

1 Introduction

Recent studies showed that full-body movement and gesture are important channels to communicate affect and people naturally express themselves through the use of their motor skills [1][2]. In this framework, segmentation of continuous motion sequences (e.g., dance fragments) in single motion units is an important step for performing expressive gesture analysis. Segmentation enables the identification of each motion unit and its representation through a set of values of relevant parameters. Higher-level analysis can then be employed to describe the qualitative components of movement in each segment. This is a fundamental step which is required in order to characterize a motion unit in terms of its contribution to the expressive content of the performance.

Our approach to segmentation of motion sequences starts from the problem of distinguishing sequences of motion and non-motion (pause) phases in a movement sequence. The present paper discusses an experiment aiming at validating an algorithm for motion segmentation implemented in the EyesWeb XMI open platform (www.eyesweb.org). Performing arts are an ideal test-bed for experiments in non-verbal communication of

M. Sales Dias et al. (Eds.): GW 2007, LNAI 5085, pp. 239–244, 2009.
© Springer-Verlag Berlin Heidelberg 2009

expressive content, since their longstanding tradition based on humanistic theories and performers' mastery of non-verbal communication channels. The experiment therefore focuses on segmentation of dance performances.

2 Segmentation of Motion Sequences

Our goal is to transform a continuous motion sequence into a sequence of motion units. Such segmentation is usually performed manually by humans, either by an expert [3] or non-expert [4] to recognize start and end of gesture patterns. Segmentation is the initial step of techniques for gesture recognition and classification. Starting from such a manual segmentation, techniques are applied for investigating body limbs trajectories and dynamics and looking for particular values (e.g. local minima, zero-crossing, values under experiment-based threshold) in low-level kinetic features (e.g. speed, acceleration). Machine learning techniques (e.g. Bayesian Classifier) are then employed for gesture classification. Results consist of semantic labels, and are validated through comparison with the classification of the same gestures performed by a sample group of subjects, i.e., results are considered to be good if gestures are classified in the same way as humans do. Another approach to gesture classification consists of finding gesture primitives whose combination results in complex gestures that are used by humans [5]. In this last case, humans may not have a conscious access to these basic patterns and evidence from motor analysis or neuroscience is needed to support the findings obtained with the computational approach.

Whereas gesture classification techniques are quite developed, the initial step of segmentation still need to be investigated in more depth. Moreover, the relation between automatic segmentation and segmentation manually performed by humans is an open issue. Our study addresses both algorithmic and perceptual issues and deals with a low-level but central aspect of gesture segmentation which has been poorly investigated: the detection of human motion activity. The distinction between motion and non-motion phases plays a central role to access motion qualities of human gesture (e.g., motion fluency, directness, impulsiveness, etc.). Some motion qualities actually rely on the comparison between the durations of motion and pause phases of a sequence, e.g. fluidity and impulsiveness, which are taken as exemplary expressive cues in the present study. A movement (e.g., a dance fragment) performed with frequent stops and restarts (i.e., characterized by a high number of short pauses and motion phases) will result less fluent than the same movement performed in a continuous way (i.e., with a few long motion phases.). In our model, the notion of fluentness/impulsiveness derives also from the Laban Movement Analysis [6] which describes qualitatively human movement in term of four main dimensions: "space", "time", "weight", and "flow". Fluentness and impulsiveness are particular linked with the "flow" dimension.

3 Perceptual Validation of Motion Segmentation

The experiment aims at the perceptual validation of our motion segmentation algorithm which is based on the *Quantity of Motion* movement cue. The QoM measure is related to the overall amount of motion which is evaluated by integrating in time the variations of the body silhouette (called Silhouette Motion Images - *SMI*). By scaling the SMI area by the most recent silhouette one, relative measures independent from the camera's distance can be obtained. QoM is computed from the following formula:

$$Quantity\_of\_Motion = Area(SMI[t, n]) / Area(Silhouette[t]).$$

QoM also includes contributions of internal motion (i.e., motion occurring in areas inside the silhouette) and weighted contributions of different parts of the silhouette (e.g., limbs and trunk have different weights). The quantity of motion is thus expressed in a range of values going from 0 to 1, in terms of fractions of the body area that moved. When a movement happens at instant *t*, it corresponds to a certain percentage of the total area covered by the silhouette. An empirically-tested based threshold on QoM is then employed to determine movement sequences and therefore to segment movement in motion and pause phases. The experiment consisted in comparing the outputs of this QoM-based algorithm with the judgements of subjects when applied to a dance sequence.

3.1 Material

A professional dancer performed the same short choreography (duration: 25s, frame rate: 25 fps) twice, with different expressive intentions: the first time the dance was performed in a fluent and smooth way (*smooth* performance), while the second performance was impulsive and jerky (*hard* performance). These dance fragments, also called 'micro-dances', were recorded with a video camera in a fixed position in front of the stage.

3.2 Subjects

The videos of the dances were presented to 11 subjects, aged between 20 and 30, without any specific experience in dance or choreography (n=11).

3.3 Method

Subjects were asked to indicate the motion and pause phases they perceived. Written instructions were provided. Subjects' task was to point out moments of pause in the micro-dance by pressing the space bar of a computer keyboard during all the pause duration and to release it when they were thinking that the pause was over (Onset/Outset detection). Both the *smooth* and the *hard* performances were shown to each subject in a randomized order. Before starting with the experiment, subjects were introduced to a training session during which they were presented with other similar videos for several times in order to overcome problems related to the reaction time to a visual stimulus and to the synchronization between vision and action. There were three pauses of different length for each expressive intention. Subjects' performances were collected and processed and then compared with the results obtained with the QoM-based algorithm. Figure 1 shows the comparison between subjects' performances and the output of the QoM-based segmentation algorithm. Left and right

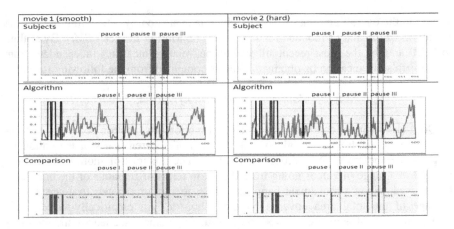

Fig. 1. Segmentation of movement sequences in pause and motion phases; from top to bottom (i)subject's judgements, (ii)Quantity of Motion values (QoM) and outputs of the automated segmentation algorithm (iii) comparison between subjects results and algorithm outputs

columns respectively show the segments/results obtained with the *smooth* and *hard* dances. Frames are labeled with '1' when belonging to a pause phase and '0' otherwise (motion phase). Human subjects' judgments were recorded as the frame at which they indicated the detection of the onset/offset of the pause. The algorithm outputs resulted from setting an empirically-tested threshold on the quantity of motion to distinguish between motion phase from pauses.

We compared the subjects and algorithm outputs by subtracting their values frame by frame. Values in the Comparison graph are therefore '–1', '0', or '1'. A frame with value '–1' means that a pause was detected only by the algorithm; a frame with value '0' value means that the algorithm matches subjects recognition of pause phases and a frame with value '1' means that only subjects recognized a pause.

Further investigation on the pause phase detection focused on the response time of the subjects. Response time was evaluated by analyzing the difference between the pause phase detection by the algorithm (considered as a reference) and the same pause phase detection by the subjects (when pressing and releasing the space bar). The time delays were then calculated in number of frames. A three-way completely within-subjects repeated measures analysis of variance (RM-ANOVA) was run in order to investigate the effects of Expressive Intention (smooth vs hard), Pause Phase (onset vs end) and Pause (1 vs 2 vs 3) and their interactions on time delay of detection.

3.4 Results

All subjects perceived the main pauses (pauses I, II and III). However, not all pause phases detected by the algorithm were pointed out by subjects. This could be explained partially by the presentation order and by the pause duration. Most pauses missed by subjects start at the very beginning of the micro-dance where subjects discovered the sequence. The other non-detected pauses were missed when their duration was under 0.2 s ($\Delta < 0.2$s). Conversely, pauses detected by subjects (pauses I, II, and III) started at least 10s after the sequence and their duration was greater than 0.4 s ($\Delta > 0.4$ s).

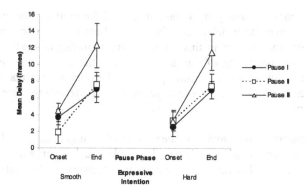

Fig. 2. Pause Phase × Expressive Intentions × Pause interaction plot. Whiskers represent 95% confidence intervals of estimated marginal means.

RM-ANOVA revealed a significant main effect of Pause Phase ($F(1, 10) = 151.64$, $p < .001$) and of Pause ($F(2, 20) = 13.96$, $p < .001$) and of the Pause Phase × Pause interaction ($F(2, 20) = 7.97$, $p = .003$). These results indicated that time delays were longer at the End, with respect to the Onset, of the Pause and, all other factors kept constant, longer for Phase 3 with respect to Phases 1 and 2 (Bonferroni-adjusted $p = .006$ and $p = .002$, respectively). However, when taking Pause Phase into account, such pattern of differences could be observed only for the End of the pause, and not for the Onset, thus accounting for the statistical significance of the interaction effect. Figure 2 shows also that no confidence interval contained 0 (i.e., no delay).

4 Discussion and Conclusions

Results suggest that it seems easier (i.e., faster) to detect a pause after a motion phase than to detect a motion after a pause phase. Further research is needed to determine whether this greater delay in end recognition is due to perceptual factors or/and to motor constraints. For instance, a pause in a sequence of movement could have priming effects on response speed and accuracy. Conversely, the observed delay could be accounted for by a deficit in key-releasing task. The two expressive intentions (*smooth* and *hard*) did not seem to affect the segmentation process. Mean delay values did not differ in pauses I and II, regardless of phase (onset/end), whereas in pause III delays were significantly larger than other pauses at the end. Greater delays concerning pause III recognition could then be accounted for by the temporal proximity between the last two pauses (pauses II and III are only distant of 1.5s) than by the quality of the dancer movement.

This paper presented a pilot experiment for the perceptual validation by subjects of a motion segmentation algorithm. The experiment showed that the developed algorithm performs a good detection of the most significant pause and motion phases in a pattern of movements and in particular in a dance fragment. It also appeared that subjects segmented dance sequence with equal ability in both types of performances. Expressive features of the motion itself did not seem to interfere with the segmentation process, either when pauses were close from one to another. We plan to investigate if the expressive content conveyed by the dancer and the motion segmentation process by subjects can give rise to learning effects. Specifically, we wonder whether (i) the motion segmentation evolves in time after a certain number of trials or if it remains constant since the beginning of the task and (ii) if the expressive content (*hard* or *smooth*) could influence such learning process. The obtained results should provide new guidelines for improving motion segmentation algorithms able to emulating human perception.

Acknowledgments. This work has been partially supported by EU-ICT Project SAME (Sound and Music for Everyone, Everyday, Everywhere, Every way, www.sameproject.eu). Thanks to the anonymous reviewers for the useful comments.

References

1. Wallbott, H.G.: Bodily expression of emotion. European Journal of Social Psychology 28, 879–896 (1998)
2. Camurri, A., De Poli, G., Leman, M., Volpe, G.: Toward Communicating Expressiveness and Affect in Multimodal Interactive Systems for Performing Art and Cultural Applications. IEEE Multimedia Magazine 12(1), 43–53 (2005)
3. Bouchard, D., Badler, N.: Semantic segmentation of motion capture using Laban Movement Analysis. In: Pelachaud, C., Martin, J.-C., André, E., Chollet, G., Karpouzis, K., Pelé, D. (eds.) IVA 2007. LNCS, vol. 4722, pp. 37–44. Springer, Heidelberg (2007)
4. Kahol, K., Tripathi, P., Panchanathan, S.: Automated gesture segmentation from dance sequences. In: Proceedings of Sixth IEEE International Conference on Automatic Face and Gesture Recognition, 2004, pp. 883–888 (2004)
5. Fod, A., Mataric, M.J., Jenkins, O.C.: Automated Derivation of Primitives for Movement Classification. Auton. Robots 12(1), 39–54 (2002)
6. Bartenieff, I., Davis, M.: Effort-Shape analysis of movement: The unity of expression and function. In: Davis, M. (ed.) Research Approaches to Movement and Personality. Arno Press Inc., New York (1972)

Signs Workshop: The Importance of Natural Gestures in the Promotion of Early Communication Skills of Children with Developmental Disabilities

Ana Margarida P. Almeida[1], Teresa Condeço[2], Fernando Ramos[1], Álvaro Sousa[1], Luísa Cotrim[2], Sofia Macedo[2], and Miguel Palha[2]

[1] Department of Communication and Arts, University of Aveiro,
Campus de Santiago, 3810-193 Aveiro
[2] Differences, Child Developmental Centre, Centro Comercial da Bela Vista,
Av. Santo Condestável, Loja 32, Via Central de Chelas, 1950-094 Lisboa

Abstract. This article emphasises the importance of natural gestures and describes the framework and the development process of the "Signs Workshop" CD-ROM, which is a multimedia application for the promotion of early communication skills of children with developmental disabilities. Signs Workshop CD-ROM was created in the scope of Down's Comm Project, which was financed by the Calouste Gulbenkian Foundation, and is the result of a partnership between UNICA (Communication and Arts Research Unit of the University of Aveiro) and the Portuguese Down Syndrome Association (APPT21/Differences).

Keywords: language and communication skills, augmented communication systems, total communication (simultaneous use of signs and language), multimedia production.

1 Introduction

The Down's Comm Project, fully financed by the Calouste Gulbenkian Foundation, is the result of a partnership between the Communication and Arts Research Unit of the University of Aveiro (UNICA) and the Portuguese Down Syndrome Association/Differences (APPT21).

This project's main objective was to research (and translate into an interactive multimedia application) examples of natural gestures from the Portuguese culture, in order to ensure the expansion and flexibility of its use by parent, educators and therapist who care for children with developmental disabilities, particularly children with difficulties in the development of speech.

Thus, it is intended to help in the creation of support strategies in order to promote the early stage of sign utilization, understood as a critical link which ensures the transition from the pre-verbal communication stage to the spoken language stage [1].

This research project resulted in the production of the Signs Workshop CD-ROM, which is clearly directed to a population target characterized by a developmental disability and speech difficulties from birth, and is assumed to be a working support

M. Sales Dias et al. (Eds.): GW 2007, LNAI 5085, pp. 245–254, 2009.

tool for parents, educators and therapists who work for the promotion of communication and interactions skills.

Within this framework, the main objectives of the Signs Workshop CD-ROM are: to promote the development of language and communication skills, at the pre-verbal stage; to enable learning and access to different natural gestures, commonly used in the Portuguese day to day culture; to provide, for each gesture, a set of information in several formats (text, sound, image, video), enabling various and personalized searches.

2   Communication Skills and Sign Communication Systems

Children with developmental difficulties, especially those with Down Syndrome, present changes in the development and use of language, with particular emphasis at the speech development level [2] [3] [4]. Hence, the subsequent difficulties to communicate surface since the pre-verbal stage, which result in a general tendency to show passivity in communicating and in a low ability to take initiative towards interacting with other individuals.

Therefore, these children's abilities to express themselves verbally are frequently inferior to those of understanding [5] [6] [7]. In some cases, children may not even be able to speak comprehensibly as the result of a deep developmental disability, great hearing loss or great motor or neuro-muscular difficulties [5] [3].

Some studies suggest that, in these cases, the bridge or link between the pre-verbal communication stage and the spoken language stage may be ensured by an early use of signs, which should thus precede the introduction of verbal signs. This should also be the time to promote a guided access and use of communication media [1] [8] [5] [9] [10] [11].

It is within this framework that Augmented Communication Systems are proposed. These systems provide an important support to message expression by the individuals who present speech difficulties, either temporary or permanent. In this context, it is important to identify Augmented Communication with all systems which supplement, support or substitute speech.

The Sign Communication Systems or Sign Language Systems, when organized in symbolic or coded signs, are examples of the Augmented Communication Systems frequently used [12]. In effect, in the specific case of children with Trisomy 21, the Augmented Communication System designated as Total Communication (simultaneous use of signs and language) is intensively used as a temporary system of transition during the early stages of speech development. This transition temporary system is particularly appropriate to children who did not initiate speech exercise around the 12-18 months of age, and who, in consequence, present signs of frustration by their incapacity of being understood by parents, siblings or other individuals [12].

The application of this Total Communication System highlights, therefore, the importance of using signs as a support to various communication functions, which would not be possible any other way: request, make questions, ask for information, express their own experiences or play.

From the viewpoint of parent-child interaction, the use of signs also enhances the communication processes and their adaptation to the child's abilities: the use of signs that represent words, by the parents, occurs in contexts where they speak slower, use shorter sentences and, probably, put into emphasis the words that are said and signalled [13]. Another significant feature of simultaneous signalling and speech is the fact that parents assure eye contact with the child while communicating with them. Parents are, thus, in a better position to observe their children's behaviour and responses, and react accordingly [13]. The simultaneous use of visual and audio communication forms may, then, facilitate information gathering and thus enhance cognitive skills [13].

3 Portuguese Cultural Daily Life Signs Standardization

The research made by the APPT21/Diferenças team, with the objective of standardizing the signs to include in the CD-ROM, was gathered among Portuguese population (continent and islands) with diagnosed Down Syndrome, who, in an early age, uses or has used, at some point, Total Communication (simultaneous use of natural gestures and speech).

To achieve its goal, the team produced an inventory built from existing national and international approaches: American Sign Language, Portuguese Sign Language Book, Portuguese Makaton, "See & Say" of the Sarah Duffen Centre of Portsmouth, and also information gathered from the experience of the APPT21/Differenças therapist team [14] [15] [16].

The mentioned inventory (figure 1) was sent to parents whose children have Down Syndrome and to therapists and educators who work with this population. They were asked to identify the signs they use in daily life and to suggest others for the presented concepts. They were also asked to provide information of other signs or concepts that were not included in the inventory.

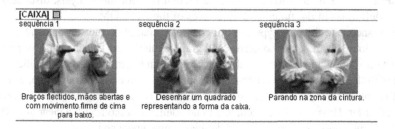

Fig. 1. Example of a sign in the inventory

After analyzing the returned inventories, the team proceeded with the data treatment: the suggested signs were added to the initial inventory, and others were modified according to the parents and therapist's recommendations. At the end of the research, the team was able to gather and standardize 184 signs.

4 Specification and Development of the Multimedia Application

Once defined the objectives and contents for the application, functional requirements specification proceeded: language selection (Portuguese, English, Spanish); sign search (alphabetically, open field and by category); user profile creation (in order for the user to store the favourite signs); user profile registration (by inserting a login); user profile edition (user can remove, add or print favourite signs); sign search according to profile (search for stored signs); sign search display (includes the sign designation, text and audio description, video and graphic display sequences); printing sign search display (includes the sign designation, text description and graphic display sequences); signs in context (permits sign viewing from the same context of the selected sign); adding signs to user profile (adds the selected sign to the user profile); help section (user support for CD-ROM interaction and navigation).

5 Functional and Technical Design

After specifying the conceptual model which resulted from the identification of the above mentioned functional requirements, the CD-ROM production was taken to the next level – the functional design [17] – and a paper script was created. This allowed not only having a clearer view of all functionalities to include in this application, but also facilitated communication among the design team.

At this point, it was also initiated a technical viability study, with the objective of beginning the parallel and iterative development of the Technical Design [17], as well as to determine which technology would be more suitable for the production of this application. In order to ensure the communication between the sign's database and the application's interface, the team decided to use Microsoft Access and Macromedia Director (with Xtras Datagrip, BuddyAPI and FileIO).

As soon as the script and the technical viability study were validated, a prototype was developed. This prototype assumed a crucial role for the analysis, discussion and correct definition of the functional objectives of the CD-ROM.

Simultaneous to the prototype creation, the team started on the communication design studies: colour schemes, symbols/icons and graphic interfaces. The challenge of providing adequate responses to specific social, technological and communicative conditions, combined with the need to create a user-friendly interface with a fast learning rate, lead to the specification of three key concepts which sustain the communication design: space, lightness and order. Having that outlined, and in an attempt to accomplish a clear and efficient visual scheme, three main colours were defined: white, green and grey.

The symbol (figure 2), based upon a line sketch and with a clear hand-like characteristic, represents two hands of a character with an open smile, and intends to create an environment of involvement. The emotional aspect of this illustration meets the sentimental feature of this application, balancing a more rational side manifested in all structural and formal aesthetic of the CD-ROM: the green colour (fresh and bright) offers it lightness and joy, and it is used as a distinguishing shade, allowing to weaken the grey's neutrality, which was chosen for the information elements.

As far as interface designing is concerned, a grid/layout was created allowing the establishment of structuring areas (navigation and contents) and of a set of navigation icons, which in coherence with the formal language represent the main functions and ensure an immediate viewing of all accessible fields (figure 3).

Fig. 2. Symbol

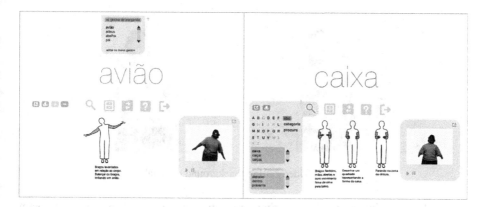

Fig. 3. Graphic Interfaces

6   Content Creation and Edition

The design of the sign's graphic representations (in different image sequences) was made from a graphic simplification and systematization of the human figure (figure 4). This figure, reduced to a contoured line, is somewhat between a realistic representation of the person who signals and a schematic representation, and adds a more rational

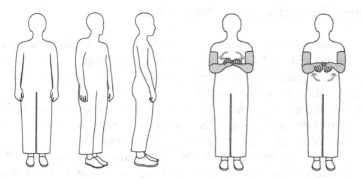

Fig. 4. Graphic systematization of the human figure and graphic representation sequence

illustrative feature to the application. From the mentioned graphic organization, was then possible to sketch the different sequences of the graphic representations of the 184 signs (figure 4).

In what concerns video contents, which show the real representation of a sign, 184 signs were captured in the APPT21 facilities: young boys and girls with Trisomy 21 executed the signs. During the process of recording and editing, the team gave special attention to the issues of light, saturation and contrast. With the objective of eliminating backgrounds (the intention was to obtain just the body outline over the application's white background), it was necessary to equalize the levels of light and to apply background removal filters (figure 5).

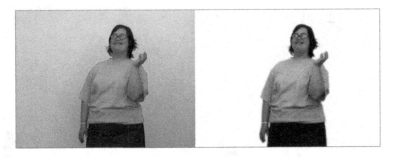

Fig. 5. Video editing (background removal)

Fulfilling the intention of integrating descriptive audio cuts of the signs, the team recorded and edited the 184 signs in the CD-ROM's three available languages: Portuguese, English and Spanish. The purpose of including audio features in the application is to support the video footage and the visual sign representations, in order to reinforce sign learning. Therefore, for each sign three distinct audio cuts can be differentiated: the sign designation, the sign's complete text description (for video support), the sign's partial text description (for supporting the graphic representation sequences).

7   Application Editing and Distribution

Once the application was concluded, the next stage was initiated: development of broadcast, distribution and support tools. To this end, a support website was created (http://www.ca.ua.pt/dc), as well as an e-mail account to establish contact lines and support to the CD-ROM's end-users (oficinadosgestos@ca.ua.pt).

The CD-ROM editing process (equally financed by the Calouste Gulbenkian Foundation) included the design of the packages and production of the 1500 copies, currently available for purchase at the APPT21/Differenças.

The package design process, CD-ROM label (figure 6) and user manual followed the same graphic elements developed by the design team, in order to bolster the visual identity of the product.

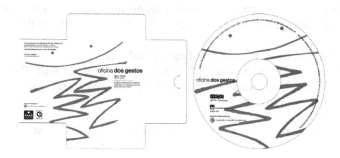

Fig. 6. CD-ROM's Package and Label

8 Case Studies Short Description

After the Signs Workshop CD-ROM development, many children with developmental disabilities have started using it, within the context of their personalized Early Intervention Programmes.

These programmes aim at promoting early communication skills, cognition and motor development and include the use of natural gestures as a Total Communication System. The familiar context is the main focus of this intervention: both family members and the child are introduced to the natural use of gesture as an effective support of the spoken word.

Early Intervention Programmes are structured in weakly sessions in which the psychologist, responsible for introducing the previous selected gestures, works with the child and the caregiver (usually, the mother or the father). Several activities and strategies that stimulate communication development are established for each weakly session and the caregivers are taught how and when to perform the gestures, so that they can use them effectively. Caregivers are also responsible for teaching the gestures to other family members and to kindergarten staff.

Case 1
Case 1 is a 21 months old boy with Down Syndrome. He's on the Early Intervention Programme since 3 months old. Natural gestures were introduced at 4 months old and he is now able to express his needs and desires, like asking for food, toys or a particular kind of game. The child has already a repertoire of 20 gestures and is already able to "respond" to questions like "What's this?" or "What are you doing?".

He stays at home with his mother, so the 20 gestures that are now part of his repertoire are used with the closer family, especially with his 4 years old sister who motivates and helps him to perform the natural gestures.

Case 2
Case 2 is a 3 years old boy with Down Syndrome that is also on the Early Intervention Programme. He was introduced to the natural gesture since 10 months old and has now a repertoire of 30 natural gestures.

This child uses natural gestures at home, with his mother, and at kindergarten to ask for some particular kind of food, to go to the bathroom, or "respond" to the caregiver.

Gestures examples used by case 1 and case 2 children
Both case 1 and case 1 children use different gestures from the Signs Workshop CD-ROM as Eat, Drink, Dog, Cow, Banana and Orange, presented in Figure 7.

Gesture	Video frame	Graphic representation Sequence	Text description
Eat			The closed hand approaches the mouth as if placing an imaginary food-stuff in it. The movement is re-peated several times.
Drink			The hand grasps an imaginary glass, the thumb close to the mouth. The hand tilts further back towards the mouth.
Dog			Flexed arms, hands close to chest with palms down. The middle finger and the index finger (in a V position) mimic the movement of walking legs.
Cow			The index fingers pointing upwards from each side of the head mimicking the horns of a cow.

Fig. 7. Gestures examples

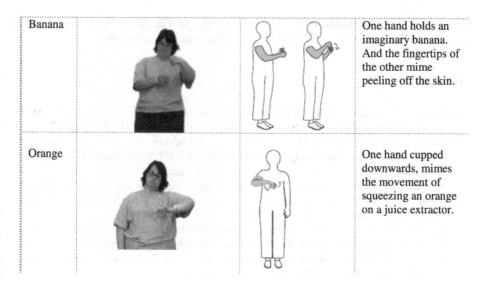

| Banana | | | One hand holds an imaginary banana. And the fingertips of the other mime peeling off the skin. |
| Orange | | | One hand cupped downwards, mimes the movement of squeezing an orange on a juice extractor. |

Fig. 7. (*continued*)

9 Conclusions

The development process of the Signs Workshop CD-ROM was frame worked within an extended methodological model, in which not only the specification and conception of a multimedia software was valued, but mainly its adequate application to the individual, social and environmental particularities of its target population.

The intensity and richness of the constant interactions with the end-users during the development process, enabled the accomplishment of the inter-disciplinary features that characterize this project, as well as widen work methods directed to the permanent contact with the natural environments of the target-group and, in consequence, develop suitable solutions to its specific universe.

By widely distributing this multimedia application, it is intended to make a positive contribution to the consolidation of knowledge on natural human signs within the context of Portuguese culture and provide to the education community a set of extended natural gestures, adequate to the development characteristics of Portuguese children with development disabilities.

Acknowledgments

The authors would like to thank to the Calouste Gulbenkian Foundation for the financial support; to the scholarship students Margarida Girão, Catarina Melo e Silva and Ana Filipa Gomes for the constant commitment and dedication to this project; to the young Teresa Palha and Henry Turquin (and families) for the participation in the video footage; to CEMED (Multimedia and Distant Learning Centre of the University of Aveiro) for the support in digital treatment and video editing; to João Miguel Lopes, José Leite, Laura Astorgano and Lina Hayek for collaborating in audio recording; to Manuela Castro, Maria João Santos and Rocio Bobadilha for the support in the translations; to

Rui Pereira, Tiago Almeida, Pedro Almeida and Diogo Valente for the technical support; and to Fernando Ferreira for support in the inventory development.

References

1. Buckley, S., Bird, G.: Teaching Children with Down's syndrome to Read. Down's Syndrome Research and Practice. The Journal of Sarah Duffen Centre 1(1), 34–39 (1993)
2. Pueschel, S.M.: Visual and Auditory Processing in Children with Down Syndrome. In: Nadel, L. (ed.) The Psychobiology of Down Syndrome, pp. 199–216. National Down Syndrome Society, Library of Congress, Mit Press, Cambridge (1988)
3. Wishart, J.G.: Early Learning in Infants and Young Children with Down Syndrome. In: Nadel, L. (ed.) The Psychobiology of Down Syndrome, pp. 1–50. National Down Syndrome Society, Library of Congress, MIT Press, Cambridge (1988)
4. Wishart, J.G.: Cognitive Development in Young Children with Down Syndrome: development strengths, development weaknesses. In: Down Syndrome in the 21st Century: 1st Biennial Scientific Conference on Down Syndrome, Down Syndrome Research Foundation and Resource Centre (1998) (accessed on: 19-01-01), http://www.altonweb.com/cs/downsyndrome/wishart.html
5. Kumin, L.: Communication Skills in Children with Down Syndrome, A Guide for Parents. Woodbine House, Bethesda (1994)
6. Miller, J.F.: The Development Asynchrony of Language Development in Children with Down Syndrome. In: Nadel, L. (ed.) The Psychobiology of Down Syndrome, pp. 167–198. National Down Syndrome Society, Library of Congress, MIT Press, Cambridge (1988)
7. Miller, J.F., Leddy, M., Leavitt, L.A. (eds.): Improving the Communication of People with Down Syndrome. Paul H. Brookes Publishing Company, Baltimore (1999)
8. Kliewer, W.: Issues Involved in Facilitated Communication and People with Down Syndrome. Facilitated Communication Digest 3(1), 8–14 (1994) (accessed on: 19-01-2001), http://www.altonweb.com/cs/downsyndrome/fcandds.html
9. Spiker, D., Hopmann, M.R.: The effectiveness of Early Intervention for Children with Down Syndrome. In: Guaralnick, M.J. (ed.) The effectiveness of Early Intervention, vol. 13. Paul. H. Brookes Publishing Company (1997) (accessed on: 19-01-2001), http://www.altonweb.com/cs/downsyndrome/eieffective.html
10. Vergason, G.A., Anderegg, M.L. (eds.): Dictionary of Special Education and Rehabilitation, 4th edn. Love Publishing Company, Denver (1997)
11. Von Tetzchner, S., Martinsen, H.: Introdução à Comunicação Aumentativa e Alternativa. Porto: Porto Editora, Colecção Educação Especial (2000)
12. Light, J., Lindsay, P.: Cognitive Science and Augmentative and Alternative Communication, Augmentative and Alternative Communication 7, 186–203 (1991)
13. Buckley, S.J.: Teaching children with Down syndrome to Read and Write. In: Nadel, L., Rosenthal, D. (eds.) Down Syndrome: Living and Learning in the Community, pp. 158–169. Wiley, New York (1995)
14. Barns, L.: ASL - American Sign Language. Harper Perennial, New York (1990)
15. SNRIPD, Gestuário de Língua Portuguesa, 2 edn. Lisboa, Secretariado Nacional de Reabilitação de Pessoas com Deficiência (1995)
16. Le Prevost., P.: See & Say, T.F.H., Stourport (1990)
17. Strauss, R.: Managing Multimedia Projects. Focal Press, Boston (1997)

The Ergonomic Analysis of the Workplace of Physically Disabled Individuals

Matthieu Aubry[1], Frédéric Julliard[1], and Sylvie Gibet[2]

[1] Université Européenne de Bretagne, LISyC
{aubry,julliard}@enib.fr
[2] Université de Bretagne Sud, Valoria
sylvie.gibet@univ-ubs.fr

Abstract. This paper presents a new gesture-based approach for the ergonomic evaluation of the workplaces of the physically handicapped. After a brief overview of tools using interactive simulation to perform ergonomic analysis, we describe the requirements to perform ergonomic analyses for the disabled. We then propose a framework unifying the synthesis and analysis of motions and integrating a model of disabilities based on constraints. Finally, we present preliminary results following the implementation of a constraint enabled kinematic controller.

Keywords: Ergonomics, Interactive simulation, Gesture, Inverse kinematics.

1 Introduction

The design of virtual environments for ergonomics has gained considerable research interest in recent years. Many tools have been developed to perform ergonomic analysis in virtual environments [4], for example: Jack [1], SAMMIE [9], MANERCOS [6] and SAFEWORK [13].

These tools are commonly used by designers to perform occupational ergonomic analysis on a virtual mock-up by immersing a virtual human controlled by direct or inverse kinematics. Within the above applications, the human models account for about 90% of the population, but those with specific needs are unfortunately excluded, especially the physically handicapped.

A new approach, called "design-for-all" [3] aims to perform accessibility tests on an even wider range of the population. To achieve this goal, a database containing the movements of physically disabled persons has been developed [9]. Using this data, it is possible to display the problems that each recorded individual is expected to experience. However, recorded behaviors cannot easily be applied to new tasks or individuals. We here present a preliminary work which aims to overcome those restrictions.

This paper is organized as follows: the first section describes the requirements necessary to perform ergonomic analysis for the disabled using an interactive simulation. The next section presents a framework dedicated to the analysis

M. Sales Dias et al. (Eds.): GW 2007, LNAI 5085, pp. 255–260, 2009.

and the synthesis of a physically disabled person's movements. The last section highlights the current status of our work and presets the preliminary results. We conclude with the progress of this study and the challenges for future work.

2 Ergonomic Analysis of a Disabled Person's Workplace

Before carrying out an ergonomic analysis, it is necessary to specify the characteristics of both the workplace, and the operator in the virtual environment.

To describe the workplace, one should prefer a functional description which simplifies the interactions between the humanoid and the objects in its environment. Both the Parametrized Action Representation proposed by Badler et al. [2] and the Smart Object framework proposed by Kallmann [8] have already been used for ergonomic analysis. To increase the realism of the interactions between the humanoid and its environment, a physical simulator can also be used.

When integrating a virtual human in this environment, there are varying notions of *virtual fidelity* [1]. Ergonomics necessitates knowledges about anthropometric data, functional ability, admissible joint angles, but also physiological data like maximum strengths, recovery time or fatigability. Modeling disabilities is discussed in the next section, which presents a framework dealing with the movements of physically disabled individuals. Ergonomic analysis can therefore be performed by simulating the operator's activity (meaning his/her motions).

Ergonomic analysis can be performed at three main levels: task level, occupational level and physiological level. At task level, empirical laws may be used to evaluate the ergonomics of a specific task from preliminary information without any simulation process. However, task analysis may require preconditions concerning the capacities of the operator that may not be verified, especially for people with disabilities. For example, the revised NIOSH equation [12] can compute a comfort score of a lifting task using only two parameters: the initial posture and load lifted, but only for healthy people.

Using simulated movements, analysis can be performed at an occupational level. Reach, accessibility or field of vision analysis are parts of the tests that can be performed here. This level has the advantage that it can be used with any individual while the motions analyzed are realistic. However, the majority of studies dealing with human movements prove the difficulty obtaining accurate data [4].

The analysis performed at physiological level deals with the forces implied by the motion to provide information like fatigue or muscular pain. For example, the joint-level model proposed in Rodriguez et al. [11] computes a coefficient of fatigue from the forces applied to the articulation. The main problem with these physiological methods is the requirement of complex models to simulate muscle activity. However, adding physical capabilities to the simulation should help retrieve forces and torques.

Using the results from the different levels of analysis, ergonomists can point out the problems in the operator's activity and try to improve the workplace. They can iterate this simulation-modification process until the workplace fits the operator's activity. However, to compare the simulations, the analysis method has to provide comparable results [10].

The next section describes a framework associated to a model of physical disabilities which both synthesizes motions and retrieves the necessary data for each level of analysis.

3   An Analysis–Synthesis Framework

After a description of our physical disabilities model, we present a framework which is used to simulate the motions of physically disabled individuals and to retrieve relevant data for ergonomic analysis.

Ergonomist are mainly interested in the consequences of the handicap on the individual's functional abilities. To model disabilities, we propose to apply a set of constraints matching those consequences on the motion controller. We categorize these constraints into three groups: effector constraints (ex: broken arm, amputation), kinematic constraints (ex: joint properties, inaccurate pointing) and physical constraints (ex: strength limits).

We now propose a motion analysis–synthesis framework (Fig 1) which integrates our constraint model. In our framework, we have a chain of four controllers. Each interaction of the simulation entered into the *interaction controller* result in variations of the virtual humanoid's posture until the interaction is achieved. The next paragraph describes and illustrates the operation of our framework.

First, the *interaction controller* conveys the interaction as a goal. As an example, we consider a *click* on a bottle would be translated as *pick up(bottle)* and transmitted to the task controller. This second controller coordinates the motor commands necessary to achieve this goal: *pick up(bottle)* → X.*reach for*(bottle), X being an effector. It also manages the effectors, and has to respect the constraints specified by the handicap model. For example, if the right hand is amputated then X will be set to left hand. The resulting motor commands are passed to the kinematic controller. This third controller is in charge of the generation of a posture from which the desired motor command may be achieved (*reach for* → *get the effector closer to the target*). The algorithm behind this controller may be function of the motor command. Kinematic constraints are passed as parameters of the controller and must be respected by the resulting posture. If

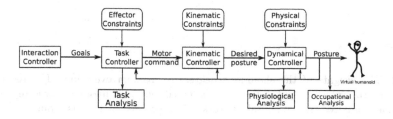

Fig. 1. The analysis–synthesis framework

a physical simulator is enabled, the dynamic controller generates forces on the humanoid to achieve the desired posture. Once again, many algorithms can be used [14] and the choice might be function of the task. The virtual humanoid must nonetheless respect the constraints passed and the rules of physics, should collisions occur. The posture obtained is given back to the task controller which determines if the goal is achieved. The kinematic controller will generate new postures while the goals are not achieved. Respecting the constraints specified in the handicap model, the synthesized motion should reproduce the capabilities of the physically disabled individual. Therefore, to provide an ergonomic analysis, goals definitions can be used for task analysis, postures for occupational analysis and forces and torques for physiological analysis.

The next section presents some preliminary results in implementing the kinematic controller part of our model.

4   Preliminary Results

Our current work deals with the implementation of a kinematic controller carrying out reaching commands. Our controller is based on that proposed by Gibet et al. [5] which already reproduces some features of human motion. This controller is based on a transposed jacobian method. It also includes a weighting process, favoring the use of specific joints in depending on time restraints. The original study showed that it was possible, using a sigmoid, to reproduce the shape of hand's speed when reaching.

We propose to enhance this weighting process to synthesize motions reflecting the physical characteristics of a person. The current study focus on extracting those weighting constraints from recorded movements and re-using them.

The skeleton used for recording has 3 degrees of freedom for each of the 4 joints used to reproduce arm motions (wrist, elbow, shoulder and a virtual joint on the spine). Therefore, for each frame of the motion, we compute a vector of 12 weights, depending on time and posture. Samples of the computed weights are shown in figure 2.

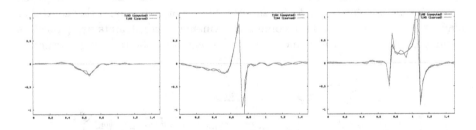

Fig. 2. The weights of the shoulder's degrees of freedom over time. The red curve represents the value computed from the captured motion. The green curve represents the value computed by the neural network using recorded motion as input.

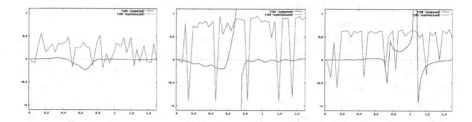

Fig. 3. The weights of the shoulder's degrees of freedom over time. The red curve represents the value computed from the captured motion. The green curve represents the value computed by the neural network taking input from the simulation.

To use the weights as a constraint, we propose the use of a feed-forward neural network [7] that would compute the weights depending on time and posture. We trained a neural network with the data extracted from a single motion. We reached 97% precision, meaning the average distance between the weight computed from the motion and the weight computed by the neural network in the same condition is below 0.03 (cf. Fig. 2).

Thus, we tried to synthesize the motion used for training using this neural network. Having a weight close to the original, we thought we would obtain the same motion. But even if the precision seemed correct, the small error at the output of the neural network led to a dysfunction of our controller. Indeed, our controller being a loop, the error at the output came back to its input and this difference at the input of the neural network completely changed its output. Finally, instead of obtaining learned curves, we obtained interference (cf. Fig. 3) which disrupted our controller and prevented it from reaching the target.

While we are currently analyzing these results and trying to solve this problem, we present some future perspectives in the conclusion.

5 Conclusion

This paper aimed to present a framework for the ergonomic analysis of the workplace of physically disabled individuals. We presented the three main requirements for performing ergonomic analysis: a functional description of the environment, a simulation using dynamics and motion synthesis reproducing the constraints caused by disabilities. Based on those essentials, we propose a framework which should enable the synthesis and analysis of the motions of disabled individuals. This framework included a constraint model able to reproduce disabilities a three levels : effector, kinematic and physical. Then, we present our preliminary results concerning the implementation of a constraint enabled kinematic controller. Constraints are expressed as weights applied to the use of degrees of freedom. To determine weights according to time and posture, we trained a neural network from a real motion. Finally, we showed that although we obtain good results during training, we cannot reproduce this motion due to the diffusion of the error in the controller.

Our future work will focus on the enhancement of our weight based constraint model. We are currently considering several enhancements to solve the disruption of our controller. In order to stabilize the weight at the output on small variations of the input, we may generalize the learning process over several motions or replace the neural network by a more stable algorithm. We are also considering the possibility of changing our evaluation method for the neural network. Instead of considering an accurate network as that which reproduces the weights extracted from the motion, we would consider it that which, when used, enables the controller to reproduce the recorded motion. We would then use a meta-heuristic to find the most appropriate network.

References

1. Badler, N.I.: Virtual Humans for Animation, Ergonomics, and Simulation. In: Non-rigid and Articulated Motion Workshop, pp. 28–36 (1997)
2. Badler, N.I., Palmer, M.S., Bindiganavale, R.: Animation control for real-time virtual humans. Commun. ACM 42, 64–73 (1999)
3. Case, K., Porter, M., Gyi, D., Marshall, R., Oliver, R.: Virtual fitting trials in design for all. Journal of Materials Processing Tech. 117, 255–261 (2001)
4. Chedmail, P., Maille, B., Ramstein, E.: Etat de l'art sur l'accessibilité et l'étude de l'ergonomie en réalité virtuelle. Mécanique Industrielle, 147–152 (2002)
5. Gibet, S., Marteau, P.F.: A self-organized model for the control, planning and learning of nonlinear multi-dimensional systems using a sensory feedback. Applied Intelligence 4, 337–349 (1994)
6. Gomes, S., Sagot, J.C., Koukam, A., Leroy, N.: MANERCOS, a new tool providing ergonomics in a concurrent engineering design life cycle. In: Euromedia 1999, pp. 237–241 (1999)
7. Hassoun, M.H.: Fundamentals of Artificial Neural Networks. MIT Press, Cambridge (1995)
8. Kallmann, M., Thalmann, D.: Modeling Objects for Interaction Tasks. In: Computer Animation and Simulation 1998, pp. 73–86 (1998)
9. Porter, J.M., Case, K., Marshall, R., Gyi, D.: Beyond Jack and Jill: designing for individuals using HADRIAN. International Journal of Industrial Ergonomics, 249–264 (2004)
10. Reed, M.P., Faraway, J., Chaffin, D.B., Martin, B.J.: The HUMOSIM Ergonomics Framework: A New Approach to Digital Human Simulation for Ergonomic Analysis. Human Factors and Ergonomics in Manufacturing 17, 475–484 (2007)
11. Rodriguez, I., Boulic, R., Meziat, D.: A Joint-level Model of Fatigue for the Postural Control of Virtual Humans. Journal of 3D Forum, 70–75 (2003)
12. Waters, T.R., Putz-Anderson, V., Garg, A., Fine, L.J.: Revised NIOSH equation for the design and evaluation of manual lifting tasks. Ergonomics, 749–776 (1993)
13. Safework, http://www.safework.com
14. Thalmann, D.: Dynamic Simulation as a Tool for Three-Dimensional Animation. New Trends in Animation and Visualization, 257–272 (1991)

Mnemonical Body Shortcuts for Interacting with Mobile Devices

Tiago Guerreiro, Ricardo Gamboa, and Joaquim Jorge

Visualization and Intelligent Multimodal Interfaces Group,
INESC-ID R. Alves Redol, 9, 1000-029, Lisbon, Portugal
{rjssg,tjvg,jaj}@vimmi.inesc.pt

Abstract. Mobile devices' user interfaces have some similarities with the traditional interfaces offered by desktop computers, which are highly problematic when used in mobile contexts. Gesture recognition in mobile interaction appears as an important area to provide suitable on-the-move usability. We present a body space based approach to improve mobile device interaction and on the move performance. The human body is presented as a rich repository of meaningful relations which are always available to interact with. Body-based gestures allow the user to naturally interact with mobile devices with no movement limitations. Preliminary studies using RFID technology were performed, validating the mnemonical body shortcuts concept as a new mobile interaction mechanism. Finally, inertial sensing prototypes were developed and evaluated, proving to be suitable for mobile interaction and efficient, accomplishing a good recognition rate.

Keywords: Gestures, Mnemonics, Shortcuts, RFID, Accelerometer, Mobile.

1 Introduction

Mobile computers are currently omnipresent, and became a part of the user's daily life. Their capabilities are diverse: communications, GPS, video and music players, digital cameras, game consoles and many other applications. The characteristics of these multiple-task devices surpass the desktop user interfaces and give more importance to new possibilities in human-computer interaction (HCI).

Mobile devices' interaction differs from the usual interaction with desktop computers due to their different physical characteristics, input/output capabilities and interaction demands. They have to be small and lightweight to be carriable therefore limiting battery resources and processor capabilities. Input and output capabilities are reduced. The interaction while mobile is also different because users' visual attention is not always focused on the device, making eyes-free and low-workload important characteristics to create a suitable mobile interface. Also, there is a core of applications that are used recurrently, and their menu access is often too slow due to the limited input capabilities. This implies the growing importance of shortcuts: users need fast application access. To achieve this goal, mobile phones provide voice and key shortcuts. Voice shortcuts are not suited to noisy environments, are too intrusive,

M. Sales Dias et al. (Eds.): GW 2007, LNAI 5085, pp. 261–271, 2009.

have a low recognition rate and low levels of social acceptance. Key shortcuts don't provide any auxiliary memorization about which shortcut is in which key.

To overcome mobile shortcuts issues and ease on-the-move mobile device interaction, a gestural input technique is proposed. Gestures are a natural and expressive method of human communication and are often combined with body hints to empathize an idea (i.e. reaching the heart to show an emotion). It is possible to apply different technologies to enhance mobile devices with gesture recognition, making those gestures a meaningful triggering method to the main functions of the device. We give special attention to the body space and related mnemonics to increase shortcut usage and therefore improve user mobile performance.

2 Related Work

There are many options to detect body or device movement and allow a response to the movement. This response may be a shortcut to an application or any other effect in internal or external applications. The most common techniques and works in gestural recognition for mobile devices were studied, namely Radio Frequency Identification (RFID), Accelerometers, Cameras, Touch Screens, Electromyography, Capacitive Sensing and Infrared Laser beams.

RFID Technology is now starting to be incorporated in mobile devices, making it possible to read a tag (a small sized chip with an antenna emitting radio frequency waves and usually storing a unique identifier) with an approximation gesture with the device. Those gestures can only be based on single/multiple point recognition as the gesture information is not recorded. A mobile gestural interaction with RFID demands a permanent presence of tags, which is possible with their embodiment (attaching it to clothes, wallets, etc.) Following this idea, Headon and Coulouris [1] created a wristband to control mobile applications with gestures, based on reading a grid of RFID tags attached to the user's shirt. The inconvenience of this solution is the need to stick tags in clothes or personal objects.

An accelerometer is a small electromechanical inertial sensor device that measures its own acceleration, and its currently being used in commercial mobile phones. With an accelerometer on a mobile device is possible to recognize gestures such as hand gestures based on vibrational [2], tap [3] and tilt [4] input or innumerous arm movements. For example, Choi et al [5] used a mobile phone with inertial sensing to recognize numbers drawn in the air to trigger phone calls or delete messages with a double lifting, while Ängeslevä et al [6] presented preliminary studies on the possibility to associate gestures with parts of the body and trigger applications using those body space mnemonics.

Pressure sensitive surfaces are commonly integrated with screens in some devices like PDAs. They are able to detect 2D gestures, such as taps, directional strokes or characters, allowing eyes-free interaction with the device. Pirhonen et al [7] prototyped a mobile music player placed on the belt, controllable with metaphorical finger gestures, like a sweep right-left to the next track or a tap to play and pause. There are other approaches: Friedlander et al [8] suggested a gestural menu selection based on directional strokes to select an entry on a concentric ring of options. However, applications in touch screens may only be used in over-sized devices and are limited to 2D gestures.

Other approaches also relevant but not so common include mobile cameras reading visual tags or processing their optical flow to recognize movement, rotation and tilting of the phone, electromyography where the user can subtly react to events by contracting a monitored muscle, capacitance sensing where the user can scroll a presentation, control a DVD or MP3 player by approaching his finger to the sensor, and laser beams also used to detect finger movements near an handheld device being even able to recognize characters.

The fact that those techniques can be implemented in mobile devices doesn't make them suitable to be used on-the-move. Current applications lack the possibility of using gestural shortcuts in mobile scenarios. Furthermore, the gesture selection does not provide enough mnemonical cues for them to be easily remembered.

3 Task Analysis

In order to capture the actual panorama considering shortcuts in mobile devices, 20 individuals were interviewed and observed. The task analysis consisted on a first part with questions about current habits on mobile phone interaction and in a second part where users were asked to reach the most used applications and contacts. It was found that 75% of the interviewed used key shortcuts, while none used voice shortcuts due to its social constraints and low recognition rates. An average of 5 key shortcuts is used, where 93% of the users execute them on a daily basis. Users with more programmed shortcuts reported difficulties in their memorization. In user observation, results show that people needed an average of 4 keystrokes to access the 3 most used applications and 5 keystrokes to call the 3 most used contacts. Key shortcuts seem to be used but observation results reflect a large number of keystrokes. Users often make mistakes or simply forget to use them and apply menu selection. Mobile device interaction still needs to find new suitable input forms to increase interaction efficiency.

4 Proposed Approach

We propose the creation of mnemonics based on the association between applications and the body space. Mobile gestural interaction has to be strongly based on a high recall of commands and the human body with its meaningful associative space offers the needed, and always available, mnemonical cues. The user should be able to create shortcuts to applications with a simple approximation to the body part associated with that specific application. For example, the user should be able to trigger a clock with a gesture towards the wrist or open the music player with an approximation to the ears (Fig. 1). These associations are intended to act as a mnemonic when recalling each application gestural command. As the body limits the number of possible associations, applications can be related with the same body parts (with a gesture or button to recall for the other applications associated with the performed gesture). The body functions as an application organizer where the user is able to keep his most used ones to easily recall them.

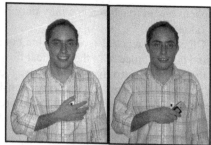

Fig. 1. Mnemonical Body Shortcuts – The expressivity of gestures

4.1 Preliminary Evaluation

To validate our approach we developed a RFID-based prototype able to associate body parts (through sticker tags) with any given mobile device shortcut (i.e. an application or a call to a certain contact). We selected RFID technology to apply our approach because it provides direct mapping, easing the creation of body shortcuts. Other solutions were clearly limited as they restrict the scope of interaction (touch screens, cameras, laser beams and EMG).

The prototype was evaluated with 20 users in a controlled environment using a Pocket LOOX 720 with a compact flash ACG RF PC Handheld Reader. In the first stage of the evaluation the users were asked to select the five most frequently tasks effectuated with their mobile phones and associate them both with a body part and a mobile device key (in their own mobile device). Considering body shortcuts, it is interesting to notice that 89%, out of 18 users, related message writing with the hand, 88%, out of 17 users, related making a call to their ear or mouth and 91%, out of 11 users, related their contacts to their chest, among other meaningful relations (Table 1). An hour later, the users were asked to access the previously selected applications,

Table 1. Most common associations gesture-application

	Mouth	Hand	Chest	Head	Wrist	Eye	Finger	Ear
SMS		10	1				6	
Call	3			1				12
Contacts		3	5	2				1
Clock					10	1		
Photos				2		8		
Calculator	3							
Mp3								2
Agenda		1	3	1				
Alarm-clock				2	2	2		3

following both approaches (body and key shortcuts). For each of the approaches the users were prompted randomly 20 times (5 for each application). Although several users selected already used key/application relations, 50% (10 users) made at least one error, with an average of 9% errors/user. Considering body shortcuts, only 15% (3 users) made a mistake with an average of 0.8% errors/user.

The results were still very favorable for Mnemonical Body Shortcuts one week later, with an error rate of 22% for key shortcuts and 6% for the gestural interaction. The results showed that, even against some established key shortcuts, gestural mnemonics had better results and may surpass the problem of low memorization of key shortcuts, providing also a wide range of possible associations, when compared with the physical limit of keys present on a mobile device.

5 Accelerometer Prototypes

Task analysis suggests that a new interaction paradigm is important to increase mobile devices' usability and evaluation of the RFID prototype demonstrated that mnemonical gestures are a good candidate solution, since it surpasses the memorization issue existent on key shortcuts. However, a RFID-based system is inconvenient regarding the need of using RFID tags on clothes or personal objects to allow an always available interaction. Following the line of the major part of the related work on this area, we decided to use accelerometers for a new prototype, mainly because of its precise measure of acceleration and self-contained hardware, already present in some mobile devices. We used a Bioplux4 wireless system and an ADXL330 MEMS tri-axial accelerometer. The three channels of the accelerometer were connected to three of the analog channels of the device that delivers the RAW data of the accelerometer through Bluetooth connection, with a sample rate of 1024 samples per second.

Focusing on mnemonical body shortcuts recognition, we followed two approaches using the accelerometer data. In both approaches the gesture starts in the chest, with the screen facing the user, and the user has to press an action button during the whole gesture. The first approach is based on the final position and rotation of each gesture, while the second one is a feature based algorithm, using a set of 12 features and classified using both Naive Bayes and K-Nearest Neighbours learners. Our goals constructing these algorithms were a high recognition rate and the importance of being lightweight to be executed on mobile devices with low processing capabilities.

5.1 Position-Based Prototype

In this prototype data was captured and processed on a Pocket LOOX 720 using .Net programming (C#). We decided to map the dislocation of the mobile device on a 2D plan, calculating the distance between an initial and fixed point (the chest) and a final point (relative position). The distance calculation was based on a double integration of the signal (Fig. 2). However, since this integration delivers some error and the mobile device may suffer some unexpected rotation, we also applied a moving average filter and a threshold to isolate the part of the signal where the real movement was present. With this processing, it was possible to detect the movement on both x and y axis.

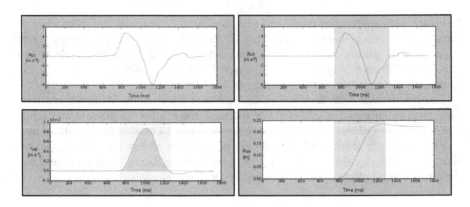

Fig. 2. Signal Processing Evolution a) Raw Signal b) Filtered c) Velocity d) Position

This approach is suitable for movements fixed in the x,y axis, but the users are likely to perform gestures that are characterized by their rotation. Those gestures are recognized taking in account the final rotation of the device (divided in six different classes) and reusing the position calculation, since it varies even when gestures have the same final rotation. Using this method, it is possible to join the recognition of gestures with or without rotation. The recognized gesture has to belong to the same final rotation class of the performed gesture and is the one with the minor Euclidean distance when compared with the position changes of the performed gesture.

There are two different modes to interact with the system:

- *Train the system and relate the given values with body parts:* The train set will be used to calculate the mean of each position results and the majority of final rotation classes. To recognize which gesture was made, the algorithm finds the nearest position of a training gesture within the same rotational class.
- *Pre-process data based on samples of correct gestures:* This mode permits default gestures based on the height of the person, thus removing the need of further training. We defined 10 default gestures, based on the body points users most referenced during the validation of the concept: Mouth, Chest, Navel, Shoulder, Neck, Ear, Head, Leg, Wrist and Eye.

5.2 Feature-Based Prototype

The first step to create a feature-based model is to choose features that characterize each gesture with accuracy. Since this was the second prototype, we already have some prior knowledge about which characteristics better define the body based gestures. We decided to choose 12 different features, considering gesture starting in the chest and finishing in a body point. Firstly, we use the maximum and the minimum values from the X, Y and Z axis. These 6 features are essential to determine the direction and position variation of the gesture. Similarly to what was done in the position-based prototype, we added 3 features with the final value of each gesture, corresponding to the final rotation. Finally, the signal's amplitude was also considered, since some gestures have different

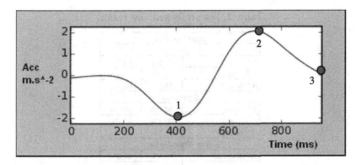

Fig. 3. Features from y axis 1) Minimum value 2) Maximum value 3) Final rotation

amplitude variation. The maximum and minimum values were added, as well as the amplitude mean value during the whole gesture (Fig. 3). The captured signal is usually noisy and not suitable for a correct feature extraction. We used a smooth algorithm based on the Hanning window, which has a better performance compared with a Moving Average approach, because each sampled signal within the window is multiplied by the Hanning function, giving more importance to the middle than those in the extremities of the window [9].

Focusing on the classification problem we had in hands, we decided to use both K-nearest-neighbors with Euclidean distance and Naïve Bayes algorithm to test the effectiveness of the selected features and to decide which was the best classifier to use.

6   Evaluation

We user evaluated the developed prototypes to distinguish which approach suits better the mnemonical body gestures scenario. These tests intend to select the solution with highest recognition rate.

6.1   Position-Based Prototype Evaluation

Both approaches present on this prototype were separately tested. User tests were made with 10 users averaging 24 years. First, default gestures were tested. After a brief demonstration of each gesture, users were prompted to perform 5 random different gestures out of the available 10 gestures, 4 times each, totaling 20 gestures. The general recognition rate was set on 82%.

Training gestures was also tested. Users were free to choose 5 free gestures and then repeat those gestures 5 times each, serving as a training set. After, they were prompted to perform 4 times each gesture, as it was done with default gestures. Results showed a recognition rate of 71%.

6.2   Feature-Based Prototype Evaluation

This prototype evaluation was based on signal acquisition of 12 default gestures. Those gestures were similar to those tested with the position-based prototype, adding

Table 2. Feature-Based Test results

User Training		
12 Gestures		
1 Training	79,5%	88,5%
2 Trainings	86,8%	92,4%
3 Trainings	91,9%	92,8%
5 gestures		
1 Training	88,2%	90,8%
2 Trainings	96,1%	98,2%
3 Trainings	96,3%	97,9%
Total Training Set		
12 Gestures	93,6%	92,8%
5 Gestures	97,3%	96,2%
Total Training Set + User Training		
12 gestures		
1 Training	93,8%	93,2%
2 Trainings	94,3%	92,4%
3 Trainings	95,8%	95,0%
5 gestures		
1 Training	97,1%	9,7%
2 Trainings	96,1%	95,8%
3 Trainings	96,8%	97,9%
	Knn	Bayes

a gesture towards the hip and the back, and they were performed while standing. A total of 20 users were asked to perform the 12 gestures, 5 times each. Then, an offline evaluation was performed, using different training and testing sets and both Naïve Bayes and KNN classifiers.

The test was divided in two phases:

User Training

In this first phase, we tested the recognition rate using as training set only the gestures performed by the user. The training set varied between 1, 2 or 3 gestures. This approach was tested using the whole set of 12 gestures but also using 5 random gestures, which was the mean number of key shortcuts a user commonly have available.

Table 3. Confusion Matrix for Total Training Set with 12 gestures 1140 gestures, Recognition Rate of 92.8%

Gestures	Mouth	Shoulder	Chest	Navel	Ear	Back	Head	Wrist	Neck	Leg	Eye	Hip
Mouth	**87,5%**	6,2%	0,0%	0,0%	5,1%	0,0%	0,0%	0,0%	0,0%	0,0%	0,0%	0,0%
Shoulder	4,2%	**90,7%**	2,0%	1,0%	0,0%	0,0%	0,0%	0,0%	0,0%	0,0%	0,0%	0,0%
Chest	0,0%	1,0%	**94,9%**	0,0%	0,0%	0,0%	0,0%	0,0%	0,0%	0,0%	0,0%	0,0%
Navel	0,0%	0,0%	3,0%	**95,8%**	0,0%	0,0%	0,0%	0,0%	0,0%	0,0%	0,0%	0,0%
Ear	4,2%	0,0%	0,0%	0,0%	**92,9%**	0,0%	0,0%	0,0%	0,0%	0,0%	0,0%	0,0%
Back	3,1%	0,0%	0,0%	1,0%	1,0%	**97,8%**	0,0%	0,0%	0,0%	0,0%	0,0%	2,9%
Head	1,0%	2,1%	0,0%	0,0%	0,0%	0,0%	**97,8%**	0,0%	0,0%	0,0%	2,0%	0,0%
Wrist	0,0%	0,0%	0,0%	0,0%	0,0%	0,0%	2,2%	**94,6%**	0,0%	0,0%	1,0%	4,8%
Neck	0,0%	0,0%	0,0%	0,0%	0,0%	0,0%	0,0%	3,3%	**100,0%**	0,0%	2,0%	0,0%
Leg	0,0%	0,0%	0,0%	0,0%	0,0%	1,1%	0,0%	0,0%	0,0%	**95,5%**	0,0%	9,5%
Eye	0,0%	0,0%	0,0%	0,0%	1,0%	0,0%	0,0%	1,1%	0,0%	0,0%	**94,9%**	0,0%
Hip	0,0%	0,0%	0,0%	2,1%	0,0%	1,1%	0,0%	1,1%	0,0%	4,5%	0,0%	**82,9%**

Table 4. Confusion Matrix for Total Training Set with 5 gestures 475 gestures, Recognition Rate of 96,2%

Gestures	Mouth	Shoulder	Chest	Navel	Ear	Back	Head	Wrist	Neck	Leg	Eye	Hip
Mouth	**89,5%**	7,0%	0,0%	0,0%	0,0%	0,0%	0,0%	0,0%	0,0%	0,0%	0,0%	0,0%
Shoulder	0,0%	**93,0%**	0,0%	0,0%	0,0%	0,0%	0,0%	0,0%	0,0%	0,0%	0,0%	0,0%
Chest	0,0%	0,0%	**100%**	0,0%	0,0%	0,0%	0,0%	0,0%	0,0%	0,0%	0,0%	0,0%
Navel	0,0%	0,0%	0,0%	**100%**	0,0%	0,0%	0,0%	0,0%	0,0%	0,0%	0,0%	0,0%
Ear	0,0%	0,0%	0,0%	0,0%	**100%**	0,0%	0,0%	0,0%	0,0%	0,0%	0,0%	0,0%
Back	5,3%	0,0%	0,0%	0,0%	0,0%	**100%**	0,0%	0,0%	0,0%	0,0%	0,0%	5,7%
Head	0,0%	0,0%	0,0%	0,0%	0,0%	0,0%	**100%**	0,0%	0,0%	0,0%	0,0%	0,0%
Wrist	0,0%	0,0%	0,0%	0,0%	0,0%	0,0%	0,0%	**93,8%**	0,0%	0,0%	0,0%	0,0%
Neck	0,0%	0,0%	0,0%	0,0%	0,0%	0,0%	0,0%	4,2%	**100%**	0,0%	0,0%	0,0%
Leg	0,0%	0,0%	0,0%	0,0%	0,0%	0,0%	0,0%	0,0%	0,0%	**100%**	0,0%	3,8%
Eye	0,0%	0,0%	0,0%	0,0%	0,0%	0,0%	0,0%	0,0%	0,0%	0,0%	**100%**	0,0%
Hip	5,3%	0,0%	0,0%	0,0%	0,0%	0,0%	0,0%	2,1%	0,0%	0,0%	0,0%	**90,6%**

Total Training Set

The second phase was based on using the whole set of training from all the users, excluding one that was discarded due to its difficulties of performing some gestures. This set of 1080 gestures worked as a training set, and each user's gestures were classified using that training set, adding none, one, two or three user trainings, also using the 12and 5 gestures set. The final results of these tests are available in Table 2 and the Confusion Matrix of 12 and 5 gesture test using only the training set (without user training) and KNN classifier are available in tables 3 and 4 respectively.

7 Discussion

After evaluation, it is clear that feature-based algorithm is a better solution, but there are some considerations to make about each prototype.

7.1 Position-Based Prototype

The evaluation on the first prototype revealed some limitations. The recognition rate of 5 different gestures was 82%, which is very considering the reduced number of gestures to be recognized. A system with such a recognition rate would probably make users unconfident and consequently drop out its use. Besides, this recognition rate is based on default gestures, which does not provide users the possibility to choose personal gestures. This option was tested in the second test phase, but the gesture recognition dropped to 71%. This lower recognition rate occurred because users sometimes chose gestures with similar final rotation and position, which were not correctly recognized. Besides, there was no outlier detection, so one training error or bad gesture spoiled some recognitions. One main conclusion is that position is not so effective to disambiguate gestures outside x,y plan, and to enhance this algorithm three things should be modified: the position calculation should work correctly even with rotations, a KNN algorithm has to be implemented and outliers should be discarded.

7.2 Feature-Based Prototype

A feature based approach achieved a high recognition rate in the majority of the tests, both using user training and the general training set of 1080 gestures. Naïve Bayes and KNN algorithms were tested, and Naïve Bayes performed better when only user training was present (low number of sample gestures), while KNN achieved better results with a large set of training.

Considering the results of isolated user training of the 12 gestures set, the best recognition was achieved with 3 trainings with 92,76%. This recognition rate, although acceptable, is still vulnerable to some possible misjudge gestures. However, we do not believe users would want to use simultaneously all the 12 gestures. The test using a reduced set of 5 gestures achieved, using Naïve Bayes, a recognition rate of 98,24% with only 2 gestures, with no positive impact of a third training. For those default gestures, user training seems to be a good approach, but it is not guaranteed the same recognition rate using free gestures. It is also problematic if users perform training gestures inconsistently, because it would reflect a lower recognition rate.

Results were also positive considering the usage of the training set of 1080 gestures (1140 gestures minus the 60 gestures performed by each user). Using all the 12 gestures, we achieved a recognition rate of 93,6%. Although not very high, this recognition rate is achieved without any user training, which is a crucial point for a good user acceptance. This value reaches 97,3% when considering 5 gestures. When we increasingly introduce the training set of the user, the recognition rate didn't increase significantly using KNN algorithm, but it influenced positively Naïve Bayes by 2 percentual points. Yet, KNN algorithm still has the best performance using the total training set. User training could be added not by explicitly asking the user to train the system, but instead using an adaptative approach: when a user correctly performs a gesture, it should be possible to enrich the training set and successively increase the recognition rate.

The study on this prototype proved the feature-based approach as the most successful and appropriate, but possible free gestures were not tested. However, we tend to believe that recognition rates would decrease but maintain an acceptable margin, capable to perform as a suitable gestural interaction algorithm.

8   Conclusions and Future Work

During previous chapters, a novel interface for mobile devices was discussed. Mobile devices interfaces are still chained to the desktop user interfaces, but there are some potentialities of mobile interaction that can be explored. Our approach, based on the creation of shortcuts using gestures and the associative potential existent in different body parts, proved to be a suitable method of interaction using a RFID based prototype. Users were more likely to remember which gesture indexes a certain application using our Mnemonical Body Shortcuts than using the common key shortcuts.

In order to accomplish a self-contained interface, we decided to create accelerometer-based prototypes. Accelerometers already exist in some mobile devices, and might be increasingly used in the future. With accelerometers, we followed two different approaches. One prototype was based on position variation and the final rotation of the device to recognize different gestures. The second approach is a feature-based prototype, using 12 different features from the inertial data, and classified using two different learners, Naïve Bayes and Knn. The first approach only achieved a recognition rate of 82% for a set of 5 pre-defined gestures and 71%, while the second had a better performance. Using only user training and Naïve Bayes algorithm, with 3 training repetitions is possible to achieve almost 93% for 12 gestures or 98% for a set of 5 recognizable gestures. We also experimented using as training the whole set of performed gestures, achieving 93,6% and 97,3% recognition rate with no user training, for 12 and 5 gestures set respectively. This results show that choosing an accelerometer to recognize mnemonical body shortcuts is a valid approach.

In the future, we will evaluate the usability of a full-developed solution (featuring audio and vibrational feedback) under real-life scenarios, namely while users are moving.

Acknowledgments. The authors would like to thank all users that participated in the studies described in this paper. Tiago Guerreiro was supported by the Portuguese Foundation for Science and Technology, grant SFRH/BD/28110/2006.

References

[1] Headon, R., Coulouris, G.: Supporting Gestural Input for Users on the Move. In: Proc. IEE Eurowearable 2003, pp. 107–112 (2003)

[2] Strachan, S., Murray-Smith, R.: Muscle Tremor as an Input Mechanism. In: Annual ACM Symposium on User Interface Software and Technology (2004)

[3] Jang, I.J., Park, W.B.: Signal processing of the accelerometer for gesture awareness on handheld devices. In: The 12th IEEE Int. Workshop on Robot and Human Interactive Communication (2003)

[4] Rekimoto, J.: Tilting operations for small screen interfaces. In: Proceedings of the 9th annual ACM symposium on User interface software and technology, pp. 167–168 (1996)

[5] Choi, E., Bang, W., Cho, S., Yang, J., Kim, D., Kim, S.: Beatbox music phone: gesture-based interactive mobile phone using a tri-axis accelerometer. In: ICIT 2005 (2005)

[6] Ängesleva, J., Oakley, I., Hughes, S., O'Modhrain, S.: Body Mnemonics: Portable Device. Interaction Design Concept, UIST (2003)

[7] Fiedlander, N., Schlueter, K., Mantei, M.: Bullseye! When Fitt's Law Doesn't Fit. In: ACM CHI 1998, pp. 257–264 (1998)

[8] Pirhonen, P., Brewster, S.A., Holguin, C.: Gestural and Audio Metaphors as a Means of Control in Mobile Devices. In: ACM-CHI 2002, pp. 291–298 (2002)

[9] Harris, F.J.: On the use of windows for harmonic analysis with the discrete Fourier-transform. Proc. IEEE 66, 51–83 (1978)

The Effects of the Gesture Viewpoint on the Students' Memory of Words and Stories

Giorgio Merola

University Roma Tre, Roma, via del Castro Pretorio 20
merogio@hotmail.com

Abstract. The goal of this work is to estimate the effects of teacher's iconic gestures on the students' memory of words and short stories. Indeed, some evidence seems to confirm the possibility that iconics help the listener, but it is unclear what are the elements that make gestures more or less useful. According to McNeill's observation that children produce many more Character Viewpoint gestures than Observer Viewpoint ones, we hypothesize that they also understand and remember better words accompanied by these gestures. The results of two experimental studies showed that iconic gestures helped students to remember words and tales better and that younger students performed better in memory tasks when their teacher used Character Viewpoint gestures.

Keywords: iconic, Character Viewpoint, effects, memory, students.

1 Introduction

The teacher's non verbal communication surely has a determining role in the regulation of the socio-emotional and relational climate in class and in the transmission of feedback and of prejudice [1], thus affecting also the learning level of the students.

The goal of the present work is to study the effects of gestures *directly* on the cognitive processes of the listener, through their conveying more information in addition to words. In particular, along with McNeill's model [2], we believe that facilitation effects are predictable on the student's comprehension and memorization processes, when the teacher uses iconic gestures [3]. While under this point of view the efficacy of deictic [4]; [5]; [6]; [7]; [8] and symbolic gestures is recognized, studies on iconic gestures are more contradictory [9].

In this paper we will try to evaluate the effects of the teacher's iconic gestures and to identify which elements make those gestures more or less useful for the students.

1.1 Critical Consideration on Related Works

The scholars who studied the effects of teachers' gestures on the students' cognitive processes started from the theoretical assumption that gestures not only support speech, but also convey additional information and help listeners to better and easily understand what the speaker means [2];[10];[11].

According to McNeill's model [2], the complete representation of the concept that a speaker wants to express is the result of the integration of the information derived

M. Sales Dias et al. (Eds.): GW 2007, LNAI 5085, pp. 272–281, 2009.

by his/her words and the gestures that respectively convey the propositional content and the visual-spatial elements of the meaning.

Learning, development and communicative processes in childhood are strongly affected by gestures [12]. Children use many gestures when they try to explain the rules of a game to adults or when they talk about very difficult tasks [13] and they comprehend and remember better the teacher's explanations when he/she uses gestures [14];[15].

To students, gestures may represent an additional resource to understand what the teacher says, for example by offering a new perspective through which they can interpret the lesson content [16].

Roth [16] reported a number of experiments showing that subjects of different age and cognitive development more or less consciously take into account the information conveyed by the speaker's gestures. Indeed, they refer to them later and reproduce the same gestures of the speaker when they have to report the same topics [15].

Goldin-Meadow, Kim and Singer [15] showed that pupils tend to remember the information conveyed by the teacher's gestures exhibited during the explanation of mathematical equations.

While studying gesture-speech mismatch, Goldin-Meadow [11] suggested that gestures semantically redundant with cooccurrent speech make students' understanding easier, while they hinder this process when they convey a different meaning from the one conveyed by words.

But the presence of a gesture-speech mismatch cannot represent the only reason why bimodal communication sometimes does not help listeners to better understand speaker's explanations, and it cannot explain why redundant gestures can be more or less useful to understand speech.

Moreover, we have to consider that Goldin-Meadow mainly studied the effects of deictic gestures, through which the speaker merely points at the referent: here gesture-speech mismatch arises when a gesture shows a different referent from that of the speech.

But other categories of gestures, like the iconics, for example, convey much information that is not expressed by cooccurrent words and the way in which they represent referents can be very complex. Therefore, beside the presence of mismatches, many factors contribute to make these gestures more or less helpful to the listener: the prominence of the information the speaker decides to convey through the gesture; the degree of similarity between gesture shape and physical characteristics of the referent; the vividness of gesture, etc.

Moreover, while many studies confirmed the function of deictics to make the understanding and remembering of verbal information easier [16]; [17]; [18]; [19]; [20], some authors (for example Krauss et al., 1991 [9]) suggested that iconics and metaphorics [2] don't help the listener in the same way. The statement that recipients acquire additional information from a speaker's iconic gestures is not unanimous: Butterworth and Hadar [21] believe that gestures ease verbal production, sometimes anticipating its significance, but not accomplishing the communicative function of adding a meaning for the listener. Rather, gestures are considered functional for the speaker in order to find the words. To prove this hypothesis, Morrel Samuels and Krauss [22] observe that, when the speaker needs to express less familiar words, the period of time between his/her gesture and his/her words becomes longer.

In three different studies, Krauss, Dushay, Chen and Rauscher [23] find experimental data that they read as a demonstration of the fact that gestures don't offer the listener any additional information besides the words.

Some evidence seems to confirm the possibility that iconics help the listener [17];[18];[10];[19], but it is unclear what are the elements that make gestures more or less useful.

As Goldin-Meadow [11] puts it: "We know that gestures can help listeners secure a message conveyed in speech when it too conveys that message, but that doesn't always help (...) At the moment we don't have any idea why gesture that is redundant with speech makes it easier to grasp the speaker's message in some cases but not in others" [3].

Holler and Beattie's studies [18] showed that the effects of iconic gestures on the listener's cognitive processes could change in conformity with the speaker's *viewpoint* [2]. McNeill [20] defines as *observer-viewpoint* those gestures in which "the hand(s) represent one or more entities in the narration (...) and the gesture space before the speaker is the space of the action, a kind of a stage or screen on which it takes place" On the other hand, "in the *character viewpoint* (CVPT), the hand(s) represent the character's hands and the speaker him/herself is inside the gesture space, performing the part of the character." [20].

McNeill [2] suggests that children produce many more Character-Viewpoint (C-VPT) gestures than Observer-Viewpoint (O-VPT) ones because C-VPT express the smaller narrative distance they assume.

Even if the participants to Holler and Beattie's experiments were adults, by considering McNeill observations about the almost exclusive production of character viewpoint by very young children, we can suppose that they understand this kind of gestures better.

2   The Effect of the Gesture Viewpoint on Children's Memory of Words and Tales

In this work we want to estimate the effect of teacher's iconic gestures on the students' memory of words and short tales. We hypothesize that iconic gestures help to remember words and tales better and that younger children perform better when their teacher uses *character viewpoint* gestures.

To test these hypotheses, two experimental studies were conducted on 359 students of 20 classes (3 first grade classes; 4 second grade; 4 third; 2 forth and 7 fifth) of 5 primary schools and their respective teachers.

2.1   First Study. GESTURE VIEWPOINT and Word Retrieval

2.1.1   Method
In the first study we estimated the effects of iconic gestures and of their viewpoint on the students' memory of words.

In a pre-test, the students' memory of words starting level was assessed: they listened to 3 lists of 8 words (5 letters, 2 syllables words, with similar use frequency and balanced imagery value) pronounced by the experimenter without cooccurrent gestures. After the listening of each list, each student wrote down all the words that he or she remembered.

In a second step, teachers of all classes pronounced other 3 lists of 8 words (5 letters, 2 syllables words, with similar use frequency and balanced imagery value; a third of each suitable to be represented with C-VPT gestures, a third with O-VPT and a third suitable to be represented both ways). On the basis of previous observations of his/her multimodal communication, each teacher was instructed to use his/her most typical modality; respectively:

N modality: to pronounce words without gestures;
C-VPT modality: to pronounce words by accompanying them with C-VPT gestures; *O-VPT modality*: to pronounce words together with O-VPT gestures.

The instructions were explained, some examples were provided to the teachers and the experimenter video-recorded the teacher's multimodal communication.

Students were assigned to one of three experimental conditions: 1) teacher using a C-VPT gesture while pronouncing each word (C-VPT condition); teacher using a O-VPT gesture while pronouncing each word (O-VPT condition); teacher not using gestures in pronouncing the words (N condition).

After listening to each list, each student wrote down all the words he remembered.

2.1.2 Results
Frequencies of remembered words in the 3 conditions were compared and the interaction with the students' age was assessed.

Fourth grade classes were cancelled from the experiment because the N-condition was missing from the beginning and the C-VPT teacher didn't respect her order.

An analysis of co-variance 3x4 (experimental condition X class grade, factors for independent measures) was conducted, with the pre-test performance as covariate. Only the words expressed by each teacher in his/her modality were considered, that means that, for example, if a C-VPT teacher accompanied a word with an O-VPT, this word was removed from the analysis.

Results show the main effects of experimental condition and class grade $(2,267)$ $=103.02$, $p<.001$, and F $(3,267) =7.02$, $p<.001$, respectively).

Moreover, also the interaction between Condition and Class grade result significant (F $(6,267) =5.98$, $p<.001$).

Whereas in N condition the children's improvement results linear from first grade to fifth grade classes, in O-VPT modality there is a low and non-linear progress, and, above all, in C-VPT condition first grade students perform as well as fifth grade students (Fig. 1).

The bimodal conditions, both C-VPT gestures and O-VPT gestures, always represent an advantage in all class levels, but this is much stronger for younger children, while it becomes weaker in the following years.

Duncan tests shows that, only in first grade students word recall frequency in C-VPT condition is statistically different from word recall frequency in O-VPT condition $(p<.05)$. Instead, the difference between C-VPT and N and the difference between O-VPT and N are statistically significant in all the classes (from $p<.001$ to $p<.0001$), but less significant in fifth grade students $(p<.05)$.

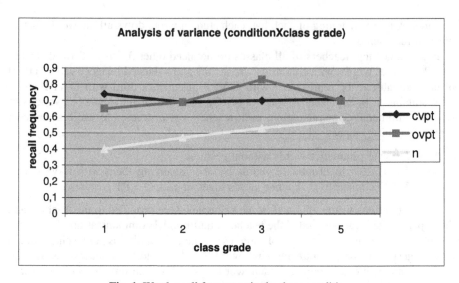

Fig. 1. Word recall frequency in the three conditions

Third grade children did better in O-VPT condition, but this was probably mostly due to the skill of the O-VPT teacher: in fact in the post-test children remembered particularly well also the few words expressed by the teacher with C-VPT gestures (those words was removed from the analysis).

2.2 Second Study – Gesture Viewpoint and Stories Retrieval

2.2.1 Method
In the second study we wanted to estimate the effects of teachers' iconic gestures and their viewpoints on the students' comprehension and memory of short stories.

After a pre-test, in which students listened to a short story read by the experimenter and answered a ten items questionnaire about it, they listened to their teacher reading a new short story in her modality (C-VPT, O-VPT or N), and, in the end, they answered another ten items questionnaire about this second story.

2.2.2 Results
In the analysis of data, only classes in which the teacher used at least 75 % of the gestures in her modality were considered: this leading, also in this test, to the exclusion of the fourth grades.

To estimate how students of different age behave in the three conditions, an analysis of variance 2X3X4 (repeated factor pre/post-test; fixed factors modality and class grade) was conducted. The interaction between the factor modality and the difference between pre and post-test resulted statistically significant (F $(2,273)$ = 6,391 (p<.005)), so as the interaction between the difference pre/post and the factors class grade and modality (F $(6,273)$ = 3,091(p<.01)).

Also for memory of story task, C-VPT gestures help younger students more than older ones. Moreover, as in the previous task, teacher's gestures seem to be more helpful for lower class grades students who in N condition performed significantly worse (Fig. 4).

First grade students are the only ones to profit more from C-VPT gestures and, in this condition, they perform significantly better in respect to the pre-test (Fig. 2). In second grade classes this advantage decreases and in the next grades C-VPT gestures lead children to poor performances, while O-VPT ones are associated with great improvements in respect to pre-test results (Fig. 3).

Character Viewpoint gestures

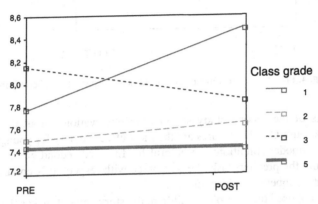

Fig. 2. Pre and post test mean score obtained by students in C-VPT condition

Observer Viewpoint Gestures

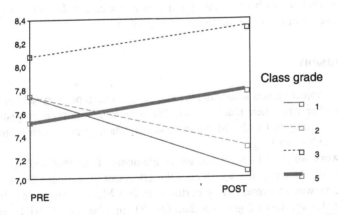

Fig. 3. Pre and post test mean score obtained by students in O-VPT condition

N condition

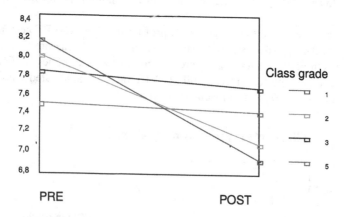

Fig. 4. Pre and post test mean score obtained by students in N condition

The results of the second study support the observations about the memory of words task, because C-VPT gestures are the most effective only for younger children.

Moreover, bimodal conditions are helpful for first and second grade students but, differently from the previous task, the advantage with respect to N condition not only decreases, but disappears in older students.

It may be supposed that, for older children, the story context makes the information conveyed by gestures less necessary, while it performs a decisive role in the memory of words, that is, in absence of a context.

Younger children instead take great help from the teacher's gestures to comprehend the context, also when this is very clear/explicit. The context described by words or even represented by observer-viewpoint gestures seems to be not enough in order to make the sense of the story totally comprehensible.

3   Conclusion

Our research objective was to assess if iconic gestures help primary school students to better remember what their teacher says. The effects of this type of gesture are not clear and, according to Goldin-Meadow, also redundant gestures can be more or less helpful for the listener [11].

In this work we tried to point out which elements of the teachers' gestures influence the pupils' memory and we studied the effects of an element that is potentially crucial: the viewpoint expressed by gestures. In fact McNeill suggested that children produce much more C-VPT gestures than O-VPT ones because C-VPT expresses the minor narrative distance they assume.

We carried out two studies to estimate the effects of the iconic gestures in general and specifically of their viewpoint on the students' memory of words and short stories. As predicted by our hypothesis, we found that the students with teachers who communicate only by speech (without gesture and signals of other modalities) obtain lower scores in words memory tests, in all class grades.

Moreover, as C-VPT gestures are more accessible to children [2], the observation of C-VPT gestures while listening at words or short stories enhanced the students' performance in memory tasks: students more frequently retrieved both words and stories accompanied by C-VPT signals. The effects were limited to younger students: results show that C-VPT gestures seem to be of higher communicative power than O-VPT gestures for younger children, and that multimodality is less necessary in older students. Data analysis in this study about viewpoint effects in story recall seems to confirm the decrease, during cognitive development, of the C-VPT positive effects.

Both studies show that the communicative value of iconic gestures already found for adults, and specifically of the gesture viewpoint, [18];[2];[10], is even higher for children. Moreover it results that younger children take advantage of the additional information provided by iconic gestures more than older ones, and that the advantage provided by character viewpoint in younger children holds not only on the production side, as found by McNeill [2], but also on the comprehension side.

We explained the different results seeing that the lack of context in words make it more important to have extra information to help memorization and it makes older children not show particular decreases in the N condition. On the contrary, younger ones continue to take advantage from the presence of gestures, in particular C-VPT gestures, also in the presence of the context described in the story.

Rather clear are the didactic and meta-didactic implications of these studies.

Primary schools teacher, especially when interacting with younger children, have to be an excellent actor; he have to "show" the things which he talk about, in order to convey the contents through all the possible modalities, by enhancing their comprehensibility and by making the recall easier, through the vividness of the images.

At the same time the teacher have to became aware of the progressive development of the abstract conceptualization, and to promote it through a more articulate and sophisticate use of verbal communication.

The individualization of other elements able to make teachers' multimodal communication more effective in the promoting of learning processes in very simple and specific tasks like the ones in these studies, could help us to collect the first indications about how to make the communication of a virtual pedagogical agent more comprehensible.

Finally, the results of our studies and the analysis of the videotapes confirm that the best way to assess the communicative effectiveness of iconic gestures is a semantic analysis that allows to consider the type of information they specifically convey. On this ground it will also be possible to re-assess the communicative effectiveness of gestures also in adults, for which the viewpoint does not seem as important.

Acknowledgments. Participation in the GW2007 was supported by HUMAINE (European Project IST- 507422).

References

1. Rosenthal, R., Jacobson, L.: Pygmalion in classroom. Holt, Rinehart & Winston, New York (1968)
2. McNeill, D.: Hand and Mind: What Gestures Reveal about Thought. University of Chicago Press, Chicago and London (1992)
3. Merola, G., Poggi, I.: Multimodality and Gestures in the Teacher's Communication. In: Camurri, A., Volpe, G. (eds.) GW 2003. LNCS, vol. 2915, pp. 101–111. Springer, Heidelberg (2004)
4. Goodwin, M.H., Goodwin, C.: Gesture and copartecipation in the activity of searching for a word. Semiotica 62(1/2), 29–51 (1986)
5. Thompson, L.A., Massaro, D.W.: Children'sintegration of speech and pointing gestures in comprehension. Journal of Experimental Child Psychology 57, 327–354 (1994)
6. Hanks, W.F.: The indexical ground of deictic reference. In: Duranti, A., Goodwin, C. (eds.) Rethinking context: language as an interactive phenomenon, pp. 43–76. Cambridge University, Cambridge (1992)
7. Haviland, J.B.: Anchoring, iconicity, and orientation in Guugu Yimithirr pointing gestures. Journal of Linguistic Anthropology 3, 3–45 (1993)
8. Levinson, S.: Language and cognition: the cognitive consequences of spatial description in Guugu Yimithirr. Journal of Linguistic Anthropology 7, 98–130 (1997)
9. Krauss, R.M., Morrel-Samuels, P., Colasante, C.: Do conversational gestures communicate? Journal of Personality and Social Psychology 61, 743–754 (1991); Language and Social Psychology 8, 221–228
10. Beattie, G., Shovelton, H.: Do iconic hand gestures really contribute anything to the semantic information conveyed by speech? An experimental investigation. Semiotica 123, 1–30 (1999)
11. Goldin-Meadow, S.: Hearing gesture. The Belknap Press of Harvard Univeristy Press (2003)
12. Piaget, J.: The language and thought of the child. Routledge & Kegan Paul, London (1959)
13. Evans, M.A., Rubin, K.H.: Hand gestures as a communicative mode in school-age children. Journal of Genetic Psychology 135, 189–196 (1979)
14. Valenzeno, L., Alibali, M.W., Klatzky, R.L.: Teachers gestures facilitate students learning: A lesson in symmetry. Contemporary Educational Psychology 28, 187–204 (2003)
15. Goldin-Meadow, S., Kim, S., Singer, M.: What the teacher's handstell the student's mind about math. Journal of Educational Psychology 91, 720–730 (1999)
16. Roth: Gesture: Their Role in Teaching and Learning. Review of Educational Research 71(3), 365–392 (2001)
17. Riseborough, M.G.: Physiographic gestures as decoding facilitators: Three experiments exploring a neglected facet of communication. Journal of Nonverbal Behavior 5, 172–183 (1981)
18. Holler, J., Beattie, G.: A microanalytic investigation of how iconic gestures and speech represent core semantic features in talk. Semiotica 142(1/4), 31–69 (2002)
19. Beattie, G., Shovelton, H.: An experimental investigation of the role of different types of iconic gesture in communication: a semantic feature approach. Gesture 1, 129–149 (2001)

20. McNeill, D.: Gesture and Thought. University of Chicago Press, Chicago (2005)
21. Butterworth, B., Hadar, U.: Gesture, speech and computational stages: A reply to McNeill. Psychological Review 96, 168–174 (1989)
22. Morrel Samuels, P., Krauss, R.M.: Word familiarity predicts temporal asynchrony of hand gestures and speech. Journal of Experimental Psychology: Learning, Memory and Cognition 18, 615–623 (1992)
23. Krauss, R.M., Dushay, R., Chen, Y., Rausher, F.: The communicative value of conversational hand gestures. Journal of Experimental Social Psychology 31, 533–552 (1995)

Author Index